The Organization of Reduction, Data Flow, and Control Flow Systems

Computer Systems
Herb Schwetman, editor

The Organization of Reduction, Data Flow, and Control Flow Systems

Werner Kluge

The MIT Press

Cambridge, Massachusetts

London, England

This book was printed and bound in the United States of America.

Library of Congress Cataloging-in-Publication Data

Kluge, Werner.
    The organization of reduction, data flow, and control flow systems / Werner Kluge.
        p.   cm. — (Computer systems)
    Includes bibliographical references and index.
    ISBN 0-262-61081-7
    1. Computer organization. 2. Data flow computing.   I. Title. II. Series: Computer systems (Cambridge, Mass.)
QA76.9.C643K58 1992
004'.3—dc20   92-3192
                                                                         CIP

Contents

Series Foreword

This series is devoted to all aspects of computer systems. This means that subjects ranging from circuit components and microprocessors to architecture to supercomputers and systems programming will be appropriate. Analysis of systems will be important as well. System theories are developing, theories that permit deeper understanding of complex interrelationships and their effects on performance, reliability, and usefulness.

We expect to offer books that not only develop new materials but also describe projects and systems. In addition to understanding concepts, we need to benefit from the decision making that goes into actual development projects; selection from various alternatives can be crucial to success. We are soliciting contributions in which several aspects of systems are classified and compared. A better understanding of both the similarities and the differences found in systems is needed.

It is an exciting time in the area of computer systems. New technologies mean that architectures that were at one time interesting but not feasible are now feasible. Better software engineering means that we can consider several software alternatives, instead of "more of the same old thing," in terms of operating systems and system software. Faster and cheaper communications mean that intercomponent distances are less important. We hope that this series contributes to this excitement in the area of computer systems by chronicling past achievements and publicizing new concepts. The format allows publication of lengthy presentations that are of interest to select readership.

Herb Schwetman

The Organization of Reduction, Data Flow, and Control Flow Systems

1 Foreword and Introduction

This book is primarily intended for graduate students of computer science and for computer professionals who are interested in basic concepts (or models) of organizing and performing computations. It is based on material which I used several times, and in varying forms, to teach graduate courses on computer organization at the Universities of Bonn and Kiel. The book is written in monograph style since it focuses on function-based system concepts, with particular emphasis on λ-calculus machines, and thus is not in line with mainstream CS courses. However, experience with students indicates that the approach outlined in this book may help to develop a better understanding of the subject than a standard text does.

The organization, architecture and design of contemporary computing systems are very well covered in numerous textbooks or monographs. Basic and advanced concepts as well as design principles are thoroughly treated [Weg71, Katz76, HiPe78, Hay78, Mye78, Baer80, Kog81, Ill82, HwBr84, Mil87, Dasgup89, HePa90], and we can also find detailed descriptions of concrete computer systems or system families that are in widespread use [AmBl64, Katz71, Rudd76, Stre78, SiBeNe82, LeEc80, Org73, ReAl80, Org83].

However, a considerable body of research work on truly novel ways of representing and performing computations has, over the last two decades, produced very encouraging theoretical and practical results. With the emergence of experimental or even prototype **data flow and reduction machines** [Veg84, Thak87, FaKe87, Ama88] there seem to be good reasons for a book that re-examines our traditional perception of computer organization and computer architecture.

This perception has been and still is dominated by the abstract concept of a **state transition machine** whose theoretical foundations have been developed by Alan Turing [Tur36], while John von Neumann has been given most of the credit for devising the basic operating principle underlying all contemporary computing systems [vNeu45, BuGoNeu46].

The state transition model requires that computations be organized as sequences of atomic state transformations. They are realized as primitive inspect-and-modify (update) operations on small partitions of the state representation which, under the control of a built-in sequencing mechanism, derive step-by-step next states from present states to effect global state changes.

The simplicity of this concept, but also pragmatic considerations, have been key factors in its amazing endurance. However, increasing size and complexity of system and application software on the one hand, and a strong trend towards non-sequential or distributed processing on the other hand, have also painfully revealed its shortcomings with respect to correct program design and program execution.

To understand the nature of these shortcomings, it must be recognized that, from an organizational point of view, programs for a state transition machine in fact constitute rather sophisticated work schedules. Besides formulating an abstract algorithm that realizes the program's intended function, the programmer must deal, at more or less granular levels of detail, with complex resource allocation and control problems that have little to do with the algorithm itself. Managing the contents of huge numbers of memory cells (the partitions of the state representation) that may be shared among many interacting parts of a large program buries the logical structure of the algorithm under some elaborate network of far-ranging causes and effects whose construction invites lots of annoying errors and, for all practical purposes, renders programming as well as program execution intractable to formal reasoning [Back78].

These ultimately organizational problems must be held responsible for what has become known as the so-called software crisis. It manifests itself in unmanageable software development projects whose products, more often than not, fail to meet their specifications in terms of function, performance and – certainly of gravest consequences – correctness and reliability.

Yet another dimension is added to these difficulties when it comes to specifying computations that can be performed non-sequentially (commonly but somewhat misleadingly referred to as 'parallel' processing) in a system of several cooperating state transition machines. Here the programmer is challenged with the even more formidable task of carefully orchestrating the activities of several independently operating components. Beyond the construction of sequential program code, this task comprises at least the explicit specification of concurrently executable program modules and the orderly flow of data and control among them [Brin77, AnSc83, Hoa85, ChMi88, Babb88, Ben90]. It may also have to include explicit resource scheduling, unless this is either handled dynamically by the operating system or can be somehow worked out and statically fixed by clever compilation. In either case, the complexity of program design and, subsequently, insecurities about program correctness grow considerably.

In short: the programmer is asked to specify not only **what** is to be computed but also **how**, in detail, the computation is to be performed by the system.

However, computing machines need not be that primitive, as is perfectly demonstrated by reduction and data flow systems. They incorporate truly alternative organizational concepts based on state-independent (applicative) models of computation which radically liberate program design from all procedural elements. As input, they accept more or less formal specifications of application problems (e.g., in the form of mathematical expressions or sets of equations), and return, as output, problem solutions. The details of executing the computations are, by the system, systematically deduced from the formal problem specifications in compliance with the resources (processing sites) that can be actually made available.

Reduction systems essentially transform problem specifications, internally rep-resented as coherent expressions, by the systematic application of a fixed set of meaning-preserving **rewrite rules** step-by-step into constant expressions (or so-called **normal forms**). This transformation process treats expressions or components there-of in an orderly manner as consumable and (re-)producible entities.

Data flow systems apply problem specifications, usually represented as constant objects, to input objects (values) which, again, by a process of systematic consump-tion and (re-)production are transformed into output objects (result values).

In either case, control over the computations is essentially exercised by making operands directly available to operators in as many copies as are necessary for the subsequent consumption. Conceptually, there is no sharing of operands. As a consequence, computations are completely liberated from side effects, which is an essential prerequisite for non-sequential program execution.

In this monograph, we strongly advocate the perception that **computer organi-zation** primarily concerns **abstract concepts** of representing and organizing compu-tations. They are characterized by little more than a **programming paradigm** (e.g., imperative vs. declarative) and the basic mechanisms of program execution (e.g., the copying and overwriting of cell contents vs. the orderly consumption and re-production of computational objects), which are two intimately correlated issues.

At the level of **operating systems**, computer organization also relates to the coordi-nation and **interaction of computational processes** within a system, to the interaction of the system with users, external equipment and processes, and to **resource schedul-ing**.

In our view, computer organization has little or nothing to do with the actual construction of a system from concrete hardware or software components and their configuration, with instruction sets, data types and addressing modes, or with so-called **software, firmware and hardware** layers.

To get these things sorted out, we need to have some informal definition or at least some clear understanding of what is meant by

computer system   organization
                 architecture
     and   implementation
                 (or engineering),

and where to draw the lines between these disciplines.

The term **organization**, as can be looked up in almost every dictionary or encyclo-pedia, refers to the **orderly cooperation** of several independently acting components of a system in order to accomplish some more or less precisely specified objective. The purpose of a system may be to

- perform a specific set of jobs or tasks, or to provide some line of services;

- manufacture, distribute or maintain a line of products;

- pursue political, military, economic or cultural goals.

It is important to understand that it is neither the purpose of a system nor the configuration and the construction of its components which characterize its organization. but the disciplines of cooperation that are being established among them. To represent these disciplines in terms that abstract from concrete implementations, it suffices to consider two classes of system components. These are

- agencies (active components) which perform transactions on (representations of) messages, documents or objects of a real world;

- channels (passive components) through which the agencies communicate with each other by the transmission of messages, documents or objects.

Computer organization is concerned with systems that support an orderly flow of information at basically two system levels which serve different purposes and objectives.

The purpose of the program execution level is to transform user-defined problem specifications, referred to as programs, into problem solutions by units of activity which are called processes or tasks. The agencies of this level are operators, and the objects carried by the channels are called operands. In addition, we may have channels through which explicit control information is passed on from operators to operators.

The cooperation of these components is characterized by

- an operational discipline which in an orderly manner supplies operators with operands;

- a control discipline which activates the operators in compliance with the logical structure inherent in the problem specification.

Compatible combinations of both disciplines define basic concepts of organizing computations [TrBrHo82]. These so-called models of computation and their realizations will be the primary concern of this monograph.

The purpose of the operating system level is to schedule the processes or tasks of the program execution level and to manage the system's resources accordingly. Its agencies are a primary and some secondary scheduling devices which operate on (representations of) processes and resources that are held in channels realized as data structures such as queues, stacks and tables. The organizational concept is mainly characterized by scheduling disciplines which are to establish fairness among the various positions of interest associated with the execution of user processes on the one hand, and to maintain a high utilization of the system's resources on the other hand.

This subject is not treated in this monograph beyond the introduction of simple process scheduling schemes and basic principles of storage management which constitute a common basis for an operating system kernel, irrespective of the particular model of computation that is being supported by the computing system. For a more detailed outline on the organization of operating systems, the interested reader must be referred to other literature.

Computer system architecture is concerned with the realization or representation of a particular model of computation on the one hand, and of an operating system concept on the other hand. Both essentially determine the appearance of the computing system to the user.

The architecture of the program execution level is characterized by the constructs of a concrete programming language which are directly supported by or wired into the (hardware of the) system. This so-called machine language includes some computationally complete set of primitive functions or instructions, means to support abstractions, e.g., in the form of composite functions or procedures, primitive and structured data types to which these functions can be applied, and some control constructs. Addressing modes, if visible to the user, as well as primitive input/output operations through which peripheral equipment can be controlled and accessed, also belong to the architecture of the program execution level.

This perception of computer architecture concurs with informal definitions that can be found elsewhere in the literature. For instance, in [Mye78] it says that '...*computer architecture is the abstraction or definition of a physical system ...as seen by a machine language programmer or compiler writer. It is the definition of the conceptual structure and functional behavior of a processor as opposed to such attributes as the ...underlying data flow and controls, logic design and circuit technology ...*'. In [AmBl64] we can read that '...*the term architecture is used to describe the attributes of a system as seen by a programmer, i.e., the conceptual structure and the functional behavior, as distinct from the organization of the data flow and controls, the logical design, and the physical implementation ...*'.

Likewise, the architecture of the operating system level is essentially characterized by the command language which provides the basic means for controlling processes and resources.

Architectures define computer system families whose members exhibit a completely identical operational behavior. They are supposed to understand and execute the constructs of and, hence, programs specified in the same language in exactly the same way [LeEc80].

Computer system implementation (or engineering), finally, refers to the physical and logical design of the individual members of a system family. It includes basic design decisions concerning production costs and technological constraints, performance, capacity and reliability requirements as well as the details of soft-, firm- and hardware engineering by which these objectives can be accomplished.

Almost all computing systems that are commercially available today follow the state transition model of computation. It is characterized by a sequential control discipline in conjunction with an operational discipline based on the unrestricted copying and overwriting of operand locations (or the sharing of channels). Typical system architectures which realize this organizational concept are the IBM/360/370 and the VAX-11 system families. They differ from each other significantly with respect to their support for subroutine (procedure) calls and with respect to their data manipulating instruction sets, control constructs, addressing modes and input/output operations. They constitute different realizations of the same computational model and, thus, different architectures [AmBl64, Katz71, Rudd76, Stre78, LeEc80].

The individual members, say, of the IBM/370 family feature widely differing hardware and firmware (control) configurations of processors, memories and input/output channels to meet different application, capacity and performance requirements. However, all members of the family are guaranteed to be at least upward compatible. Programs that run on the smaller systems also run on the bigger ones. This upward compatibility extends into the more recent IBM/43xx and /30xx series [Tuc86]. The members of the /370 system family are different implementations of the same architecture [IBM78].

In this monograph we will systematically study three basic models of organizing deterministic computations and how they relate to the underlying programming paradigms: demand flow (as inherent in the concept of reduction), data flow, and control flow (or state transition). For each model, we will study how language concepts and organizational principles translate into architectures (or abstract machines), and how architectural features translate into concrete system implementations. We will also try to relate these architectures and their implementations to each other in order to identify characteristic features which they have in common and those in which they differ.

Our focus will be primarily on a functional programming paradigm based on a full-fledged operational λ-calculus and on its realization by various reduction systems. We will also show to which extent this formally clean concept must be compromised in functional systems based on various forms of compilation to 'efficiently' executable code (compiled graph reduction and data flow), and in control flow systems which realize an imperative programming paradigm.

The possible courses of reading through this monograph are graphically depicted in fig. 1.1. In order to get a fairly complete picture, the reader is advised to follow

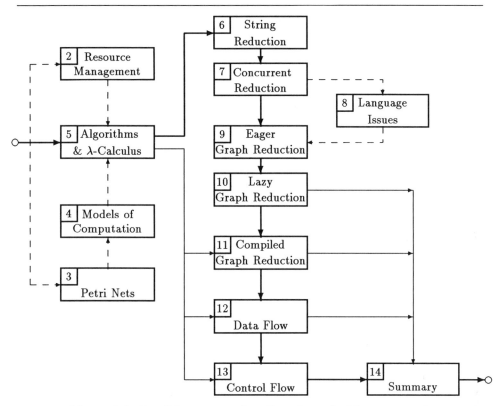

Figure 1.1: Possible courses of reading through this monograph

at least the route of the thick arrows. However, shortcuts may be taken along any of the thin arrows since the summary includes an overview over the concepts and machineries described in the chapters that are bypassed. Complementary material may be found along the dashed arrows, of which the route through chapters 3 and 4 is the more important one with respect to the remainder of the text.

In chapter 2 we give a brief outline of the overall configuration of a computing system and of an operating system kernel. It primarily serves to define some basic terminology and to introduce the basic concepts of process scheduling and storage management. The reader who is familiar with this subject may simply skip this part.

In chapter 3 we introduce some elements of the theory of **Petri-nets** as modeling tools for non-sequential systems and processes. They allow us to describe in abstract terms of causes and effects the mechanisms and phenomena involved in the interaction of agencies (or operators) and channels (as carriers of operands).

A simple form of higher-order Petri-nets will be used in chapter 4 to identify, largely by means of examples, the operational and control disciplines which govern the organization of reduction, data flow and control flow computations.

Though not an essential reading, chapters 3 and 4 should nevertheless be studied with some care in order to get acquainted with the basic ideas and with the formal background for the line of reasoning along which we plan to proceed.

Chapter 5 is the first that belongs to the hard core of the book. It introduces the notions of abstract algorithms and of reductions, and gives an overview over their formal basis, the theory of the λ-calculus This theory of computable functions deals with elementary properties of operators and their application to operands, addresses the concept of variables and variable scoping, execution orders and termination problems, and defines in a clean setting what is meant by the semantics of programs. It constitutes the formal basis of the functional programming paradigm (or of functional languages), and to some extent of the imperative paradigm as well.

Computing engines which directly and completely realize the reduction semantics of a full-fledged λ-calculus are the subject of chapters 6 to 10, which form the main part of this book. The three engines under consideration are different implementations of essentially the same architecture. They share the same kernel machinery but differ with respect to evaluation mechanisms, internal program representations, and run-time environments. In order to understand how these engines relate to each other, they should be studied strictly in the given sequence.

In chapter 6 we first describe a string reduction engine which transforms λ-terms step-by-step to constant terms (or normal forms) by the literal substitution of (sub-)terms by others, using a complete and correct implementation of the β-conversion rule as its basic operational mechanism. Every transformation (or reduction) step returns a legitimate λ-term as a complete specification of an intermediate state of the computation.

In chapter 7 we also introduce a concept for the non-sequential (or concurrent) execution of λ-terms based on a recursive term partitioning scheme, and outline its implementation on a system of cooperating string reduction machines.

Chapter 8 addresses some supplementary language and complexity issues which primarily motivate the need for more efficient implementation techniques based on graph reduction.

In chapters 9 and 10 we will have a close look at two alternative graph reduction engines which again realize the reduction semantics of an applied λ-calculus, genuinely transforming graph representations of λ-terms by high-level interpretation.

One is based on an eager reduction regime (or a call-by-value semantics) which passes operands in evaluated form to operators. This reduction order is fairly simple to implement, and it also lends itself quite naturally to non-sequential program execution.

The other supports a **lazy reduction regime** (or a **call-by-need** semantics) which postpones the evaluation of operands until it becomes absolutely necessary to do so in order to produce the desired results. This reduction order consequently avoids redundant computations and guarantees termination for all meaningful programs. It also allows for an elegant style of programming finite problems with infinite structures. However, the price to be paid for these features consists in decidedly more complex machinery that is necessary to deal with nested environment structures and with unevaluated λ-terms whose graph representations may have to be shared among several program parts.

The material presented in the remaining chapters, other than including references to and comparisons with that of chapters 5 through 10, is more or less self-contained and may therefore be read in any order.

Chapter 11 discusses two decidedly more popular concepts of implementing the functional programming paradigm, the G-machine and SKI combinator reduction. Both realize a lazy evaluation regime based on **compiled graph reduction**. The idea is to compile functional programs to some abstract machine code which can be efficiently implemented (or interpreted) on conventional machinery. However, we will see that these ends can only be achieved if the flavors of a full-fledged λ-calculus are to some extent sacrificed.

Yet another concept of performing functional computations based on compiled code is **data flow**, which will be investigated in chapter 12. The emphasis here is predominantly on the potential of functional program specifications for fine-grain concurrent execution in systems comprising large numbers of cooperating processing sites. Data flow is generally based on a **call-by-value** semantics (or **eager evaluation**).

The chapter includes a brief outline of three basic data flow **execution models** followed by a detailed description of a **tagged token data flow** system. It realizes the most versatile of the three execution models both in terms of the language concept it supports and in terms of exploiting program-inherent concurrency.

In chapter 13 we will study the classical **control flow** concept and how it relates to the imperative programming paradigm. Execution models based on control flow are essentially sequential. Non-sequential computations must be explicitly organized by the programmer as part of the problem specification.

Control flow architectures usually support only a very low level of programming directly. Other than a built-in sequencing scheme they provide, in the form of primitive bit-string manipulating and control instructions, just the bare essentials for efficiently generating, traversing, interpreting and modifying complex computational structures. They are well suited as targets for the compilation of **typed programming languages**, declarative (functional) or imperative, whose programs show a fairly static behavior in the sense that detailed plans for their execution can be completely worked out beforehand.

We will describe in detail a typical control flow architecture (basically a VAX-11 system) whose instruction set and addressing modes are closely tailored to the needs of compiling modern imperative languages into reasonably compact code. We will also address the basic principles of machine level programming.

In the last chapter we summarize the basic properties of the described architectures and make an attempt to classify them with respect to the semantic models they support.

Very little will be said about the details of designing hardware machinery. In fact, we assume that the reader is familiar with the construction and working of basic hardware components and modules such as arithmetic/logic units, counters, register sets etc. and with hard-wired or micro-programmed control units. Also, we are not too concerned with efficiency considerations, optimization techniques, and absolute or comparative performance figures. These subjects relate to a considerable extent to implementation details which are outside the scope of this book.

Acknowledgements

Writing this book turned out to be an experience which was more demanding and time-consuming than I expected. I would not have been able to get the job done without the support and advise of many others.

I owe a lot to my graduate students and research assistants here in Kiel and to my former colleagues at GMD in Bonn who provided material, searched the literature, shared the proof reading, and through many discussions helped to shape the contents of the book and its overall organization.

I am particularly indebted to Klaus Berkling who stimulated my interest in reduction systems and who I had the privilege to work with for a long time. His research contributed significantly to the technical substance of the book, both directly and indirectly.

I am also indebted to those whose research work and concepts I have taken the liberty of including in the book.

Finally, I wish to thank Claudia Schmittgen who spent a considerable amount of her time on this project. She did some very careful proof reading, without which a few serious errors would have slipped in, and I also relied heavily on her valuable expertise and untiring support in getting the manuscript TEXed.

Kiel, May 1992   Werner Kluge

2 Resource Management

In this chapter we will briefly outline the basic organizational concepts underlying an operating system kernel. They apply irrespective of the model of computation which is supported at the program execution level as all computing systems essentially feature the same configuration of abstract and concrete components. We will concern ourselves primarily with resource management, i.e., with the allocation of processing units and memory space to executable processes. The emphasis will be on principles, not on the details of management policies and their performance.

For a more thorough treatment of operating system principles and concrete implementations, the reader must be referred to other books, e.g., [Brin73, CoDe83, Com84, Org85, Bach86, Krak88].

In a computing system we can typically identify the following abstract components:

- an aggregate of one or several processing engines (PEs) which are to execute user-specified programs (procedural or declarative problem specifications);

- an aggregate of one or several input/output engines (IOEs) through which the system transfers data to or from its peripheral equipment and communicates messages;

- an operating system engine (OSE) which, in entities called computational processes (or tasks), supervises and schedules the activities of the processing and input/output engines, and manages their resources.

These engines are realized by concrete computing machines (or systems) which include the following physical resources:

- a directly accessible (addressable) storage medium, called the working memory, which holds code and data of active programs;

- one or several functional (instruction) processing units (FPUs) which execute PE- or OSE-programs;

- one or several input/output processing units (IOPUs) which execute input/output programs;

- a variety of peripheral devices such as disc and tape memories, alpha-numerical and graphical display terminals, printers, etc. which, by the operating system, are uniformly considered storage media which are logically subdivided into volumes and files.

A hard-wired configuration comprising physical memory, functional and in-put/output processing units, as well as some essential peripheral equipment consti-tutes a real computing machine or system. It may support several so-called virtual computing machines simultaneously. A virtual machine is made up from the tem-porary allocation of one or several physical or logical memory units (including files residing on peripheral devices) and by processing units. It may be considered an instantiation of an engine in a real system.

The operating system engine may be thought of as being in sole possession of all physical resources. However, the ownership of resources may be temporarily transferred to virtual machines on a leasing basis. Processing units are allocated to competing virtual machines in intervals of time, whereas memory is allocated in units of space. Allocation and de-allocation are governed by more or less elaborate schemes that attempt to establish some degree of fairness among the demands of the various virtual machines that need to be accommodated.

A system featuring the described configuration is called

- a mono-processor system if it is equipped with just one FPU, which in this case is commonly referred to as central processing unit (CPU);

- a multi-processor system otherwise.

A configuration comprising several mono- or multi-processor systems which are connected to a common local or non-local communication network is called a dis-tributed system. The connections to the network are established by so-called network controllers which may be considered special IOPUs.

2.1   Programs and Processes

Computer programs are executable specifications of user or operating system func-tions (or, more precisely, of function applications), or of standardized input/output operations. They are represented as code (possibly including data) that can be directly executed by the respective processing units. Processes (or tasks) are in this context considered units of activity which execute programs or parts thereof in a strictly sequential manner, requiring exactly one processing unit. A process comprises both the executable representation of a program (and its data) and a virtual machine in which the program can actually run. Apart from the availability of a processing unit, the virtual machine may be viewed as an instantiation of the logical address space of a program in one or several (not necessarily contiguous) por-tions of the real (or physical) address space of the memory. The logical address space typically comprises one or several contiguous address segments which accommodate

- static parts such as the program code itself, constant values, input data sets and buffer areas of constant size etc;

- dynamic parts whose sizes and structures change while the program actually operates on them.

Processes are represented within a computing system by so-called process context blocks. A context block contains, in condensed form, information pertaining to

- the identification of the process within the system;

- the virtual machine allocated to the process;

- the status of the computation executed by the process;

- the authority the operating system has over the process with respect to the allocation and de-allocation of resources that must be shared among all processes within the system (processing units, memory).

In addition, a process is characterized by its global status which may be either

- *executing* (being in possession of a processing unit);

- *executable* (lined up for the allocation of a processing unit);

- *waiting* (for synchronization with other processes);

- *terminated* or *non-existent* (i.e., not in possession of a virtual machine);

The operating system exercises control over the processes by means of their respective context blocks. For each resource or resource type, it maintains one or several queues of service requests whose entries are (pointers to) the context blocks of the processes to which it must be allocated.

Using a largely self-explanatory PASCAL-like notation, we can specify a typical process context block as a record of the following kind:

TYPE *process_context* =
    RECORD
                    identity : *process_identifier;*[1]
              virtual_machine : *descriptor;*
                    status : *state_of_computation;*
                  waiting : *boolean;*
            interrupt_mask : *array_of_boolean;*
                  priority : *priority_range;*
    END_OF_RECORD

---

[1] The identity of a process usually includes also that of its father process, and possibly the identities of son processes.

TYPE   *descriptor* = (* (pointer to) a data structure specifying the memory
                                segments or files allocated to the virtual machine *)
        state_of_computation = (* concise description of the actual focus of control at
                                which program execution has arrived, including regis-
                                ter contents, condition codes etc. *)
            process_index = $(0, \ldots, p-1)$
                                (* assuming an upper limit p on the number of pro-
                                cesses that may coexist within the system *)
            priority_range = $(1, \ldots, k)$.

Resource scheduling, particularly the allocation and de-allocation of processing
units, is essentially governed for each process by the record fields *interrupt_mask*
and *priority*.

The interrupt mask specifies by which of several potential causes an executing
process may be suspended in order to yield the processing unit it holds in possession
to some other, possibly more urgent process. By means of the process priority,
the operating system decides to which of several competing executable processes
a processing unit which has become available is to be allocated. Thus, both the
interrupt mask and the priority define, in fact, the authority the operating system
may exercise over a process.

2.2   Process Scheduling

Process scheduling is concerned with the allocation of resources of type processing
unit to executable processes. Scheduling disciplines must not only aim at a high
utilization of scarce resources but also may have to establish some degree of fairness among the various needs and positions of interest associated with individual
processes. Unfortunately, these objectives are not necessarily congruent.

In order to serve both objectives reasonably well, we usually have

- a short-term scheduling discipline (or policy) which simply allocates processing units to executable processes as soon as they become available, possibly
  following some priority regime;

- a medium-term scheduling discipline (or policy) which allocates virtual machines, assigns identities and priorities to processes, and supervises process
  creation, execution, suspension and termination in compliance with the process status or, if the programs to be executed belong to the operating system,
  by function and purpose.

Short-term disciplines are concerned with the efficient utilization of processing
units, while medium-term disciplines try to allocate the physical resources of the
system to competing processes on a reasonably fair basis.

We are here primarily interested in short-term disciplines which need be supported more or less directly by hardware-implemented mechanisms. These mechanisms form the basis of an **operating system kernel**.

Short-term disciplines basically fall into two categories.

Non-preemptive scheduling produces the least overhead for resource management and makes the most efficient use of the processing capacity, while almost totally neglecting fairness considerations. This discipline simply keeps a processing unit (and all other essential resources) allocated to an executing process until it suspends itself. Self-suspensions are usually effected by

- the orderly termination of a process;

- explicit requests for services from the operating system, e.g., to have another resource allocated without which the process cannot continue;

- the occurrence of an error condition either within the program executed by the process or within the hardware.

Representative for non-preemptive scheduling disciplines are **batch processing systems** (or subsystems). The simplest versions process all programs to completion strictly in their order of submission and one at a time. It is obvious that these systems tend to get completely monopolized by programs requiring long run-times while short programs may be delayed beyond tolerable limits. Some degree of fairness may, however, be introduced by **priority rules** which give preference to the programs with the shortest expected run-times.

Non-preemptive scheduling must be applied to most input/output processes, e.g., to

- high speed data block transfers from and to semi-mechanical peripheral equipment (e.g., disc or tape drives) which, once started, must continue to completion in order to avoid the loss of data;

- line-printer processes which must produce contiguous output on paper.

Preemptive scheduling, at the expense of a higher process management overhead, is primarily concerned with the quasi-simultaneous execution of several independent processes under reasonably fair conditions, using a so-called **time-sharing** principle. The idea is to allocate processing units to executable processes cyclically (or **round robin**) for constant **time slices** which are decidedly shorter than average program execution times. Thus, every process generally requires several to many such time slots to complete its computation.

This interleaved execution of several processes is also called processor multiplexing. In more advanced systems it is used in conjunction with process priorities, i.e., time-slices are allocated to processes with the highest actual priority level. This simple strategy ensures that all of, say, n processes which are at this level proceed with approximately $1/n$ of the processing speed, irrespective of their total computation time. Processes with lower priorities proceed at a decidedly slower speed.

To obtain acceptable average response times for all processes, priority-controlled preemptive scheduling must be backed up by a medium-term discipline which assigns high priorities to processes running small programs and low priorities to processes running large programs. The progress of low priority processes, however, must be steadily enhanced by stepping up their priorities with elapsing time (or as they age).

In more general terms, preemptive scheduling may be viewed as a discipline by which active processes can be suspended in reaction to conditions which are brought about by processes or events occurring somewhere else inside or outside the system. They include

- time-out conditions generated by a system clock which signal the elapse of time slices, whereupon new processes must be scheduled;

- synchronization conditions concerning the communication of messages between processes (such as the termination of or exceptional conditions arising in input/output processes), in which case an active process must be temporarily sidelined in favor of an operating system routine which handles the communication and, if necessary, changes the global status of the receiving process accordingly;

- operator or user intervention, e.g., to terminate a process prematurely.

Fig. 2.1 schematically illustrates, in a somewhat idealized form, the components of a simple preemptive scheduling scheme for one processing unit. It includes, besides the processor, an array of FIFO (first-in/first-out) queues *ready_queue*[1 .. k], another FIFO queue *released_queue*, and a *wait_table*. The entries of these data structures are assumed to be pointers to process context blocks held in a *process_table* which is not shown. In particular, the entries in

- the *ready_queues* represent executable processes, ordered by their priority levels (with priorities decreasing from 1 to k);

- the *wait_table*[2] represent processes waiting for synchronization conditions

---

[2]It should be pointed out here that the *wait_table* is introduced merely for illustration purposes. As we will see later, it is not required in an actual implementation since processes waiting for synchronization conditions are distinguished by the *waiting*-field entries in their context blocks.

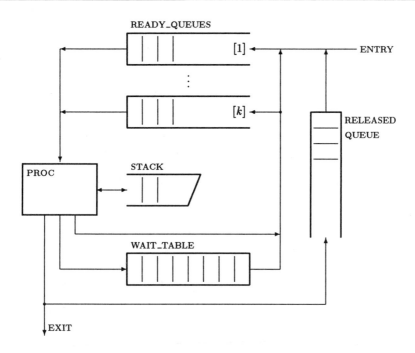

Figure 2.1: Process scheduling scheme for a mono-processor system

which indicate the completion of services requested from the operating system (e.g., the transfer of a file from a peripheral storage device) or the arrival of a message;

- the *released_queue* are pointers to context blocks which have been de-allocated from terminating processes and can be re-used by new processes entering the system.

In addition we have associated with the processing unit a LIFO (last-in/first-out) stack, the so-called system stack, which holds the context blocks of processes that need be temporarily suspended.

Whenever an executing process is suspended by

- an elapsing time slice, (the pointer to) its context returns to the end of the *ready_queue* which corresponds to its priority level;

- a service request to the operating system, its context is usually placed into the *wait_table*;

- orderly termination, user or operator intervention, its context is placed into the *released_queue*;

- all other conditions, its context is temporarily saved on the *stack* and reactivated or released from there.

In all cases but the last one, a new process is scheduled for execution on the processing unit. It is taken from the head of the non-empty *ready_queue* with the highest priority. The scheduler continues with the process topmost on the stack after having dealt with synchronization conditions involving processes in a wait state. Continuation after hardware or program errors may be made dependent on the ability of the system to recover from such a situation in the particular process state. In general, the suspended processes are aborted.

This process scheduling scheme constitutes an operating system (OS-)kernel. With some modifications, such a kernel can be used to govern the circulation of processes in a multi-processor system as well. The modifications primarily concern the introduction of a so-called monitor which controls the shared access of several processing units to the queues and tables maintained by the OS-kernel.

The various conditions leading to the suspension of active processes are commonly referred to as interrupt conditions (or interrupts for short). They are uniformly processed by an interrupt subsystem which is partly integrated into the processing unit(s). It provides

- some basic hardware support for the communication of interrupt conditions to the processing unit(s) and for swapping process contexts;

- a set of standardized interrupt handling routines which, upon occurrences of the respective interrupt conditions, are activated by the context swapping mechanism.

There are essentially two classes of interrupts that must be dealt with.
Internal interrupts are those which cause the self-suspension of active processes. They originate from

- requests for operating system services which, in the program text of the executing process, are specified as OSE-call instructions;

- exceptions arising from erroneous program code or data, from protection violations, or from the exhaustion of resources (e.g., page faults).

External interrupts may be generated by processes which run somewhere else. They relate to events which either the active process or one of the suspended processes must be notified of. The operating system must deal with them at least as an intermediary. These interrupts include

- synchronization conditions concerning the communication of messages among processes;

- user or operator intervention;

- timer interrupts signaling the elapse of pre-specified intervals of time.

In addition, we may have interrupts due to hardware malfunctions.

Irrespective of their origins, interrupt conditions are to change global process states, e.g., from *non-existent* to *existent* and vice versa, from *executable* to *executing*, from *executing* to *waiting* or *executable* etc., which directly relate to process scheduling. They are in fact primitive messages which either implicitly or explicitly specify destination processes and the state changes that have to be effected on them.

Interrupt conditions cause the hard-core interrupt mechanism to

- suspend the active process by pushing its context block into the system stack;

- install instead in the processing unit the context of the respective interrupt routine (which is obtained from a special interrupt table maintained by the os-kernel).

An interrupt routine typically interprets the message associated with the interrupt condition and modifies the global state of the destination process accordingly. It does so by moving (the pointer to) the context block of this process to the respective data structure of the scheduler. The routine eventually terminates by

- either installing in the processing unit another executable process (whose context is taken from the non-empty *ready_queue* with the highest priority) after having saved the context of the suspended process in its *process_table* location or disposed of it;

- resuming the execution of the suspended process by retrieving its context from the system stack otherwise.

The former case primarily applies to OSE-calls and to time-out interrupts, whereas the latter case mainly applies to interrupts caused by synchronization conditions which relate to processes that are in a wait state. The continuation after all other interrupt conditions depends on the process states affected by them and on the current state of the os-kernel.

2.3   Memory Management

In our discussion of the OS-kernel we have implicitly assumed that executable processes lined up in the *ready_queues* have sufficient memory space allocated to them so that they can actually run for some time once they have got hold of a processing unit.

Technological and economical constraints usually necessitate a hierarchical configuration of several physical memory components whose access times and capacities increase from top to bottom whereas their specific costs decrease in the same direction. A typical hierarchy of this kind is shown in fig. 2.2.

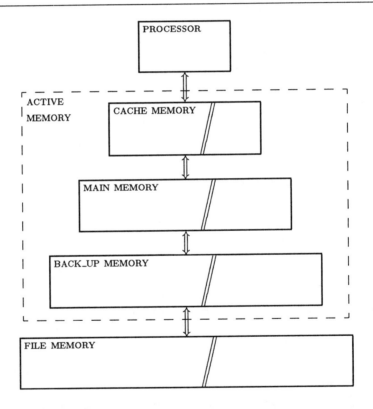

Figure 2.2: Hierarchical memory configuration of a computing system

At the top, we have a cache memory to which the processing unit has direct access at a rate that is compatible with its operating speed. Access time and capacity of a cache are usually in the order of 10 nanoseconds (1 nanosecond $= 10^{-9}$ seconds) and up to about 100 kilobytes (1 kilobyte $= 2^{10}$ bytes), respectively. In a multi-processor system each processing unit is equipped with its private cache memory to reduce access conflicts.

The main memory makes up the second level of the hierarchy. It provides the real (or physical) address space of a computing system as it is seen by the processing unit. This address space is usually smaller (in a few older systems it is larger) than the range of addresses that can be generated by the processor. Thus there must be means to map logical into physical addresses. Access times and capacities usually range from 50 to 200 nanoseconds and from about 10 to 100 megabytes (1 megabyte $= 2^{20}$ bytes), respectively. The main memory is shared among all processing units of a multi-processor system.

Both the cache memory and the main memory are implemented as so-called random access storage devices: access to all locations (addresses) requires the same time.

At the third level we find a back-up memory which in some high-performance systems is implemented as a large-capacity random access memory with access times of about 2 to 8 microseconds (1 microsecond $= 10^{-6}$ seconds). The majority of large systems, however, uses head-per-track discs (or drums) with capacities usually not exceeding 1 gigabyte (1 gigabyte $= 2^{30}$ bytes) and access times in the order of 1 to 10 milliseconds (1 millisecond $= 10^{-3}$ seconds).

These three hierarchical levels form what earlier has been referred to as the working (or active) memory of a computing system in which program execution actually takes place. It supports the virtual machine environment for all processes that are under the control of the os-kernel and thus are in circulation for the allocation of processing units.

The back-up memory constitutes its lowest hierarchical level. It holds so-called images of the static and dynamic program components of all processes. An executing process has at least an essential part of these components, commonly referred to as the working set, copied into the main memory. It is swapped in from the back-up memory as demand arises and address space can be made available. A relatively small portion of the program code and of the data set which constitutes the actual focus of activity (or control) of the program execution is copied from the main memory into the cache to which the processing unit has direct and very fast access.

The basic idea here is to have pieces of code and data gradually ascend to the top of the hierarchy as the focus of activity moves towards it, and to have it gradually descend from the top (and eventually swapped back into the back-up memory) as the focus of activity moves away from it. Climbing up means that address space must be allocated at the hierarchically higher level and code or data be copied in from the lower level. Climbing down means that address space be released at the higher level and data (or changeable parts in general) be copied back into their original locations at the lower level.

The fourth level of the hierarchy essentially comprises an aggregate of moving-arm disc memories which, in the form of files, stores inactive programs and data of the operating system and of all users. At the next lower level we find magnetic tape units which are primarily used for input/output and system back-up purposes, and also for the storage of large volumes of infrequently used data.

This memory hierarchy is representative for large, high-performance multi-user systems. In smaller systems, there may be no cache memory, and the back-up memory may be realized as a sufficiently large partition of a moving-arm disk which otherwise serves as a file store. However, these are implementation details which have little bearing on the hierarchical organization of the memory.

A large computer program is usually composed of several more or less independently constructed components. Besides the main program, we may have (recursively nested) procedures or functions, modules, and various fixed-sized data structures (pre-defined arrays, tables, etc.). They are considered the static parts of the program. Once specified, their memory demands never change. In addition, we may have dynamically expanding and contracting data structures such as stacks, queues and linked lists which are either explicitly specified in the program or created by the run-time system. They are considered the dynamic or changeable parts of the program. Their memory demands cannot, in general, exactly be à priori predicted.

The changeable parts of conventional (procedural) programs typically include

- a run time-stack which holds the activation records (i.e., the actual parameters and local variables) of nested procedure or function calls;

- a heap section to support dynamically changing data structures, e.g., built up from pointer chains.

The representation in memory of the static as well as of the dynamic program parts involves up to three levels of addressing. These are

- the logical address spaces of the individual program components, also referred to as logical segments, in which addresses are generated relative to the base zero;

- the virtual address space of the program (or its virtual memory), in which the logical address segments of its components are assembled relative to a base of zero;

- the **real address space** of the main memory into which the virtual address space or the logical segments of the program must be mapped for execution.

The simplest way of mapping virtual into real address space is to partition the main memory into **regions** of standard size and to realize the virtual memories of programs as equally sized **virtual regions**. These regions may come in sizes of, say, 100 kilobytes for small programs, 1 **megabyte** for medium-sized programs, and 10 **megabytes** or more for very large programs.

Executable programs (or processes) must have their complete virtual regions **swapped in** from the back-up memory into physical regions of the main memory. Processes suspended by OSE-calls, which subsequently go into a it wait state, have their complete regions **swapped out** into the back-up memory. If main memory space is tight, even low priority processes suspended by timer interrupts may get their regions moved out.

Addresses within a virtual region are relative to zero, i.e., they are within an interval $[0 .. region\_size - 1]$. The mapping of addresses from virtual into real space is done once when the virtual region of a process is loaded for the first time into an allocated physical region. All virtual addresses are then **bound** to the physical addresses by a special program called **loader**, and the process executes directly in place. The addresses remain bound until the process terminates. Thus, whenever it is swapped out before completion, it must be swapped back into the same physical region.

A program region is typically divided into two major sections, as schematically shown in fig. 2.3. The one in the upper part of the address space usually accommodates the static components of the program, whereas the one in the lower part accommodates the dynamic components, i.e., the **run-time stack** at one end and the **heap** at the other end. As indicated by the arrows, the stack grows towards decreasing addresses, starting at the upper boundary of this section, and the heap basically grows towards increasing addresses, starting at the lower boundary.

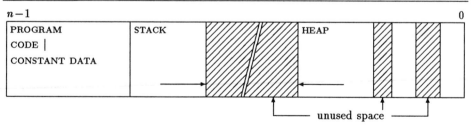

Figure 2.3: Typical layout of the virtual memory region of a program

However, there is a significant difference between the stack and the heap. As the stack keeps track of recursively nested procedure/function calls, it grows and shrinks only at the top and thus always occupies a contiguous address segment. The heap, however, may develop holes of unused space as heap structures are usually produced and consumed in a rather arbitrary order.

To manage the region-internal heap space efficiently, we can try

- to place a new heap structure into one of several fitting holes or, if this fails,

- to reorganize (or compact) the heap so that all unused fragments on the one hand and all occupied fragments on the other hand form contiguous segments again,

in this order. If demands for more memory space cannot be met then, the process is in a deadlock and must be aborted.

Thus, some housekeeping of the address space assigned to the stack/heap section is necessary. It must cope with the dynamic allocation and de-allocation of variably sized pieces of memory, with the unification of unused contiguous pieces, and with heap compaction, if this should become necessary. The latter, of course, requires that all heap objects be relocatable, which generally cannot be easily accomplished.

We will address heap space management in more detail later on in connection with graph reduction systems.

A severe problem with fixed-sized regions is that the simplicity of allocating real to virtual regions must be dearly paid for in terms of poor memory utilization which, in turn, degrades performance. Whatever region sizes are chosen, they will never be right with respect to the actual demands of the programs. On average, a considerable portion of the region-internal memory space will be left unused and thus wasted – a phenomenon which is also referred to as internal fragmentation.

This problem can be overcome by supporting regions of variable sizes (or segments) which can be more closely adapted to the expected memory demands of the programs (or processes). However, memory space must then be managed in essentially the same way as region-internal heap space. To do so, the os-kernel maintains a cyclically linked list of records which identify free memory segments (or holes). These records are generally updated, in some cases removed from or added to the list, as physical regions are allocated or de-allocated, respectively. From time to time, the free memory space must also be compacted as it gradually splits up into smaller and smaller pieces. This phenomenon is called external fragmentation. It is due to the fact that virtual regions hardly ever fit exactly into available physical memory space. There are almost always unused pieces of smaller sizes left over.

Memory compaction requires that virtual regions be relocatable; i.e., there must be no permanent binding of virtual to real address space as with regions of fixed size. Instead, there must be a dynamic address translation scheme which takes the virtual addresses of a program (or process) as offsets relative to its base address in the real address space.

Besides considerable degrees of fragmentation, region-based memory management suffers from yet another problem. It always swaps complete regions between the back-up and the main memory. However, in an actual program run several of the program and data segments, due to particular actual parameters, may not be needed at all. Thus, both memory space and input/output processing time are wasted. Moreover, we may have the problem that in extreme cases the memory demands of a single process exceed the size of the main memory.

In order to deal with these problems, memory space must be managed in entities smaller than regions, and virtual addresses must be dynamically (i.e., at run-time) translated into physical addresses in order to render these entities relocatable. This can be accomplished by essentially two memory management schemes which may or may not be combined with each other.

One is called segmentation. It maintains the logical structure of programs, e.g., in terms of the modules of which they are composed, by dynamically mapping logical segments from the virtual into the real address space. Segments may be scattered about the real memory wherever free space of sufficient size can be located. In contrast to the region approach, we now have the advantage that a process may start executing with only some of its segments in the main memory. Further segments may be swapped in as demand arises, segments that are no longer needed may be swapped out, and some segments may never be swapped. Moreover, segments of re-entrant code (e.g., of library routines) may be shared among several executing processes. However, while memory utilization improves, there is also a decidedly higher overhead involved in the management of free memory space and in the translation of virtual into real addresses.

Segmentation requires process-specific segment tables which for each segment specify

- its presence or absence in main memory and,

- if present, its base address and its size;

- if absent, some data which identify its location in the back-up memory.

An access to a segment not resident in main memory suspends the active process by a segment fault interrupt. The interrupt routine takes the back-up memory location found in the particular segment table entry to start an I/O process which loads the missing segment. In the meantime, the suspended process remains in a wait state.

The other memory management scheme is called **paging**. It completely separates the logical structure of programs from the physical structure of the memory. It partitions virtual and real address space into **pages** of equal size and dynamically maps virtual or real pages into real pages. Pages are decidedly smaller than regions or even segments; they usually come in sizes of 2^{10}, 2^{11} or 2^{12} **bytes**. Cache pages may even be smaller than that, e.g., from 2^6 to 2^8 **bytes**.

Paging utilizes memory space very efficiently in that it

- avoids a great deal of the internal and external fragmentation of the main memory space that comes with regions and segments;

- allows arbitrary scattering of consecutive pages of a virtual address space about the pages of the real address space without there being a major space management problem;

- renders it possible to execute a process with less than its complete set of pages (the working set) in memory.

The latter allows for a smooth ascent and descent of program and data pages in the memory hierarchy as the focus of activity changes. However, the penalty that is to be paid for this consists in fairly frequent interrupts of the active process due to the generation of addresses which cannot be mapped into valid pages in memory. These **page faults** are treated in essentially the same way as segment faults: while the suspended process is put into a wait state, the missing page is loaded into the main memory.

The pages of a process are administered by a process-specific **page table** whose entries map virtual into real page addresses (or into back-up memory locations if the pages are not resident in main memory). If segmentation is combined with paging, the entries of a process-specific segment table are pointers to segment-specific page tables.

A considerable problem with paging concerns **page replacement** strategies. As all page frames of the main memory may eventually become occupied by pages belonging to executable processes, demands for new pages can only be satisfied at the expense of other pages which must be forced out. There are several more or less speculative schemes to render a decision as to just which pages these should be. They are all based on some kind of book-keeping on the frequency of accesses that have been made to the pages in memory. Best known are LRU and LFU strategies which respectively identify the **least recently** or **least frequently** used page as the victim which has to be moved out. Both work on the speculation that what happened in the recent past will likely happen in the near future. Pages whose contents have not been changed while in the main memory are preferred as victims over pages which have been updated. In the former case, the page frame may simply be over-written by the new page; in the latter case, the page has to be copied back into its location in the back-up memory in order to bring its image up to date before the new page can be moved in.

More details on these memory management concepts can be found in the litera-ture referenced at the beginning of this chapter.

3   Abstract Models for Processes and Systems

In order to develop some basic understanding of how to organize computations at the program execution level, it is useful to introduce a few elements and concepts of the theory of Petri nets [Petri62, Petri80, Peson81, GeLaTh80, Rei85, BrReRo87]. This theory provides a formal apparatus which allows us to model and reason about concurrency in processes and systems strictly in terms of causes and effects. Petri nets are invariant against different positions of an observer and against the notion of time. They also abstract completely from conceivable implementations, exposing just logical (or causal) dependencies among the agencies (active components) and channels (passive components) of a process (or system). Of particular interest for our purposes will be a high-level variant of Petri nets, so-called Predicate/Transition (PrT-) nets, by which the operational semantics of computations can be included into process models at various levels of refinement.

3.1   Conditions, Events and Cases

When modeling the behavior of processes or systems, it generally suffices to consider only states and state changes. In complex systems with many activities distributed over space and time, the state is not a monolithic thing which changes as a whole. It partitions into atomic conditions which may or may not hold. State changes are effected by atomic events which change these conditions. More precisely, we define

- a state of a system as a maximal subset of conditions that hold coexistently;

- a state change or a state transition as the occurrence of one or several independent events, each of which coincidently terminates pre-conditions belonging to the current state and brings into existence post-conditions that belong to the next state.

The term state may be replaced by the more general term case which simply refers to some abstract phenomenon that exists in space and time. A process may then be perceived as a sequence of event occurrences which changes whatever is the case [Petri73].

With these notions at hand, we formally define a so-called case-graph-system by means of a quadruple (B, C, E, r), where

- $B = \{b_0, b_1, b_2, \ldots\}$ denotes the set of conditions;

- $K = P(B)$ is the power set of B which denotes the set of constellations (or the set of all conceivable combinations of conditions that may hold coexistently);

- $C \subseteq K$ denotes the set of **cases**, which is the subset of constellations that specify correct system behavior;

- $E = \{e_0, e_1, e_2, \ldots\}$ denotes the set of **events**;

- $r \subseteq C \times E \times C$ specifies the **reachability** relation: if $(c_1, e, c_2) \in r$, then the event e is said to change the case c_1 into the case c_2.

Given the set of conditions B and the set of events E, the dynamic behavior of a case-graph-system is in fact determined by the reachability relation r or, more precisely, by the restrictions imposed on r.

We will in the following primarily consider systems which follow the principle of **context-free substitution** (or the **extensionality principle**). It demands that an event $e \in E$ be completely defined by the conditions it changes.

Let $(c_1, e, c_2) \in r$, then these conditions comprise

- the set of **pre-conditions** of e which belong to c_1 but not to c_2, denoted as ${}^\bullet e = c_1 \setminus c_2$, and thus cease to hold

- the set of **post-conditions** of e which belong to c_2 but not to c_1, denoted as $e^\bullet = c_2 \setminus c_1$, and thus begin to hold

upon the occurrence of the event e.

Alternatively, we may formulate the extensionality principle as follows:

$$(\forall\, c_1, c_2, c_3, c_4 \in C)\, ((c_1, e, c_2) \in r \wedge (c_3, e, c_4) \in r)$$

$$\Leftrightarrow (c_3 \setminus c_4 = c_1 \setminus c_2 \wedge c_4 \setminus c_3 = c_2 \setminus c_1)$$

This principle states that all conditions $b \in c_1 \cap c_2$ or $b \in c_3 \cap c_4$ have no influence on and are not influenced by the occurrence of e. It is therefore irrelevant for the occurrence of e whether or not these conditions hold.

Based on these definitions, we can conclude that an event $e \in E$ is **enabled (activated)** or **has concession** to take place under a case $c_1 \in C$ if and only if

- all its pre-conditions hold;

- all its post-conditions don't hold;

i.e., iff ${}^\bullet e \subseteq c_1 \wedge e^\bullet \cap c_1 = \emptyset$.

The extensionality principles may be considered an idealization of real system behavior: the occurrence of an event consumes all its pre-conditions and produces all its post-conditions. Moreover, it establishes symmetry in the sense that e may also take place in reverse direction, with $e^\bullet$ being the set of pre-conditions and ${}^\bullet e$ being the set of post-conditions.

This idealization makes good sense. Consider, as an example, two conditions $b_1 \in B$ and $b_2 \in B$ whose respective interpretations are the propositions 'the glass is filled with wine' and 'the glass is empty'. An event $e \in E$ with the interpretation 'the glass is being emptied' would require b_1 to be a pre-condition and b_2 to be a post-condition. Clearly, the occurrence of the event e invalidates (or consumes) the valid pre-condition b_1 and validates (produces) the post-condition b_2, which prior to it was invalid. When taking place in reverse direction, the event e simply needs to be interpreted as 'the glass is being filled with wine', which perfectly complies with the interpretation of the conditions b_1 and b_2.

However, sometimes it appears useful to deviate, for pragmatic reasons, from the extensionality principle and to include so-called **side conditions** into the specification of events. To do so, we assume, with respect to an event $e \in E$, the existence of a non-empty subset of conditions

$$\widehat{e} = {}^{\bullet}e \cap e^{\bullet} \subset c_1 \cap c_2 \neq \emptyset.$$

In order to maintain the symmetry of the event e, we demand that

$$c_1 \setminus {}^{\bullet}e = c_2 \setminus e^{\bullet}.$$

This equation partitions the set $c_1 \cap c_2$ into the subsets $\widehat{e}$ and $c_1 \cap c_2 \setminus \widehat{e}$ in which case $\widehat{e}$ is said to be the set of **side conditions**. They are both pre- and post-conditions of the event; i.e., they are required to hold in order to enable the event but continue to hold after its occurrence. All conditions from the subset $c_1 \cap c_2 \setminus \widehat{e}$ have nothing to do with the event e: they may or may not hold.

An obvious side condition in our glass-of-wine example is the existence of a glass. It clearly is a pre-condition **and** a post-condition of the event 'the glass is being emptied' or of its reverse 'the glass is being filled'.

However, as side conditions have no impact on the **dynamic** behavior of a system, they may simply be assumed to hold implicitly and, hence, be ignored in the system model.

3.2 Condition/Event (CE-)Systems

We now switch to a more amenable representation of the concepts discussed in the previous section. It is based on **bipartite graphs** or **nets** which use two types of nodes to represent conditions and events, and directed arcs to represent the partial ordering among them [GeSta80, GeLaTh80].

A triple $N = (S, T; F)$ is said to denote a **directed net** iff

- $S \cap T = \emptyset$

- $S,\, T \neq \emptyset$

- $F \subseteq (S \times T) \cup (T \times S)$

- $domain(F) \cup codomain(F) = S \cup T$

and
S is the set of S-elements,
T is the set of T-elements,
$X = S \cup T$ is the set of elements of N,
F is the flow relation whose elements are the directed arcs of N.

In a graphical representation of N, we use the following symbols:

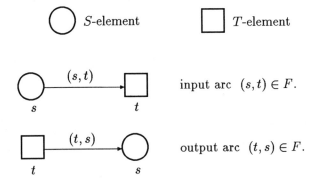

Let $N = (S, T; F)$ be a directed net, and $x, y \in X = S \cup T$, then we call

$$
\begin{aligned}
{}^\bullet x &= \{y \in X \mid (y, x) \in F\} \quad \text{the pre-set of } x\,, \\
x^\bullet &= \{y \in X \mid (x, y) \in F\} \quad \text{the post-set of } x\,.
\end{aligned}
$$

The net N is said to be

- simple iff no two elements have the same pre- or post-set:

$$
(\forall x, y \in X)\, (({}^\bullet x = {}^\bullet y) \wedge (x^\bullet = y^\bullet) \Rightarrow (x = y))\,;
$$

- pure iff

$$
(\forall x \in X)\, ({}^\bullet x \cap x^\bullet = \emptyset)\,.
$$

In a simple net, there are no multiple representations of elements that have pre- and post-sets in common. In a pure net, we have no cyclical interconnections between T-elements and S-elements.

It is a rather straightforward matter to use these nets as abstract system models. All we need to do is to represent, say, conditions by S-elements and events by T-elements. By appropriate arcs, the pre-condition set ${}^\bullet e$ and the post-condition set $e^\bullet$ of an event $e \in E$ must then be made the pre-set ${}^\bullet t \subseteq S$ and the post-set $t^\bullet \subseteq S$, respectively, of the corresponding T-element $t \in T$. We use the presence or absence of a single marking or token in an S-element to indicate whether or not the corresponding condition holds.

Formally, we can define a quadruple $\sum = (B, E; F, C)$ which models a condition/event system (CE-system) iff the following holds:

- $(B, E; F)$ is a pure and simple net whose elements $b \in B$ are called conditions and whose elements $e \in E$ are called events.

- C is a non-empty proper subset of $K = P(B)$, the elements $c \in C$ are called cases. They are represented as markings of the subset $c \subseteq B$ of conditions.

- $(\forall e \in E)\,(({}\exists c \in C)\,({}^\bullet e \subseteq c \wedge e^\bullet \cap c = \emptyset))$,
  i.e., each event has concession to take place in at least one case.

- $(\forall b \in B)\,(({}\exists c_1, c_2 \in C)\,(b \in c_1 \wedge b \notin c_2))$,
  i.e., each condition holds in at least one case and does not hold in at least another case.

- $(\forall c \in C)\,(({}\exists e \in E)\,({}^\bullet e \subseteq c \wedge e^\bullet \cap c = \emptyset))$,
  i.e., under each case there is at least one event which has concession.

- C is an equivalence class of the transitive closure of the reachability relation as defined in the previous section.

The requirement that the net $(B, E; F)$ be pure, in fact, excludes side conditions; i.e., CE-systems follow the extensionality principle.

With respect to the occurrence of events in a CE-system we make the idealizing assumptions that

- an event may take place once it has concession. The time at which this happens, however, can neither be determined nor is it enforced, e.g., by a clock;

- the occurrence of an event takes no time, which is to say that the termination of its pre-conditions coincides with the beginning of its post-conditions.

These abstractions eliminate any notion of time from our considerations, i.e., the behavior of systems is strictly represented in terms of causes and effects. In particular, the second assumption excludes a proposition of the form that any two or more events occur at the same time.

We will now proceed to study by means of net models some characteristic situations or phenomena that may occur in CE-systems. Since the absence of side conditions establishes symmetry with respect to the occurrence of events, all models may be considered in forward and backward direction.

Concession for the occurrence of an event $e \in E$ under a case $c \in C$, as we already know, is defined by

$$\bullet e \subseteq c \wedge e^\bullet \cap c = \emptyset \quad \text{in forward direction;}$$
$$e^\bullet \subseteq c \wedge \bullet e \cap c = \emptyset \quad \text{in backward direction.}$$

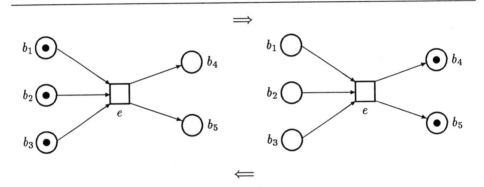

Figure 3.1: Concession for the occurrence of an event

Fig. 3.1 shows an event $e \in E$ whose pre- and post-condition sets are

$$\bullet e = \{b_1, b_2, b_3\} \text{ and } e^\bullet = \{b_4, b_5\},$$

respectively. On the left-hand side, we have concession in forward direction as the pre-conditions b_1, b_2, b_3 are marked by tokens, whereas the post-conditions carry no tokens. The occurrence of the event brings about the case shown on the right-hand side, which constitutes concession in backward direction.

Concurrency between two events $e_1, e_2 \in E$ under a case $c \in C$ is a situation in which both events have concession and are totally independent of each other with respect to their pre- and post-conditions. It is formally defined as

$$\bullet e_1 \cap \bullet e_2 = e_1^\bullet \cap e_2^\bullet = \emptyset \quad \text{and}$$

$$\bullet e_1 \subseteq c \wedge \bullet e_2 \subseteq c \wedge e_1^\bullet \cap c = e_2^\bullet \cap c = \emptyset \quad \text{in forward direction;}$$

$$\bullet e_1 \cap c = \bullet e_2 \cap c = \emptyset \wedge e_1^\bullet \subseteq c \wedge e_2^\bullet \subseteq c \quad \text{in backward direction.}$$

The two concurrent events may take place in either order, i.e., with e_1 preceding e_2 or with e_2 preceding e_1, or in one step. As their pre- and post-conditions are non-overlapping, all orders produce the same successor case. In this sense, concurrency results in deterministic system behavior.

Fig. 3.2 shows two concurrent events e_1 and e_2 which, on the left-hand side, are enabled in forward direction. The occurrence of both events produces the situation shown on the right-hand side which enables them in backward direction.

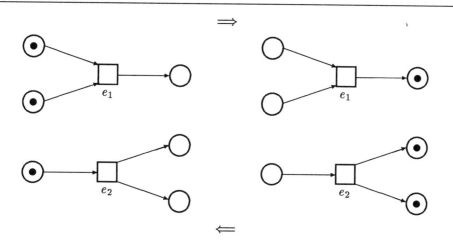

Figure 3.2: Concurrency between two events

Concurrency is a binary relation

$$conc \subseteq E \times E$$

which is symmetric but neither reflexive nor transitive. This is to say that

- no event $e \in E$ is concurrent to itself:

$$(\forall e \in E)\, ((e, e) \notin conc);$$

- e_2 is concurrent to e_1 iff e_1 is concurrent to e_2:

$$(\forall e_1, e_2 \in E)\, (((e_1, e_2) \in conc) \Longleftrightarrow ((e_2, e_1) \in conc))$$

- from concurrency between e_1 and e_2 on the one hand and between e_2 and e_3 on the other hand, it can not be concluded that e_1 and e_3 are concurrent; i.e., we may have events e_1, e_2, $e_3 \in E$ such that

$$((e_1, e_2), (e_2, e_3) \in conc \wedge (e_1, e_3) \notin conc) \, .$$

A conflict between two events $e_1, e_2 \in E$ under a case $c \in C$ arises if both have concession to take place but share pre- or post-conditions. In such a situation, the occurrence of one of the conflicting events terminates the concession for the respective other event.

We define

$$ {}^\bullet e_1 \cap {}^\bullet e_2 \neq \emptyset \vee e_1^\bullet \cap e_2^\bullet \neq \emptyset \quad \text{and} $$

$$ {}^\bullet e_1 \subseteq c \wedge {}^\bullet e_2 \subseteq c \wedge e_1^\bullet \cap c = e_2^\bullet \cap c = \emptyset \qquad \text{as a forward conflict;} $$

$$ {}^\bullet e_1 \cap c = {}^\bullet e_2 \cap c = \emptyset \wedge e_1^\bullet \subseteq c \wedge e_2^\bullet \subseteq c \qquad \text{as a backward conflict.} $$

As there is nothing that would force an enabled event to take place at a particular time, it cannot be predicted which of the two conflicting events actually occurs. Within the scope of the conditions that are taken into consideration, no information to this effect is available. We have two alternative succeeding cases into which the conflict eventually resolves. However, the choice between the two is made completely at random or, as we may also say, by arbitration. Thus, conflicts result in non-deterministic system behavior.

Fig. 3.3 illustrates the effect of a forward and a backward conflict between two events e_1 and e_2, based on the same net structure. The events are in conflict with respect to the pre-condition b_1 and the post-condition b_4.

It is interesting to observe that forward and backward conflicts are, in this example, not symmetric. Neither of the conflict resolutions brings about a successor case that would constitute a conflict in the opposite direction.

The occurrence of either event under both the forward and the backward conflict situation brings about a conflict-free case, under which this event is enabled in reverse direction. Its occurrence re-establishes the original conflicting case.

This observation is generally true for all conflicting events that have either only pre-conditions or only post-conditions in common, or feature, as in the example, at least some form of asymmetry with respect to common pre- and post-conditions.

Moreover, we observe that, by inspection of the valid (marked) pre- and post-conditions of two potentially conflicting events, it can obviously be decided in an objective manner whether or not they are the result of a conflict resolution and, if so, which way this conflict has actually been resolved. This information has apparently entered our scope of consideration (or our system model) since it was not available before. It is therefore said to have emerged out of nothing or to have been brought in from the environment [Petri73, Petri76].

We interpret this gain of information as the consequence of a decision. If this decision is being reversed, say, by an occurrence in opposite direction of the event that brought it about, then the information is said to disappear or to be lost into the environment.

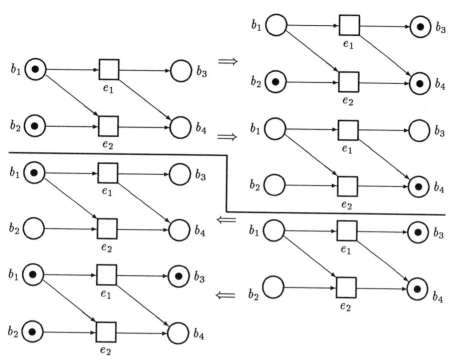

Figure 3.3: Forward and backward conflicts between two events

Confusion is a situation that arises between conflicting and concurrent events. It is characterized by the creation of cases from which the resolution of conflicts can not be objectively stated.

In a case $c \in C$, two events $e_1, e_2 \in E$ may concurrently have concession. However, due to the occurrence of, say, the event e_1, the event e_2 either gets into or out of a conflict with a third event $e_3 \in E$.

These situations are illustrated in fig. 3.4. On the left-hand side, we have both e_1 and e_2 concurrently enabled, as a consequence of which they may take place in any order. Either order produces the case $\{b_2, b_5\}$. However, this case is the result of a conflict resolution between e_2 and e_3 if e_1 happens to occur before e_2, and the result of a conflict-free sequence of events if e_2 occurs before e_1.

On the right-hand side, we have again e_1 and e_2 concurrently enabled, as both events have neither pre- nor post-conditions in common. Either order of occurrences produces the case $\{b_3, b_5\}$. However, having reached this case, it cannot any more

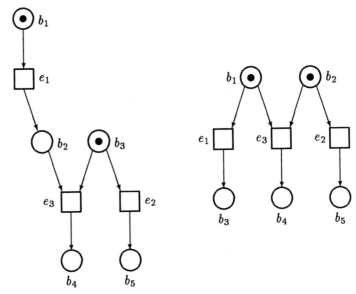

Figure 3.4: Confusion between two events

be decided whether a conflict has been resolved between e_1 and e_3, as consequence of which e_2 has been taken out of its conflict situation with e_3, or between e_2 and e_3, as a consequence of which e_1 has been moved out of its conflict with e_3.

Thus, in a system featuring confusion, the occurrence of conflict situations does not only depend on the net structure, but also on the particular sequence of event occurrences.

The condition/event net of fig. 3.5 models a small system which features all the phenomena we have just discussed. A conceivable sequence of event occurrences which starts from the initial case $\{b_1, b_2, b_3\}$ is as follows:

b_1			b_1	b_1			b_5	b_2	b_1	
b_2	e_1 b_1	e_5	b_5	e_2 b_2	e_1	b_4	e_4 b_7	e_2 b_9	e_7 b_2	$\cdots$
b_3	e_3 b_6		b_8	b_8		b_8	b_8	e_6 b_{10}	e_8 b_3	

In this sequence, cases are represented as columns of the respective enabled conditions. To the right of each case representation, we find a column of events which are enabled under this case. Conflicting events are symbolized as pairs $\underline{e_i} \not\!\phi_j$, of

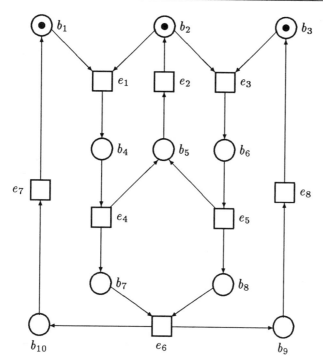

Figure 3.5: Example of a CE-net featuring concurrent and conflicting events

which e_i is the event that is assumed to occur and ϕ_j is the event which loses its concession. Concurrent events are symbolized as $e_i\ e_j$. The columns to the right of event columns represent the cases that emerge from the occurrence of the events.

This sequence of events is one out of two possible sequences that, given the initial case, characterize the behavior of the system. Each of these sequences is said to be a process. Both processes reproduce the initial case and are therefore said to be cyclic or reproducing processes. In cases of concurrency between any two events e_i and e_j, the sequences e_i, e_j and e_j, e_i are not considered alternatives of the system behavior. Both constitute occurrences of the same single-step process. Alternative system or process behavior results only from conflict situations which are resolved by arbitration.

A CE-net is called

- a state transition graph iff all events have exactly one pre-condition and one post-condition, i.e., $(\forall e \in E)\ (|{}^\bullet e| = |e^\bullet| = 1)$,

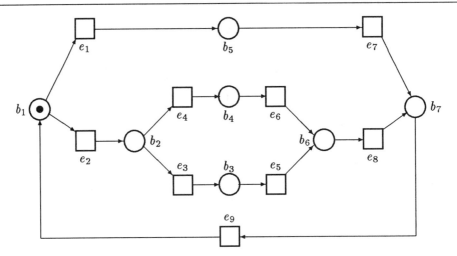

Figure 3.6: A state transition graph modeling an automaton

- a synchronization graph iff all conditions have exactly one input event and one output event, i.e., $(\forall b \in B)\ (|{}^{\bullet}b| = |b^{\bullet}| = 1)$.

A typical state transition graph which models a **state transition machine** (or an **automaton**) is shown in fig. 3.6. As branching (and merging) of paths through the graph is confined to conditions, the net is token-preserving. In the case of just one token circulating about the net, each place represents a state of the machine. Each state transition is accomplished by the occurrence of exactly one event. Two (or more) events may be in conflict with each other but never be enabled concurrently. The net is **live** as each state has a successor state. This is a consequence of the cyclic structure of the net and of the fact that each forward conflict is offset by a corresponding backward conflict. In particular, the information that enters the net on the resolution of the forward conflict between e_1 and e_2 exits on the occurrence of the backward conflict between e_7 and e_8, and the information gained by the resolution of the forward conflict between e_3 and e_4 is lost on the occurrence of the backward conflict between e_5 and e_6.

Synchronization graphs model the branching (or splitting) of a process into concurrent threads and the synchronization of these threads.

In the synchronization graph shown in fig. 3.7, the occurrence of e_1 creates two concurrently executable threads A and B, of which A is further split up into the threads $A1$ and $A2$ by the occurrence of the event e_2. The corresponding instances of synchronization are the occurrences of the events e_6 (for the threads $A1$ and

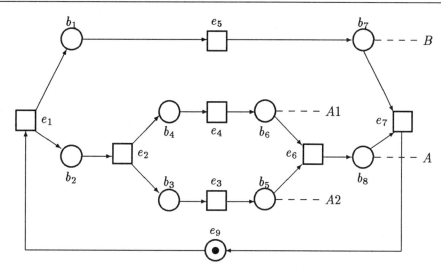

Figure 3.7: A synchronization graph

$A2$) and e_7 (for the threads A and B). Note that this synchronization graph is fully complementary to the state transition graph of fig. 3.6 in that all events and conditions are completely interchanged.

3.3   Predicate-Transition (PrT-) Nets

Condition/event nets are the simplest form of Petri nets. Conditions and events are formally treated as indistinguishable units or entities whose function, purpose or meaning is beyond the scope of these models and, hence, can be freely interpreted.

It appears to be a rather straightforward matter to work with informal inscriptions to associate an interpretation with the components of the net structure (S-units, T-units, arcs), i.e., on the static parts of the system (process) model. Inscriptions of this kind may include natural language text, special literals, variables, graphical symbols, or formal expressions representing, for instance, pieces of some computation. However, it turns out to be generally quite difficult to deal in a consistent manner with inscribed tokens that would help to distinguish individual items or pieces which, as they pass through the same net, essentially undergo the same treatment by the system, unless there is some formal basis available for it.

In the absence of such a basis, we would be forced to design nets featuring repetitively occurring subnets of identical structure which distinguish individual system instantiations that belong to the same scheme. It takes little imagination to realize that such nets, even when modeling rather simple systems, would be hopelessly overloaded with unnecessary structural details.

A formal framework for inscribing the static and dynamic parts of CE-nets in a consistent manner can be deduced from a systematic approach towards folding subnets with identical structures into a single net scheme. Its various instantiations are distinguished by constant inscriptions of tokens. They are bound to variable inscriptions of net components in compliance with logical formulas that specify the legitimate instantiations of the scheme.

This folding technique rests on the following interpretation of condition/event nets [GeLa78, Gela81, Gen87].

The conditions may be considered atomic propositions of propositional logic. They are either true (holding) or false (not holding) which is reflected by the presence or absence of markings (tokens) in the respective S-units.

In first-order logic, the atomic propositions are replaced by predicates. These predicates denote properties of individual items which constitute the components of a system or process, or relations that exist between these items. The predicates are formed from symbols or literals denoting properties and from names, expressions or values by which the individual items can be identified.

The occurrence of an event, in this interpretation, is to be understood as

- the invalidation of the propositions associated with its pre-conditions;

- the coincident validation of the propositions associated with its post-conditions.

As a very simple example, let us consider the condition/event net of fig. 3.8 which features two disjoint subnets of identical structure. The conditions of this net are distinguished by predicates formed from the property symbols P, Q, R and from the set of individuals $\{a, b\}$. The particular marking of the net represents the propositions

- 'individual a has the properties P and Q';

- 'individual b has the property Q but not the property P';

- 'individual b is in relation R to individual a' but
  'individual a is not in relation R to individual b'.

The occurrence of the enabled event causes a to lose its property P and b to lose its property Q, while forcing a into the relation R with b. Thus, we say that the properties P, Q and R are predicates with changing extensions.

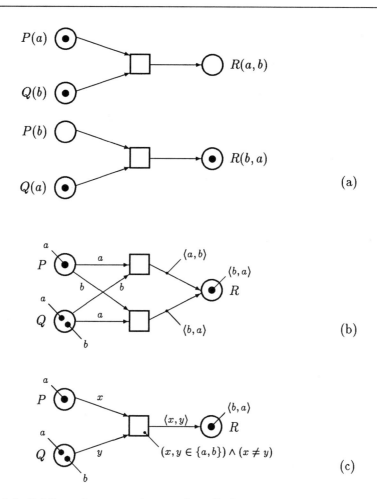

Figure 3.8: Folding of a CE-net into an inscribed PrT-net scheme

In fig. 3.8.a we observe that each of the predicates P, Q, R appears twice in order to be able to represent the properties P and Q for each of the individuals a and b, and the relation R for each pair that can be formed from a and b.

However, instances of the same predicates can be folded into predicate schemes in which instantiations by individuals are represented as tokens that are inscribed with their names. In our example, we obtain the folded net shown in fig. 3.8.b. The arcs of this net need to be labeled by the names of the individuals in compliance with the propositions that are being changed by the events.

In a similar way, we can fold both events of the net into one **event scheme**, as they are connected to the same predicate schemes in the same way, except for the labels on the arcs. The result of this folding step is shown in fig. 3.8.c. The arcs must now be inscribed with **variables** or **tuples of variables** which substitute for members of the set of individuals that may assume properties associated with the places to which they are connected.

The range of the variables and the instantiations of the event scheme are specified by the logical formula with which the T-unit is inscribed. A particular instance of the event scheme derives from the consistent substitution (or binding), in compliance with the logical formula, of the variables with individuals from the respective input predicate schemes P and Q.

Having sketched out the underlying idea, we can now proceed to define more rigorously what we mean by a simple variant of a **predicate/transition (PrT-) net** so-called **first-order predicate schemes** of CE-nets [Gela81]. Its constituents are

- a directed net $(S, T; F)$, where S is a set of **first-order predicate schemes**, T is a set of **transition schemes**, and F is the **flow relation** by which elements from T and S are interconnected;

- a **structure** $\sum$ which comprises sets of individuals and operations and relations defined over these individuals;

- a **labeling** of all arcs from the set F with n-tuples of variables, where n is the arity of the predicate schemes that are connected to the arcs; with a zero-tuple (denoted as ϕ) specifying a no-arguments predicate scheme, or an ordinary place which carries plain tokens. Examples of inscribed arcs are:

- inscriptions in (some of) the transition schemes which are logical formulas constructed from the operations and relations of the structure $\sum$, from the set of individuals and from the variables that appear in the inscriptions of the incoming and outgoing arcs of the transition scheme. If (part of) such a formula has the form $v = t$, where v is a variable and t is a term, then all occurrences of v on incoming and outgoing arcs may be replaced by copies of the term t.

Examples of inscriptions in transition schemes are:

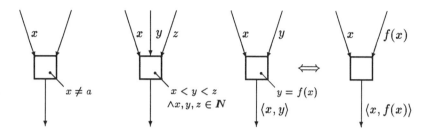

- some initial marking M_0 of the predicate schemes of S with n-tuples of individual items, such as

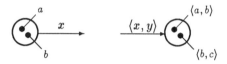

(note that a predicate scheme may be marked with at most one copy of a particular individual).

A transition scheme is enabled to take place iff:

- the variables on its input arcs can be instantiated with individuals from the respective input predicate schemes so that its logical formula is satisfied;

- none of the output predicate schemes carries copies of the individuals which the particular instantiation produces as output.

Consider, for an illustration of these definitions, the transition scheme defined in fig. 3.9. The underlying structure $\sum$ is specified by the set of individuals $\{a, b, c\}$ and by the precedence relation $<$, which is assumed to order the individuals as $a < b < c$. Under the particular marking, two instantiations of the transition scheme are enabled, namely $(x = a \wedge \langle y, z \rangle = \langle b, c \rangle)$ and $(x = b \wedge \langle y, z \rangle = \langle b, c \rangle)$. However, as both instantiations are in conflict with each other with respect to the item $\langle b, c \rangle$, only one of them may actually occur. We have chosen this to be the former instantiation, as a consequence of which the markings of the predicate schemes change as shown: the item a and the item $\langle b, c \rangle$ are withdrawn from the upper and lower input predicate schemes, respectively, while the item $\langle a, b \rangle$ and a plain token are added to the upper and lower output predicate schemes, respectively.

If no ambiguities can arise, we will also refer to predicate and transition schemes simply as places and transitions.

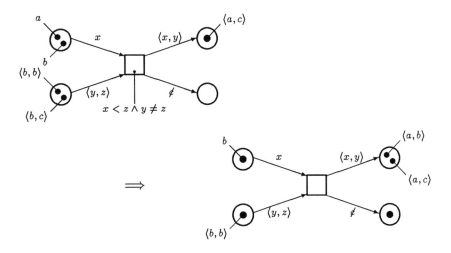

Figure 3.9: Occurrence of a transition scheme of a PrT-net

Full-fledged PrT-nets generally allow for more concise system models. They feature predicate schemes which may be instantiated with several copies of an individual item, possibly up to a certain upper bound (or capacity), and arcs that may be inscribed with **formal sums** of n-tuples of variables. Instances of transition schemes

- withdraw as many individuals from the input places as are necessary to satisfy the formal sums on the respective input arcs;

- put as many individuals in the output places as are specified by the formal sums on the respective output arcs (provided there is enough capacity left).

System states and state changes can thus be specified and modeled in a form that is more closely adapted to the needs of dealing with objects, messages or resources that come in several copies or units, and of reasoning about system invariance properties.

4 Models of Computation

We now use the modeling tools developed in the preceding chapter to systematically derive from a common root three basic concepts of organizing deterministic computations.[3] Generally speaking, these computations can be defined in terms of (algorithms which realize) functions or function applications modeled by means of synchronization graphs. The underlying organizational concepts or, as we may alternatively say, models of computation are characterized by [TrBrHo82]

- control disciplines specifying the mechanisms by which computations are driven ahead step-by-step;

- operational disciplines specifying the mechanisms that supply operators with operands.

The PrT-net models used throughout this chapter feature the following general properties:

- The individuals denoted by the variables are assumed to be from the same set U. The logical formulas inscribed into the transitions are composed of these variables, equality and the operators and predicate symbols associated with the set U.

- The arcs are just labeled with variables, not tuples, in compliance with the properties (or predicate schemes) associated with the places they are connected to.

- The places carry at most one copy of an individual item.

4.1 A Functional Model

From a conceptual point of view, deterministic computational processes may simply be thought of as occurrences of abstract or real operators that accept interpretable (or executable) specifications of functions and arguments as operands, and return function values as results.

Conventional computing machines may be considered real operators whose functions and arguments need to be specified as procedural (or imperative) programs and input data sets, respectively. The programs constitute specific instantiations (or occurrences) of the operators (machines) which transform the respective input data sets, internally represented as initial states, into output data sets, represented as terminal states, by sequences of incremental state transitions.

---

[3]The contents of this chapter can in large parts be found in [Klu86].

Instantiations of operators may be considered at several levels of refinement or abstraction. We may either be interested in the details of incremental state transitions or in global state changes (from initial to terminal states) only. Accordingly, the operators may be seen as being instantiated by orderly sequences of primitive function applications (e.g., instructions) that effect n-step processes or, alternatively, by composite function applications (programs) that effect one-step processes.

We learned in the previous chapter that PrT-nets are perfect tools to model processes at various levels of abstractions and to move freely between these levels without loss of information. Structural information generally transforms into more specific inscriptions of transitions, places, arcs and tokens as the level of abstraction increases, and information contained in inscriptions transforms into more specific net structures, as the level of abstraction decreases.

PrT-net models of computational processes enable us to exhibit their operational semantics. The objects of a computation can be modeled by inscribed tokens which instantiate predicate schemes, and the transformations to be performed on these objects can be expressed by logical formulas specifying transition schemes [GeLa78, Gela81, Gen87].

These ideas can best be captured by devising a basic PrT-net primitive for an abstract operator which accepts function specifications of arity n which are from the set

$$F^{(n)} \subset X^n \times Y \ .$$

X and Y respectively denote sets of arguments and function values and X^n denotes the n-fold Cartesian product of X. The distinction between functions, arguments and function values is of a more or less artificial nature. It merely serves to identify the property of an object with respect to a particular instantiation of an abstract operator. We denote the set of computational objects under consideration by U, with

$$X = Y = U \ \ \text{and} \ \ F \subset U \ .$$

where $F = F^{(1)} \cup F^{(2)} \cup \ldots$. Thus, all objects may occur as legitimate arguments and function values. In particular, we allow for higher-order functions at least to the extent that functions may be applied to functions as parameters.

A general scheme for computing the value of a function for some n arguments may be denoted as

$$y = f(x_1, \ldots, x_n) \ .$$

This equation specifies the variables $x_1, \ldots, x_n \in X$, $f \in F$, $y \in Y$ as formal parameters (or placeholders) for actual parameters (arguments, functions and function values), respectively.

The operational aspect can be made more explicit using the notation

$$y = \mathbf{op}^{(n)} f \, x_1 \ldots x_n \ ,$$

in which $\mathbf{op}^{(n)}$ represents an $(n+1)$-place abstract operator. This operator is said to apply whatever object actually substitutes for the formal parameter f to whatever objects substitute for the formal parameters $x_1, \ldots, x_n$. The right-hand side of this equation constitutes an expression which is also referred to as an **application**. Its value substitutes for the formal parameter y.

An application can be straightforwardly translated into the PrT-net primitive AP shown in fig. 4.1.

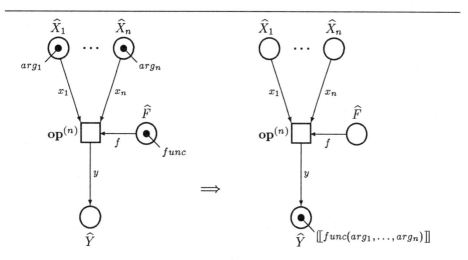

Figure 4.1: PrT-net representation AP of an application

In this net primitive, we model the abstract operator $\mathbf{op}^{(n)}$ as a transition scheme which is connected to $n + 1$ input predicate schemes $\widehat{X}_1, \ldots, \widehat{X}_n$ and $\widehat{F}$, and to one **output predicate scheme** $\widehat{Y}$. These predicate schemes respectively represent the properties **argument object, function object** and **function value object**. We will henceforth refer to them simply as **input** and **output places**, or sometimes also as **channels** via which the operator receives its operands and sends out its result value. The formal parameters $x_1, \ldots, x_n, f, y$ appear as inscriptions of the connecting arcs. Inscribed tokens represent individuals from the set U of computational objects.

The instantiations of the input places with inscribed tokens, in fact, model the bindings of the **formal input parameters** $x_1, \ldots, x_n$ and f to **actual parameters** and, thus, an activation of the operator $\mathbf{op}^{(n)}$.

In the case shown on the left-hand side of fig. 4.1, $\mathbf{op}^{(n)}$ is enabled with

$$x_1 = arg_1, \ x_2 = arg_2, \ \ldots, \ x_n = arg_n \ \text{ and } \ f = func \,.$$

Its occurrence consumes the tokens from the input places and produces in the output place a token inscribed with $y = [\![func(arg_1, \ldots, arg_n)]\!]$, which denotes the result of applying the object $func$ to the objects $arg_1, \ldots, arg_n$. This case is shown on the right-hand side of fig. 4.1.

The transition scheme $\mathbf{op}^{(n)}$ must be inscribed with some logical formula which precisely specifies the mapping of actual instantiations of the input places into the corresponding instantiation of the output place (or of operand objects into a result object). This specification must be based on a concrete set F of legitimate functions and their respective domains/codomains. In particular, the formula must include conditionals requiring that

- the instantiation of $\widehat{F}$ be from the set F (i.e., the object in function position is a legitimate function);

- the instantiations of all $\widehat{X}_i$ be within the domain of the function (i.e., the function is applied to legitimate arguments);

- the arity of the function matches the arity of the operator.[4]

Otherwise, the output place $\widehat{Y}$ must be instantiated with some bottom token indicating that the object in function position is not applicable at all, or not applicable to the objects in the argument positions, or not supplied with the correct number of arguments. Thus, the logical formula for $\mathbf{op}^{(n)}$ in fact defines the operational semantics of a simple functional programming language.

As essential ingredients of such a language, we introduce here rather informally a small set of primitive functions, including

- the binary arithmetic functions $+$, $-$, $*$, $/$ which are assumed to map decimal numbers into decimal numbers;

- the binary predicate functions LT (less than), EQ (equal), GE (greater or equal), GT (greater than) etc. which map decimal numbers into the Boolean constants TRUE and FALSE;

- the logical functions NAND, NOR which map Boolean constants into Boolean constants;

---

[4]This restriction is introduced as a matter of convenience which keeps the net models free of details that are not relevant in this context. It excludes from consideration r-ary applications of n-ary functions with $n \neq r$, which are to return

- functions of arity $n - r$ if $n > r$,
- applications of arity $r - n$ if $r > n$.

The full implications of these cases are somewhat difficult to include into simple net models.

- an IF-THEN-ELSE clause which takes a Boolean constant as a selector function for either the consequence or the alternative.

Let us now consider, as an example, the conditional expression

$$\text{IF } (u \text{ GE } v) \text{ THEN } (u - v) \text{ ELSE } (v - u)$$

which for each pair of numbers substituted for the variables u and v computes the absolute value of their difference.

In our applicative notation this expression assumes the form

$$\mathbf{op}^{(2)} \ \mathbf{op}^{(2)} \ \text{GE } v \ u \ \mathbf{op}^{(2)} \ - \ v \ u \ \mathbf{op}^{(2)} \ - \ u \ v \ .$$

The outermost $\mathbf{op}^{(2)}$ takes the applicative version of the predicate as a function and applies it to the applicative versions of the consequence and the alternative in its argument positions.

This applicative notation can be turned directly into the PrT-net shown in fig. 4.2 which features two levels of application primitives with overlapping input/output places. Annotations of the form u/x on the arcs denote the renaming of the standard inscription x into the variable u taken from the expression.

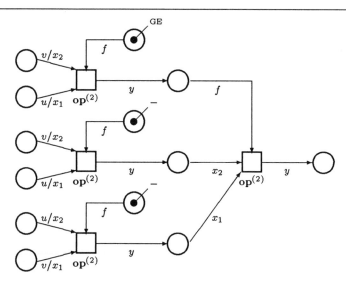

Figure 4.2: PrT-net model for the computation of
$$\text{IF } (u \text{ GE } v) \text{ THEN } (u - v) \text{ ELSE } (v - u)$$

We note that in this net none of the input places for arguments is as yet instantiated. This reflects the fact that the expression from which this net derives contains
variables rather than numerical values in the respective syntactical positions, in
which case no evaluation is possible.

In order to model a semantically correct computation, all input places whose
outgoing arcs are inscribed with the same variable (either u or v in the particular
example) must be instantiated with identical copies of value tokens. This can
be accomplished in one conceptual step by completing the net with a **substitution
scheme** (or a **substitution operator**) which injects and thereby replicates argument
tokens.

Adding a substitution operator is conceptually equivalent to forming a composite
function which may be applied to arguments in the same way as primitive functions.

Let $expr$ be an expression which is specified in terms of the variables $x_1, \ldots, x_n$,
then

$$f = \mathbf{sub}^{(n)} \langle x_1 \ldots x_n \rangle \; expr$$

denotes a function (or an **abstraction**) of n formal parameters. The substitution
construct $\mathbf{sub}^{(n)} \langle x_1 \ldots x_n \rangle$ is said to be the function (abstraction) **header**. It binds
free occurrences of the variables $x_1, \ldots, x_n$ in the function (abstraction) **body** $expr$.
Variable occurrences in $expr$ are considered free if they are not preceded by other
substitution constructs inside $expr$ that bind them.

In order to allow for a simple form of **recursive functions**, the function name f
may be included into the list of variables bound by the substitution operator:

$$f = \mathbf{sub}^{(n)} \langle f \mid x_1 \ldots x_n \rangle \; expr \; .$$

It denotes the binding of free occurrences of f in $expr$ to the entire function expression on the right-hand side.

The application of such a defined function to n arguments takes the form

$$y = \mathbf{op}^{(n)} \; \mathbf{sub}^{(n)} \langle f \mid x_1 \ldots x_n \rangle \; expr \; arg_1 \ldots arg_n \; .$$

It is supposed to return as a result the value of the function body in which all free
occurrences of f are substituted by the function expression and all occurrences of
$x_1, \ldots, x_n$ are substituted by the respective arguments. We denote this as

$$y = \llbracket expr[f \Leftarrow \mathbf{sub}^{(n)} \langle f \mid x_1 \ldots x_n \rangle \; expr; \; x_1 \Leftarrow arg_1, \ldots, x_n \Leftarrow arg_n] \rrbracket \; .$$

This substitution scheme can be modeled by means of the PrT-net primitive SUB
shown in fig. 4.3. It connects the input places $\widehat{X}_1, \ldots, \widehat{X}_n$ and $\widehat{F}$ to sets of output
places $S\_\widehat{X}_1, \ldots, S\_\widehat{X}_n$ and $S\_\widehat{F}$ through arcs inscribed with the variables $x_1, \ldots, x_n$
and f, respectively. The places belonging to the sets $S\_\widehat{X}_1, \ldots, S\_\widehat{X}_n$ and $S\_\widehat{F}$ are

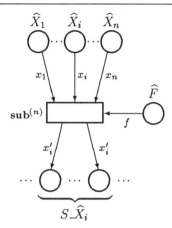

Figure 4.3: PrT-net primitive SUB for the substitution scheme $\mathbf{sub}^{(n)}$

to model free occurrences of the variables bound by $\mathbf{sub}^{(n)}$ in a function body expression. Each of these sets may be empty. An occurrence of SUB reproduces the token instantiations of its input places in the respective sets of output places.

With this substitution primitive, the computation of a defined function can be modeled by a PrT-net of the general form depicted in fig. 4.4. Its input and output places perfectly map onto those of an application primitive which supplies it with the necessary argument and function tokens. This enables us to represent the same computation at two different levels of abstraction (or refinement). The occurrence of an apply-operator $\mathbf{op}^{(n)}$ instantiated with a defined function may be considered

- either as a **one-step process** (or as an atomic event), in which case we are interested merely in the input/output mapping and, therefore, ignore the details of computing the function body;

- or as a **k-step process**, in which case we refine $\mathbf{op}^{(n)}$ by substituting in its place the PrT-net which explicitly models the computation of the function body.

In either case, the token eventually produced in the output place $\widehat{Y}$ carries the same inscription, i.e., it represents the same resulting object.

Thus, we define the **refinement** of an operator $\mathbf{op}^{(n)}$ as the **consistent** replacement by the PrT-net which models the computation specified by the function expression it is instantiated with. The attribute **consistent** relates to the input/output- and semantic-preserving property of the replacement.

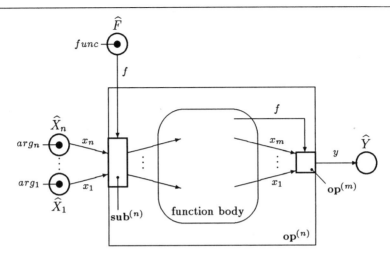

Figure 4.4: PrT-net module scheme for the computation of defined functions

The primitive functions informally introduced earlier and the defined functions (or abstractions) that can be constructed by means of the substitution operator $\mathbf{sub}^{(n)}$ form a reasonably complete set F of functions. The precise specification of the transformations that are effected by these functions when applied to arguments takes the form of the following logical formula with which the transition scheme $\mathbf{op}^{(n)}$ must be inscribed:

$$y = \begin{cases} [\![(x_2 \; f \; x_1)]\!] & \text{if } (n = 2) \\ & \text{and } ((x_1, x_2 \in D \text{ and } f \in \{+, -, *, /, \text{LT}, \text{EQ}, \text{GE}, \text{GT}\}) \\ & \text{or } (x_1, x_2 \in \{\text{TRUE}, \text{FALSE}\} \text{ and } f \in \{\text{NAND}, \text{NOR}\})) \\[6pt] [\![x_1]\!] & \text{if } (n = 2) \text{ and } (f = \text{TRUE}) \\ [\![x_2]\!] & \text{if } (n = 2) \text{ and } (f = \text{FALSE}) \\[6pt] [\![expr[f \Leftarrow \mathbf{sub}^{(n)}\langle f \mid x_1 \ldots x_n \rangle \; expr; x_1 \Leftarrow arg_1, \ldots, x_n \Leftarrow arg_n]]\!] \\ & \text{if } (n \geq 1) \text{ and } f = \mathbf{sub}^{(n)}\langle f \mid x_1 \ldots x_n \rangle \; expr \\ & \text{and } (\forall i \in \{1, \ldots, n\}) \, (x_i = arg_i) \\[6pt] \bot & \text{else} \end{cases}$$

D denotes the set of decimal numbers.

This formula lists from top to bottom

- applications of primitive binary arithmetic, predicate and logical functions;

- the IF-THEN-ELSE clause;

- applications of defined functions;

- the generation of a bottom symbol ⊥ if none of the above cases applies with respect to the instantiations of the input places.

It specifies the operational semantics of a simple functional programming language or, if this language is directly supported by a functional computing system, the architecture of that system.

We are now ready to take another look at and complete our example of computing the absolute value of the difference of any two numbers. To do so, we turn the expression specifying this computation into a defined function of two formal parameters and apply it to actual arguments, say 3 and 4:

$$y = \mathbf{op}^{(2)} \ \mathbf{sub}^{(2)} \ \langle f \mid u \ v \rangle$$
$$\mathbf{op}^{(2)} \ \mathbf{op}^{(2)} \ \text{GE} \ v \ u$$
$$\mathbf{op}^{(2)} - v \ u$$
$$\mathbf{op}^{(2)} - u \ v$$
$$3 \quad 4$$

This equation can be directly transformed into the PrT-net model depicted in fig. 4.5.

When ignoring the refinement of the big transition box, the net models the computation as a one-step process which, upon the occurrence of $\mathbf{op}^{(2)}$, coincidently consumes the input tokens and produces an output token which is inscribed with the decimal value $+1$.

Taking the refinement into consideration, the net models the same computation as a three-step process, of which

- the first step fires the substitution operator $\mathbf{sub}^{(2)} \langle f \mid u \ v \rangle$ to inject duplicates of the argument tokens into the places that represent the argument positions of the three innermost application primitives.

- the second step comprises the concurrent occurrence of the three innermost operators $\mathbf{op}^{(2)}$ which model the computations of the predicate expression and of both alternatives of the IF-THEN-ELSE clause. As a result, we obtain a token inscribed with the Boolean value TRUE in the function position and tokens inscribed with the decimal values $+1$ and -1 in the first and second argument position, respectively, of the outermost operator $\mathbf{op}^{(2)}$.

- the third step fires this operator to reproduce the instantiation $+1$ of its first argument position in the output place $\widehat{Y}$, while consuming without reproduction the instantiation of the second argument position.

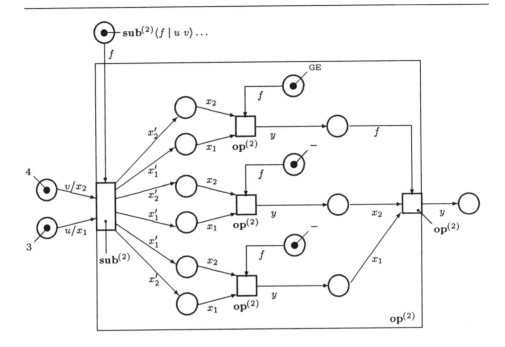

Figure 4.5: PrT-net model for the computation of the absolute value of the difference between two decimal numbers

We note that this PrT-net models a **process** which is completely controlled by the
orderly consumption and (re-)production of operands (object tokens) by operators.
As none of the channels (places) via which the operands are being moved is shared
between any two operators, we have in fact a **synchronization graph** which behaves
deterministically.

However, our example also reveals a somewhat annoying problem that comes
with the need to instantiate all input places in order to activate an operator. In the
case of the IF-THEN-ELSE clause, this activation model is bound to effect redundant
computations as both the consequence and the alternative constitute arguments of
the outermost operator $\mathbf{op}^{(2)}$ and, hence, need to be evaluated. Only one of the
alternatives, however, contributes to the result of the function application, while
the other one is simply consumed by the operator.

This kind of redundancy need not necessarily be rejected as unacceptable. Other
than wasting resources, no harm is done as long as the computations are guaranteed

to produce correct results.

However, in conjunction with recursive functions, our execution model for the IF-THEN-ELSE clause also creates a severe problem whose consequences cannot at all be tolerated: non-termination.

Meaningful recursive functions include IF-THEN-ELSE clauses whose predicates specify termination conditions. The recursive calls occur either only within the consequence or within the alternative.

A typical example is the computation of the factorial function, which may be recursively defined as

$$fac(n) = \text{IF} \quad (n \text{ GT } 1)$$
$$\text{THEN} \ (fac(n-1) * n)$$
$$\text{ELSE} \quad 1$$

The equivalent applicative notation, when applied to some argument value, say 9, has the form:

$$\mathbf{op}^{(1)} \ \mathbf{sub}^{(1)} \ \langle fac \mid n \rangle$$
$$\mathbf{op}^{(2)} \ \mathbf{op}^{(2)} \ \text{GT } 1 \ n$$
$$\mathbf{op}^{(2)} * n \ \mathbf{op}^{(1)} \ fac$$
$$\mathbf{op}^{(2)} - 1 \ n$$
$$1$$
$$9$$

This applicative expression transforms directly into the PrT-net model of fig. 4.6. As a refinement of the outermost operator $\mathbf{op}^{(1)}$, we have a PrT-net FAC which models the computation of the recursive function specified by the token in its input place $\widehat{F}$. Since there is also an argument token carrying the value 9 in the input place $\widehat{X}$, $\mathbf{op}^{(1)}$ is enabled to take place.

The execution of this PrT-net eventually leads to the instantiation of the inner $\mathbf{op}^{(1)}$, symbolized by $\boxed{}$, with tokens representing

- a copy of the recursive function expression in $\widehat{F'}$;

- the argument value, decremented by one, in $\widehat{X'}$.

The occurrence of this operator creates in itself another recursive refinement by the PrT-net FAC. These refinements continue without termination as the outermost operator of FAC expects one of its argument tokens from the recursively instantiated operator $\mathbf{op}^{(1)}$, which never delivers it.

In order to rectify this problem we obviously must modify the execution model of the IF-THEN-ELSE clause. What we need is some control discipline which enforces

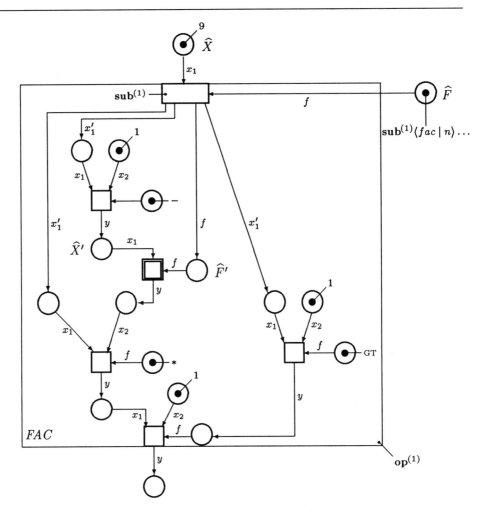

Figure 4.6: PrT-net model for the recursive computation of the factorial function

- first the computation of the predicate expression, and

- then only the computation of the clause selected by the predicate value, while the computation of the respective complementary clause must be suppressed, as demanded semantically.

There are essentially two control disciplines by which this can be accomplished. Both disciplines, in fact, define two different functional models of computation which have in common an operational discipline governed by the orderly consumption and reproduction of computational objects.

4.2 Control by Demand

This control discipline renders the activation of every operator $\mathbf{op}^{(n)}$ (and subsequently of every $\mathbf{sub}^{(n)}$) dependent on another pre-condition, modeled by an additional input place $\widehat{D}$. It represents a demand for its execution or, more precisely, for the type of the result token(s) that must be produced. $\widehat{D}$ may be instantiated with individuals from the set $\{\top, \bot\}$ of demand tokens, of which only the bottom token $\bot$ belongs to the set U as well.

The operator $\mathbf{op}^{(n)}$, when instantiated by a demand token

- $\top$, transforms all legitimate function applications, represented as instantiations of the input places $\widehat{X}_1, \ldots, \widehat{X}_n$ and $\widehat{F}$, according to the logical formula specified in the previous section, thereby producing a non-trivial result token in the output place $\widehat{Y}$;

- $\bot$, produces a bottom token $\bot$ in $\widehat{Y}$ irrespective of the tokens in $\widehat{X}_1, \ldots, \widehat{X}_n$ and $\widehat{F}$.

Thus, $\top$ represents a demand for the normal execution of $\mathbf{op}^{(n)}$, while $\bot$ just forces the trivial firing of an operator which merely serves to clean the net from tokens.

In a PrT-net which models the computation of a complex function application, demand tokens are recursively propagated from outermost to innermost, i.e., opposite to the flow of object tokens. This demand token flow is supposed to activate only those operators by $\top$ whose occurrences actually contribute to the function value, while all others are activated by $\bot$.

Since an operator $\mathbf{op}^{(n)}$ must receive a function token and n argument tokens, the demand for executing it may have to be replicated up to $(n+1)$ times in order to enable the subnets which compute these objects. No demand tokens are, however, required for constant objects.

To model the demand propagation properly, the application primitive AP of fig. 4.1 must be augmented as shown in fig. 4.7. This demand controlled application primitive DAP includes, in addition to the operator $\mathbf{op}^{(n)}$, a distribution scheme $\mathbf{ds}^{(m)}$ for demand tokens. A token residing in the input place $\widehat{D}_I$ is reproduced by $\mathbf{ds}^{(m)}$ in

- the internal place $\widehat{D}$ to enable $\mathbf{op}^{(n)}$,

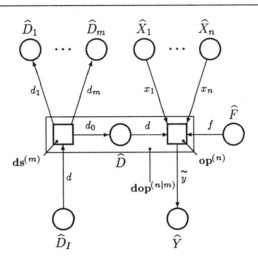

Figure 4.7: PrT-net primitive DAP for a demand-controlled application

- the output places $\widehat{D}_1, \ldots, \widehat{D}_m$ via which the demand is driven into $m \leq n+1$ subnets which eventually produce tokens in $\widehat{X}_1, \ldots, \widehat{X}_n$ and $\widehat{F}$ (or in any subset of these input places).

The net structure made up from the transition schemes $\mathbf{op}^{(n)}$ and $\mathbf{ds}^{(m)}$ and the internal place $\widehat{D}$ forms a **demand-controlled operator** $\mathbf{dop}^{(n|m)}$.

Executing an IF-THEN-ELSE clause under demand control requires a more elaborate scheme for the replication and propagation of demand tokens. It can be modeled by the PrT-net primitive DIF shown in fig. 4.8. The transition scheme $\mathbf{ifop}^{(2)}$ includes

- an operator $\mathbf{dop}^{(2|1)}$ made up from the transition schemes $\mathbf{dp}^{(1)}$ and $\mathbf{op}^{(2)}$ which, in a first phase, propagates a demand token arriving in $\widehat{D}_I$ into the subnet that computes the predicate value. In a second phase, it produces a result token in the output place $\widehat{Y}$ from subsequent instantiations of its input places $\widehat{X}_1, \widehat{X}_2$ and $\widehat{F}$.

- a demand generator $\mathbf{dg}^{(2)}$ which, depending on the predicate value token arriving in $\widehat{F}$, instantiates its output places thus:

$$d_1 = \begin{cases} \top & \text{if } f = \text{TRUE} \\ \bot & \text{else} \end{cases} \quad \text{and} \quad d_2 = \begin{cases} \top & \text{if } f = \text{FALSE} \\ \bot & \text{else .} \end{cases}$$

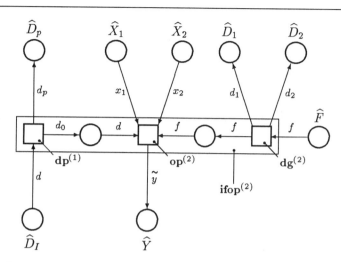

Figure 4.8: PrT-net primitive *DIF* for a demand-controlled IF-THEN-ELSE clause

These demand tokens are propagated into the subnets for the computation of the consequence and the alternative, respectively, which deliver the value tokens for the argument positions $\widehat{X}_1$ and $\widehat{X}_2$ of the operator $\mathbf{op}^{(2)}$.

If an operator $\mathbf{dop}^{(n)}$ is instantiated with a defined function of the form

$$\mathbf{sub}^{(n)}\langle f \mid x_1 \ldots x_n \rangle \; expr$$

in $\widehat{F}$, then a demand token $\top$ in $\widehat{D}_I$ results in a refinement of $\mathbf{dop}^{(n)}$ in which the demand is distributed as schematically shown in fig. 4.9. The subset of operators which becomes enabled with demand tokens $\top$ forms a coherent subnet that computes the actual function value, whereas the object tokens are soaked up without computation from all operators enabled with tokens $\bot$. In particular, a demand token $\bot$ terminates recursive function applications as it always produces the bottom symbol $\bot$ in the output place $\widehat{Y}$ of the particular operator $\mathbf{op}^{(n)}$, irrespective of the instantiation of function and argument predicate schemes.

Fig. 4.10 shows, as an example, a PrT-net for the demand-controlled computation of the factorial function. When executing the demand-controlled operators as described, $\mathbf{ifop}^{(2)}$ produces demand tokens $\top$ for the computation of the consequence and, hence, for the recursive refinement of the transition box $\boxdot$, as long as the predicate expression $(n \; \text{GT} \; 1)$ evaluates to TRUE. If $(n \; \text{GT} \; 1)$ turns FALSE, the consequence receives a bottom token $\bot$ which causes all its operators to produce $\bot$ as output tokens. The operator $\mathbf{op}^{(2)}$ in $\mathbf{ifop}^{(2)}$ thus becomes instantiated with $\bot$

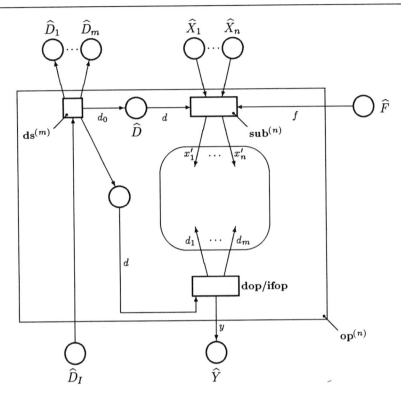

Figure 4.9: Demand distribution within the PrT-net of a defined function

and 1 in its first and second argument position, respectively, and with FALSE in its function position. This instantiation produces a token inscribed with the value 1 in $\widehat{Y}$. Subsequently, the entire net that has emerged from recursive refinements of □ terminates by the recursive propagation of result tokens from innermost to outermost.

Control by demand, as we will see later on, is primarily exercised in reduction systems as it follows in a natural way from the recursive definition of the reduction semantics underlying functional programs. It is generally applied to control computations which involve so-called non-strict terms. These are all program components which, depending on the outcome of certain decisions, may or may not have to be (fully) evaluated in order to arrive at meaningful results. The alternative expressions of IF-THEN-ELSE clauses are just the most obvious examples in kind. Others

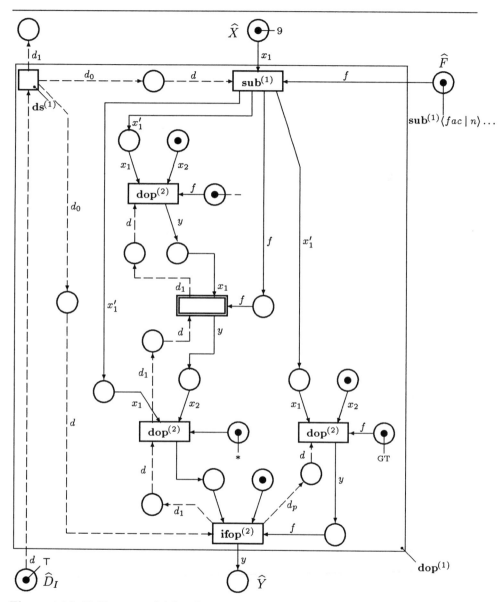

Figure 4.10: PrT-net model for the recursive computation of the factorial function under demand control

include data structures which contain unevaluated components or are potentially unending. To deal with the later case, control by demand may also be employed in data flow systems [AmHa84, PiAr85].

As for reductions, the PrT-net models which we have developed here give only a partly correct picture.[5] They insinuate the existence of token flow structures which, other than recursively expanding, do not change in the course of program execution. However, reduction relates to meaning-preserving transformations of program expressions which would have to be modeled by modifications of the respective net structures, e.g., by removing entire application primitives upon operator occurrences. Since this is not possible within the framework of PrT-nets, they can model reduction processes correctly only with respect to operator occurrences, including the orderly consumption and re-production of operand objects, but not with respect to the transformation of expressions.

4.3   Control by Availability

Control by demand is absolutely necessary to prevent redundant or non-terminating computations when unconditionally substituting operand (argument) tokens into all components of an IF-THEN-ELSE clause. The demand tokens conditionally propagated into the clause selected by the predicate value serve as additional trigger tokens for the operators enabled by the presence of operand tokens, whereas the bottom tokens propagated into the complementary clause in fact neutralize the activation due to the injected operand tokens.

However, these ends may be achieved by more direct means which avoid the flow of demand tokens altogether.

All we need to do is to introduce a more sophisticated scheme by which substitutions into the components of IF-THEN-ELSE clauses are realized.

Basically, the application of function expressions of the general form

$$\mathbf{sub}^{(n)}\langle x_1 \ldots x_n \rangle \ \ldots \quad \begin{array}{ll} \text{IF} & pred\_expr \\ \text{THEN} & true\_expr \\ \text{ELSE} & false\_expr \ \ldots \end{array}$$

must follow an execution model which uses

- an unconditional substitution operator $\mathbf{sub}^{(n)}$ to inject argument (and function) tokens into all components of the function body expression, including $pred\_expr$ but excluding $true\_expr$ and $false\_expr$ of an IF-THEN-ELSE clause;

---

[5]They do model reasonably well what is known as compiled graph reduction where all functions are treated as constant objects (see chapter 11).

- two complementary conditional substitution operators **sub_true**$^{(n)}$ and **sub_false**$^{(n)}$ which, under the control of the Boolean constant that emerges from the evaluation of *pred_expr*, inject argument (and function) tokens either into the consequence *true_expr* or into the alternative *false_expr*.

Fig. 4.11 schematically illustrates the complementary use of conditional substitution in a recursive function.

The unconditional substitution scheme **sub**$^{(n)}$ replicates, as before, argument and function instantiations from $\widehat{X}_1, \ldots, \widehat{X}_n$ and $\widehat{F}$ into the sets $S\_\widehat{X}_1, \ldots, S\_\widehat{X}_n$ and $S\_\widehat{F}$, respectively. At most one place of each set serves as input place for the subsequent conditional substitution operators **sub_true**$^{(n)}$ and **sub_false**$^{(n)}$. For all bound variables occurring in both the consequence and in the alternative, the respective input places are shared between **sub_true**$^{(n)}$ and **sub_false**$^{(n)}$. The operator **op**$^{(n)}$ which computes *pred_expr* is enabled to take place as soon as **sub**$^{(n)}$ has occurred. It produces an instantiation of the control predicate scheme $\widehat{C}$ with either of the Boolean constants TRUE or FALSE (or with some other individual from U). If $c =$ TRUE, then **sub_true**$^{(n)}$ is enabled to take place, but not **sub_false**$^{(n)}$. If $c =$ FALSE, then **sub_false**$^{(n)}$ is enabled to take place, but not **sub_true**$^{(n)}$.

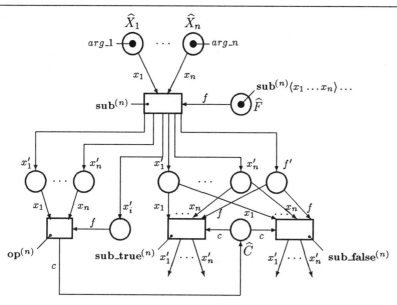

Figure 4.11: PrT-net model for conditional substitution

Thus, substitution and, hence, activation occurs only in either the consequence or the alternative but not in both. Should *pred_expr* evaluate to some individual from U other than TRUE or FALSE, then either **sub_true**$^{(n)}$ or **sub_false**$^{(n)}$ fires, injecting bottom tokens into the respective subnets. Eventually, they produce $\perp$ as the value of the entire IF-THEN-ELSE clause.

With this concept of conditional substitution, we can exercise control by availability of operand objects. The operational mechanism, i.e., the orderly consumption and reproduction of operand objects, remains the same as in the demand-controlled model. Thus, control by availability constitutes an alternative functional model of computation which avoids unnecessary computations by other means.

Fig. 4.12 shows, as an example, the PrT-net model for computing the factorial function under control by availability. Note that in this model the conditional substitution operator **sub_false**$^{(1)}$, if enabled, absorbs both its first argument and the function token, and reproduces the constant value 1, which is the second argument, in its output place.

Exercising control over operator occurrences by the availability of operand tokens characterizes the computational model underlying data flow systems. They come in essentially three versions, called execution models [Denn84], of which all have in common that executable programs are represented in the form of graph structures which are very similar to our PrT-nets. They are referred to as data flow graphs.

In the more traditional static data flow execution model, functions may only be applied to data objects, returning data objects as function values. There is no concept of higher-order functions. Primitive as well as user-defined functions are treated as non-consumable/non-reproducible objects, i.e., they are in fact realized as individualized operators.

When excluding functions from the set of consumable/reproducible objects, we have no general concept for recursion either. Indeed, the static data flow model provides only a CALL operator for non-recursively defined functions. Occurrences of the CALL operator, prior to executing the program, are statically expanded by the function expressions (or by the equivalent PrT-nets) referred to by inscribed names (identifiers). There is no recursive expansion of static data flow nets. This model allows only for tail-end recursions represented as iteration loops. The respective data flow graphs are used repeatedly by the direct feedback of output tokens into input parameter positions.

The other two data flow models include a general recursion concept and are therefore also referred to as being dynamic.

The recursive execution model comes closest to the concepts outlined by means of our PrT-net models. It is based on the recursive refinement (or expansion) of operators by data flow graphs which realize recursive functions. The recursive model does not allow for cyclic net structures as in the static model, thus ruling out

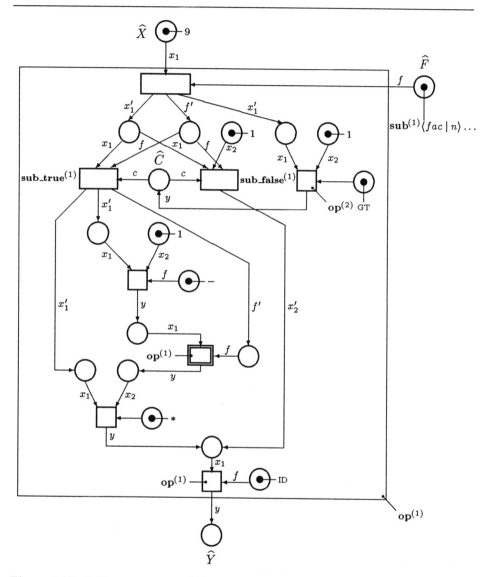

Figure 4.12: PrT-net model for the computation of the factorial function under control by availability

the realization of tail-end recursions by means of iteration loops. Every operator of the recursively expanding data flow graph therefore occurs at most once.

The **tagged token model** supports both recursion and iteration. In particular, iterations may occur within recursions and recursions may occur within iterations, and successive cycles through an iteration loop may overlap. Also, in contrast to the recursive model, different instances of recursive functions use the same data flow graphs rather than explicitly copying them recursively into themselves. Tokens that belong to different function or iteration loop instances are distinguished by special tags attached to them.

4.4   Control Flow

The acyclic synchronization graphs used throughout the preceding sections model functional (deterministic) computations at a level which completely abstracts from conceivable implementations. Operator occurrences are governed by the orderly consumption and (re-)production of object tokens communicated via unique channels. Each operator occurs at most once, and each channel is used at most once for the passage of a token between a producing and a consuming operator.

An entirely different model of computation emerges if, for reasons of an efficient implementation, we dispense with the explicit consumption and (re-)production of computational objects, and if we also try to share channels for the passage of tokens among several producing and consuming operators. To achieve both ends, we simply need to realize channels as **structural side conditions** of operators so that

- instantiations of (tokens in) input channels are restored,

- instantiations of output channels are modified (updated),

upon operator occurrences. All channels may then be used as inputs or outputs of several operators.

The problem with this approach is that it assumes the permanent instantiation of all channels with tokens. This would render all operators executable all the time, i.e., we would have total chaos.

To restore order among operator occurrences, we need to superimpose an additional **control structure** which activates operators based on the orderly consumption and reproduction of explicit **control tokens**. This control structure must realize a **synchronization graph** which establishes the same logical ordering among operators as given by the flow of object tokens in an equivalent functional net model.

A PrT-net primitive which models an operator under **control flow** is depicted in fig. 4.13.

Control over $\mathbf{cop}^{(n)}$ is exercised solely by the availability of a plain control token $\cent$ in the input control place C_i. The occurrence of $\mathbf{cop}^{(n)}$ passes this control token

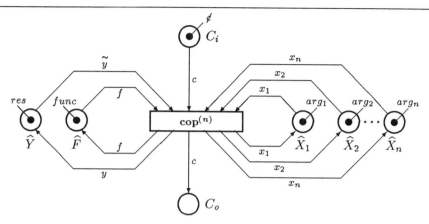

Figure 4.13: PrT-net primitive of an abstract operator under control flow

on to the output control place C_o (which coincides with the control input of the next operator in sequence).

What we have in fact modeled here is the familiar concept of instruction execution in a conventional computer.

The places $\widehat{F}, \widehat{X}_1, \ldots, \widehat{X}_n$ and $\widehat{Y}$ connected to the operator $\mathbf{cop}^{(n)}$ model memory cells. Their instantiations represent actual cell contents (values) which can be either copied without destruction or replaced (overwritten) by other values. In particular, an instantiation of $\widehat{F}$ specifies an instruction, and instantiations of $\widehat{X}_1, \ldots, \widehat{X}_n$ and $\widehat{Y}$ represent operand or result values, respectively. The passage of a control token through $\mathbf{cop}^{(n)}$ models the incrementation of the instruction counter by which the focus of control is moved from one instruction to the next in sequence. Whenever an operator is activated by a control token, it occurs with whatever the actual instantiations of the operand positions $\widehat{X}_1, \ldots, \widehat{X}_n$ and $\widehat{F}$ are. These instantiations merely determine the value of the resulting token which replaces the one removed from the output place $\widehat{Y}$.

Fig. 4.14 illustrates the three possible forms of channel sharing between two operators $\mathbf{cop}_1^{(3)}$ and $\mathbf{cop}_2^{(4)}$. We have the channel (place)

- P_1 in function position of $\mathbf{cop}_1^{(3)}$ and in function value position of $\mathbf{cop}_2^{(4)}$;

- P_2 as a common argument position of $\mathbf{cop}_1^{(3)}$ and $\mathbf{cop}_2^{(4)}$;

- P_3 in argument position of $\mathbf{cop}_2^{(4)}$ and in function value position of $\mathbf{cop}_1^{(3)}$.

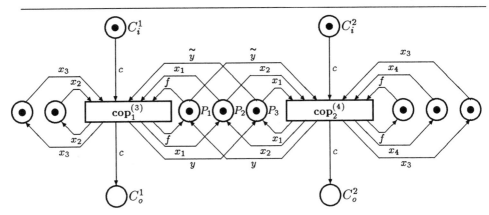

Figure 4.14: The sharing of operand predicate schemes between two control flow operators

If both operators belong to independent **control flow threads** and hence can be performed in either order, then

- the operator $\mathbf{cop}_1^{(3)}$ may change the token in P_3 either before or after it is being used as argument by $\mathbf{cop}_2^{(4)}$;

- the operator $\mathbf{cop}_2^{(4)}$ may change the token in P_1 either before or after it is being used as a function by $\mathbf{cop}_1^{(3)}$;

i.e., we may get different resulting instantiations of P_1 and P_3.

Thus, the **sharing of channels** among concurrently executable operators is bound to cause **non-determinism** if their instantiations are modified by at least one of the operators involved. Non-determinism can only be avoided if

- the control flow is strictly sequential;

- the execution order among concurrent operations that change the instantiation of a shared channel is irrelevant (i.e., the operations are associative);

- sharing among concurrently executable operators is confined to input channels whose instantiations remain unchanged.

The instantiations of channels that are shared among producing and consuming operators (which most of them are) have no meaningful interpretation of their own. They depend on the flow of control tokens, along which they may be modified by several operator occurrences. Control flow computations are therefore said to be history-sensitive (or dependent on side effects). They require that the instantiations of channels be carefully orchestrated with the flow of control tokens in order to ensure semantically correct (and in the case of threaded control flow determinate) results.

Though the control flow model dispenses with the explicit replication of object tokens, it includes a special n-ary copy-operator to pass in an orderly form argument and result tokens in and out of invocations of user-defined functions. Moreover, we need

- two complementary control operators T-*gate* and F-*gate* for the conditional passage of control tokens, of which a standard configuration is shown in fig. 4.15. Depending on the instantiation of the place $\widehat{C}$ with TRUE or FALSE, either the T-*gate* or the F-*gate* is enabled to pass a control token ϕ from the common input place C_i to either of the output places C_o^{T} or C_o^{F}, respectively;

- two complementary operators fork and join which respectively are to branch from one to several concurrent control flow threads and to synchronize them again.

We note that there are some fundamental differences between the control flow model on the one hand and functional models of computation on the other hand.

The orderly consumption and reproduction of tokens, which is what governs the occurrences of operators and, hence, the entire process behavior, is,

- in all functional models, an integral part of the operational discipline by which the objects of the computation are being manipulated;

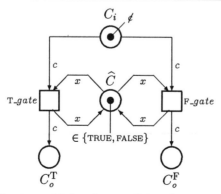

Figure 4.15: PrT-net model for the conditional passage of control tokens

- in the control flow model, completely separated from the world of computational objects and artificially set up as a control structure.

Whereas both the control discipline and the operational discipline are intimately correlated with each other in the functional models, the operational discipline hardly matters with respect to the control discipline that underlies the control flow model. More precisely, the control flow model is characterized by

- a control discipline based on the orderly consumption and reproduction of control tokens, as a consequence of which we may (or may not) have

- an operational discipline based on the sharing of channels whose instantiations may be copied and modified without any constraints.

The point to be made here is important enough to re-phrase it: the complete separation of the control discipline from the operational discipline provides the freedom of choice for the latter. The most chaotic form of it is the unrestricted sharing of channels which constitutes the conceptual basis for the assignment statement of conventional (procedural) programming languages. This operational discipline is ultimately responsible for the need to specify explicitly which operations are to be performed on which operand objects in which state of control in order to perform semantically correct computations.

4.5   A Preliminary Classification of Computational Models

The objective of this study was to identify the operational and control disciplines which characterize the underlying organizational concepts.

We saw that the control disciplines essentially subdivide into control

- by demand for result objects

- by availability of operand objects

- by availability of control tokens.

The operational disciplines are based on

- the orderly consumption and (re-)production of computational objects communicated via non-shared channels;

- the representation of computational objects as side conditions which may be shared among several operators.

The pairing of each control discipline with each operational discipline would yield six different models of organizing computations. The explicit sharing of objects, however, is not compatible with control by the demand for or by the availability of objects. Both control disciplines are intimately related with the orderly consumption and reproduction of objects. This leaves us with four combinations, of which another one appears to be redundant. Little is gained by artificially superimposing a flow of control tokens if control can, in fact, be exercised by the operational mechanism.

The remaining three organizational concepts are in fig. 4.16 classified with respect to their operational and control disciplines [TrBrHo82].

Both reduction and data flow are functional concepts (or models) which share the same operational discipline. The computational processes are free of side effects and hence history-insensitive. There is no state involved with which the processes interact and in which traces are left, e.g., in the form of intermediate objects, of terminated computations. Conceptually, we have no memory to support computations.

Reduction combines the unconditional substitution of formal by actual function parameters with demand control in order to avoid unnecessary computations in

control	operations on	
by	*consumable/reproducible objects*	*modifiable objects*
demand for objects	reduction	incompatible
availability of objects	data flow	
availability of control tokens	redundant	control flow

Figure 4.16: Classification of computational models

alternative components of a program. Data flow achieves the same ends by the combination of conditional substitution into alternative program components with control by availability of object tokens.

The control flow concept performs operations on shared objects which are treated as side conditions. The collection of these side conditions constitutes the state with which the computational process interacts. As the side conditions survive the processes that create them, we have side effects which to some extent reflect the histories of computations. Conceptually, there is a memory by which the computations are supported.

There is no doubt that, for obvious pragmatic reasons, all practical computing systems need to have some considerable amount of memory in order to support data bases, program libraries, system back-up etc. A computing system that cannot remember things which have been done in the past is of no use at all.

It would therefore seem that conventional control flow systems are the only alternative left. This supposition is true to the extent that functional systems have no useful existence of their own, but only as components of control flow systems.

The problem at hand simply is to decide

- whether the computational processes are to interact on a step-by-step basis with a state in order to effect global state changes by user-specified sequences of incremental state changes, as is the case with conventional computing systems;

- or whether the processes should be organized so as to accomplish global state changes without any intermediate interactions with the state, as in all functional systems.

A functional system may be viewed as a processing engine of a control flow system which in one conceptual step performs the global state transformation specified by an entire program, rather than the incremental state change of primitive instructions.

Thus, what both functional models and the control flow model have in common is the basic cycle depicted in fig. 4.17 which partitions into a functional and a state transition world.

Control flow computations run through this cycle at the level of assignment statements: the functional part of executing them consists in evaluating the expressions on their right-hand sides (after having copied the respective data values from the current state), whereas the state transition part corresponds to overwriting the variables on their left-hand sides.

Functional computations may for this purpose simply be considered very complex assignment statements which perform this cycle just once: the programs correspond to the expressions on their right-hand sides, and the state changes are effected either

FUNCTIONAL WORLD | STATE TRANSITION WORLD

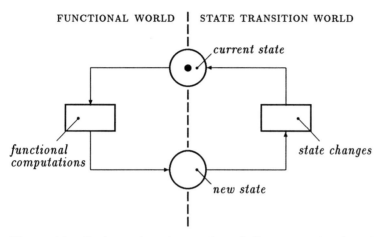

current state

functional computations

state changes

new state

Figure 4.17: Basic modus of operation of all computational models

by explicit PRINT commands or by an implicit output routine which transfers the results of the program runs to some output file (which is equivalent to assigning values to variables).

5 Abstract Algorithms, Reduction and the λ-Calculus

In chapter 4 we investigated three models of computation based on the supposition that deterministic computational processes transform problem specifications represented in the form of function applications into problem solutions represented as constant objects (or function values). Function applications constitute complete problem specifications in an algorithmic form: they prescribe partially or totally ordered sequences of transformation steps which produce determinate results.

We will refer to an algorithm as being

- abstract (or pure) if it is specified in terms of purely mathematical concepts and notations such as equations and expressions;

- a computer program if it can be executed by a concrete class of computing systems that realizes a particular model of computation.

The transformation of an abstract algorithm into a computer program is a rather straightforward matter which, either by compilation or by simple transliteration, may be carried out by the computing system itself.

In general, abstract algorithms specify only partially ordered transformation steps. If necessary, a sequential order of execution among mutually independent transformation steps must be established either as part of the compilation process or, if the abstract algorithm can be more or less directly used as an executable program, by a sequencing scheme built into the system.

The purpose of this chapter is to study some basic theoretical issues concerning the specification and execution of algorithms which could not be adequately treated within the framework of the rather simple organizational models developed in chapter 4. They primarily relate to the concept of variables and variable scoping, in particular to the problem of naming conflicts and their orderly resolution (or avoidance), to transformation (evaluation) strategies, termination problems, and non-sequential (or concurrent) program execution. These issues need to be fully understood in order to be able to develop representative architectures for computing systems which realize the computational models identified in chapter 4 and, hence, the programming paradigms supported by them.

In the sequel, we will first engage in an informal discussion of abstract algorithms to develop, largely by means of examples, an intuitive understanding of the problems involved. This is followed by a formal introduction to the concept of reduction and to the theory of the λ-calculus.

5.1   Function Equations as Abstract Algorithms

An abstract algorithm may be specified by an expression which typically has the form

$$expr = \text{DEFINE}$$

$$\vdots$$

$$f(x_1, \ldots, x_n) = f\_expr$$

$$\vdots$$

$$h(y_1, \ldots, y_l) = h\_expr$$

$$\vdots$$

$$\text{IN } s\_expr .$$

It includes a set of recursive function equations and a so-called goal expression s_expr constructed from applications of these functions whose value is to be computed. In compliance with the terminology used in chapter 4, we refer to the left-hand sides of the function equations as function headers and to the right-hand sides as function body expressions or defining expressions [Turn81].

For instance, the function header $f(x_1, \ldots, x_n)$ declares f to be a function of n variables (or formal parameters) $x_1, \ldots, x_n$. The function body expression f_expr specifies an algorithm for the computation of function values of f in terms of

- the variables $x_1, \ldots, x_n$ and f (in which case the function is recursive);

- applications of subfunctions of f;

- applications of functions declared at the same level as f, e.g., the function h.

These DEFINE constructs may recursively appear as defining expressions. For instance, f_expr may be specified as

$$\text{DEFINE}$$

$$\vdots$$

$$g(v_1, \ldots, v_m) = g\_expr$$

$$\vdots$$

$$\text{IN } f\_expr' ,$$

where the function g and all other functions defined at this and lower levels are subfunctions of f. All variables defined in a particular function are also defined in its subfunctions. All function names specified under a particular DEFINE construct must be unique.

A more appropriate notion for the status of a variable is that of its binding level. With respect to an abstract algorithm specified in the above form, binding levels may be roughly defined as follows:

- the formal parameters $x_1, \ldots, x_n$ are bound in the function f but free in its subfunctions, e.g., in the function g;

- the formal parameters $v_1, \ldots, v_m$ are bound in g but, again, free in the subfunctions of g;

- function names are mutually recursively bound in all functions defined at the same hierarchical level; they are also bound in the goal expression: g is bound in f_expr', and f and h are bound in s_expr.

We will henceforth refer to

- variables which are free in subfunctions but bound higher up as being relatively free;

- functions containing only bound variables as being closed, and open otherwise.

The specification of an algorithm can be considerably simplified if only closed functions are permitted. Due to the absence of relatively free variables there is no need to define functions as subfunctions of others. An algorithm may then be represented in flat form, i.e., without recursively nested DEFINE constructs. All functions may cross-reference each other in a completely symmetric way, as all function names are declared at the same level.

In addition to functions that are given names, we also admit non-recursive nameless (or anonymous) functions of the form

$$\text{SUB} \left(x_1, \ldots, x_n \right) \text{ IN } expr$$

where $x_1, \ldots, x_n$ again denote formal parameters and $expr$ denotes the function body expression.

Other expressions may be recursively constructed from

- function applications, denoted as $func(arg\_1, \ldots, arg\_r)$, where $func$ is the name of a function defined by an equation, a nameless function or a symbol representing a primitive function, and $arg\_1, \ldots, arg\_r$ are argument expressions;

- WHERE clauses as special forms of nameless function applications

$$expr \text{ WHERE}$$

$$\vdots$$

$$x = x\_expr$$

$$\vdots$$

$$y = y\_expr$$

$$\vdots$$

which specify the (values of) x_expr and y_expr as substitutes for free occurrences of the variables x and y, respectively, in $expr$;

- IF-THEN-ELSE clauses of the form

$$\begin{array}{ll} \text{IF} & pred\_expr \\ \text{THEN} & true\_expr \\ \text{ELSE} & false\_expr \end{array}$$

of which $pred\_expr$, $true\_expr$ and $false\_expr$ are also referred to as the predicate, the consequence and the alternative, respectively (IF-THEN-ELSE clauses represent special function applications in a syntactically more amenable form);

- lists or sequences of expressions, denoted as

$$<expr\_1, \ldots, expr\_n>$$

as a means for representing structured objects.

The set of primitive functions is assumed to include the familiar binary arithmetic, logic and relational operations, applications of which are denoted as $(arg\_2 \text{ OP } arg\_1)$, and some structuring and predicate functions applicable to lists, such as FIRST, REST, APPEND, EMPTY, etc.

The abstract algorithms that can be constructed from these expressions may be considered programs of a high-level functional language. The transformation rules by which these program expressions can be evaluated define an abstract functional computing machine. Since we will use this functional language as a kernel language throughout the remainder of this monograph, we will refer to it in abbreviated form as HLFL . In varying syntactical forms, the elements and constructs of HLFL form an essential basis of all functional (or function-based) programming languages proposed and implemented to date, e.g., MIRANDA [Turn85, Turn86], SASL [Turn76], VAL [AcDe79],VALID [AmHaOn84], ID [ArGoPl78, Nikh88], SCHEME [Dyb87], ML [Miln84, Harp85, HaMcQMi86, HaMiTo88] and HASKELL [HuWa88].

5.1.1   The Transformation of Function Applications

The mechanical evaluation of HLFL expressions requires machinery which somehow computes values for instances of function applications of the general form:

$$func(arg\_1, \ldots, arg\_r)$$

A direct way of doing this is by the following transformations: if $func$ is either the name of a function defined by an equation or a nameless function, then the application must be replaced in one conceptual step by the respective defining expression, wherein all free occurrences of formal parameters are being substituted by the respective argument expressions. We will use the term expansion for this transformation step. Applications of primitive functions are directly replaced by their values.

As a simple example that illustrates expansion, let us first consider a recursive algorithm for the computation of the greatest common divisor of two integer numbers, using only closed function definitions:

> DEFINE
> $gcd(x, y)$ = IF $(x$ EQ $y)$
> THEN x
> ELSE IF $(x$ GT $y)$
> THEN $gcd(y, mod(x, y))$
> ELSE $gcd(x, mod(y, x))$
> $mod(x, y)$ = IF $(x$ LEQ $y)$
> THEN x
> ELSE $mod((x - y), y)$
> IN $gcd(4, 6)$

By the systematic expansion of applications of defined functions as outlined above, and by the substitution of applications of primitive functions by their values, this algorithm produces the following transformation sequence:

> $gcd(4, 6)$
> ⇓
> IF $(4$ EQ $6)$
> THEN   4
> ELSE   IF $(4$ GT $6)$
> THEN $gcd(6, mod(4, 6))$
> ELSE $gcd(4, mod(6, 4))$
> ⇓

```
IF       FALSE
THEN     4
ELSE     IF        (4 GT 6)
         THEN      gcd(6, mod(4, 6))
         ELSE      gcd(4, mod(6, 4))
                        ⇓
IF       (4 GT 6)
THEN     gcd(6, mod(4, 6))
ELSE     gcd(4, mod(6, 4))
                ⇓
         gcd(4, mod(6, 4))
                ⇓
gcd(4,   IF        (6 LEQ 4)
         THEN      6
         ELSE      mod((6 − 4), 4))
                        ⇓

                        ⋮
                        ⇓
         gcd(4, mod(2, 4))
                ⇓
gcd(4,   IF        (2 LEQ 4)
         THEN      2
         ELSE      mod((2 − 4), 4))
                        ⇓

                        ⋮
                        ⇓
              gcd(4, 2)
                ⇓
IF       (4 EQ 2)
THEN     4
ELSE     IF        (4 GT 2)
         THEN      gcd(2, mod(4, 2))
         ELSE      gcd(4, mod(2, 4))
                        ⇓

                        ⋮
              2
```

Unfortunately, expansion cannot be done in this naive form if the algorithm is defined in terms of open subfunctions.

To convey the nature of the problem, let us consider an algorithm which computes the product of all integer numbers within an interval $[m..n]$ $(0 \leq m \leq n)$ by a so-called divide-and-conquer technique: the product is recursively split up into two subproducts for the intervals $[m..par]$ and $[(par+1)..n]$, where par denotes the largest integer number smaller than or equal to $(n-m)/2 + m$. This algorithm may be specified as follows:

> DEFINE
> > $prod(n,m) =$ DEFINE
> > > $split(par) = (prod(n,(par+1)) * prod(par,m))$
> > > IN IF $(n$ GT $m)$
> > > THEN $split((\text{TRUNC}(((n-m)/2)) + m))$
> > > ELSE n
>
> IN $prod(7,2)$

(the primitive function TRUNC cuts the fractional part off its argument, provided it evaluates to a number).

We note that the function $prod(n,m)$ is defined by means of a subfunction $split(par)$, in which n and m occur relatively free. Open subfunctions constitute an integral part of the specification of defined functions. The expansion of function applications by their defining expressions must therefore include the substitution of formal parameters throughout all subfunctions in which they occur free.

When executing the application $prod(7,2)$ in this way, we obtain

$$prod(7,2)$$
$$\Downarrow$$

> DEFINE
> > $split(par) = (prod(7,(par+1)) * prod(par,2))$
> > IN IF $(7$ GT $2)$
> > THEN $split((\text{TRUNC}(((7-2)/2)) + 2))$
> > ELSE 7

$$\Downarrow$$

> DEFINE
> > $split(par) = (prod(7,(par+1)) * prod(par,2))$
> > IN $split(4)$

$$\Downarrow$$
$$(prod(7,5) * prod(4,2))$$

i.e., the computation proceeds as expected.

Careful inspection of this algorithm also reveals that we have a perfect candidate for non-sequential or concurrent execution. Every recursive call of the function $prod$

creates two independent applications of it to different sets of arguments; i.e., we obtain a hierarchy of concurrently executable function applications which may be conveniently partitioned at any hierarchical node. Applications which are not in a predecessor/successor relationship with each other may be transformed in any order, as conceptually there is no sharing of subexpressions among them.

The execution of the algorithms discussed so far is governed by a so-called call-by-value regime: arguments of function applications are evaluated before they are substituted for formal parameters.

While this evaluation strategy does have its merits in some cases, it may inflict redundant computations in others. Consider, as another example, the algorithm

$$
\begin{aligned}
&\text{DEFINE}\\
&\quad find\_last(list) = \text{IF} \quad \text{EMPTY}(\text{REST}(list))\\
&\qquad\qquad\qquad\quad \text{THEN FIRST}(list)\\
&\qquad\qquad\qquad\quad \text{ELSE} \;\; find\_last(\text{REST}(list))\\
&\quad \text{IN} \; find\_last(<expr\_1, \ldots, expr\_n>) \,,
\end{aligned}
$$

which is supposed to produce as a function value the last component of the argument list; i.e., (the value of) $expr\_n$.

Under the call-by-value regime, all expressions of the argument list are evaluated before the function is applied to it, even though the components $expr\_1, \ldots,$ $expr\_(n-1)$ are one by one discarded in consecutive recursion steps.

Redundant computations can in this and similar cases be prevented by a so-called call-by-name regime. It substitutes arguments as they are, i.e., in unevaluated form.

However, the choice between either of the regimes does not only depend on the expected number of transformation steps that need to be carried out in order to arrive at a function value. Even more critical is the problem of whether or not the computation eventually terminates with a function value at all.

We will investigate this problem in more detail in subsection 5.1.3.

5.1.2 Naming Conflicts

Since we have placed no particular restrictions on the choice of arguments so far, we could decide to apply the function $prod(n, m)$ as defined in the preceding subsection to variables, e.g., $prod(par, 2)$. If this application is naively expanded, we get:

$$prod(par, 2)$$
$$\Downarrow$$

DEFINE

$split(par) = (prod(\boxed{par}), (par + 1)) * prod(par, 2))$

IN IF $(par$ GT $2)$
   THEN $split((\text{TRUNC}(((par - 2)/2)) + 2))$
   ELSE par

Among other problems which need to be discussed later, we have in this expression created a naming conflict (or a name clash). The encircled occurrence of the variable name par within the defining expression of $split(par)$ constitutes a parasitic binding of a variable that originally was free. It has been produced by the naive substitution into a function body in which the same variable name is already bound. Parasitic bindings change the binding status of a variable and, subsequently, the meaning of a function definition. If we were to substitute the parameter par by the value 7 later on, we would obtain an incorrect value for $prod(7, 2)$. These naming conflicts must therefore be consequently avoided in order to maintain the functional character of the algorithm.

The most convincing solution in this particular case appears to be the complete elimination of relatively free variables from abstract algorithms by a consequent conversion of open into closed function definitions. To do so, we simply need to add to the list of formal parameters in the header of an open function definition all the variables that occur relatively free in it, and to modify applications of the function accordingly.

In the case of the algorithm $prod(n, m)$, we obtain two closed function definitions which call on each other in a completely symmetric way:

DEFINE

$prod\_c(n, m)$ $=$ IF $(n$ GT $m)$
                     THEN $split\_c(n, m, (\text{TRUNC}(((n - m)/2)) + m))$
                     ELSE n

$split\_c(n, m, par) = (prod\_c(n, (par + 1)) * prod\_c(par, m))$

IN $prod\_c(7, 2)$

The execution of this algorithm sets out with

$$prod\_c(7, 2)$$
$$\Downarrow$$

IF   (7 GT 2)
THEN $split\_c(7, 2, (\text{TRUNC}(((7 - 2)/2)) + 2))$
ELSE   7

$$\Downarrow$$
$$split\_c(7, 2, 4)$$
$$\Downarrow$$
$$(prod\_c(7, 5) * prod\_c(4, 2))$$

and proceeds correctly, eventually terminating with the value 5040.

Suppose now we were to compute $prod\_c(par, 2)$, performing expansions where possible. Then, after two transformation steps, we would get:

$$prod\_c(par, 2)$$
$$\Downarrow$$

IF $(par$ GT 2$)$
THEN $split\_c(par, 2, (\text{TRUNC}(((par - 2)/2)) + 2))$
ELSE par

$$\Downarrow$$

IF $(par$ GT 2$)$
THEN $(prod\_c(par, ((\text{TRUNC}(((par - 2)/2)) + 2) + 1)) *$
           $prod\_c((\text{TRUNC}(((par - 2)/2)) + 2), 2))$
ELSE par

No name clashes occur now between bound occurrences of the variable par in the function $split\_c$ and the actual parameter par with which the function $prod\_c$ is called. If we substitute occurrences of par in this expression by the value 7, we again get, after the evaluation of the IF-THEN-ELSE clause and of the applications of TRUNC:

$$(prod\_c(7, 5) * prod\_c(4, 2)) \ .$$

This particular example is somewhat artificially set up to convey the basic nature of the problem. However, naming conflicts may occur in a decidedly less trivial form when applying functions to functions in order to compute new functions. This concept of higher-order functions is an important feature of all functional languages which allows for concise and elegant problem specifications.

Consider as a simple example the application

$$twice(square, 2)$$
$$\text{WHERE } twice \ = \ \text{SUB}(f, x) \text{ IN } f(f(x))$$
$$square = \text{SUB}(x) \text{ IN } (x * x)$$

The function *twice* constructs a two-fold application of its first argument, the function *square*, to its second argument 2:

$$twice(square, 2)$$
$$\Downarrow$$
$$square(square(2))$$
$$\Downarrow$$
$$square((2 * 2))$$
$$\Downarrow$$
$$(4 * 4)$$
$$\Downarrow$$
$$16$$

While this works just fine, a serious problem arises with the following example:

$$double\_twice(square, 2)$$
WHERE *double_twice* $= twice(twice)$
WHERE *twice* $= $ SUB(f, x) IN $f(f(x))$
$square$ $= $ SUB(x) IN $(x * x)$

Here we apply *twice* to itself in order to compute a new function *double_twice* which is supposed to construct the four-fold application of *square* to the argument 2. The self-application *twice(twice)* is said to be partial in the sense that the binary *twice* in function position receives just one argument. When performing naive substitutions, this application expands as follows:

$$twice(twice)$$
$$\Downarrow$$
SUB(f, x) IN $f(f(x))$ $(twice)$
$$\Downarrow$$
SUB(x) IN $twice(twice(x))$
$$\Downarrow$$
SUB(x) IN $twice($SUB(f, x) IN $f(f(x))$ $(x))$
$$\Downarrow$$
SUB(x) IN $twice($SUB(x) IN $x(x(x)))$

At this point, we have obviously created a name clash by the partial application of *twice* to the variable x: it is substituted for occurrences of f in the body of *twice* and thus parasitically bound to the remaining SUB(x). When transforming this term further, we get eventually

$$double\_twice = \text{SUB}(x) \text{ IN SUB}(x) \text{ IN } x(x(x)) \, (x(x(x))) \, (x(x(x))))$$

which is obviously wrong: all occurrences of x in the body of this binary function are bound to the innermost $\text{SUB}(x)$, no variable occurrences are bound to the outermost $\text{SUB}(x)$. Thus, when expanding

$$double\_twice(square, 2) \, ,$$

we obtain

$$2(2(2)) \ (2(2(2)) \ (2(2(2)))) \, .$$

However, this problem can be easily corrected simply by renaming the bound variable x in different occurrences of *twice*, say, by priming them. We thus get:

$$twice(twice') = \text{SUB}(f, x) \text{ IN } f(f(x)) \ (twice')$$
$$\Downarrow$$
$$\text{SUB}(x) \text{ IN } twice''(twice'(x))$$
$$\Downarrow$$
$$\text{SUB}(x) \text{ IN } twice''(\text{SUB}(f, x') \text{ IN } f(f(x')) \ (x))$$
$$\Downarrow$$
$$\text{SUB}(x) \text{ IN } twice''(\text{SUB}(x') \text{ IN } x(x(x')))$$
$$\Downarrow$$
$$\text{SUB}(x) \text{ IN } \text{SUB}(f, x'') \text{ IN } f(f(x''))(\text{SUB}(x') \text{ IN } x(x(x')))$$
$$\Downarrow$$
$$\text{SUB}(x) \text{ IN } \text{SUB}(x'') \text{ IN } \text{SUB}(x') \text{ IN } x(x(x'))(\text{SUB}(x') \text{ IN } x(x(x'))(x''))$$
$$\Downarrow$$
$$\text{SUB}(x) \text{ IN } \text{SUB}(x'') \text{ IN } \text{SUB}(x') \text{ IN } x(x(x'))(x(x(x'')))$$
$$\Downarrow$$
$$\text{SUB}(x) \text{ IN } \text{SUB}(x'') \text{ IN } x(x(x(x(x''))))$$

This term now is truly a function in two variables (x and x'') for *double_twice* which, when applied to the arguments *square* and 2, yields the desired four-fold application of *square*:

$$square(square(square(square(2))))$$

The difficult part with this approach is that the renaming must be done mechanically by the evaluating system. It must be able to dynamically detect potential instances of name clashes and to convert conflicting variable names uniquely into others based, say, on an indexing scheme.

5.1.3   Typing and the Termination Problem

We have so far investigated only the operational aspect of evaluating abstract algorithms constructed from function definitions and function applications. In doing this, we have more or less ignored that

- functions are mathematical objects which map domain sets into range sets, i.e., function values are formally defined only if the arguments of function applications are from the respective domain set(s);

- in a very precise sense the defining expressions specify algorithms for the computation of function values but not the functions themselves.

This poses two major problems, namely

- to make sure that an algorithm realizes the intended function;

- to find out whether or not an algorithmic function definition is applied to legitimate arguments.

The former problem is outside the scope of this monograph for it concerns program correctness and its verification. The latter is of a more pragmatic nature and can be dealt with in either of the following ways.

We can play it safe and introduce type declarations for all formal parameters of defined functions which in fact specify their domain sets. Function applications may then be expanded if and only if all arguments are of a compatible type. We can even do an à priori type check which at least makes sure that all declared variable types are compatible with the primitive functions used in the respective defining expressions. Primitive functions always require arguments of a particular type: arithmetic functions such as $+$, $-$, . . . are only applicable to numbers, structuring functions such as FIRST, REST, . . . are only applicable to lists etc. But even then we have no guarantee that the function applications produce function values for the functions may be only partially defined over their domain sets, or the algorithms may not realize the desired functions. Thus, while type declarations may help to increase the confidence in the correctness of algorithms, there are still problems.

We may therefore look at the problem of typing from a less rigid point of view and simply say that the algorithmic specifications of functions also define their domain sets (or argument types). This renders all type declarations for formal parameters superfluous, i.e., we can use a type-free substitution of formal by actual parameters. Put another way: all legitimately constructed HLFL expressions may occur as arguments of non-primitive functions.

Undefined function applications may now appear in one of the following forms: we may have applications of

- primitive functions to arguments which are not of a compatible type (or are outside the functions' domains);

- expressions or names which cannot be identified as legitimate primitive or defined functions;

- defined functions which either contain or, by substitution of formal by actual parameters, create undefined components.

In the process of executing abstract algorithms mechanically, these undefined applications should be dealt with in some systematic way in order to be able to identify the particular causes of their occurrences.

We may, as in chapter 4, propose to substitute these applications by so-called **bottom symbols** $\bot$ and to enforce **bottom preservation**: occurrences of the symbol $\bot$ within an expression cause the entire expression to be transformed into $\bot$. However, this solution,

- insinuates the presence of an error after the occurrence of which it does not appear to be expedient to continue with further computations. While this supposition is true for expressions like $(x+\text{TRUE})$ or $\text{REST}(3)$ etc., it can hardly be justified for, say, $(x + y)$, $(x + 3)$, $\text{FIRST}(x)$. Though primitive functions are not applicable to variables (which, in the context of abstract algorithms, represent nothing but themselves), these expressions ought to be treated as irreducible rather than as errors for the variables may be substituted by type-compatible terms later on.

- is too rigid insofar as $\bot$ may occur within subexpressions whose values do not contribute to the computation of the actual function value and therefore can be safely ignored.

- as will be demonstrated later, is not practical in the case of recursive functions which are being applied to arguments not belonging to their domains.

It should therefore be rejected.

From a pragmatic as well as from a formal point of view it appears more appropriate to treat undefined applications of primitive functions or applications of undefined function names as a form of **constant expressions** and leave them as they are, except for further transformations that can be carried out within their subexpressions. Thus, we may have the following transformations:

$$
\begin{array}{rcl}
(x + y) & \Rightarrow & (x + y) \\
((x + 3) * (3 - 2)) & \Rightarrow & ((x + 3) * 1) \\
\text{REST}(\text{FIRST}(<a\ b\ c>)) & \Rightarrow & \text{REST}(a)
\end{array}
$$

When transforming IF-THEN-ELSE clauses in this way, we would need to compute

- first the value of the predicate expression and then

- either the consequence or the alternative depending on whether the predicate value is TRUE or FALSE, respectively;

- both the consequence and the alternative in the context of the complete IF-THEN-ELSE construct if the predicate value is neither TRUE nor FALSE.

Hence, we would have

$$\begin{array}{ll} \text{IF} & (2 \text{ GT } 1) \\ \text{THEN} & (3+2) \\ \text{ELSE} & ((3-2)+\text{`abc'}) \end{array} \quad \Rightarrow \quad 5$$

but

$$\begin{array}{ll} \text{IF} & (\text{`abc' GT } 1) \\ \text{THEN} & (3+2) \\ \text{ELSE} & ((3-2)+\text{`abc'}) \end{array} \quad \Rightarrow \quad \begin{array}{ll} \text{IF} & (\text{`abc' GT } 1) \\ \text{THEN} & 5 \\ \text{ELSE} & (1+\text{`abc'}) \end{array}$$

where 'abc' denotes a character string.

Unfortunately, this approach has a fatal consequence: IF-THEN-ELSE clauses are essential constructs of meaningful recursive function definitions. Their predicate expressions, in conjunction with occurrences of the recursively bound variables either in the consequence or in the alternative, specify termination conditions, provided the functions are applied to arguments from their intended domains.

However, with a type-free substitution, it is perfectly legitimate to apply functions intended to be defined, say, over the domain of natural numbers to character strings, or functions intended to be defined over the domain of lists to numbers, character strings, or even variables.

Consider, as an example, the application of the function *gcd*, as defined in the previous section, to a character string in the first argument position, say *gcd('abc', 6)*. It produces the following sequence of transformations:

$$gcd(\text{`abc'}, 6)$$
$$\Downarrow$$

$$\begin{array}{ll} \text{IF} & (\text{`abc' EQ } 6) \\ \text{THEN} & \text{`abc'} \\ \text{ELSE} & \begin{array}{ll} \text{IF} & (\text{`abc' GT } 6) \\ \text{THEN} & gcd(6, mod(\text{`abc'}, 6)) \\ \text{ELSE} & gcd(\text{`abc'}, mod\,(6, \text{`abc'})) \end{array} \end{array}$$
$$\Downarrow$$

IF   ('abc' EQ 6)
THEN   'abc'
ELSE   IF   ('abc' GT 6)
       THEN $gcd(6,$ IF   ('abc' LEQ 6)
                      THEN   'abc'
                      ELSE $mod(('abc' - 6), 6))$
       ELSE $gcd('abc', mod(6,'abc'))$
                       ⇓

IF   ('abc' EQ 6)
THEN   'abc'
ELSE   IF   ('abc' GT 6)
       THEN $gcd(6,$ IF   ('abc' LEQ 6)
                      THEN   'abc'
                      ELSE   IF   (('abc'−6) LEQ 6)
                                 THEN   ('abc' − 6)
                                 ELSE $mod((('abc' - 6) - 6), 6))$
       ELSE $gcd('abc', mod(6, 'abc'))$
                       ⇓
                       ⋮

This sequence of recursive function calls never terminates since none of the predicate expressions of the IF-THEN-ELSE clauses ever evaluates to a Boolean constant. The obvious cause of the problem is the type-incompatibility of the character string 'abc' with numbers in the context of applications of the relational functions EQ, GT, LEQ and of subtractions.

We can of course easily rectify this particular problem by demanding that both consequences and alternatives of IF-THEN-ELSE clauses remain unevaluated if their predicates transform to constant expressions other than TRUE or FALSE.

However, non-termination simply reflects the fact that character strings are not within the domain of the recursive function *gcd* (or more precisely, in the particular realization of this function). Function values are not defined for these arguments and can therefore not be computed by finite sequences of transformations. We can also say that these function applications are meaningless.

This is in the particular example also true for all negative integers. Though they are type-compatible with the primitive functions in terms of which the predicates are specified, the predicate values never terminate the recursions.

Consider, as an example, the computation of $gcd(-4, -6)$ which proceeds as follows:

$$gcd(-4, -6)$$
$$\Downarrow$$
$$\vdots$$
$$\Downarrow$$
$$gcd(-6, mod(-4, -6))$$
$$\Downarrow$$
$$\vdots$$
$$\Downarrow$$
$$gcd(-6, mod(2, -6))$$
$$\Downarrow$$
$$\vdots$$
$$\Downarrow$$
$$gcd(-6, mod(8, -6))$$
$$\Downarrow$$
$$\vdots$$
$$\Downarrow$$

We note that this sequence is getting trapped in recursive calls of the function *mod* since the monotonically increasing first argument keeps forever FALSE the predicate value of its IF-THEN-ELSE clause.

Thus, the particular algorithm obviously confines the domain of the function *gcd* to positive integers, for which we have transformation sequences terminating with function values.

We may even specify recursive functions which very obviously have an empty domain. Typical examples are the function definitions

$$h(n) = (h((3 * n)) + 1)$$

and

$$g(n) = \quad \text{IF} \qquad \text{ODD}(n)$$
$$\text{THEN} \quad g(((3 * n) + 1))$$
$$\text{ELSE} \quad g((n/2))$$

neither of which ever terminates for any legitimate argument expression. The defining expression of $h(n)$ contains no IF-THEN-ELSE clause at all. In the defining expression of $g(n)$ we have recursive function calls in both the consequence and the alternative of the IF-THEN-ELSE clause.

Unfortunately, we may also have function definitions whose domains cannot as easily and completely be identified as in the preceding examples. Consider for instance the function definition

$$f(n) = \quad \text{IF} \quad (n \text{ EQ } 1)$$
$$\text{THEN} \quad 1$$
$$\text{ELSE} \quad \text{IF} \quad \text{ODD}(n)$$
$$\text{THEN} \quad f(((3 * n) + 1))$$
$$\text{ELSE} \quad f((n/2))$$

which, for obvious reasons, is known as the so-called **roller-coaster** function : applications to argument values other than $n = 2^k$ seem to oscillate incessantly between the consequence and the alternative of the innermost IF-THEN-ELSE clause. There is no formal way of deciding whether or not the computation of this function terminates for some other subset of integer numbers, i.e., whether or not it has a domain that includes elements other than from the subset $\{2^k \mid k \in I\!N_0\}$ and just what that subset might be.[6]

Since the termination problem cannot be decided in general, computing systems must include a halting mechanism which, after some prespecified number of transformation steps, terminates the computation of a function application which by then has not yet produced a function value. Ideally, the actual state of computation at that point should be exhibited in some intelligible form to the user who must decide whether or not to continue with further transformations. This decision cannot be made by the system.

This so-called **Entscheidungsproblem** is also the pragmatic reason for rejecting the substitution of undefined function applications by bottom symbols, as proposed earlier. It simply cannot be done in a mechanized way as there is generally no criterion by which non-terminating recursions can be recognized.

The termination problem has yet another facet: complex algorithms may allow for several alternative transformation sequences, of which some terminate and the others don't.

A typical example of this kind is the application of the function $find\_last$ to a list of at least two components which, say, in its first component contains an application of a recursive function with an empty domain. Execution under the **call-by-value** regime, which demands the evaluation of all components of the argument list, causes non-termination, whereas execution under the **call-by-name** regime returns, after a finite number of transformation steps, the last component of the argument list as the correct function value.

---

[6]By brute-force evaluation it has been shown that this function terminates for all integers up to 2^{40}.

Thus, there obviously exists a function value if at least one of several alternative transformation sequences terminates. The problem that needs to be solved, then, is

- to organize the actual transformation sequence in such a way that it is guaranteed to terminate if a function value exists, i.e., the function is applied to arguments from its (non-empty) domain;

- to ensure that all terminating transformation sequences for a particular function application yield the same function value.

5.2   The Concept of Reductions

The direct program transformations described in the preceding section characterize HLFL as a so-called reduction language. Following a classification given by Backus [Back72, Back73], reduction languages form a subclass of functional languages which are

- complete in the sense that '... *their semantics specify for many programs a result which is the meaning of the original program and is itself a program* ...';

- primary in the sense that '... *(they have) a transition function defined for (their) programs ... which, when repeatedly applied to a (program), will ultimately produce a (program) which is the meaning of the original, if a meaning exists. Thus the meaning of a program is found by transitions entirely within the space of programs. Primary languages are necessarily complete* ...'.

They can be formally defined by triples

$$L = (E, C, m)$$

where

- E is a set of expressions,

- $C \subset E$ is a set of constant expressions,

- $m : E \longrightarrow C$ is the meaning or semantic function of L which is partial over E.

For all meaningful expressions $expr \in E$, we have $m[\![expr]\!] = c \in C$. All constant expressions are their own meanings: $m[\![c]\!] = c \in C$; i.e., C is the set of fixed points of m.

A complete realization CR of a language L is defined by a triple

$$CR = (E, C, \tau),$$

in which E and C are as above, and τ is a binary relation $\tau \subset E \times E$ which specifies the transformation of expressions into expressions and is total in its left component.

If an expression $expr \in E$ has a meaning, then there exists some integer n such that

$$\tau^{(n)}(expr) = m \left[\!\left[expr \right]\!\right] \in C,$$

i.e., $m \left[\!\left[expr \right]\!\right]$ can be computed with a finite number of transformation steps. C is therefore also the set of fixed points of τ.

The tuple $\mathcal{R} = (E, \tau)$ in fact defines a **reduction calculus**: E is the set of **well-formed formulas** and τ is the set of **rewrite rules**, also referred to as **one-step reductions**.

Let $expr\_1, expr\_2 \in E$, then

- $expr\_1$ is said to be **reducible** to $expr\_2$ in one step iff $(expr\_1, expr\_2) \in \tau$;

- $expr\_1$ is said to be **irreducible** iff for all $expr\_2 \in E$ with $expr\_1 \neq expr\_2$ we have $(expr\_1, expr\_2) \notin \tau$.

A sequence of expressions (or terms) $expr\_1, \ldots, expr\_n \in E$ is called a **reduction sequence** for $expr\_1$ iff $(expr\_i, expr\_(i+1)) \in \tau$ for all $i \in [1 \mathinner{..} (n-1)]$.

Let τ^* denote the **transitive closure** of τ, then $expr\_1 \in E$ is said to be reducible to $expr\_n \in E$ iff $(expr\_1, expr\_n) \in \tau^*$.

A reduction calculus $\mathcal{R}$ features the so-called **Church-Rosser property** iff for all terms $expr\_0, expr\_1, expr\_2 \in E$ with

$$(expr\_0, expr\_1) \in \tau^*, \ (expr\_0, expr\_2) \in \tau^*$$

there exists another term $expr\_3 \in E$ such that

$$(expr\_1, expr\_3) \in \tau^*, \ (expr\_2, expr\_3) \in \tau^*.$$

This property is essential for deterministic (or functional) computations: it guarantees that all terminating reduction sequences applied to a legitimate term of the calculus return the same constant term.

With these definitions and propositions at hand, we can say that reduction languages are functional languages whose semantics are completely and directly defined by the rewrite rules of a reduction calculus.

Reduction language expressions suitable for a mechanical evaluation are usually represented in a so-called **constructor syntax**

$$CS = (A, K)$$

where $A \subset E$ denotes a subset of atomic expressions and K denotes a set of constructors.

Each constructor $\mathbf{k}^{(n)} \in K$ realizes a mapping of some subset $Sk^n \subseteq E^n$ (with $n \geq 0$) into E. An expression is either atomic or composed of a unique constructor $\mathbf{k}^{(n)} \in K$ and n unique expressions $expr\_1, \ldots, expr\_n \in E$, i.e., we have either $atom \in E$ or $\mathbf{k}^{(n)} expr\_1 \ldots expr\_n \in E$.

A constructor-syntax expression may be considered a pre-order linearized representation of an n-ary tree structure, with the constructor $\mathbf{k}^{(n)}$ occupying the root node position, and with the expressions $expr\_1, \ldots, expr\_n$ forming the subtrees:

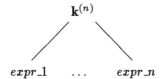

A reduction language L with the constructor syntax CS is said to be applicative iff:

- $A \subseteq C$

- there exists a constructor $\mathbf{ap}^{(n)} \in K$ such that for all expressions $expr\_1, \ldots, expr\_n \in E$

$$ m \left[\!\left[\mathbf{ap}^{(n)} expr\_1 \ldots expr\_n \right]\!\right] = m \left[\!\left[\mathbf{ap}^{(n)} m \left[\!\left[expr\_1 \right]\!\right] \ldots m \left[\!\left[expr\_n \right]\!\right] \right]\!\right] $$

- for all other constructors we have

$$ m \left[\!\left[\mathbf{k}^{(n)} expr\_1 \ldots expr\_n \right]\!\right] = \mathbf{k}^{(n)} m \left[\!\left[expr\_1 \right]\!\right] \ldots m \left[\!\left[expr\_n \right]\!\right] .^7 $$

The expression $\mathbf{ap}^{(n)} expr\_1 \ldots expr\_n$ represents the application of a function expression to some $n - 1$ argument expressions. The syntactical position of the function expression is specified by the constructor $\mathbf{ap}^{(n)}$. It is usually the first subexpression of the application. The constructor $\mathbf{ap}^{(n)}$, also referred to as an applicator, is the sole operator of an applicative language, its subterms are considered the operands.[8]

We note that the meaning of an expression is recursively defined by and, hence, must be recursively computed from the meanings of its subexpressions. In the case

---

[7] In the sequel, we will use $m \left[\!\left[expr \right]\!\right]$ to denote both the meaning of an expression $expr$ and also the syntactical representation of its normal form.

[8] Note that this syntax essentially is the one we used in chapter 4, with what we called the universal operator $\mathbf{op}^{(n)}$ instead of $\mathbf{ap}^{(n)}$.

of non-applicative expressions, the meaning is thus completely defined. However, the meaning of an application cannot be determined without specifying, outside the framework of the language L, which functions are represented by constant expressions or, more precisely, how function values are to be computed for constant expressions appearing in function position.

To do so, we introduce the notion of **closed applicative languages** which defines the semantics of applications by associating a function with each constant expression.

An applicative language is said to be **closed** iff there exists a function $R \in [C \longrightarrow [C^{n-1} \longrightarrow E]]$ such that

- R is total over C

- $(\forall c \in C)\, ((R(c) \in [C^{n-1} \longrightarrow E])$ is total over $C^{n-1})$

- $(\forall a, b, \ldots, p \in C)\, (m \, [\![\mathbf{ap}^{(n)}\, a\, b \ldots p]\!] = m \, [\![\mathbf{ap}^{(n)}\, R(a)\, b \ldots p]\!])$

The **representation function** R in fact specifies the hard-core reduction rules for applications of primitive, composite and defined functions. They need to be realized in a real reduction system as the equivalent of the instruction set of a conventional computer.

However, demanding that R be total over C, for all practical purposes, does not seem to be very useful. It would mean that R be defined for such items as numbers, character strings (variables), even lists of constant expressions, etc. Consistent with the way we have dealt with undefined components of applications in section 5.1, we decide to define the realization function R for all other than a very specific subset of constant expressions as follows:

$$((\forall a \in C)\, (R(a) \notin [C^{n-1} \longrightarrow E]))\, (m \, [\![\mathbf{ap}^{(n)}\, a\, b \ldots p]\!] = \mathbf{ap}^{(n)}\, a\, b \ldots p)$$

(where $b, \ldots,\ p$ are also constant). Rather than producing an error symbol in case of an undefined operator expression, the application remains unchanged, and computations may continue elsewhere in the expression. Eventually, the system returns an expression in which applications with undefined components can be readily detected.

Closed applicative languages constitute the most restricted forms of complete languages. They are primarily characterized by the

- **extended Church-Rosser property:**
  every terminating sequence of reductions performed on an expression yields the same constant expression. If an expression has a meaning, then *all* reduction sequences applied to it must terminate;

- reduction property:
  if an expression has a meaning, then all subexpressions have a meaning. If any
  subexpression is replaced by its meaning, then the meaning of the expression
  remains unchanged.

5.3 The λ-Calculus

The λ-calculus, first published by Alonzo Church [Chur32, ChRo36, Ros84], is the
most general reduction calculus which formalizes the concept of evaluating abstract
algorithms by program transformations.[9] It is primarily a theory of computable
functions which deals with elementary properties of operators, with applications of
operators to operands, and with the systematic construction of complex operators
(functions/algorithms) from more primitive ones.

In fact, the λ-calculus is based on little more than a well-defined concept of
substituting variables by expressions with strictly functional properties. This concept
suffices to develop a precise understanding of the problems discussed in section 5.1.
Moreover, since the λ-calculus is a closed language, its semantics can be defined
based on the equivalence of λ-terms and thus completely within its own domain.

The λ-calculus may be considered the paradigm for all functional programming
languages and, with some restrictions, for many imperative programming languages
as well [Lan65, Lan66a, Lan66b].

We will here introduce the λ-calculus only as far as is necessary to understand the
machine concepts and implementations discussed in the remainder of the book. For
a more comprehensive study the reader is referred to [CuFe58, CuHiSe72, Bar81,
HiSe86], another brief introduction may be found in [Weg71].

The term λ-calculus derives from the notation that is being used to represent
functions. This notation appears to be rather unusual when compared to (recursive)
function equations. However, as the λ-calculus does not really distinguish between
operators and operands other than by syntactical positions within an expression,
the λ-notation greatly facilitates the representation of a function as an object of
either kind. Moreover, the λ-notation allows a precise definition of the binding
status of variable occurrences.

The representation of functions in the λ-calculus is almost identical to the one
we introduced in chapter 4.

Let

$$f(x_1, \ldots, x_n) = expr$$

---

[9]The contents of this section are in part based on notes privately communicated by W. Lippe
and F. Simon [LiSi86].

define f as a non-recursive function of n variables $x_1, \ldots, x_n$. In the λ-calculus, f is equivalently denoted as

$$f = \lambda x_1 \ldots x_n.expr \ .$$

The right-hand side of this equation is said to be an **abstraction** (of the variables $x_1, \ldots, x_n$ from $expr$): $\lambda x_1 \ldots x_n$ specifies a **binder** for **free** occurrences of the variables $x_1, \ldots, x_n$ in the function **body** expression $expr$.

An application

$$f(arg\_1, \ldots, arg\_r)$$

assumes in the λ-notation the form

$$(f \ arg\_1 \ldots arg\_r) = (\lambda x_1 \ldots x_n.expr \ arg\_1 \ldots arg\_r)$$

(where r must not necessarily be equal to n). In particular, we have

$$(f \ x_1 \ldots x_n) = (\lambda x_1 \ldots x_n. \ expr \ x_1 \ldots x_n) = expr \ .$$

In order to keep the formal apparatus simple and concise, the λ-calculus considers, without loss of generality, functions of one variable only. This is possible due to a discovery by Curry and Schoenfinkel [Scho24, Curr29], according to which functions of n variables may be equivalently represented as n-fold nestings of functions of one variable (i.e., of unary functions):

$$f = \lambda x_1 \ldots x_n.expr \equiv \lambda x_1.\lambda x_2. \ \ldots \lambda x_n.expr \ .$$

Using this so-called **curried notation**, we may specify the application of f to one argument, say arg_1, as

$$(f \ arg\_1) = (\lambda x_1. \ \ldots \lambda x_n. \ expr \ arg\_1) \ ,$$

and its application to r arguments $arg\_1, \ldots, \ arg\_r$ as an r-fold nesting of applications of unary functions:

$$(f \ arg\_1 \ldots arg\_r) \equiv (\ldots ((f \ arg\_1) \ arg\_2) \ldots arg\_r) \ .^{10}$$

When using only unary functions, we have the following syntax for the construction of **well-formed formulas** of the λ-calculus, also referred to as λ-**expressions** or λ-**terms**: let V be a finite set of variables and C be a finite set of constants other than variables, i.e., $V \cap C = \emptyset$. Then

---

[10] In an equivalent constructor syntax notation the parentheses surrounding an application would have to be replaced by an applicator preceding it:

$$\mathbf{ap}^{(r+1)} f \ arg\_1 \ldots arg\_r \equiv \mathbf{ap}^{(2)} \ldots \mathbf{ap}^{(2)} \ \mathbf{ap}^{(2)} \ f \ arg\_1 \ arg\_2 \ldots arg\_r \ .$$

- all variables $x \in V$ and constants $c \in C$ are atomic λ-terms;

- $(M \ N)$ is a λ-term called **application**, if M and N are λ-terms;

- $\lambda x.M$ is a λ-term called **abstraction**, if $x \in V$ is a variable and M is a λ-term.[11]

In the following we will use

- capital letters to denote λ-terms,

- the lower case letters u, v, w, x, y, z to denote variables,

- all other lower case letters, character strings, numbers and special (function) symbols to denote constants,

- E_λ to denote the set of legitimate λ-terms.

The application $(M \ N)$ represents the result of applying the λ-term M to the λ-term N. M and N are respectively called **operator** and **operand** (or **rator** and **rand** for short). Alternatively, we may consider M and N to be a function and an argument, respectively, although this interpretation is somewhat misleading.

The λ-term $\lambda x.M$ definitely constitutes a function (of the variable x). Its value for some argument N is computed by the substitution of all free occurrences of x in M by N. This can, however, only be accomplished by an application of the form

$$(\lambda x.M \ N)$$

in which $\lambda x.M$ is in operator position and N is in operand position.

Consider, as an example, the application

$$(\lambda x.(x \ x) \ \lambda y.y)$$

which transforms, in two steps, into $\lambda y.y$.

If the λ-terms within the application are interchanged, we obtain

$$(\lambda y.y \ \lambda x.(x \ x))$$

and, after one transformation step, $\lambda x.(x \ x)$.

---

[11]Note that in some of the standard literature on the λ-calculus abstractions are also denoted as $(\lambda x \ M)$.

In either case, we apply a function to a function and reproduce, as a result, the function in operand position.[12]

Parentheses in λ-terms may be omitted as applications are, in compliance with the curried notation, assumed to be left-associative.

Literal or syntactical equality of two λ-terms M and N will be denoted as

$$M =_s N.$$

It is assumed that

$$((M\ N) =_s (P\ Q)) \Rightarrow ((M =_s P) \wedge (N =_s Q))$$

and

$$(\lambda x.M =_s \lambda y.P) \Rightarrow ((x =_s y) \wedge (M =_s P)).$$

The λ-calculus is said to be **pure**, if the set of constants is **empty**, i.e., $C = \emptyset$, otherwise it is said to be **applied**.

In the **pure λ-calculus**, we have only functions of the form $\lambda x.M$. The substitution of free occurrences of bound variables in functions is its sole legitimate operation (or transformation). Nevertheless, the pure λ-calculus constitutes a complete formal model which provides the bare essentials for a formal reasoning about abstract algorithms. Numbers, truth values, even list structures, as well as value-transforming or structuring functions to be performed on them can be represented as (admittedly rather formidable, hardly intelligible) pure λ-terms.

In the sequel we will be primarily concerned with the concept of substitution. It therefore suffices to consider only the pure λ-calculus even though it is way too primitive to study non-trivial computational problems in a comprehensible form.

5.3.1   Reduction

We learned that the application $(\lambda x.M\ N)$ is supposed to represent the result of applying the operator $\lambda x.M$ to the operand N. This result must be computed by the substitution of free occurrences of the variable x in M by N, denoted as $M[x \Leftarrow N]$.

The transformation

$$(\lambda x.M\ N) \longrightarrow_\beta M[x \Leftarrow N]$$

---

[12]Note that we are in a conflict here with respect to the proper terminology. In applicative languages, applicators are considered the sole (universal) operators, and its components are considered the operands. This complies with the terminology used in chapter 4. However, the λ-calculus distinguishes between operators and operands with respect to the components of applications (which are implicitly represented as pairs of brackets). In the following, we will use the terms operator and operand as in the λ-calculus. Alternatively, we will refer, somewhat sloppily, to operators as functions and to operands as arguments as well.

is called β-reduction or β-contraction. It is said to simplify or reduce the β-redex $(\lambda x.M \; N)$ to its contractum $M[x \Leftarrow N]$.

In order to formally define substitution, we first need to define, in the context of the λ-calculus, what is meant by the binding status of a variable.

Let M be a λ-term, and let $FV(M)$ be the set of free variables, $BV(M)$ the set of bound variables in M. Then we have

$$FV(M) = \begin{cases} \{x\} & \text{if } M =_s x \in V \\ FV(P) \cup FV(Q) & \text{if } M =_s (P \; Q) \\ FV(P) \setminus \{x\} & \text{if } M =_s \lambda x.P \end{cases}$$

$$BV(M) = \begin{cases} \emptyset & \text{if } M =_s x \in V \\ BV(P) \cup BV(Q) & \text{if } M =_s (P \; Q) \\ BV(P) \cup \{x\} & \text{if } M =_s \lambda x.P \end{cases}$$

A variable x in a λ-term M is said to be free iff $x \in FV(M)$ and bound iff $x \in BV(M)$. In a λ-term $\lambda x.M$, the term M is called the scope of the binder λx.

In compliance with our informal definition of open and closed functions in section 5.1, we say that a λ-term M is closed (or a combinator) iff $FV(M) = \emptyset$, otherwise it is open.

Examples of primitive combinators include

$$\begin{aligned} \Omega \quad &=_s \quad \lambda x.(x \; x) \\ S \quad &=_s \quad \lambda x.\lambda y.\lambda z.((x \; z)(y \; z)) \\ K \quad &=_s \quad \lambda x.\lambda y.x \\ I \quad &=_s \quad \lambda x.x \; . \end{aligned}$$

The most important of these are the combinators S, K, I which were independently introduced by Schoenfinkel [Scho24] and by Curry [Curr29, Curr34, Curr36] as a basis for what is called combinatory logic. They are computationally complete in the sense that they suffice to represent all computable functions: the combinator I reproduces its argument, the combinator K reproduces its first and consumes its second argument, and the combinator S duplicates its third argument. Thus, we have an identity operation, as well as annihilation and duplication of λ-terms[13].

The SKI combinators, together with a few other primitive combinators, define another powerful reduction calculus which has proved to be a suitable basis for the implementation of functional languages [Turn79]. We will study such an implementation later on.

---

[13] In fact, the combinator I is even redundant for it can be equivalently represented as SKK.

We are now ready to define the substitution by β-reduction of a λ-term N for free occurrences of a variable x in a λ-term M as follows:

$$M[x \Leftarrow N] = \begin{cases} N & \text{if } M =_s x \in V \\ h & \text{if } M =_s h \in V\backslash\{x\} \\ (P[x \Leftarrow N]\, Q[x \Leftarrow N]) & \text{if } M =_s (P\, Q) \\ \lambda x.P & \text{if } M =_s \lambda x.P \\ \lambda y.P[x \Leftarrow N] & \text{if } M =_s \lambda y.P \\ & \text{and } (y \notin FV(N)) \vee (x \notin FV(P)) \\ \lambda v.(P[y \Leftarrow v])[x \Leftarrow N] & \text{if } M =_s \lambda y.P \\ & \text{and } (y \in FV(N)) \wedge (x \in FV(P)) \\ & \text{where } v \in V \\ & \text{and } (v \notin FV(P) \cup FV(N))\,. \end{cases}$$

The most important case of this definition is the last one: in order to avoid naming conflicts between free occurrences of the variable y in N and P, occurrences of y in P are renamed by substituting another variable $v \neq y$ for them which occurs neither in P nor in N.

If we were to perform a naive substitution

$$(\lambda y.P)[x \Leftarrow N] =_s \lambda y.(P[x \Leftarrow N])$$

in case of a name clash, we would obtain a parasitic binding of free occurrences of y in N by λy.

The consequences of such name clashes have been extensively discussed in subsection 5.1.2. In the context of the λ-calculus, this problem may be illustrated again by a simple example: the λ-term $\lambda y.x$ is a constant function: when applied to whatever argument, it returns the variable x as the function value. A naive substitution of x in $\lambda y.x$ by N would yield:

$$(\lambda y.x)[x \Leftarrow N] =_s \lambda y.N.$$

If $N =_s w \in V$, then we get $\lambda y.w$ which, again, is a constant function. However, if $N =_s y \in V$, we get the identity combinator $\lambda y.y$ which reproduces its argument rather than consuming it. Thus, the meaning of the function has changed as a consequence of changing the status of the variable y from free to (parasitically) bound.

The renaming of bound variables in λ-terms by the transformation

$$\lambda y.P \longrightarrow_\alpha \lambda v.(P[y \Leftarrow v])$$

which the substitution rule requires in the case of name clashes is called α-conversion. It derives from β-reducing the application

$$(\lambda u.\lambda v.(u\ v)\ \ \lambda y.P)$$
$$\downarrow_\beta$$
$$\lambda v.(\lambda y.P\ v)$$
$$\downarrow_\beta$$
$$\lambda v.(P[y \Leftarrow v])\,,$$

where $\lambda u.\lambda v.(u\ v)$ is said to be the α-conversion function.

The renaming of variables in case of name clashes proves to be the most difficult and complex part in mechanizing the β-reduction

$$(\lambda x.M\ N) \longrightarrow_\beta M[x \Leftarrow N]\,.$$

For every binder penetrated in M, the mechanism must find out whether

- the variable bound by this binder appears free in N, and whether

- there is a free occurrence of the variable to be substituted in its scope,

in which case an α-conversion must be performed. The new variable name must be generated by the system in some unique way, e.g., based on the enumeration of one name by consecutive indices derived from a counting device which is being incremented on each renaming instance.

The complexity of substitution can be substantially reduced if all bound variables are uniquely renamed à priori, again following some global enumeration scheme which assigns static indices, or if all open λ-terms are converted into closed λ-terms (or combinators) by the abstraction of free variables. In either case, the potential for name clashes disappears completely at the expense of modifying the representation of the entire λ-expression without, of course, changing its meaning.

A more elegant solution to the naming problem which preserves both the binding status and the names of variables may be based on an unbinding concept which is a symmetric complement to λ-binding.

Variable occurrences in a λ-term may be preceded by sequences of some i unbinding operators $\backslash$ (called λ-bars) to protect them against the innermost i binders for the particular variable name.

Let $\underbrace{\backslash\backslash\ldots\backslash}_{i}x = \backslash_{(i)}\ x\ (i \in \{0,1,\ldots\})$ denote an occurrence of the variable x with i-fold protection, and let $j \in \{0,\ 1,\ldots\}$ enumerate nested binders λx, counted from the variable occurrence outwards. Then, with respect to the j-th binder λx, an occurrence of $\backslash_{(i)}\ x$ in the body expression is said to be

- protected if $i > j$,   • free if $i = j$,   • bound if $i < j$.

The index i in fact identifies the binding level (or binding status) of the variable occurrence. Protected variables in a λ-expression which are bound higher up are also referred to as relatively free variables.

The β-reduction of an application $(\lambda x.M\ N)$ can now be defined as follows: an occurrence of $\backslash_{(i)}\ x$ in

- the function body term M

  - decrements its protection index i by one if it is protected;
  - is substituted by the argument term N if it is free;
  - remains unchanged if it is bound;

- the argument term N

  - increments its protection index by l if it is free or protected,
  - remains unchanged if it is bound,

  when substituting it into the scope of some $l > 0$ nested binders λx within the term M.

As an example, we consider the β-reduction of the λ-term

$$(\lambda u.\underbrace{(\lambda w.(\ldots u \ldots w \ldots (\lambda w.(\ldots u \ldots w \ldots \backslash w \ldots)\ a))\ b)}_{M}\ \underbrace{w}_{N})\ .$$

Its outermost application is supposed to substitute a free occurrence of the variable w in operand position for free occurrences of u in the function body expression M, thereby penetrating the scope of up to two nested binders λw against which the operand w must be protected in order to maintain its binding status. When reducing the redexes from outermost to innermost, we obtain the sequence

$$(\lambda u.(\lambda w.(\ldots u \ldots w \ldots (\lambda w.(\ldots u \ldots w \ldots \backslash w \ldots)\ a))\ b)\ w)$$
$$\downarrow_\beta$$
$$(\lambda w.(\ldots \backslash w \ldots w \ldots (\lambda w.(\ldots \backslash\backslash w \ldots w \ldots \backslash w \ldots)\ a))\ b)$$
$$\downarrow_\beta$$
$$(\ldots w \ldots b \ldots (\lambda w.(\ldots \backslash w \ldots w \ldots b \ldots)\ a))$$
$$\downarrow_\beta$$
$$(\ldots w \ldots b \ldots (\ldots w \ldots a \ldots b \ldots))\ .$$

In the resulting redex-free expression, all occurrences of w which have been substituted for u are free again.

The advantages of this unbinding concept are twofold:

- the protection indices realize a dynamic enumeration scheme for occurrences of identically named bound variables which uniquely identifies their binding levels, rather than renaming à priori all bound variables globally, following some static enumeration scheme;

- in the course of β-reductions, binding levels change dynamically based on simple, locally applicable decrement- and increment-rules, which facilitates the mechanization in a machine.

Free occurrences of variables in a λ-term merely serve as **place-holders** (or dummies) for λ-terms which, by β-reduction, are substituted for them. We are therefore free to rename bound variables by α-conversion without changing the meaning of the λ-term. What really matters is the binding level of a variable occurrence.

Since binding levels of occurrences of identically named variables can be uniquely identified by protection indices, we may

- systematically rename all bound variables into one variable name by α-conversion, and subsequently

- drop the variable name altogether,

thereby obtaining a λ-term with nameless binders, and with nameless protection indices (or binding levels) in the places of variable occurrences.

We will refer to these indices (in reference to their inventors) as **Berkling/de Bruijn indices**, or as **number variables** [Brui72, BeFe82a, BeFe82b].

Consider, as an example, the λ-term

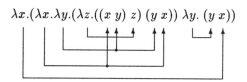

$$\lambda x.(\lambda x.\lambda y.(\lambda z.((x\ y)\ z)\ (y\ x))\ \lambda y.\ (y\ x))$$

in which the binding structure is represented by arrows pointing from the binders to the respective variable occurrences.

When applying the α-conversion function $\lambda u.\lambda v.(u\ v)$ to, say, all λy first, we obtain:

$$\lambda x.(\lambda x.(\lambda u.\lambda v.(u\ v)\ \lambda y.(\lambda z.((x\ y)\ z)\ (y\ x)))\ (\lambda u.\lambda v.(u\ v)\ \lambda y.(y\ x)))$$
$$\downarrow_\beta$$
$$\lambda x.(\lambda x.\lambda v.(\lambda y.(\lambda z.((x\ y)\ z)\ (y\ x))\ v)\ \lambda v.(\lambda y.(y\ x)\ v))$$
$$\downarrow_\beta$$
$$\lambda x.(\lambda x.\lambda v.(\lambda z.((x\ v)\ z)\ (v\ x))\ \lambda v.(v\ x))$$

Applying the α-conversion to λz we get:

$$\lambda x.(\lambda x.\lambda v.((\lambda u.\lambda v.(u\ v)\ \lambda z.((x\ v)\ z))\ (v\ x))\ \lambda v.(v\ x))$$
$$\downarrow_\beta$$
$$\lambda x.(\lambda x.\lambda v.(\lambda v.(\lambda z.((x\ \backslash v)\ z)\ v)\ (v\ x))\ \lambda v.(v\ x))$$
$$\downarrow_\beta$$
$$\lambda x.(\lambda x.\lambda v.(\lambda v.((x\ \backslash v)\ v)\ (v\ x))\ \lambda v.(v\ x))$$

Applying the α-conversion to the innermost λx yields

$$\lambda x.((\lambda u.\lambda v.(u\ v)\ \lambda x.\lambda v.(\lambda v.((x\ \backslash v)\ v)\ (v\ x)))\ \lambda v.(v\ x))$$
$$\downarrow_\beta$$
$$\lambda x.(\lambda v.\lambda v.(\lambda v.((\backslash\backslash\ v\ \backslash v)\ v)\ (v\ \backslash v))\ \lambda v.(v\ x))$$

and, finally, to the outermost λx, we get

$$\lambda v.(\lambda v.\lambda v.(\lambda v.((\backslash\backslash\ v\ \backslash v)\ v)\ (v\ \backslash v))\ \lambda v.(v\ \backslash v))$$

If we now drop all variables and introduce nameless binding symbols Λ, we obtain

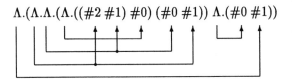

$$\Lambda.(\Lambda.\Lambda.(\Lambda.((\#2\ \#1)\ \#0)\ (\#0\ \#1))\ \Lambda.(\#0\ \#1))$$

where all $\#i$ represent Berkling/de Bruijn indices (or number variables) which, in terms of binding levels, exhibit the same binding structure as the original λ-term.

The β-reduction of this term from outermost to innermost produces the transformation steps

$$\downarrow_\beta$$
$$\Lambda.\Lambda.(\Lambda.((\Lambda.(\#0\ \#3)\ \#1)\ \#0)\ (\#0\ \Lambda.(\#0\ \#2)))$$
$$\downarrow_\beta$$
$$\Lambda.\Lambda.((\Lambda.(\#0\ \#2)\ \#0)\ (\#0\ \Lambda.(\#0\ \#2)))$$
$$\downarrow_\beta$$
$$\Lambda.\Lambda.((\#0\ \#1)\ (\#0\ \Lambda.(\#0\ \#2)))\ .$$

Particularly interesting with respect to the transformation into Berkling/de Bruijn indices are closed λ-terms (or combinators).

Let $\lambda z_1.\ \ldots\lambda z_i.\ \ldots\lambda z_n.expr$ denote a closed λ-abstraction, i.e., its body *expr* contains no free variables other than $z_1,\ldots,z_n$. It is called a **supercombinator** iff all λ-abstractions that occur in its body are closed as well [Hugh82, John85, Peyt87]. By α-conversion of the bound variables $z_1, \ldots, z_n$ of this supercombinator into v we get

$$\lambda v. \ldots \lambda v.expr'$$

where $expr'$ is obtained from $expr$ by replacing, for all $i \in \{1, \ldots, n\}$, free occurrences of the variable z_i by $\backslash_{(n-i)} v$. After dropping v, we have

$$\underbrace{\Lambda \ldots \Lambda}_{n}.\#expr = \Lambda_{(n)}.\#expr \ ,$$

where $\Lambda_{(n)}$ denotes a sequence of n nameless binders, and $\#expr$ derives from $expr'$ by the substitution $\backslash_{(j)} v \Leftarrow \#j$ for all $j \in \{0, \ldots, n-1\}$.

Thus, the binding levels represented by the Berkling/de Bruijn indices in $\#expr$ are from the interval $[0 \ldots (n-1)]$, where n is the number of binders. When β-reducing the supercombinator application

$$(\ldots((\Lambda_{(n)}.\#expr \ N_1) \ N_2) \ldots N_r), \ (r \geq n) \ ,$$

systematically from innermost to outermost, the binders Λ are consumed from left to right so that the binding indices in $\#expr$ never change: they represent a static binding structure in which, for all $i \in \{1, \ldots, r\}$, occurrences of the indices $\#(n-i)$ are substituted by the respective operand terms N_i.

It is also important to note that free binding indices which may occur in the operand terms N_i will not have changed once all β-reductions are done. This is due to the fact that all Λ-binders whose scopes may have been penetrated by β-reductions have then disappeared.

Consider as a simple example the stepwise reduction of the supercombinator application

$$(((\Lambda\Lambda\Lambda.(\#2 \ \#1 \ \#0) \ (\#2 \ \#3)) \ b) \ a)$$
$$\downarrow_\beta$$
$$((\Lambda\Lambda.((\#4 \ \#5) \ \#1 \ \#0) \ b) \ a)$$
$$\downarrow_\beta$$
$$(\Lambda.((\#3 \ \#4) \ b \ \#0) \ a)$$
$$\downarrow_\beta$$
$$((\#2 \ \#3) \ b \ a)$$

Here we see that the binding indices in the operand term $(\#2 \ \#3)$, when substituted for the index $\#2$ in the abstraction in operator position, are first incremented by 2, and subsequently decremented to their original values as the binders that have been crossed disappear due to further β-reductions.

Thus, when β-reducing supercombinator applications to full argument sets in one conceptual step, all substitutions can in fact be done naively.

The mechanization of this substitution scheme in a graph reduction system becomes extremely simple: pointers to λ-terms in operand positions may in their order of application, simply be pushed into a stack; occurrences of de Bruijn indices within the supercombinator body are taken as offsets relative to the top of this stack to access the particular operand terms which must be substituted in their places.

We will see later on that supercombinators and supercombinator reductions play an important role in implementing functional languages.

5.3.2   Reduction Sequences and the Church-Rosser Property

With a precise definition of β-reduction at hand, we will now have a closer look at some important properties of reduction sequences.

If P is a λ-term which contains a redex $(\lambda x.M\ N)$, and P' is a λ-term which emerges from P by the β-reduction of this redex, then P is said to be β-reducible to P' in one step, denoted as

$$P \longmapsto_\beta P' \ ,$$

A λ-term P is β-reducible to a λ-term Q, denoted as

$$P \longmapsto\!\!\!\!\!\longrightarrow_\beta Q \ ,$$

iff P can be transformed into Q by a finite sequence of β-reductions and α-conversions.

Based on these definitions, we can formalize what is meant by the **semantic equivalence** of λ-terms: two λ-terms P and Q are semantically equivalent (or have the same **meaning**), denoted as $P = Q$, iff P can be transformed into Q by a finite, possibly empty sequence of β-reductions or reverse β-reductions and α-conversions. This is to say that there ought to exist a finite sequence of λ-terms $P_0, \ldots, P_i, \ldots, P_n\ (n \geq 0)$ such that $P_0 = P$ and $P_n = Q$ and

$$(\forall i \in \{0, \ldots, n-1\})\ ((P_i \longmapsto_\beta P_{i+1}) \vee (P_{i+1} \longmapsto_\beta P_i) \vee (P_i \longrightarrow_\alpha P_{i+1})).$$

We say that a λ-term is in **normal form** (or β-normal form) iff it contains no β-redexes. If a λ-term P is β-reducible to Q, and Q is in normal form, then Q is said to be the normal form (*NF*) of P.

To exhibit some basic properties of reduction sequences, we consider as a first example the reduction of the λ-term $(\lambda x.(\lambda y.(x\ (x\ y))\ u)\ v)$. It may proceed along two different paths, as the redexes can be reduced in any order:

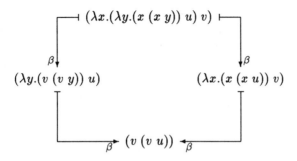

We note that both reduction sequences terminate with the λ-term $(v\ (v\ u))$, which is the normal form of all λ-terms preceding it. Moreover, all λ-terms have the same meaning (or are semantically equivalent), as they can obviously be transformed into each other by at most two β-reductions (or reverse β-reductions).

As a second example, let us consider the application $(\Omega\ \Omega) =_s (\lambda x.(x\ x)\ \lambda x.(x\ x))$. It causes a non-terminating sequence of β-reductions as it incessantly reproduces itself:

$$(\lambda x.(x\ x)\ \lambda x.(x\ x))$$

$$\downarrow \beta$$

$$(\lambda x.(x\ x)\ \lambda x.(x\ x))$$

$$\downarrow \beta$$

$$(\lambda x.(x\ x)\ \lambda x.(x\ x))$$

$$\vdots$$

Non-terminating sequences never produce a normal form. All λ-terms of such a sequence have the same meaning. However, the meaning, as we will learn later, is undefined.

The discussion of these two examples raises two interesting questions: given some λ-term,

- does it have a normal form at all, i.e., is there at least one reduction sequence which terminates after some finite number of steps?

- do all terminating sequences produce a unique normal form?

These questions, which have already been brought up in section 5.1.3, essentially relate to the existence of a function value for a function application.

The existence of a normal form for a given λ-term is generally not decidable, as we have already stated earlier. It would mean that there is some way of finding out whether or not after some finite number of β-reductions a normal form can be reached. Unfortunately, an upper limit for such a number cannot be specified [Tur36, Chur36, ChRo36].

However, the uniqueness of normal forms is guaranteed by the most important theorem of the λ-calculus, the **Church-Rosser theorem** [ChRo36]: it states that for any three λ-terms M, P, Q we have

$$((M \longmapsto_\beta P) \wedge (M \longmapsto_\beta Q)) \Rightarrow (\exists R) ((P \longmapsto_\beta R) \wedge (Q \longmapsto_\beta R))$$

where R is also a λ-term (see also section 5.2).

The essence of this theorem may be illustrated by the following simple diagram (which reflects the same structure as the one for the β-reduction of the λ-term $(\lambda x.(\lambda y.(x\ (x\ y))\ u)\ v)$):

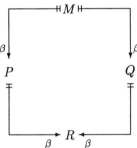

If any two λ-terms P and Q can be deduced from a λ-term M by finite sequences of β-reductions, then there exists another λ-term R, to which P and Q can be reduced. P and Q must not necessarily be syntactically different, and R must not necessarily be a normal form since none may exist.

We omit the proof of this theorem for its length. A recent version which has been accepted as being correct may be found in [HiSe86].

From this theorem we can immediately conclude that P and Q are α-convertible, denoted as $P =_\alpha Q$, if they are both normal forms of M.

This follows from the fact that normal forms do not contain redexes. Hence, P and Q must be α-convertible into R, which is also in normal form, and therefore be α-convertible into each other. Put differently: disregarding α-conversions, any two terminating sequences of β-reductions applied to a λ-term M always produce a unique normal form and thus realize strictly functional computations.

In another form, the **Church-Rosser theorem** states that for any two λ-terms P, Q we have

$$(P = Q) \Rightarrow (\exists N) ((P \longmapsto_\beta N) \wedge (Q \longmapsto_\beta N)),$$

i.e., the semantic equivalence of two λ-terms P and Q implies the existence of a third λ-term N into which both can be transformed by finite sequences of β-reductions and α-conversions.

This theorem can be rather straightforwardly proved by induction over the sequence of λ-terms $P_0, \ldots, P_{n-1}, P_n$ via which $P = P_0$ can be transformed into $Q = P_n$, and vice versa [Bar81, HiSe86].

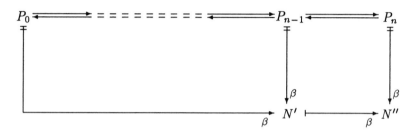

For $n = 0$, the proof is trivial. For the induction step from $n - 1$ to n, we assume that either $P_{n-1} \longmapsto_\beta P_n$ or $P_n \longmapsto_\beta P_{n-1}$, and that there exist λ-terms N' and N'' such that $P_0 \longmapsto_\beta N'$, $P_{n-1} \longmapsto_\beta N'$ and $N' \longmapsto_\beta N''$, $P_n \longmapsto_\beta N''$.

If $P_n \longmapsto_\beta P_{n-1}$, then we also have $P_n \longmapsto_\beta N'$ and, hence, $N = N'$.

If, however, $P_{n-1} \longmapsto_\beta P_n$, then we apply the Church-Rosser theorem in its original form, with P_{n-1}, N', P_n, N'' substituting for M, P, Q, R, respectively, and obtain $N = N''$.

Following this theorem, it is easy to see that P can be β-reduced to Q if P and Q are semantically equivalent, and Q is a normal form.

Furthermore, if P and Q are semantically equivalent, then both have either the same normal form, or no normal form at all.

This proposition may be verified by the following consideration: let $\overline{P}$ and $\overline{Q}$ be the normal forms of P and Q, respectively. From $P = Q$ follows $\overline{P} = \overline{Q}$ and $P \longmapsto_\beta \overline{Q}$. Since $\overline{P}$ is in normal form, we also have $\overline{P} =_\alpha \overline{Q}$.

Suppose now there exists a normal form $\overline{Q}$ for Q but none for P. From $P = Q$ and $Q \longmapsto_\beta \overline{Q}$ follows, however, that $P = \overline{Q}$ and, hence, $P \longmapsto_\beta \overline{Q}$, which contradicts our supposition.

5.3.3   Reduction Disciplines

The objective of transforming λ-terms by sequences of β-reductions is to deduce their normal forms (if they at all exist) in order to represent their meanings in the simplest possible form. In general, λ-terms may contain several redexes which may be reduced in any order, i.e., we have a transformation relation $\tau \subset E_\lambda \times E_\lambda$

which is total in its left component. For a λ-term that has a meaning, however, the Church-Rosser property guarantees that all terminating sequences of β-reductions yield a unique normal form.

With respect to a redex $(\lambda x.M \ N)$ we basically have the choice between two alternative reduction disciplines.

Applicative order reduction requires that the operand λ-term N be reduced to its normal form before the operator $\lambda x.M$ is applied to it. The idea is to transform N exactly once before its substitution for possibly many occurrences of the variable x in the λ-term M. It corresponds to a **call-by-value** parameter passing discipline in conventional programming languages.

When applying this discipline recursively to all subterms of a λ-term, say R, the transformation relation τ becomes a function $\tau_A \subset E_\lambda \times E_\lambda$ which is defined as follows:

$$\tau_A(R) = \begin{cases} x & \text{if } R =_s x \in V \\ \lambda x.\tau_A(P) & \text{if } R =_s \lambda x.P \\ \tau_A'(\tau_A(P) \ \tau_A(Q)) & \text{if } R =_s (P \ Q) \text{ and } P \neq_s \lambda x.P' \\ \tau_A'(P \ \tau_A(Q)) & \text{if } R =_s (P \ Q) \text{ and } P =_s \lambda x.P' \end{cases}$$

where

$$\tau_A'(R) = \begin{cases} \tau_A(P[x \Leftarrow Q]) & \text{if } R =_s (\lambda x.P \ Q) \\ (P \ Q) & \text{if } R =_s (P \ Q) \end{cases}$$

The function τ_A is recursively driven from outermost to innermost into a λ-term. It substitutes operands in normal form, if they can be produced, and generates non-terminating β-reductions otherwise.

Normal order reduction of a redex $(\lambda x.M \ N)$ requires that the operator be applied to the operand as it is, with the consequence that the λ-term N may have to be reduced several times inside the λ-term M. It corresponds to a **call-by-name** parameter passing discipline in conventional programming languages.

Normal order reduction applied to a λ-term R is recursively defined by the function $\tau_N \subset E_\lambda \times E_\lambda$ as follows:

$$\tau_N(R) = \begin{cases} x & \text{if } R =_s x \in V \\ \lambda x.\tau_N(P) & \text{if } R =_s \lambda x.P \\ \tau_N'(\tau_N(P) \ Q) & \text{if } R =_s (P \ Q) \text{ and } P \neq_s \lambda x.P' \\ \tau_N'(P \ Q) & \text{if } R =_s (P \ Q) \text{ and } P =_s \lambda x.P' \end{cases}$$

where

$$\tau_N'(R) = \begin{cases} \tau_N(P[x \Leftarrow Q]) & \text{if } R =_s (\lambda x.P \ Q) \\ (P \ \tau_N(Q)) & \text{if } R =_s (P \ Q) \end{cases}$$

It recursively enforces the reduction of the leftmost redex within a λ-term.

The difference between these two reduction disciplines which really matters is that

- applicative order reduction attempts to reduce operands to their normal forms irrespective of whether or not they are being inserted into operators;

- normal order reduction attempts to generate normal forms of operands only if they contribute to the normal forms of the λ-terms they are part of.

Hence, normal order reduction applied to λ-terms that have a meaning is bound to yield normal forms, while applicative order reduction may fail to do so by getting trapped in non-terminating substitutions.

The existence of terminating and non-terminating sequences of β-reductions, as we already learned in the preceding subsection, is always caused by redexes of the form

$$K\ A\ B =_s \lambda x.\lambda y.x\ A\ B \qquad \text{or} \qquad \overline{K}\ A\ B =_s \lambda x.\lambda y.y\ A\ B\ ,$$

if the λ-term B in the first case and the λ-term A in the second case contains at least one redex which has no normal form.

Applicative order reduction would get trapped in endless transformations of B and A, respectively, while normal order reduction would perform the transformations

$$K\ A\ B \longmapsto_\beta A \qquad \text{and} \qquad \overline{K}\ A\ B \longmapsto_\beta B\ .$$

Neither of these disciplines is optimal in the sense that they produce normal forms with the least number of β-reductions. Applicative order reduction may inflict redundant transformations if the normal form of an operand λ-term is consumed by the operator without reproduction; normal order reduction may inflict redundant transformations if the operand λ-term is reproduced more than once within the operator.

Besides these two basic reduction disciplines, there are variants of normal order reduction which are called lazy and fully lazy evaluation. They essentially avoid the repeated transformation of several copies of the same operand λ-term inside an operator by sharing its reduction to normal form. This, however, is an implementation principle which is outside the scope of the λ-calculus and will therefore not be treated here.

5.3.4   Recursion

Recursion constitutes a fundamental concept of the λ-calculus. It is based on the reproduction of applications of λ-terms to themselves by means of β-reductions (for which the redex $(\Omega\ \Omega) =_s (\lambda x.(x\ x)\ \lambda x.(x\ x))$ is a simple example).

The formal treatment of recursion in the λ-calculus derives from the so-called fixed-point theorem.

It states that for all λ-terms F there exists a λ-term Q such that $(F\ Q) = Q$, where Q is the fixed point of F.

A closed λ-term M is said to be a fixed-point combinator iff for all λ-terms F we have

$$(M\ F) = (F(M\ F)),$$

i.e., $(M\ F)$ is the fixed point of F.

This equation can be solved by the so-called Y-combinator, one valid form of which is given as

$$Y =_s (P\ P) \text{ where } P =_s \lambda x.\lambda y.(y\ ((x\ x)\ y)) ,$$

since

$$
\begin{aligned}
(Y\ F) \quad =_s \quad & ((\lambda x.\lambda y.(y\ ((x\ x)\ y)))\ P)\ F) \\
= \quad & (\lambda y.(y\ ((P\ P)\ y))\ F) = (F\ ((P\ P)\ F)) = (F\ (Y\ F)) .
\end{aligned}
$$

The Y-combinator applies, by substitution of the bound variable x, the combinator P to itself and reproduces, by substitution of the variable y, the λ-term F which is assumed to represent a recursive function.

Consider, as an example, the λ-term

$$F =_s \lambda x.\lambda y.(((F\ x)\ y)\ ((F\ y)\ x))$$

which is recursively defined by itself. We may rewrite this equation as

$$F = (\lambda f.R\ F)$$

with $R =_s \lambda x.\lambda y.(((f\ x)\ y)\ ((f\ y)\ x))$.

Following the definition of the fixed-point combinator Y, a solution for this equation must be of the form

$$F = (Y\ \lambda f.R)$$

in order to get

$$(Y\ \lambda f.R) = (\lambda f.R\ (Y\ \lambda f.R)) .$$

In general, we have the following proposition: let R be a λ-term containing free occurrence of the variable f, then there exists a λ-term F such that

- $F = (\lambda f.R\ F)$

- $F \longmapsto_\beta R[f \Leftarrow F]$.

The proof is trivial.

This proposition specifies all recursive functions F as fixed points of abstractions of the form $\lambda f.R$, and the β-reduction $F \longmapsto_\beta R[f \Leftarrow F]$ as a rule of computation for recursive functions.

The universal character of the Y-combinator derives from the fact that it reproduces the abstraction $\lambda f.R$ as a by-product of reproducing itself on each recursion step. The additional β-reductions that reproduce the Y-combinator can, however, be avoided if recursion is realized by more direct means.

Rather than transforming a recursive function definition F into $F = (Y \ \lambda f.R)$, we could simply define F to be a self-application of the form

$$F = (F^* F^*) \text{ with } F^* =_s \lambda f.R^*,$$

where R^* derives from R in that all free occurrences of f are being replaced by applications $(f \ f)$.

It can easily be verified that the redex $(F^* \ F^*)$ effects, by means of a single β-reduction, the direct reproduction of F in itself.

In the case of the above example we have

$$F =_s \lambda x.\lambda y.(((F \ x) \ y) \ ((F \ y) \ x)) = (F^* F^*)$$

with $F^* =_s \lambda f.\lambda x.\lambda y.((((f \ f) \ x) \ y) \ (((f \ f) \ y) \ x))$.

When extending the λ-calculus by a special recursion operator α, recursive λ-terms may be specified even more concisely as

$$F = \alpha f.R \ .$$

The recursive binder αf is to effect the direct substitution of free occurrences of f in R in a way that is fully equivalent to β-reducing the application

$$(\lambda f.R \ \alpha f.R) \longmapsto_\beta R[f \Leftarrow \alpha f.R] \ .$$

Other than avoiding superfluous β-reductions, the recursion operator α also solves another rather annoying problem: the Y-combinator $Y =_s (P \ P)$ cannot be used under an applicative order reduction regime. Following its definition in the preceding subsection, it can easily be verified that under this regime the self-application $(P \ P)$ engages in endless recursions for it reproduces itself incessantly in the operand position of an application. The α-operator prevents this by the direct substitution of $\alpha f.R$ in itself in unreduced form, which is equivalent to reducing the Y-combinator in normal order.

Sets of mutually recursive functions which have the general form

$$F_1 = \ldots F_1 \ldots F_i \ldots F_k \ldots$$
$$\vdots$$
$$F_i = \ldots F_1 \ldots F_i \ldots F_k \ldots$$
$$\vdots$$
$$F_k = \ldots F_1 \ldots F_i \ldots F_k \ldots$$

may be transformed into λ-terms in a similar way. When abstracting, say from F_i, the function names $F_1, \ldots, F_i, \ldots, F_k$, we obtain

$$F_i = (\lambda \vec{f}.R_i\ F_1 \ldots F_i \ldots F_k)$$

where $\lambda \vec{f}.\ R_i = \lambda f_1.\ \ldots \lambda f_i.\ \ldots \lambda f_k.\ \dashv \ldots f_1 \ldots f_i \ldots f_k \ldots \vdash$ (with $\dashv \vdash$ denoting the delimiters of the body expression R_i). When abstracting F_i again, we get

$$F_i = (\lambda f_i.(\lambda \vec{f}.R_i\ F_1 \ldots f_i \ldots F_k)\ F_i)$$

and as a solution for this equation,

$$F_i = (Y\ \lambda f_i.(\lambda \vec{f}.R_i\ F_1 \ldots f_i \ldots F_k))\ .$$

Using the recursion operator α instead of the Y-combinator, we have

$$F_i = \alpha f_i.(\lambda \vec{f}.R_i\ F_1 \ldots f_i \ldots F_k)\ .$$

In either case, the λ-term on the right-hand side reduces to

$$F_i = (\lambda \vec{f}.R_i\ F_1 \ldots (Y\ \lambda f_i.(\lambda \vec{f}.R_i\ F_1 \ldots f_i \ldots F_k)) \ldots F_k)$$
$$= (\lambda \vec{f}.R_i\ F_1 \ldots F_i \ldots F_k)$$

(after three β-reductions)

or to

$$F_i = (\lambda \vec{f}.R_i\ F_1 \ldots \alpha f_i.(\lambda \vec{f}.R_i\ F_1 \ldots f_i \ldots F_k) \ldots F_k)$$
$$= (\lambda \vec{f}.R_i\ F_1 \ldots F_i \ldots F_k)$$

(after one recursion step),

respectively.

Thus, our set of mutually recursive function definitions can, in terms of λ-expressions, equivalently be represented as

$$F_1 = (\lambda \vec{f}.R_1 \ F_1 \ldots F_i \ldots F_k)$$

$$\vdots$$

$$F_i = (\lambda \vec{f}.R_i \ F_1 \ldots F_i \ldots F_k)$$

$$\vdots$$

$$F_k = (\lambda \vec{f}.R_k \ F_1 \ldots F_i \ldots F_k) .$$

5.3.5   The Meaning of λ-Terms

Based on the notion of semantic equality of λ-terms which we introduced in subsection 5.3.2, we can formalize what is meant by the semantics of λ-terms.

A first definition was given by Church in 1941 [Chur41]: let E_λ denote the set of λ-terms, $C_\lambda \subset E_\lambda$ the set of normal forms, and $m \subset E_\lambda \times C_\lambda$ a partial function, then the semantics or meaning of a λ-term $M \in E_\lambda$ is defined as

$$m \left[\!\left[M \right]\!\right] = \begin{cases} N \in C_\lambda & \text{if } N \text{ is the normal form of } M \\ undefined & \text{otherwise} . \end{cases}$$

This definition causes problems with λ-terms containing non-terminating components.

Consider, as an example, the λ-term

$$K \ I \ (\Omega \ \Omega) \quad \text{with} \quad \begin{aligned} K &=_s \lambda x.\lambda y.\lambda x \\ I &=_s \lambda x.x \\ \Omega &=_s \lambda x.(x \ x) \end{aligned}$$

The existence of a normal form can only be determined by reducing the term, which can be done in two different ways:

- if we apply the outermost combinator K to its arguments as they are, we obtain a normal form after two β-reductions:

$$K \ I \ (\Omega \ \Omega) \longmapsto_\beta I$$

- however, if we try to reduce the arguments of the combinator K first, we end up with a non-terminating reduction sequence:

$$K \ I \ (\Omega \ \Omega) \longmapsto_\beta K \ I \ (\Omega \ \Omega) \longmapsto_\beta \ \ldots$$

Thus, we have λ-terms which can be reduced to normal forms. However, the normal forms can not be reached with every possible reduction sequence.

To overcome these difficulties, Church has, in a very rigid interpretation of the above definition, demanded that a λ-term has a meaning if and only if all of its subterms have a meaning (or can be transformed to normal forms). This demand is, in very restrictive form, satisfied by the terms of the so-called λI-calculus. However, it rules out all abstractions $\lambda x.M$ with $x \notin FV(M)$ and thus the K-combinator. Without it, selection among alternatives, which is essential for the specification of terminating recursions, cannot be accomplished by direct means.[14] From a pragmatic point of view, the λI-calculus is therefore not very useful.

In the extended so-called λK-calculus, a meaning is defined for all λ-terms which are **solvable** or have a **head normal form** in compliance with the following definitions [Bar81]:

A closed λ-term (or combinator) M is said to be solvable iff there exist λ-terms $N_1, \ldots, N_n$ such that

$$(M \; N_1 \ldots N_n) = I \;,$$

i.e., M applied to $N_1, \ldots, N_n$ yields the identity combinator.

An open λ-term M with the set of free variables $FV(M) = \{z_1, \ldots, z_q\}$ is said to be solvable iff

$$M' =_s \; \lambda z_1. \ldots \lambda z_q.M$$

is solvable.

Thus, solvability of a λ-term M requires the existence of at least one set of arguments, the one for which the function M produces the combinator I as function value.

Examples of solvable λ-terms are

- S since $S \; I \; I = I$

- $\lambda x.((x \; I)\Omega)$ since $(\lambda x.((x \; I)\Omega) \; K) = I$

- $\lambda x.(x \; (M \; \Omega))$ since $(\lambda x.(x \; (M \; \Omega)) \; (K \; I)) = I$

We consider now a λ-term of the general form

$$P =_s \lambda x_1. \ldots \lambda x_n.(z \; M_1 \ldots M_m) \; ; \; (m, n \geq 0, \; z \in \{x_1, \ldots, x_n\}) \;.$$

---

[14] An abstraction equivalent to the K-combinator may be constructed from applications to I-combinators so that the λ-term in its second argument position is systematically 'eaten up', whereas the first argument term is reproduced. A simple example is the abstraction $K' =_s \lambda x.\lambda y.(((y \; I)I)x)$. The reader may convince himself that the application $((K' \; M)N)$ with $N =_s \lambda u.\lambda v.(u \; v)$ reproduces M and consumes N (see also [Bar81]).

It is easy to see that this term can only be reduced to a λ-term

$$P^* =_s \lambda x_1. \ldots \lambda x_n.(z\ M_1^* \ldots M_m^*)$$

with

$$(\forall i \in \{1, \ldots, m\})\ (M_i \longmapsto_\beta M_i^*)\ .$$

We note that the head part $\lambda x_1. \ldots \lambda x_n.(z \ldots$ remains unchanged.

The λ-term P is therefore said to be in **head normal form**.

A λ-term M is said to **have** a head normal form iff there exists a λ-term P in head normal form and $M = P$. If a λ-term P' is not in head normal form, then it has the form

$$P' =_s \lambda x_1 . \ldots \lambda x_n. ((\lambda y.Q\ M_0)\ M_1 \ldots M_m)\ ;\ (m, n \geq 0)\ ,$$

where $(\lambda y.Q\ M_0)$ is called the **head-redex**.

This definition leads us to conclude that a λ-term has a head normal form iff there is a reduction sequence which, when applied to the head-redex, terminates.

A normal form is, of course, also a head normal form, but not necessarily vice versa. Thus, the existence of a head normal form is a decidedly weaker property than the existence of a normal form.

From the theorem which says that a λ-term is solvable iff it has head normal form we may deduce the following propositions regarding the **semantics** (or **meaning**) of terms of the λK-calculus:

- the meaning of a λ-term is undefined iff it is not solvable;

- a λ-term is not solvable iff it has no head normal form;

- a λ-term without a head normal form is also without a normal form, but not vice versa.

Using these propositions, we define the meaning m of a λ-term M in a less rigorous way than Church as

$$m\ [\![M]\!] = \begin{cases} N & \text{if it is the normal form of } M; \\ undefined & \text{if } M \text{ has no head normal form;} \\ P & \text{else} \end{cases}$$

where P is a head normal form of M.

The pragmatism of this definition deserves some further interpretation: a λ-term M which can be reduced to a head normal form $P =_s \lambda x_1. \ldots \lambda x_n.(z\ M_1 \ldots M_m)$ in fact represents a function of n variables. The solvability of this function is defined by the existence of a set of n arguments $N_1, \ldots, N_n$ for which the function produces a particular value (the identity combinator I). If the function is indeed solvable, it (also) has a non-empty domain. To verify solvability it suffices to show that the function has a head normal form. If it has one, it also is assumed to have a meaning.

Thus, the definition declares all functions meaningful which have a non-empty domain comprising at least the (sets of) argument λ-terms which yield the identity combinator as a function value.

5.3.6 An Applied λ-Calculus

We learned throughout the preceding subsections that the pure λ-calculus provides a formal model for executing abstract algorithms (or rules of computation). It allows us to exhibit and reason about basic properties of functions and function applications at a very high level of abstraction.

However, the pure λ-calculus is not suited as a practical programming language. Though it is possible to represent numbers, truth values and lists as combinator terms and to specify abstractions which effect the equivalent of arithmetic, relational, logical and structuring operations on these representations, the resulting λ-terms are difficult, if not impossible to interpret. Moreover, they tend to become extremely complex for applications of only moderate size, inflicting a multiple of β-reductions for all the primitive operations that need to be performed.

Even a primitive version of an applied λ-calculus can be expected to remedy this problem to some considerable extent. In its set of constants, it should include at least decimal numbers, character strings, the Boolean constants TRUE and FALSE, and the symbols $<,>$ for the construction of lists on the one hand, and primitive function symbols for arithmetic, logic and list operations on the other hand.

Following the recursive construction of λ-terms in the form of nested operator-operand pairs, we need to represent

- binary operations of the form $(arg\_2 \text{ OP } arg\_1)$ as $((\text{OP } arg\_1) \, arg\_2)$,

- unary operations of the form $\text{OP}(arg)$ as $(\text{OP } arg)$.

Thus, we have the equivalent representations

$$(3 \text{ EQ } 2) \equiv ((\text{EQ } 2)3)$$
$$((4-1) * (2+3)) \equiv ((* ((+ 3) \, 2)) \, ((- 1) \, 4))$$
$$(5 \text{ GT } 3) \equiv ((\text{GT } 3) \, 5)$$
$$\text{FIRST}(<a, b, c>) \equiv (\text{FIRST } <a, b, c>) .$$

The transformation of λ-terms that specify applications of primitive functions such as $+ \mid - \mid \ldots \mid \text{GT} \mid \text{EQ} \mid \ldots$ etc. is called δ-reduction.

Let $M, N \in L$ be terms of an applied λ-calculus, then M is said to be δ-reducible to N in one step, denoted as $M \longmapsto_\delta N$, iff

- $M =_s (a\ M_1 \ldots M_n)$, where $a \in PF \subset C$, $M_1, \ldots, M_n \in L$, and PF is the set of primitive functions;

- the λ-terms $M_1, \ldots, M_n$ are irreducible with respect to β- and δ-reductions;

- and $FV(M) = FV(N) = \emptyset$.

This definition in fact demands that δ-reductions be executed after completion of all β-reductions that affect free occurrences of bound variables in M, and strictly in applicative order. The pragmatism of this derives from the fact that all primitive functions can only be applied to arguments that are within their respective domains, to which neither variables nor applications belong.

IF-THEN-ELSE clauses have, in the applied λ-calculus, the general form $((P\ M)\ N)$. This is based on the supposition that the Boolean constants TRUE and FALSE, to either of which the predicate term P is expected to reduce, realize the combinators K and $\overline{K}$, respectively; i.e., we have

$$\text{TRUE} \quad \equiv K \quad =_s \lambda x.\lambda y.x$$
$$\text{FALSE} \quad \equiv \overline{K} \quad =_s \lambda x.\lambda y.y \ .$$

A λ-term of the applied λ-calculus is in normal form iff it contains neither β-redexes nor δ-redexes.

We consider now, as an example for the representation and transformation of an algorithm in the applied λ-calculus, a recursive specification of the factorial function. In the notation used throughout section 5.1 of this chapter, it has the form

$$
\begin{aligned}
fac(n) = \quad &\text{IF} \quad && (n \text{ GT } 1) \\
&\text{THEN} \quad && (n * fac((n-1))) \\
&\text{ELSE} \quad && 1 \ .
\end{aligned}
$$

This recursive equation translates into the λ-term

$$fac =_s \lambda n.((\text{GT } 1\ n)\ (* (fac\ (-\ 1\ n))\ n)\ 1) \ .$$

By abstraction of the recursively defined variable fac we obtain

$$fac =_s (\lambda f.\lambda n.((\text{GT } 1\ n)\ (* (f\ (-\ 1\ n))\ n)\ 1)\ fac) \ ;$$

i.e., fac is a fixed point of the λ-term $\lambda f.\lambda n.(\ldots)$:

$$fac =_s (Y\ \lambda f.\lambda n.((\text{GT } 1\ n)\ (* (f\ (-\ 1\ n))\ n)\ 1)) \ .$$

The application of this λ-term to the argument value 3 reduces as

$$(fac\ 3)$$
$$\Downarrow$$
$$((Y\ \lambda f.\lambda n.((\text{GT}\ 1\ n)\ (*\ (f\ (-\ 1\ n))\ n)\ 1))\ 3)$$
$$\Downarrow$$
$$(((\lambda x.\lambda y.(y\ ((x\ x)\ y))\ P)\ \lambda f.\lambda n.((\text{GT}\ 1\ n)\ (*\ (f\ (-\ 1\ n))\ n)\ 1))\ 3)$$
$$\Downarrow$$
$$((\lambda y.(y\ ((P\ P)\ y))\ \lambda f.\lambda n.((\text{GT}\ 1\ n)\ (*(f\ (-\ 1\ n))\ n)\ 1))\ 3)$$
$$\Downarrow$$
$$((\lambda f.\lambda n.(\ldots)\ (Y\ \lambda f.\lambda n.(\ldots)))\ 3)$$
$$\Downarrow$$
$$(\lambda n.((\text{GT}\ 1\ n)\ (*\ ((Y\ \lambda f.\lambda n.(\ldots))\ (-\ 1\ n))\ n)\ 1)\ 3)$$
$$\Downarrow$$
$$((\text{GT}\ 1\ 3)\ (*((Y\ \lambda f.\lambda n.(\ldots))\ (-\ 1\ 3))\ 3)\ 1)$$
$$\Downarrow$$
$$(K\ (*\ ((Y\ \lambda f.\lambda n.(\ldots))\ 2)\ 3)\ 1)$$
$$\Downarrow$$
$$(*\ ((Y\ \lambda f.\lambda n.(\ldots))\ 2)\ 3)$$
$$\Downarrow$$
$$(*\ (*\ 1\ 2)\ 3)$$
$$\Downarrow$$
$$6\ .$$

Note that in this sequence the Y-operator is reduced in normal order while all other applications are reduced in applicative order.

When using the operator α instead of the Y-combinator, recursion can be accomplished by more direct means. The factorial function then takes the form

$$fac\ =_s\ \alpha f.\lambda n.((\text{GT}\ 1\ n)\ (*\ (f\ (-\ 1\ n))\ n)\ 1)\ ,$$

and the application to the argument value 3 proceeds as follows:

$$(fac\ 3)$$
$$\Downarrow$$
$$(\alpha f.\lambda n.((\text{GT}\ 1\ n)\ (*\ (f\ (-\ 1\ n))\ n)\ 1)\ 3)$$
$$\Downarrow$$
$$(\lambda n.((\text{GT}\ 1\ n)\ (*\ (\alpha f.\lambda n.(\ldots)\ (-\ 1\ n))\ n)\ 1)\ 3)$$
$$\Downarrow$$

$$((\text{GT } 1\ 3)\ (*\ (\alpha f.\lambda n.(\ldots)\ (-\ 1\ 3))\ 3)\ 1)$$

$$\Downarrow$$

$$\vdots$$

$$\Downarrow$$

$$6\ .$$

When comparing both reduction sequences, we note that it takes four β-reductions to perform recursion by means of the Y-combinator, while just one transformation equivalent to a β-reduction is necessary to achieve the same ends by means of the α-operator.

5.3.7   Brief Outline of a Typed λ-Calculus

Types introduce into programming languages the notion of functions as mappings from domain sets to range sets. This contrasts with the theory of the untyped λ-calculus which primarily deals with the operational aspects of transforming function applications. However, both views can be united within the framework of a typed λ-calculus which extends λ-terms by type expressions [HiSe86].

Typing may be seen as a means to introduce more formal rigor into programming and to facilitate reasoning about program correctness. However, it is also of considerable practical relevance. Since almost all contemporary computing machines have no built-in type checking facilities, high-level programs must include at least to some extent type declarations in order to make sure that they are well-typed (i.e., do not produce type-incompatibilities at run-time) and to aid the compiler in transforming these programs into correct machine code.

Type expressions are recursively constructed from atomic types, function types and union types. The atomic types denote sets, say, of Boolean values, numbers, characters etc., and the function types denote mappings from domain sets to range (codomain) sets. Atomic types are denoted as $\alpha, \beta, \ldots$, function types as $(\alpha \rightarrow \beta)$, and union types as $(\alpha_1 \cup \alpha_2 \cup \ldots \cup \alpha_n)$, where $\alpha_1, \ldots, \alpha_n$ are types.

Using this basic notion of so-called monomorphic types, we can define a typed λ-calculus as follows: let x and c denote a variable and a constant other than a variable, respectively, then

- $x:\alpha$ and $c:\alpha$ are typed λ-terms of type α;

- $(M:(\alpha \rightarrow \beta)\ N:\alpha):\beta$ is a typed application of type β if M and N are typed λ-terms of the types $(\alpha \rightarrow \beta)$ and α, respectively;

- $(\lambda x:\alpha.\ M:\beta):(\alpha \rightarrow \beta)$ is a typed abstraction of type $(\alpha \rightarrow \beta)$ if x is a variable of type α and M is a λ-term of type β.

Some of the type annotations in abstractions and applications may be dropped since they can in an obvious way be inferred from other types. Likewise, if no ambiguities can occur, we may drop parentheses from nested function types and write

$$\alpha_1 \to \alpha_2 \to \ldots \alpha_{n-1} \to \alpha_n \text{ instead of } (\alpha_1 \to (\alpha_2 \to \ldots (\alpha_{n-1} \to \alpha_n) \ldots)),$$

implying association to the right.

A typed β-reduction is defined as

$$(\lambda x. M : (\alpha \to \beta) \ N : \alpha) \longmapsto_{\beta_t} M[x : \alpha \Leftarrow N : \alpha] : \beta \,,$$

i.e., it is carried out in the same way as a type-free β-reduction provided that the type of the operand matches the type of the λ-bound variable (or the domain type) of the operator. Otherwise, the application remains as it is.

It is important to note that in a typed β-redex the operator must be of a 'higher' type (containing at least one more type constructor $\to$) than the operand, i.e., both λ-terms cannot be the same. This rules out self-applications and thus the realization of the Y-combinator (unless we allow for recursive types). Without it, there can be no recursive λ-terms. A typed λ-calculus is therefore said to be strongly normalizing: every typed λ-term has a normal form into which it can be transformed by a finite sequence of typed β-reductions. This being the case, it can also be decided whether or not two typed λ-terms are semantically equivalent (which requires that they can be converted into each other by finitely many β-reductions (or reverse β-reductions) and α-conversions).

However, strong normalization is not at all desirable from a pragmatic point of view. The absence of a recursion operator severely limits the expressive power of a typed λ-calculus. Since all functions are in fact totally defined, we can essentially compute polynomials only.

The problem with recursion is not primarily caused by typing itself, but by its implication on self-applications. We can infer a type for every fixed-point combinator μ which satisfies $(\mu \ F) = (F \ (\mu \ F))$ (see section 5.3.4), including the Y-combinator. Assuming the types α for $(\mu \ F)$ and $\alpha \to \beta$ for F, we have

$$(\mu \ F) : \alpha = (F : (\alpha \to \beta) \ (\mu \ F) : \alpha) : \beta \,.$$

By unification of the types of the λ-terms on both sides of the equation, we get $\alpha = \beta$ and subsequently

$$(\mu : ((\alpha \to \alpha) \to \alpha) \ F : (\alpha \to \alpha)) : \alpha = (F : (\alpha \to \alpha) \ (\mu \ F) : \alpha) : \alpha \,,$$

i.e., μ has a type $((\alpha \to \alpha) \to \alpha)$.

So, in order to support general recursions in a typed λ-calculus, it is obviously necessary to realize the fixed-point combinator μ as a primitive operator rather than by means of an explicit self-application. In fact, the **recursion operator** α (not to be confused with the type α) which we introduced in section 5.3.4 is exactly what we are looking for. It performs recursion by the direct substitution

$$\alpha f.R \longmapsto R[f \Leftarrow \alpha f.R]$$

of a term in itself.

The monomorphic types we have used so far are not too well suited for λ-terms which apply uniformly to all arguments irrespective of their types. Typical examples are the *SKI* combinators and the recursion operator α which simply duplicated or consume their arguments. To deal with such λ-terms in the framework of a typed λ-calculus, we need to introduce the concept of **polymorphic types** (or **type schemata**). They are usually denoted as $*\alpha, *\beta, \ldots$ etc., representing propositions of the form **for all types** α, **for all types** $\beta, \ldots$ etc., respectively. Thus, we have for instance the following type annotations for the *SKI* combinators:

$$
\begin{aligned}
I &: \quad (*\alpha \rightarrow *\alpha) = (\lambda x : *\alpha.\, x : *\alpha) : (*\alpha \rightarrow *\alpha) \\
K &: \quad (*\alpha \rightarrow *\beta \rightarrow *\alpha) = (\lambda x : *\alpha.\, \lambda y : *\beta.\, x : *\alpha) : (*\alpha \rightarrow *\beta \rightarrow *\alpha) \\
S &: \quad ((*\alpha \rightarrow *\beta \rightarrow *\gamma) \rightarrow (*\alpha \rightarrow *\beta) \rightarrow *\alpha \rightarrow *\gamma) = \\
&\quad\ (\lambda x : (*\alpha \rightarrow *\beta \rightarrow *\gamma).\, \lambda y : (*\alpha \rightarrow *\beta).\, \lambda z : *\alpha.\, ((x\ z)\, (y\ z))) : \\
&\quad\ ((*\alpha \rightarrow *\beta \rightarrow *\gamma) \rightarrow (*\alpha \rightarrow *\beta) \rightarrow *\alpha \rightarrow *\gamma)\ .
\end{aligned}
$$

Polymorphic type schemata require that all occurrences of the same schema identifier be instantiated with the same type.

This polymorphic type concept, which in reference to their inventors is referred to as the **Hindley/Milner type system** [Hin69, Miln78], has become a standard for many functional (or function-based) languages, e.g., MIRANDA, SML or HASKELL.

When introducing type annotations (or declarations) into HLFL , they typically have the form

- $expr : \alpha$
  for expressions in general;

- $f(x\_1 : \alpha_1, \ldots, x\_n : \alpha_n) : \beta = expr$ or $f(x\_1 : \alpha_1, \ldots, x\_n : \alpha_n) = expr : \beta$
  for recursive function definitions;

- SUB $(x\_1 : \alpha_1, \ldots, x\_n : \alpha_n)$ IN $expr : \beta$
  for non-recursive function definitions;

- $x : \alpha = expr$ or $x = expr : \alpha$
  for local variable definitions;

- IF $pred\_expr : \alpha_p$ THEN $true\_expr : \alpha_t$ ELSE $false\_expr : \alpha_f$
  for IF-THEN-ELSE clauses with the union type $(\alpha_t \cup \alpha_f)$ and with
  $\alpha_p = \{\text{TRUE}, \text{FALSE}\}$.[15]

- $< expr\_1 : \alpha_1, \ldots, expr\_n : \alpha_n >$ or $< expr\_1, \ldots, expr\_n > \!\!\times\!\! < \alpha_1, \ldots, \alpha_n >$
  for lists with individual component types and
  $< expr\_1, \ldots, expr\_n > : list\_of\ \alpha$
  for lists with uniformly typed components (or well-typed lists).

All type identifiers other than the type α_p for the predicate of an IF-THEN-ELSE clause may be replaced with polymorphic type identifiers.

The atomic type identifiers typically include the basic types *dec_number*, *int*, *boolean*, *char_string*, etc.

Other type identifiers may be defined as

$$\text{TYPE } \alpha = type\_expr,$$

where *type_expr* typically specifies an interval of numbers, a set of elements of an enumerative type such as the colors of the rainbow or the days of the week, but also records, union or function types etc.

The scopes of **type annotations** coincide with **binding scopes**: type annotations to

- λ-bound variables hold within the respective abstraction bodies;

- expressions hold for the expressions.

Type definitions of the form TYPE $\alpha = type\_expr$ may appear anywhere within the scopes in which they are supposed to be valid.

The rules for consistent type annotations for the terms of a formal calculus (or for programs of a concrete language) are defined by a **type system**. These rules specify the realization of a **type checker** (or of a **type inference** algorithm) [Peyt87].

In a **static type system**, all type checking is done before executing a term (program). **Dynamic type systems** do the type checking at run-time.

A term (program) is said to be **safe** (or **well-typed**) if no type inconsistencies (errors) can occur at run-time. A type system is **sound** if every term (program) that is typed according to its rules is also **safe**. Sound type systems allow for static type checking. It essentially ensures that all primitive operators are applied to operands with compatible types. However, it can not statically detect type errors, say, due to division by zero, overflow conditions etc. which are of a dynamic nature and therefore must be dealt with at run-time.

---

[15] Well-typed expressions require that $\alpha_t = \alpha_f$ in conditionals.

A language (calculus) is said to be **strongly typed** if the type checker accepts only well-typed programs (terms). Legitimate programs of **weakly typed** languages may produce type incompatibilities at run-time.

It should be noted here that typing, though widely claimed to introduce more confidence into the correctness of programs, may also cause some rather unpleasant problems which do not occur in untyped languages. Other than outlawing self-applications, the respective type checkers also fail to infer types for a variety of higher-order functions and partial applications.

For instance, a polymorphic type checker infers for the function

$$twice = \text{SUB}(f, x) \text{ IN } f(f(x))$$

the type

$$twice : (*\alpha \rightarrow *\alpha) \rightarrow *\alpha \rightarrow *\alpha \, ,$$

i.e., the function substituted for f has to be of the type $*\alpha \rightarrow *\alpha$ and the argument substituted for x has to be of the type $*\alpha$ in order to produce a result of type $*\alpha$. This type perfectly unifies with

- the type of
  $$square : int \rightarrow int = \text{SUB}(x) \text{ IN } (x * x)$$
  and the type int for the value 2 in the application
  $$twice(square, 2) \, ,$$
  instantiating $*\alpha$ with int,

- the type of
  $$\text{REST} : list\_of * \beta \rightarrow list\_of * \beta$$
  and the type $list\_of \, \alpha$ for the list $< a\_1, \ldots, a\_n >$ in the application
  $$twice(\text{REST}, < a\_1, \ldots, a\_n >) \, ,$$
  instantiating $*\alpha$ with $list\_of \, \alpha$.

However, the application

$$twice(\text{FIRST}, < a\_1, \ldots, a\_n >) \, ,$$

causes a type incompatibility since the type $list\_of * \beta \rightarrow *\beta$ for FIRST cannot be unified with $*\alpha \rightarrow *\alpha$.

Similar typing problems may arise with applications of the same function identifier in different contexts. Consider as an example the combinator

$$S' =_s \lambda f.\lambda x.\lambda y.(f\ x\ (f\ x\ y))$$

for which a polymorphic type can be inferred as

$$(*\alpha \rightarrow *\beta \rightarrow *\beta) \rightarrow *\alpha \rightarrow *\beta \rightarrow *\beta\ ,$$

i.e., f must be of type $(*\alpha \rightarrow *\beta \rightarrow *\beta)$, x must be of type $*\alpha$ and y must be of type $*\beta$ for a result of type $*\beta$.

However, if this combinator is modified to

$$S'' =_s \lambda f.\lambda x.\lambda y.(f\ x\ (f\ y))\ ,$$

then the type checker fails for it tries unsuccessfully to infer for the first occurrence of f a type $*\alpha \rightarrow *\beta \rightarrow *\gamma$ and for the second occurrence of f a type $*\alpha \rightarrow *\beta$, and to unify both types (or more precisely the types $*\beta$ and $*\beta \rightarrow *\gamma$). The problem here obviously is that f is considered both a binary and a unary function in S'', whereas in S' it is taken as a binary function in both occurrences.

For a programmer not too familiar with the intricacies of polymorphic type systems these type errors are hardly comprehensible, particularly when occurring in a large program. The standard error messages produced in the above cases are usually of the form

> type clash in : *expr*
> looking for an : $*\alpha$
> I have found an : $*\alpha \rightarrow *\beta$ (or *list_of* $* \alpha \rightarrow *\alpha$),

meaning that the type checker failed to unify in the expression *expr* (which may be of considerable size) the types $*\alpha$ and $*\alpha \rightarrow *\beta$ (or *list_of* $* \alpha \rightarrow *\alpha$).

5.3.8   The *SECD* Machine

Landin [Lan64] introduced an abstract machine which has proved to be a suitable basic model for concrete evaluators of λ-expressions and, in more or less modified form, for expressions (terms) of concrete programming languages as well [Lan65, Lan66b]. This so-called *SECD* machine derives its name from the fact that it supports, as a run-time environment, four list structures for the representation and manipulation of λ-expressions or of components thereof. These are

- a control structure C which, in the form of a list whose components are λ-terms, holds what may be considered the executable code (or the program text);

- a run-time stack S which temporarily holds evaluated arguments (constants) as well as partially evaluated abstractions;

- an environment E whose entries are name (identifier)/value pairs which represent the substitution of formal by actual parameters;

- a dump D to store away the entire state of the machine, represented by the quadruple (S, E, C, D), upon entering into the evaluation of a new function application.

In fact, all list structures may be considered push-down stacks as well.

The machine operations are specified in terms of a state transformation function

$$\tau : (S, E, C, D) \longrightarrow (S', E', C', D')$$

which, essentially under the control of the first (topmost) component of the control structure C, maps a current state (S, E, C, D) into a next state (S', E', C', D').

We use the following simple syntax of binary list structures to define this function for the evaluation of expressions of the pure λ-calculus:

$$
\begin{aligned}
List \quad &:= <L\_expr, List> \\
L\_expr \quad &:= expr \mid (x, expr) \mid [E, x, expr] \\
expr \quad &:= x \mid \lambda x.expr \mid (expr \; expr)
\end{aligned}
$$

In this syntax, the expression

- $(x, expr)$ denotes a name/value pair;

- $[E, x, expr]$ denotes a so-called closure, i.e., an object which may be considered the *value* of the λ-term $\lambda x.expr$ in the environment E.

The symbol x stands for any variable.

The *SECD* machine employs applicative order reduction. The state transformation function is defined in terms of the syntactical components that may show up in the head position of the control structure C. In the case of

- an empty control list $<>$, the evaluation of a function application is assumed to be completed (the value returned by it is the head element S_1 in the structure S) and a new machine state needs to be restored from the dump D in order to continue with the evaluation of the enclosing application if there is one, or to terminate the machine if the dump is empty;

- of a variable x, the associated value must be retrieved from the environment structure E and pushed into the run-time stack S; if no entry is found in E, then x is free and, hence, its own value;

- an abstraction $\lambda x.expr$, a closure must be put on top of S;

- of an application $(expr\_1\ expr\_2)$, its components need to be reconfigured on top of C so as to have the operand evaluated before the operator (applicative order reduction) and to introduce an explicit applicator ap as a control symbol;

- the applicator ap in conjunction with a closure on top of S a new name/value pair must be set up in E for the variable of the closure, and the entire machine state must be saved on the dump D;

- the applicator ap in conjunction with a value other than a closure on S the application must be restored as *value* from the first two components of S.

Thus, we can define τ by the mapping rules:

(1) $(<S_1, S_2>, E, <>, (S', E', C', D')) \longrightarrow (<S_1, S'>, E', C', D')$

(2) $(S, E, <x, C>, D) \longrightarrow (<value(x, E), S>, E, C, D)$
(where $value(x, E)$ denotes the value of x in E, and $value(x, E) = x$ if x is free)

(3) $(S, E, <\lambda x.expr, C>, D) \longrightarrow (<[E, x, expr], S>, E, C, D)$

(4) $(S, E, <(expr\_1\ expr\_2), C>, D)$
$\qquad \longrightarrow (S, E, <expr\_2, <expr\_1, <ap, C>>>, D)$

(5) $(<[E', x, expr], <S_1, S_2>>, E, <ap, C>, D)$
$\qquad \longrightarrow (<>, <(x, S_1), E'>, <expr>, (S_2, E, C, D))$

(6) $(<S_1, <S_2, S_3>>, E, <ap, C>, D) \longrightarrow (<(S_1\ S_2), S_3>, E, C, D)$
(where S_1 is not a closure).

The applicative order reduction regime of the *SECD* machine is bound to cause termination problems with recursive functions which in the pure λ-calculus need to be realized using the Y-combinator (see section 5.3.4). An application of the general form $((Y\ F)\ R)$ reduces under this regime as

$$((Y\ F)\ R) \longmapsto_\beta ((F\ (Y\ F))\ R) \longmapsto_\beta ((F\ (F(\dots(F\ (Y\ F))\dots)))\ R) \longmapsto_\beta \dots$$

i.e., it is getting trapped in non-terminating recursions.

Normal order reduction can, however, be enforced for particular redexes by taking advantage of the fact that the *SECD* machine does not evaluate closures unless they are applied to arguments. The trick that needs to be played is to modify the redex so that

- the operand becomes an abstraction of a variable which does not occur free in it;

- in the body of the operator, all free occurrences of its bound variable are applied to some arbitrary term (e.g., to the variable abstracted from the operand) in order to obtain occurrences of the operand in its original form.

Consider, as an example, the redex $(\lambda x. \dashv \ldots x \ldots x \ldots \vdash R)$. Normal order reduction can be accomplished by reducing in applicative order

$$(\lambda x. \dashv \ldots (x\ z) \ldots (x\ z) \ldots \vdash \lambda z.R)$$
$$\longmapsto_\beta \dashv \ldots (\lambda z.R\ z) \ldots (\lambda z.R\ z) \ldots \vdash$$
$$\longmapsto_\beta \dashv \ldots R \ldots R \ldots \vdash$$

To prevent, by the same technique, endless recursions of the Y-combinator, we need to modify it to

$$Y =_s \lambda y.(A\ A) \text{ where } A =_s \lambda x.(y\ \lambda z.(x\ x\ z))\ .$$

An application of the general form $((Y\ F)R)$ reduces in applicative order as follows:

$$
\begin{aligned}
((Y\ F)\ R) \quad &=_s \quad ((\lambda y.(A\ A)\ F)\ R) \\
&=_s \quad ((\lambda y.(\lambda x.(y\ \lambda z.(x\ x\ z))\ A)\ F)\ R)
\end{aligned}
$$

$$\downarrow \beta$$

$$((\lambda x.(F\ \lambda z.(x\ x\ z))\ A')\ R)$$
$$(\text{where } A' \quad =_s \quad \lambda x.(F\ \lambda z.(x\ x\ z))\ )$$

$$\downarrow \beta$$

$$((F\ \lambda z.(A'\ A'\ z))\ R)$$

At this point we realize that the λ-term F is assumed to be of the form $F = \lambda f.F'$. Hence, the λ-term $\lambda z.(A'\ A'\ z)$ which is to reproduce F in itself, is being substituted in unevaluated form for free occurrences of the variable f in F'. Moreover, we recognize that applications of the form $(f\ Q)$ in F', after substitution of f by $\lambda z.(A'\ A'\ z)$, yield $(A'\ A'\ Q)$. Thus, the bound variable z is in fact used to pass along the argument of the function F.

The conscious reader will have noticed that the $SECD$ machine does not perform full β-reductions. Variables that occur free on top of the control stack C are naively substituted by the respective environment entries (rule 2). Parasitic bindings are solely prevented by turning λ-abstractions into closures (rule 3) which are not evaluated until they can be applied to argument terms (rule 5).

As a negative consequence, the *SECD* machine does not realize a full-fledged λ-calculus insofar as it cannot return abstractions as normal forms (values) of λ-expressions. For instance, when evaluating the application of a function of n formal parameters to some $r < n$ arguments the machine terminates, after exhaustion of the control structure C, with a closure containing a function of $n - r$ parameters in its expression part and a list of r name/value entries in its environment part, which is set up on top of stack S. Unless it becomes the argument of an enclosing application (whose status is to be retrieved from the dump), the machine stops with this closure in S.

6   The Mechanization of a Full-Fledged λ-Calculus

Abstract algorithms based on the reduction semantics of an untyped λ-calculus are an interesting paradigm for specifying and performing deterministic computations. This is primarily for the following reasons:

- Programming is based on clean mathematical concepts which feature a well-defined semantics. Programs need to be specified merely in terms of recursive function equations and function applications (or λ-expressions).

- Variables are treated as full λ-terms which are their own meanings. Name clashes between free and bound variable occurrences are correctly resolved. This may even be done without changing variable names. Simple symbolic computations may thus be realized with λ-terms containing free variables.

- In an untyped λ-calculus we have full support for higher-order functions, including self-applications: functions may be freely applied to functions in order to create new functions. In particular, functions of n parameters may be partially applied to some $r < n$ arguments to compute functions of $n - r$ parameters.

- The Church-Rosser property of β-reduction renders abstract algorithms perfect candidates for non-sequential (or concurrent) execution in a system of several cooperating processing sites.

- Conceptually, programs are executed by processes of meaning-preserving transformations which are governed by the β-reduction rule of the λ-calculus. Every transformation step returns a legitimate program of the language.

Of particular relevance is the latter aspect: it allows for stepwise program transformations under user control as an ideal means to validate, e.g., during the design phase, the correctness of a program or subprogram, and to modify it, if necessary. The entire state of the computation is contained in the program expression itself; there is conceptually no environment that needs to be inspected.

Our objective in this and the following four chapters is to systematically develop architectures for computing systems which, by a rigorous support for the reduction semantics of a full-fledged λ-calculus, truly and completely incorporate these characteristics.

The reduction language and the string reduction machine to be discussed in this chapter have been proposed by Berkling in 1974 [Berk75, Berk78], stimulated by Backus' earlier work on reduction languages [Back72, Back73]. A first simulator version was implemented in IBM/360-assembler code by 1976 [Hom77], and a

prototype hardware machine developed at GMD in Bonn was operational in 1978
[Klu79, KlSc80]. It was the first full-fledged reduction machine ever built world-
wide. It included a high-level interface for syntax-directed editing and interactively
controlled execution of programs with an HLFL syntax [Hom80].[16]

6.1   A Machine-Level Reduction Language

We introduce here a reduction language called OREL/0 (for OUr REduction Language) which we will take as the machine language for the reduction engines to be
discussed in the sequel. It is based on an n-place constructor syntax as introduced in
section 5.2 in order to facilitate its interpretation by fairly simple recursive mechanisms. Functional programs specified in HLFL may be converted into OREL/0 more
or less by straightforward transliteration. In this section, we will confine ourselves
to some essential subset of OREL/0 which suffices to convey the basic operating
principles of the kernel machinery. Later on, the language will be upgraded by
more powerful constructs.

The constructors of OREL/0 include

- two $(n + 1)$-place applicators $@^{(n)}$ and $\overline{@}^{(n)}$ which are to enforce applicative
  and normal order reductions, respectively;

- an $(n + 1)$-place binding constructor (or binder) $\lambda^{(n)}$ for n formal parameters,
  and a two-place recursive binding constructor α;

- an $(n + 1)$-place list constructor $<^{(n)}$;

- a two-place constructor Δ which forms an operator expression from the consequence and the alternative of an IF-THEN-ELSE clause;

- a one-place unbinding constructor $\backslash_{(i)}$ which specifies the binding level of a
  variable.

The atoms of the language are

- primitive (special single character) atoms representing function symbols such
  as

$$+ \mid - \mid * \mid / \mid \ldots \mid \wedge \mid \vee \mid \neg \mid \ldots \mid \top \; (\text{TRUE}) \mid \bot \; (\text{FALSE})$$

---

[16] Another intriguing string reduction concept was proposed by Mago in 1979 [Mag79]. It is
based on a tree-structure of processing elements which is capable of performing several reductions
simultaneously on string representations of Backus' FP-expressions [Back78]. The program strings
are held in the elements that form the base (leaf nodes) of the tree; control over the string
manipulations is in a rather complicated way exercised by the processing elements in the upper
tree levels.

$|\ldots|\longleftarrow$ (FIRST) $|\longrightarrow$ (REST) $|\uparrow$ (SELECT)

and the end-of-list symbol $>$;

- composite atoms (or character strings) representing variables, text, decimal numbers (including a decimal point), etc.

Expressions are either atomic or recursively constructed as

- applications of the general form

$$@^{(r)}arg\_r \ldots arg\_1 \ func$$

$$\overline{@}^{(r)} func \ arg\_1 \ldots arg\_r$$

where $arg\_1, \ldots, arg\_r$ and $func$ are expressions which are considered the operands (arguments) and the operators (functions), respectively. The applicator $@^{(r)}$ takes its last subexpression as the operator and all others preceding it as operands, whereas the applicator $\overline{@}^{(r)}$ takes its first subexpression as the operator and the following components as operands. This syntax is chosen in compliance with the control mechanism which will be used to serialize reductions:

- λ-abstractions (defined functions) of n formal parameters which are either of the form

$$\lambda^{(n)}x_1 \ldots x_n \ expr$$

in which case we have a nameless (or anonymous) non-recursive function, or of the form

$$\alpha \ f \ \lambda^{(n)} \ x_1 \ldots x_n \ expr$$

in which case we have a recursive function whose name is f;

- lists of n expressions

$$<^{(n)}expr\_1 \ldots expr\_n>$$

with an obligatory end-of-list symbol $>$;

- applications of the special form

$$@^{(1)}pred\_expr \ \Delta \ true\_expr \ false\_expr$$

which realize IF-THEN-ELSE clauses;

- protected variables, e.g., $\backslash_{(i)} \ x$.

We note that, contrary to the original definition in section 5.2, the arity indices of constructors, if explicitly specified as superscripts, are one less than the actual arities. This is a convenience with respect to the implementation of the language, but it also improves the readability of the expressions. The arity indices equal, in the case of

- applications the number of operands;

- λ-abstractions the number of formal parameters;

- lists the number of component expressions.

The meanings of these expressions are generally defined as in section 5.2. Exceptions relate to

- the meanings of normal-order applications which are defined as

$$m \left[\!\left[\overline{@}^{(r)} func\ arg\_1 \ldots arg\_r \right]\!\right] = m \left[\!\left[\overline{@}^{(r)} m \left[\!\left[func \right]\!\right] arg\_1 \ldots arg\_r \right]\!\right] ,$$

  i.e., the normal form of the operator expression is applied to unreduced operands;

- the meanings of λ-abstractions which, for pragmatic reasons that become clear later on, are defined as

$$m \left[\!\left[\boldsymbol{\lambda}^{(n)} x_1 \ldots x_n\ expr \right]\!\right] = \boldsymbol{\lambda}^{(n)} x_1 \ldots x_n\ expr$$

  and as

$$m \left[\!\left[\alpha\ f\ \boldsymbol{\lambda}^{(n)} x_1 \ldots x_n\ expr \right]\!\right]$$
$$= \boldsymbol{\lambda}^{(n)} x_1 \ldots x_n\ expr[f \Leftarrow \alpha\ f\ \boldsymbol{\lambda}^{(n)} x_1 \ldots x_n\ expr] ,$$

  i.e., we do not reduce in abstraction bodies.[17] We also note that recursion is treated as a pseudo-application: it is executed without there being an explicit applicator.

Special consideration must be given to the meaning of an application in which the arity of the applicator and, hence, the number of operands (arguments) does not match the arity of the function in operator position. The application of a defined function (λ-abstraction) reduces in compliance with the λ-calculus to

- an application of arity $r - n$ if $r > n$, i.e., if the λ-abstraction needs fewer arguments,

---

[17] In the terminology of the λ-calculus, abstractions whose bodies may contain redexes are said to be in weak normal form (*WNF*).

- a new (non-recursive) λ-abstraction of $n - r$ formal parameters if $r < n$, i.e., the original λ-abstraction needs more arguments than are tied up to the applicator.

This must be defined as follows:

$$m \left[\!\left[@^{(r)}\ arg\_r \ldots arg\_1\ \alpha\ f\ \lambda^{(n)} x_1 \ldots x_n\ expr \right]\!\right]$$

$$= \begin{cases} m \left[\!\left[expr[f \Leftarrow \alpha\ f\ \lambda^{(n)} x_1 \ldots x_n\ expr, \\ \qquad x_1 \Leftarrow m \left[\!\left[arg\_1 \right]\!\right], \ldots, x_n \Leftarrow m \left[\!\left[arg\_r \right]\!\right] \right] \right]\!\right] & \text{if } n = r \\[2mm] m \left[\!\left[@^{(r-n)}\ m \left[\!\left[arg\_r \right]\!\right] \ldots m \left[\!\left[arg\_(n+1) \right]\!\right] \right. \\ \qquad m \left[\!\left[expr[f \Leftarrow \alpha\ f\ \lambda^{(n)} x_1 \ldots x_n\ expr, \right. \\ \qquad\qquad \left. \left. x_1 \Leftarrow m \left[\!\left[arg\_1 \right]\!\right], \ldots, x_n \Leftarrow m \left[\!\left[arg\_n \right]\!\right] \right] \right] \right]\!\right] & \text{if } n < r \\[2mm] \lambda^{(n-r)} x_{r+1} \ldots x_n\ expr[f \Leftarrow \alpha\ f\ \lambda^{(n)} x_1 \ldots x_n expr, \\ \qquad x_1 \Leftarrow m \left[\!\left[arg\_1 \right]\!\right], \ldots, x_r \Leftarrow m \left[\!\left[arg\_r \right]\!\right]] & \text{if } n > r \end{cases}$$

where $expr[\ldots, x \Leftarrow expr', \ldots]$ denotes the substitution of occurrences of the variable x in $expr$ by $expr'$, following the β-reduction rule of the λ-calculus.

$m \left[\!\left[@^{(r)} \alpha\ f\ \lambda^{(n)} x_1 \ldots x_n\ expr\ arg\_1 \ldots arg\_r \right]\!\right]$ can be defined likewise simply by replacing $m \left[\!\left[arg\_i \right]\!\right]$ with arg_i within the respective intervals of indices, and by reversing the ordering of function and argument expressions.

In the case of non-recursive function applications, we simply need to drop the substitution $f \Leftarrow \alpha\ f \ldots$ from the definition.

The meaning of an IF-THEN-ELSE clause is defined as

$$m \left[\!\left[@^{(1)}\ pred\_expr\ \Delta\ true\_expr\ false\_expr \right]\!\right]$$

$$= \begin{cases} m \left[\!\left[true\_expr \right]\!\right] & \text{if } m \left[\!\left[pred\_expr \right]\!\right] = \text{TRUE} \\[2mm] m \left[\!\left[false\_expr \right]\!\right] & \text{if } m \left[\!\left[pred\_expr \right]\!\right] = \text{FALSE} \\[2mm] @^{(1)}\ m \left[\!\left[pred\_expr \right]\!\right]\ \Delta\ true\_expr\ false\_expr \\[1mm] \qquad \text{if } m \left[\!\left[pred\_expr \right]\!\right] \notin \{\text{TRUE}, \text{FALSE}\} \end{cases}$$

It specifies the conditional $\Delta\ true\_expr\ false\_expr$ as a typed unary function whose domain is the set of boolean constants $\{\text{TRUE}, \text{FALSE}\}$. For all argument expressions outside this domain, the application of the conditional is undefined and hence remains as it is. When in operator position of an applicator with arity $r > 1$, the conditional is simply applied to the innermost (first) operand, returning an application of its meaning to the remaining $r - 1$ operands. Likewise, primitive arithmetic, logic, relational and list structuring functions may be considered typed functions(or combinators) of fixed arities which are hard-wired into the system. The meanings of their applications are then definable in essentially the same way as those of non-recursive λ-abstractions. When in operator position of an applicator with arity r, we obtain

- a new application of arity $r - n$ if $r > n$;

- a new (intermediate) function of arity $n - r$ if $r < n$;

and if the arguments are within the function's domain; otherwise the application is left unchanged.

To illustrate these concepts, we consider various applications of the binary function $+$ which is defined over the domain of decimal numbers. We have

$$@^{(3)}\ 4\ 2\ 3\ + \qquad\qquad \longmapsto_\delta\quad @^{(1)}\ 4\ 5$$

$$@^{(1)}\ 4\ @^{(2)}\ 2\ 3\ + \qquad\qquad \longmapsto_\delta\quad @^{(1)}\ 4\ 5$$

$$@^{(2)}\ 4\ 2\ @^{(1)}\ 3\ + \qquad\qquad \longmapsto_\delta\quad @^{(2)}\ 4\ 2\ (+3) \qquad \longmapsto_\delta\ @^{(1)}\ 4\ 5$$

$$@^{(1)}\ 4\ @^{(1)}\ 2\ @^{(1)}\ 3\ + \quad \longmapsto_\delta\quad @^{(1)}\ 4\ @^{(1)}\ 2\ (+3) \quad \longmapsto_\delta\ @^{(1)}\ 4\ 5$$

$$@^{(1)}\ 4\ @^{(2)}\ a\ 3\ + \qquad\qquad \longmapsto_\delta\quad @^{(1)}\ 4\ @^{(1)}\ a\ (+3)$$

where $(+3)$ denotes an intermediate unary function which adds the value 3 to its argument.

It makes good sense to use the applicative order reduction regime as a default option in a real system. In the case of applications of

- defined functions (λ-abstractions) the arguments are reduced to their normal forms exactly once before being substituted for possibly several occurrences of the respective variables in the body expression;

- conditionals and primitive arithmetic, logic and relational functions, the arguments need to be reduced to values in order to be able to compute function values. These functions are therefore also referred to as being strict with respect to their arguments.

In the case of β-redexes, the applicative order regime clearly constitutes a compromise as it may cause redundant or even non-terminating reductions, while a normal order regime always yields normal forms, if they exist. However, the penalty that may have to be paid for the normal order reduction regime consists in repeated reductions of identical copies of subexpressions, unless a lazy evaluation strategy is applied.

The recursive definition of the meaning function implies a control discipline which drives a demand for the reduction of applications recursively from outermost to innermost into an expression. This demand can be satisfied by reducible applications (or redexes). They are characterized by

- expressions in operator position which can be identified by the system as legitimate primitive, composite or defined functions (λ-abstractions); i.e., expressions which belong to the domain of the representation function R;

- expressions in operand position which in the case of

  - primitive function applications must be in the functions' domain,

  - applications of λ-abstractions may be all legitimate expressions of the language, since β-reduction is assumed to be type-free.

6.2 A String Reduction Engine

The basic mechanisms of an abstract reduction engine derive from the operational and control disciplines that govern the transformation of program expressions in general, and from the syntax and semantics of the concrete machine language in particular. Following the discussion of these issues in the preceding sections, our reduction engine must provide the means to

- uniquely represent, in a suitable storage structure, the syntactical structure of OREL/0 program expressions;

- exercise a demand-driven control discipline which in compliance with the syntax of applications must be realized as a pre-order traversal of the program expressions

- identify, during the pre-order traversal, instances of reductions (redexes);

- execute redexes by consuming their components and by substituting the respective resulting expressions in their places;

- resume, after the completion of β- or δ-reductions, the pre-order traversal in search for further reducible applications until the traversal position returns to the topmost constructor of the expression.

This can be readily accomplished either by string reduction or by graph reduction. In the former case, a program expression is represented as a (pre-order-linearized) character string and reduced by the systematic literal substitution of substrings representing redexes. In the latter case, the program is represented as a recursively constructed pointer structure. Reductions are carried out largely by re-arranging pointers.

While graph reduction is decidedly more efficient in terms of the computational complexity involved, we nevertheless set out with the design of a string reduction engine to study in a clean setting the implementation of

- a pre-order traversal as a versatile control mechanism for sequencing and performing reductions as well as for moving expressions from source locations to sink locations;

- a full-fledged β-reduction as the basic operational mechanism by which operators are supplied with operands.

Both the pre-order traversal mechanism and, to some lesser extent, full β-reductions will also play a key role in the realization of the graph reduction engines to be described later on.

An elegant way of implementing the pre-order traversal is based on a recursive shunting yard mechanism which uses three push-down stacks named X, Y and M. It transforms the character string representation of an expression into its left-right transposed form, using either of the stacks X or Y as the source and the other as the sink location, and the stack M as an intermediate store for constructor symbols. This mechanism transfers syntactically complete expressions from source to sink. Repetition with source and sink stack interchanged restores the expression in its original (non-transposed) form.

Considering the stacks as binary list structures of the general form

$$list := \ <item, \ list>$$
$$item := \mathbf{k}^{(n)} \ | \ atom \ | \ \%$$

(where $\mathbf{k}^{(n)}$, $atom$, $\%$ respectively denote $(n+1)$-place constructors, atomic expressions and a special termination symbol), we can specify the traversal mechanism – similar to the *SECD* machine – in terms of a state transition function:

$$trav : (X, Y, M, c) \longrightarrow (X', Y', M', c') \ .$$

Here, X, Y and M respectively denote the list structures representing the source-, sink- and M-stack, and c specifies one of the following four control states:

$$c = \begin{cases} \left. \begin{array}{ll} en & : \ \text{entry into} \\ ex & : \ \text{exit from} \end{array} \right\} & \text{the traversal of an expression} \\ \\ m : \ \text{inspect top of the } M\text{-structure} \\ x \ : \ \text{inspect top of the } X\text{-structure} \end{cases}$$

Using this notation, *trav* can be defined by the following rules:

(1) $(X, Y, M, en) \longrightarrow (X, Y, <\%, M>, x)$

(2) $(<\mathbf{k}^{(n)}, X>, Y, M, x) \longrightarrow (X, Y, <\mathbf{k}^{(n|n)}, M>, x)$

(3) $(<atom, X>, Y, M, x) \longrightarrow (X, <atom, Y>, M, m)$

(4) $(X, Y, <\mathbf{k}^{(n|i>0)}, M>, m) \longrightarrow (X, Y, <\mathbf{k}^{(n|(i-1))}, M>, x)$

(5) $(X, Y, <\mathbf{k}^{(n|0)}, M>, m) \longrightarrow (X, <\mathbf{k}^{(n)}, Y>, M, m)$

(6) $(X, Y, <\%, M>, m) \longrightarrow (X, Y, M, ex)$

After pushing the special termination symbol % into stack M, this traversal mechanism starts with the inspection of the topmost symbol in the source stack X.

Constructor symbols are moved from X to M. The arity indices are duplicated in M, and the copies are used as count indices that follow up on the movement of the subexpressions from X to Y. Control returns to X.

An atom is directly moved from X to Y; subsequently the count index of the topmost constructor in M is decremented, whereupon control returns to X. If the count index is found to be zero, the topmost constructor of M is moved to Y, thereby completing the traversal of a non-atomic (sub-)expression, and control returns to M.

The mechanism terminates with the symbol % re-appearing on top of M, whereupon it is popped out.

Fig. 6.1 shows a few snap-shots taken from the stacks while traversing the expression

$$@^{(2)} a\_3 \, \overline{@}^{(2)} f\_1 \, a\_1 \, a\_2 \, f\_2$$

from X to Y, where it builds up as

$$@^{(2)} \, \overline{f\_2} \, \overline{@}^{(2)} \, \overline{a\_2} \, \overline{a\_1} \, \overline{f\_1} \, \overline{a\_3} \,,$$

with $\overline{expr}$ denoting the left-right transpose of *expr*.

It is interesting to note that this traversal mechanism recursively brings about constellations as in figs. 6.1.c and 6.1.d in which the operator expression and the applicator of an application respectively reside on the tops of the stacks X and M. In the case of an

- applicator $@^{(n)}$ we find its count index to be zero, with the operand expressions stacked up in reverse order and in transposed form in Y (fig. 6.1.d);

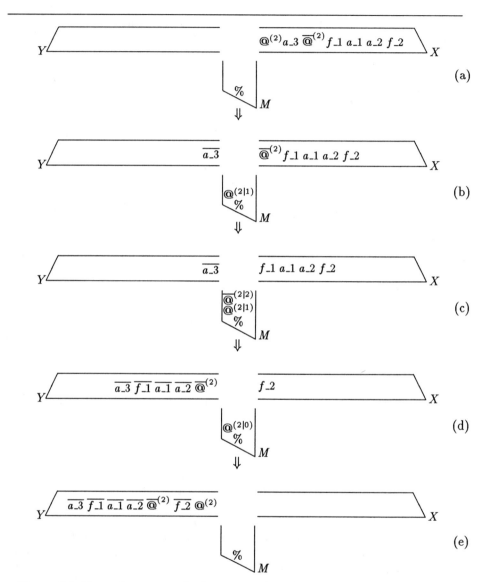

Figure 6.1: Pre-order traversal of an expression about three push-down stacks

- applicator $\overline{@}^{(n)}$ the count index equals its arity since all of its subexpressions are still stacked up in X (fig. 6.1.c).

These constellations constitute potential instances of reductions which can be executed whenever the topmost expression in X is indeed a function (i.e., it is defined under the representation function R) and the arguments are found to be within its domain.

This being the case, the pre-order traversal is suspended and control switches to what may be considered **micro-programs** which actually perform the transformations specified by the **representation function** R, with control eventually returning to the pre-order traversal.

Reductions generally involve rather simple recursive mechanisms, most of which are derivative forms of the pre-order traversal such as

- the **deletion** of an expression, which is a traversal without a sink stack;

- the **duplication** of an expression, which is a traversal with two sink stacks;

- the **comparison** of two expressions, which is a traversal with two source stacks.

To provide sufficient space and flexibility for the decomposition of applications, for the duplication and comparison of (sub-)expressions and for the execution of operations on numbers and character strings, it is convenient to have a few more stacks available. In addition, we need a control stack which governs the sequencing of the micro-programs (subroutines) that interpret the reduction rules.

Control over the stack operations is exercised by means of a **reduction unit** which accommodates the micro-programs. It inspects the topmost items of selected stacks and, depending on the particular pattern of symbols found, it selects stacks to be pushed, popped and inspected next, and specifies, if necessary, the symbols required for push-operations.

There are also **input/output** facilities through which expressions may be loaded and unloaded, and via which the user may control the engine.

A complete block diagram of such a string reduction engine is shown in fig. 6.2. It includes the **working stacks** E, A, B, U, V and M, and the **control stack** C. Expressions or subexpressions may be traversed with any one of the stacks E, A, B, U, V serving as source or sink, and with the stack M as the intermediate stack for constructor symbols.

Instances of reductions are, by convention, always searched for while traversing a program expression from stack E to A. All other stacks get involved only during the execution of reduction rules.

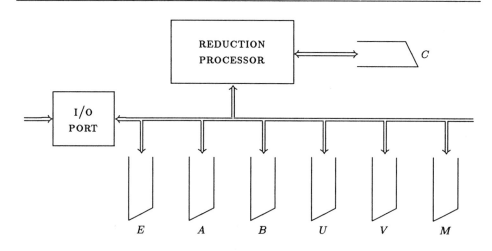

Figure 6.2: Block diagram of a string reduction engine

Stack E serves as the input/output stack through which expressions are moved in and out of the engine. Expressions are expected to reside there in non-transposed form.

The reduction unit also includes a so-called reduction counter. Its primary purpose is to halt the engine in some orderly manner in case of non-terminating recursions. Prior to submitting a program expression to the engine, this counter is initialized with some user-specified value. During program execution, it is decremented on each β-reduction (and optionally on each δ-reduction as well). The engine terminates whenever

- either the program expression is transformed into its normal form,

- or the counter value is decremented to zero,

whichever happens first. In either case, the engine returns an OREL/0 expression.

This counter may also be used to control the engine when reducing expressions in a step-by-step mode for the inspection and modification of intermediate expressions.

6.2.1 Stack Control Diagrams

To specify more precisely the string reduction mechanics we have just outlined, we introduce a special graphical notation for the control programs that operate the stacks as well as registers (counters) containing status information. These so-called **stack control diagrams** lend themselves more elegantly to

- the specification of primitive push, pop and inspect operations on formatted stack entries,

- the representation of complex control programs in terms of simpler ones,

- the inclusion of procedures (subroutines) not entirely related to stack operations,

than state transition functions as we have used earlier [Berk75, Hom77].

It is important to realize that, in a concrete hardware machine, we have to deal with entries of fixed size (or formats) corresponding, in our case, to the widths of the stacks rather than with objects of arbitrary (but finite) length.

Without being too specific about the exact formats, we commit ourselves to the following: an entry in one of the stacks E, A, B, U, V may accommodate

- a constructor symbol, including its arity index;

- a primitive function symbol;

- a fixed number of characters (say from one to four) of a composite atom.

An entry into the stack M is assumed to accommodate a constructor symbol, including its duplicated arity index.

Composite atoms are character strings of finite length representing variables, text or decimal numbers. To represent these strings in stacks whose entries may accommodate some $k > 1$ characters, we introduce a syntax for what we call **stack strings**. Assuming an alignment to the right, we must take into account that the first (leading) entry of the string may have to be partially filled with some $l \in \{0, \ldots, k - 1\}$ empty characters. As for the specification of control programs, we can in the overwhelming majority of cases ignore the existence of empty characters in the first entry and simply consider a stack string as a sequence of entries of the form

$$\langle: stack\_string :\rangle \ := \ \langle: entry^0 :\rangle \mid \langle: entry^1 :\rangle \langle: stack\_string :\rangle .$$

The last string entry is earmarked by a ^{0}, and all other entries (if any) are earmarked by a ^{1} in order to be able to identify the end of a string while traversing it.

For every stack that participates in the execution of a control program, we have one **horizontal stack line** each to represent pop and push operations. Horizontal stack lines may be interconnected by **vertical control flow lines** which specify the transfer of control between the stacks. This may or may not include the transfer of a stack entry. The control lines may be intercepted by **boxes** specifying calls for

- other stack control programs,

- subroutines not entirely related to stack operations,

- primitive operations,

- tests of conditions.

Fig. 6.3.a illustrates these elements for a **pop-line** of some stack X and a **push-line** of some stack Y.

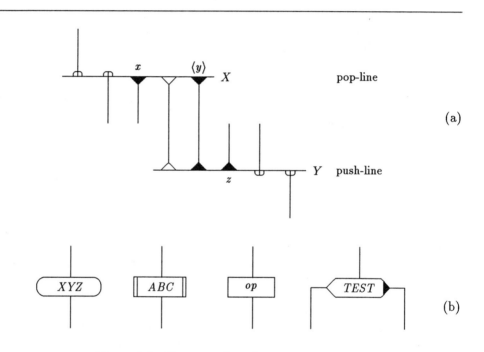

Figure 6.3: Elements of stack control programs

Pop-lines are characterized by control lines leaving through downwards pointing triangles and arriving through upwards pointing half-circles. Push-lines have control lines arriving at upwards pointing triangles and leaving at downwards pointing half-circles. Solid triangles specify pop- or push-operations either on individual stack entries, denoted by terminal symbols (such as x), or on all members of a particular class of stack entries, identified by non-terminal symbols (such as $\langle y \rangle$). An empty triangle on a pop-line specifies pop-operations on all stack entries not specified by the solid triangles on this line. Empty triangles on a push line must be connected to empty triangles on pop-lines in order to specify the class of entries that is to be pushed. The same applies to solid triangles on push-lines which are labeled by non-terminal symbols identifying classes of stack entries.

Control lines beginning or ending at a half-circle transfer control from a push-line or to a pop-line, respectively, without moving a stack entry.

Push- and pop-lines may be labeled by two stack names, in which case the respective operations have to be carried out on both stacks simultaneously. Correspondingly, the solid triangles on these lines may have to be labeled by pairs of symbols.

Fig. 6.3.b shows the boxes that may intercept a control line. They represent, from left to right, a call for another stack control program named XYZ, for an open subroutine named ABC, for a primitive operation op, and a test for a condition, with the *yes*-exit marked by a solid triangle.

All stack control programs, in one way or another, move syntactically complete expressions from source to sink locations. They have unique entry and exit points which are respectively marked by pushing or popping a termination symbol % into or out of stack M.

Fig. 6.4 shows the stack control diagram for the **pre-order traversal** of an expression from a source to a sink stack which on page 143 has been specified in terms of a state transition function. The class symbols $\langle pf \rangle$ and $\langle se \rangle$, respectively, denote primitive function symbols and string entries.

In the context of another control program this traversal is symbolized as $\overline{(XY)}$ where X and Y, respectively, name source and sink stack.

Essentially the same diagram specifies the duplication of an expression from a source stack X into two sink stacks Y and Z, symbolized as $\overline{(XYZ)}$. All we need to do is to add the name Z to the push-line for stack Y, and to duplicate the symbols labeling the solid triangles on Y.

Deleting an expression may be accomplished by traversing it without a sink stack. The corresponding stack diagram may be obtained from the one for the pre-order traversal by removing the push-line of stack Y, and by terminating all control lines leading to it at the pop-line of stack M. Deletion is symbolized as $\overline{(\delta X)}$, where X again denotes the source stack.

It is important to note that all three forms of the traversal move only the topmost syntactically complete expression from the source stack. If its contents are, say

$$\underline{@^{(2)} \; @^{(1)} \; arg\_2 \; f\_2 \; arg\_1 \; f\_1} <^{(n)} expr\_1 \; \ldots \; ,$$

then the traversal removes the underlined expression but leaves the following list structure untouched. Removing the topmost applicator $@^{(2)}$ renders its left subex-

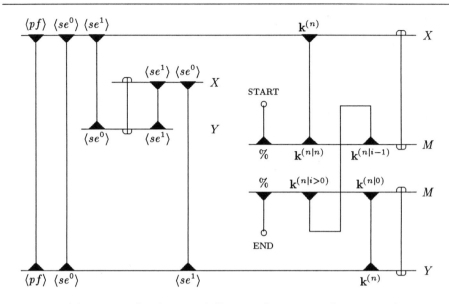

Figure 6.4: Stack control diagram for a pre-order traversal

pression $@^{(1)}$ arg_2 f_2 the topmost expression; adding, say, a two-place constructor at the top includes the list structure into the topmost expression.

These traversals constitute the most basic string manipulation mechanisms. They are repeatedly called upon when performing reductions.

6.2.2   The Implementation of Reduction Rules

Our reduction engine is assumed to reduce expressions while traversing them from stack E to stack A. During this traversal, instances of reducible applications (redexes) must be intercepted and executed.

We recall that redexes are identifiable by **stack constellations** with

- either of the applicators $@^{(r|0)}$ or $\overline{@}^{(r|r)}$ on top of stack M;

- a primitive function symbol from the class $\langle pf \rangle$ or a defined function as the topmost expression in the source stack (E).

Defined functions can easily be recognized by their head symbols which are either $\lambda^{(n)}$ or α.

To include reductions into a traversal from E to A, we therefore simply need to

- insert subroutine boxes for all δ-reduction rules into the control line via which primitive function symbols are moved from E to A;

- separate from the control line which transfers constructors from E to M two individual control lines for $\lambda^{(n)}$ and α, and insert into these lines subroutine boxes specifying the respective reduction rules.

We thus obtain the global structure of the reduction control program $\boxed{EAR}$ as shown in fig. 6.5.

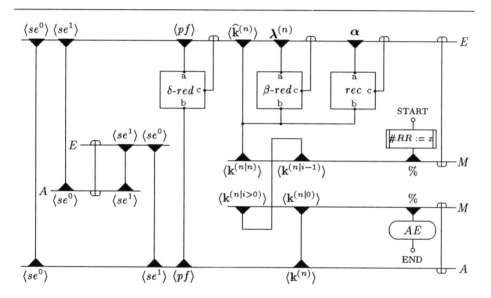

Figure 6.5: Stack diagram for the reduction control program $\boxed{EAR}$

The entry line into this program includes, as a primitive operation, the initialization of the reduction counter register $\#RR$ with some user-specified value. The exit line includes a traversal of the reduced expression from $\grave{A}$ to E in order to have it set up in E in non-transposed form for output.

Each reduction rule box is equipped with one entry point a and two exit points b and c. Control leaves a box through

- exit c on the successful completion of the particular reduction, whereupon the traversal of the expression continues with the topmost subexpression in E, which happens to be the result of this reduction;

- exit b if the reduction must be aborted and the original stack constellation must be restored for one of the following reasons:

  - the reduction counter $\#RR$ is decremented to zero, in which case $\overparen{EAR}$ continues as a traversal of the remaining expression from E to A;

  - there is a constructor other than an applicator on top of M;

  - the function expression on top of E is not in operator position of the applicator, i.e., we have either $@^{(r|i>0)}$ or $\overline{@}^{(r|i<r)}$ on top of M;

  - in the case of a δ-reduction, the operand (argument) expression(s) is (are) not within the domain of the function.

We will now be concerned primarily with the contents of the β-reduction box $\boxed{\beta\text{-red}}$ which constitutes the most fundamental and complex operation of the engine. Recursion is just a special case of β-reduction.

Fig. 6.6 shows the part of the β-reduction box which controls the entry into the actual interpretation of the reduction rule within the subroutine box $\boxed{\beta\text{-red\_ex}}$. On entering through point a it is tested whether the reduction counter value $\#RR$

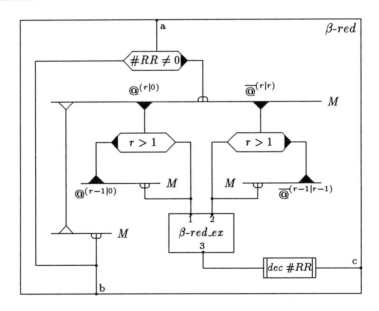

Figure 6.6: Entry into the stack control program for β-reduction

is greater than zero and, subsequently, whether the topmost entry in M is either $@^{(r|0)}$ or $\overline{@}^{(r|r)}$. If one of these tests fails, control leaves through exit b. Otherwise, control splits into a branch each for applicative and normal order reduction to enter the box $\boxed{\beta\text{-}red\_ex}$ at the points 1 and 2, respectively. This distinction is necessary insofar as, in the former case, the operand expression resides on top of A while, in the latter case, it follows the operator expression in E. The arity test of the applicator in both branches is to decide whether the arity must be decremented or whether the applicator must be removed. The exit from the $\boxed{\beta\text{-}red\_ex}$ box includes the decrementation of the reduction counter value $\#RR$.

A first refinement of the subroutine box $\boxed{\beta\text{-}red\_ex}$ is shown in fig. 6.7. We note immediately that the branches for applicative and normal order reduction differ

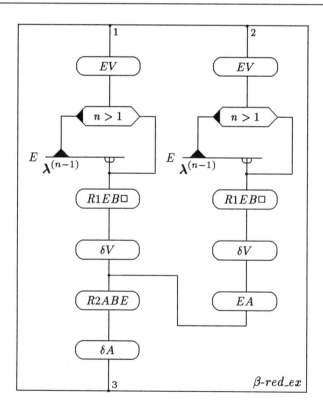

Figure 6.7: Stack control program for β-reduction

only with respect to the call for a traversal (of the argument) from E to A in the latter.

To follow this control program from the entry points we need to remember that the first step in entering the subroutine box $\boxed{\beta\text{-}red}$ was to pop the binding constructor $\boldsymbol{\lambda}^{(n)}$ from E. As a result, the stack E holds all components that were hooked up to it as isolated expressions, with the variable that is to be substituted in its topmost position. This variable is by the control program $\widehat{EV}$ moved to stack V.

If the arity n of the binding constructor $\boldsymbol{\lambda}^{(n)}$ is greater than one, meaning that more bindings follow, then it is restored in E as $\boldsymbol{\lambda}^{(n-1)}$, otherwise no binding is left in front of the function body.

The control program $\widehat{R1EB\square}$ now prepares the body expression of the binding instance currently executed for the substitution of the argument by traversing it from E to B. While doing this, each variable occurrence is compared with the variable set up in V. If the comparison is successful and the variable occurrence is bound, then its position in the expression that builds up in B is replaced by a so-called **protection list** L which lists all variables that are bound in this place. The list is completed by a **place-holder symbol** $\square$ for the argument. The control program also removes a protection key $\backslash$ from each free or protected occurrence of the variable that is being searched for.

After the completion of $\widehat{R1EB\square}$, the variable in V is deleted by executing $\widehat{\delta V}$.

Having moved the function body expression to B, we have in the normal order reduction branch the argument of the substitution set free on top of E. Traversing it into A by $\widehat{EA}$ creates the same stack constellation as the one which so far has been reached in the applicative order reduction branch. Both branches can now be joined.

The control program $\widehat{R2ABE}$ traverses the expression residing in transposed form in B back to E. For each occurrence of the place-holder symbol $\square$, however, a copy of the argument expression which (also in transposed form) resides in A is traversed into E. A protection key $\backslash$ is added to every free occurrence of a variable in the argument for every occurrence of it in the particular protection list. Subsequently, this list is deleted.

After the completion of $\widehat{R2ABE}$, the program $\widehat{\delta A}$ removes the argument from stack A, and control exits from the subroutine $\boxed{\beta\text{-}red\_ex}$ (and subsequently from the subroutine $\boxed{\beta\text{-}red}$) with the resulting expression set up on top of stack E.

The example shown in fig. 6.8 may help to illustrate what the control programs $\widehat{R1EB\square}$ and $\widehat{R2ABE}$ accomplish. We set out with the expression shown in fig. 6.8.a, which is represented as a tree structure to exhibit its transformation more clearly.

The first instance of reduction detected during the execution of $\widehat{EAR}$ is the

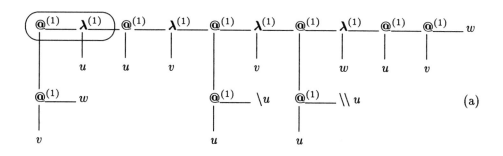

(a)

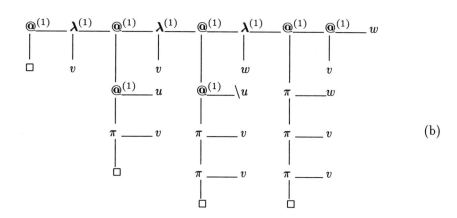

(b)

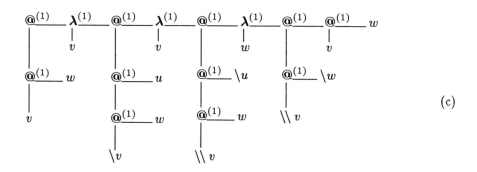

(c)

Figure 6.8: The treatment of name-clashes during β-reductions

outermost β-redex. When entering the control program $\overline{(R1EB\square)}$, the encircled applicator–lambda pair is removed, the argument expression $@^{(1)}$ v w occupies, in transposed form, the topmost position in A, and the variable u is on top of stack V. The execution of $\overline{(R1EB\square)}$ on the remaining function body produces in stack B the transpose of the expression in fig. 6.8.b.

We recognize that each free occurrence of the variable u that was bound by the binder which is about to be reduced is now replaced by a protection list. While traversing the expression from E to B, a variable entry is added to this list for every binding scope penetrated. The special two-place constructor π belongs to the realization of the β-reduction, it is not an element of the constructor set K of the language OREL/0.

After running the control program $\overline{(R2ABE)}$ on this expression (with the transpose of the argument in stack A), we obtain in stack E the expression of fig. 6.8.c, in which all occurrences of free variables within the arguments are properly protected in their places of substitution. The number of protection keys added equals the number of occurrences of the variable in the respective protection lists.

Notwithstanding its considerable complexity which primarily arises from the correct treatment of naming conflicts, the control program $\boxed{\beta\text{-}red}$ realizes a full-fledged β-reduction as defined in section 5.3. Rather than changing conflicting variable

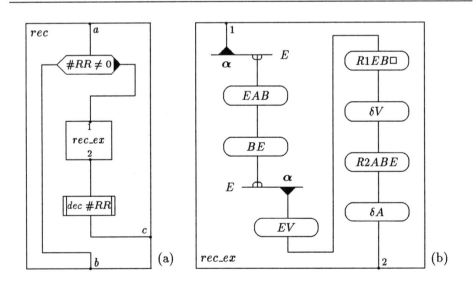

Figure 6.9: Stack control program for recursion

names statically, this realization adopts the more elegant solution of preserving the original variable names and distinguishing different binding levels by dynamically changing numbers of protection keys (λ-bars). Among other advantages relating to stepwise program execution, we thus can easily transform an expression into its de Bruijn representation by systematic α-conversion. Using number variables instead of individual variable names considerably reduces the complexity of $\boxed{\beta\text{-red}}$, particularly of the control programs $\overparen{R1EB\Box}$ and $\overparen{R2ABE}$, as neither time-consuming comparisons of variable names need be carried out nor protection lists need be constructed, copied and repeatedly inspected.

Recursion differs from β-reduction only insofar as it is realized as a self-application of α v expr. Figs. 6.9.a and 6.9.b show that the entry from the subroutine $\boxed{rec}$ into the subroutine $\boxed{rec\_ex}$ passes only through the test of the reduction counter $\#RR$. The entry into the β-reduction path inside $\boxed{rec\_ex}$ is preceded by the traversals

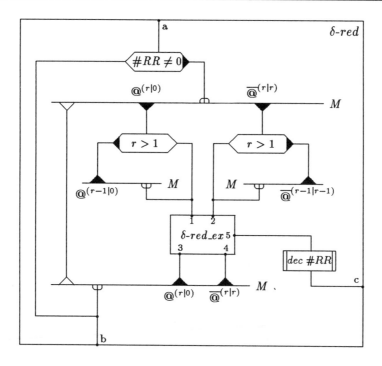

Figure 6.10: Entry into the stack control program for δ-reductions

$\boxed{EAB}$ and $\boxed{BE}$ which produce a copy of the recursive function expression as its own argument in stack A.

The entry into the control program $\boxed{\delta\text{-}red}$ for δ-reductions, which is shown in fig. 6.10, differs from that for β-reductions insofar, as tests for the compatibility of the argument types with the primitive functions must be performed. Additional exits must be provided from the subroutine box $\boxed{\delta\text{-}red\_ex}$ in order to restore the original application in case of type incompatibilities.

As a simple example of a δ-reduction rule, we have in fig. 6.11 given the control diagram for the application of the list function FIRST ($\longleftarrow$). Type checking is performed by inspecting the head symbol of the argument which in the applicative order reduction path resides in stack A, and in the normal order reduction path resides in stack E. If this symbol is a list constructor, the reduction proceeds as desired, with control leaving through exit 5. Otherwise, the argument remains as it is, and control leaves through either of the exits 3 or 4 in order to restore the respective applicator on M.

Control programs for other δ-reduction rules follow essentially the same scheme: having entered the subroutine box $\boxed{\delta\text{-}red\_ex}$ and successfully passed the type check,

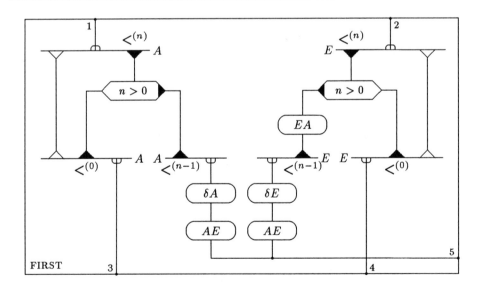

Figure 6.11: Stack control program for the reduction of applications of the list function FIRST

the argument expression(s) is (are) operated on as specified by the function, possibly involving additional stacks, and the resulting expression is, after deletion of the argument(s), set up in stack E, whereupon control exits to it.

6.2.3 Machine Realizations

The string reduction engine which we have studied so far may be considered an abstract high-level interpreter for OREL/0 programs. Very little has been said about actual (hardware) machinery beyond the need to put stack entries into certain formats.

We may think of essentially two ways of realizing such a reduction engine as a concrete computing machine.

One alternative would be a tailor-made hardware design in which

- the reduction unit is directly implemented as the processing unit, and

- the working memory is realized as a set of hardware stacks, of which at least two can be accessed simultaneously.

This solution has the advantage that the processing unit can be equipped with fast arithmetic/logic facilities capable of handling decimal numbers, letter strings and text of unbounded length on the one hand, and with a high-band-width control store so that several stack accesses can be performed in one machine cycle on the other hand [Klu79].

However, there are some drawbacks to this solution as well. Hardware stacks are rather wasteful in terms of the total memory capacity expended. As an entire program expression must, in extreme cases, fit almost completely into every stack except M and C, at most 15 % of the total memory capacity can be utilized during the program execution.

Moreover, a virtual machine concept cannot be conveniently supported by hardware stacks. While virtual machines can, in any state of distribution of their expressions over the stacks, easily be pushed on top of each other, only the actual topmost virtual machine can be executed. Thus, the stack system enforces a LIFO scheduling discipline which is neither fair nor efficient as virtual machines may block each other for considerable periods of time.

The other alternative would be to use fairly traditional machinery in which

- the reduction unit can be emulated on a suitable conventional processor which effectively supports stack addressing modes;

- the stacks are realized as (not necessarily contiguous) segments of a conventional addressable memory which, by some paging facility, can be dynamically expanded and contracted on demand.

While the performance of this approach in terms of program execution times may not be competitive with tailor-made hardware, it has the advantage that memory space can be more economically administered and that full support can be given to the virtual machine concept.

Undoubtedly, a compromise can be found between both alternatives insofar as a tailor-made reduction processor can be hooked up to a bank of physical memory units whose address space is dynamically administered.

The demands of several virtual machines for memory space may be satisfied so that

- the total memory capacity within the memory bank is rather evenly allocated;

- each of them has simultaneous access to several of its stacks with a low probability for conflicts.

7 Performing Reductions Concurrently

The orderly cooperation of several concurrently acting components within a large system has been widely accepted as a natural way of getting complex things done efficiently.[18] It has also been recognized that well-organized systems requiring little overhead have the following characteristic features:

- they are structured as hierarchies of subsystems;
- the subsystems are only loosely coupled;
- the internal components of a subsystem are highly cohesive.

In terms of computational problems this means that recursively constructed programs which at execution time can be recursively partitioned into hierarchies of smaller, mutually independent subprograms (or tasks) from top to bottom and synchronized from the bottom up are highly suitable candidates for concurrent (or non-sequential) processing.

If the tasks in different branches of the hierarchy are totally independent of each other, then causes and effects are locally confined (or of short range), and the tasks interact only through well-defined interfaces provided by the root nodes of the hierarchical structure. The decision to split a task into smaller, self-contained subtasks can be made locally and without regard for other parts of the hierarchy. This property makes a recursive task partitioning (or divide-and-conquer) scheme particularly attractive for dynamically evolving task hierarchies whose structures and sizes depend on actual parameters and, hence, cannot be anticipated à priori. Moreover, hierarchical structures are known to cause neither deadlocks nor starvation.

Reduction language expressions appear to be perfectly suited for this purpose. From sections 5.2 and 6.1 we remember that the meaning of a non-atomic expression is recursively defined by and, hence, must be recursively computed from the meanings of its subexpressions. As these subexpressions are completely independent of each other, their meanings can be computed concurrently, i.e., in any order. A particularly interesting class of expressions are applicative order applications whose meanings are defined as

$$m [\![@^{(r)} \; arg\_r \ldots arg\_1 \; func]\!] = m [\![@^{(r)} \; m [\![arg\_r]\!] \ldots m [\![arg\_1]\!] \; m [\![func]\!]]\!]$$

Assuming that the expression $func$ is a non-recursive λ-abstraction of the form $func = \lambda^{(n)} x_1 \ldots x_n \; expr$, then this definition, in fact, specifies the following rule of computation: in order to obtain the normal form of the application, we

---

[18]The material contained in this chapter has been published in [Klu83].

- first need to compute the normal forms of the argument expressions, which may be done concurrently;

- next reduce the application of the λ-abstraction (which by definition is its own meaning) to the reduced arguments;

- then continue with the computation of the resulting expression.

This rule of computation may be employed as a standard scheme for exploiting concurrency in program expressions in the following way: let

$$expr = \dashv \ldots sub\_expr\_1 \ldots sub\_expr\_n \ldots \vdash$$

denote an expression built up from some n mutually independent subexpressions sub_expr_1, ..., sub_expr_n which need not necessarily be directly tied up to the outermost constructor (again, the meta symbols $\dashv, \vdash$ are to denote the left and right delimiters, respectively, of the expression on the right hand side).

To compute $m \llbracket expr \rrbracket$, we may apply the following meaning-preserving transformation steps:

$$m \llbracket \dashv \ldots sub\_expr\_1 \ldots sub\_expr\_n \ldots \vdash \rrbracket$$

$\qquad \downarrow$ by abstraction

$$m \llbracket @^{(n)} \; sub\_expr\_n \ldots sub\_expr\_1 \; \lambda^{(n)} t_1 \ldots t_n \dashv \ldots t_1 \ldots t_n \ldots \vdash \rrbracket$$

$\qquad \downarrow$ by reduction of the arguments

$$m \llbracket @^{(n)} \; m \llbracket sub\_expr\_n \rrbracket \ldots m \llbracket sub\_expr\_1 \rrbracket \; \lambda^{(n)} t_1 \ldots t_n \dashv \ldots t_1 \ldots t_n \ldots \vdash \rrbracket$$

$\qquad \downarrow$ by β-reduction

$$m \llbracket \dashv \ldots m \llbracket sub\_expr\_1 \rrbracket \ldots m \llbracket sub\_expr\_n \rrbracket \ldots \vdash \rrbracket$$

This scheme may be given the following interpretation in terms of abstract reduction engines: the computation sets out with an engine which is supposed to reduce the expression $\dashv \ldots sub\_expr\_1 \ldots sub\_expr\_n \ldots \vdash$ to its meaning. In the course of abstracting the subexpressions, this engine assumes the position of a master engine which creates n slave engines to compute $m \llbracket sub\_expr\_1 \rrbracket, \ldots, m \llbracket sub\_expr\_n \rrbracket$ The expression that is left under the control of the master engine essentially is a λ-abstraction and thus constant, which puts the master engine in a *wait* state.

The subsequent β-reductions transform the expression of the master engine into $\dashv \ldots m \llbracket sub\_expr\_1 \rrbracket \ldots m \llbracket sub\_expr\_n \rrbracket \ldots \vdash$, as a result of which the master engine may continue with further reductions. Hence, these β-reductions may be

considered instances of synchronization of the master with the slave engines, whereupon the latter cease to exist and the former returns to a *ready* state.

All slave engines may, in the course of computing the meanings of their subexpressions, recursively create (and synchronize with) further slaves of their own. We
thus obtain a hierarchy of abstract engines which dynamically expands from top to
bottom and contracts from the bottom up.

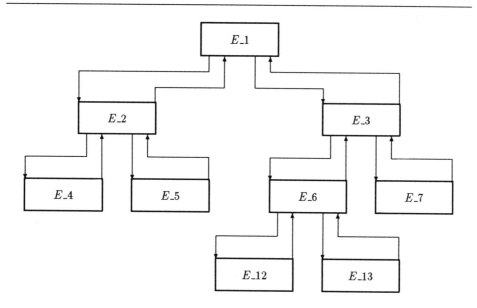

Figure 7.1: Hierarchy of abstract reduction engines that participate in the reduction
            of an expression

A typical hierarchy of reduction engines that, at some time, may have developed
in the course of reducing an expression is schematically shown in fig. 7.1. The engines are enumerated following the usual tree enumeration scheme. It is interesting
to note that this hierarchy conceptually exhibits an extremely simple communication pattern, as is indicated by the arrows. All communication is strictly confined
to that between masters and their immediate slaves. We have just one communication (of the abstracted subexpression) from a master to a slave which coincides
with the creation of the slave, and one communication (of the normal form of the
subexpression) from a slave to its master, which coincides with the termination of
the slave (or its synchronization with the master).

In a real system comprising several processing sites, hierarchies of abstract engines must be realized as hierarchies of processes. Following the terminology introduced in section 2.1, we consider here a process as a unit of activity comprising both an expression (or subexpression) and a virtual machine in which the expression can be executed. To do so, we need to take into consideration a few pragmatic points concerning

- the identification, in a given program, of subterms that are suitable for concurrent execution;

- a favorable ratio of useful computations versus the organizational overhead involved in the management of the processes;

- the economy of resource utilization.

They suggest that

- the subexpressions selected for concurrent execution constitute self-contained function applications of sufficient complexity;

- all free occurrences of bound variables within these subexpressions be substituted before processes are being created to ensure that a maximum number of reductions can indeed be performed;

- instances of creation yield at least two concurrently executable slave processes for every de-activated master process;

- processes be created only on demand in order to avoid redundant computations;

- the number of processes which at any time exist within the system be kept within reasonable bounds relative to the number of processing sites in order to avoid excessive organizational overhead without a gain in performance.

These criteria evidently relate to properties of the program expressions and to the reduction regime on the one hand, and to organizational measures that keep an upper limit on the number of processes (or virtual machines) within the system on the other hand.

In the sequel we will discuss these issues in the context of the string reduction machinery outlined in the preceding chapter. However, the concepts and concrete solutions presented here are also applicable, in more or less the same form, to graph reduction. They are primarily of an organizational nature and thus to a large extent independent of particular implementations.

In fact, the divide-and-conquer scheme is common to all reduction-based forms of concurrent program execution as it follows directly from the highly recursive construction of functional programs [DaRe81, Kel85, Peyt87, AuJo89, GrWo89]. Differences primarily relate to evaluation strategies, workload partitioning, distribution and balancing, and to suitable ways and means of limiting the total number of concurrently executable processes.

7.1 Controlling the Division of Workload

Program expressions suitable for non-sequential execution appear to be applications of λ-abstractions to λ-abstractions provided that, in the body of the λ-abstraction in operator position, we have at least two free occurrences of the bound variable in operator positions of applications.

A typical expression of this kind has the form

$$\overline{@}^{(1)} \quad \lambda^{(1)} v \dashv \ldots @^{(r)} \, a\_r_1 \ldots a\_1_1 \, v \ldots @^{(r)} \, a\_r_n \ldots a\_1_n \, v \ldots \vdash$$
$$\lambda^{(r)} w_1 \ldots w_r \dashv \ldots w_1 \ldots w_r \ldots \vdash .$$

We note that the body of the λ-abstraction in operator position of the outermost application contains some $n > 1$ applications of the bound variable v to r arguments $a\_1_i, \ldots, a\_r_i$ ($i \in \{1, \ldots, n\}$). When β-reducing the outermost application, we obtain n concurrently executable applications of the r-ary λ-abstraction that is in its operand position. These applications may be considered sufficiently complex to justify the creation of processes since each needs to perform at least some r β-reductions in order to substitute formal by actual parameters. Moreover, the body of the λ-abstraction can be expected to yield further β-reductions and δ-reductions as well.

In order to prepare such an application for concurrent execution, we have the following choice: the reduction engine can do it dynamically at run-time, using a modified implementation of the β-reduction rule which returns the expression

$$\dashv \ldots \overline{@}_p \Uparrow @^{(r)} \, a\_r_1 \ldots a\_1_1 \, \lambda^{(r)} w_1 \ldots w_r \dashv \ldots w_1 \ldots w_r \ldots \vdash \ldots$$
$$\ldots \overline{@}_p \Uparrow @^{(r)} \, a\_r_n \ldots a\_1_n \, \lambda^{(r)} w_1 \ldots w_r \dashv \ldots w_1 \ldots w_r \ldots \vdash \ldots \vdash .$$

The subexpressions that are to be reduced concurrently now appear in operand positions of normal order applications of the general form $\overline{@}_p \Uparrow sub\_expr$, where $\Uparrow$ denotes a primitive function which is to effect the abstraction of sub_expr. These applications are supposed to reduce to unique place-holder variables, creating as side effects processes for the computation of the abstracted expressions.

The necessary modifications of the subroutine $\boxed{\beta\text{-}red\_ex}$ for β-reductions relate to

- the control program $\boxed{R1EB\square}$ which must count the number of occurrences of the bound variable in operator positions of applications within the expression that is being traversed from stack E to B;

- the identification of a λ-abstraction of some r formal parameters while traversing the operand expression from stack E to A;

- the control program $\boxed{R2ABE}$ which subsequently must construct applications of $\Uparrow$ whenever multiple substitutions of λ-abstractions into operator positions of applications are carried out, provided the arity of the λ-abstraction is matched or exceeded by the arities of the applicators.

Alternatively, we can employ a **pre-processor** to identify potential instances of process creation by a **static program analysis** and to insert the appropriate applications of $\Uparrow$ à priori. This solution is decidedly more economical in terms of the overall processing time expended, but contradicts to some extent the idea of direct interpretation as realized by our string reduction engine.

A process executing an expression

$$\dashv \ldots \overline{@}_p \Uparrow sub\_expr \ldots \vdash$$

becomes, after the abstraction of sub_expr and the creation of the corresponding slave process, a master process. Eventually, it must produce the complementary application

$$\overline{@}_p \Downarrow t \dashv \ldots t \ldots \vdash m \left[\!\left[sub\_expr \right]\!\right]$$

in order to terminate (or synchronize with) the slave. Instead of λ, we can use a **primitive binding operator** $\Downarrow$ which effects the **naive substitution** of $m \left[\!\left[sub\_expr \right]\!\right]$ for the single occurrence of t in $\dashv \ldots t \ldots \vdash$. Naive substitution is admissible since all place-holder variables are assumed to be unique and distinguishable from user-specified variables; hence, no name clashes can occur.

The special applicator $\overline{@}_p$, in conjunction with the operators $\Uparrow$ and $\Downarrow$, specifies so-called **pseudo-applications** which serve strictly organizational purposes. They do not belong to the reduction language OREL/0 but to its realization.

Fig. 7.2 schematically illustrates the creation and termination (synchronization) of n slave processes $p_1^s, \ldots, p_n^s$ by a master process p^m which executes the expression

$$\dashv \ldots \overline{@}_p \Uparrow sub\_expr\_1 \ldots \overline{@}_p \Uparrow sub\_expr\_n \ldots \vdash .$$

The reduction of its pseudo-applications yields

- a **skeleton expression** $\dashv \ldots t_1 \ldots t_n \ldots \vdash$ (which is treated as constant) under the control of the master process;

- **tuples** of the form $(t_1, sub\_expr\_1), \ldots, (t_n, sub\_expr\_n)$ under the control of slave processes.

Carrying the place-holder variables with the slave processes and returning tuples $(t_i, m[\![sub\_expr\_i]\!])$ enables the master process to construct and reduce the synchronizing pseudo-applications

$$\overline{@}_p \Downarrow t_i \dashv \ldots t_i \ldots \vdash m [\![sub\_expr\_i]\!]$$

in any order, e.g., in the order of terminating slaves.

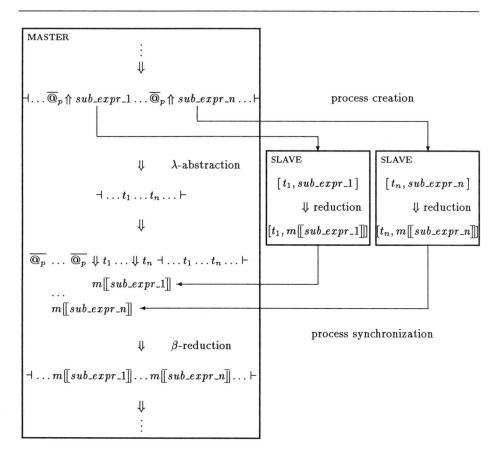

Figure 7.2: The creation and termination of slave processes by a master process

Reducing pseudo-applications in the normal course of executing the control program $\widehat{EAR}$ ensures that slave processes are being created only on demand and that a maximum number of reductions can indeed be performed within the expressions that are under their control.

We consider, as an example, a recursive function application of the general form

$$@^{(r)} \; arg\_r \ldots arg\_1$$
$$\alpha \; v \; \lambda^{(r)} w_1 \ldots w_r \dashv \ldots @^{(1)} \; pred\_expr$$
$$\Delta \dashv \ldots @^{(r)} \; brg\_r \ldots brg\_1 \; v \ldots$$
$$\vdots$$
$$\ldots @^{(r)} \; crg\_r \ldots crg\_1 \; v \ldots \vdash$$
$$false\_expr \ldots \vdash$$

which is an ideal candidate for non-sequential execution: every recursion step produces at least another two applications of the recursive function since the recursively bound variable v occurs at least twice in operator positions of applications within the consequence of the IF-THEN-ELSE clause.

The control program $\widehat{EAR}$ executes this expression by first reducing the operand expressions of the outermost application and by performing a recursion step. We thus obtain

$$@^{(r)} \; m \left[\!\left[arg\_r \right]\!\right] \ldots m \left[\!\left[arg\_1 \right]\!\right]$$
$$\lambda^{(r)} w_1 \ldots w_r \dashv \ldots @^{(1)} \; pred\_expr$$
$$\Delta \dashv \ldots \overline{@}_p \Uparrow @^{(r)} \; brg\_r \ldots brg\_1$$
$$\alpha \; v \; \lambda^{(r)} w_1 \ldots w_r \dashv \ldots \vdash \ldots$$
$$\vdots$$
$$\ldots \overline{@}_p \Uparrow @^{(r)} \; crg\_r \ldots crg\_1$$
$$\alpha \; v \; \lambda^{(r)} w_1 \ldots w_r \dashv \ldots \vdash \ldots \vdash$$
$$false\_expr \ldots \vdash$$

The subsequent r β-reductions yield

$$\dashv \ldots @^{(1)} \; pred\_expr[\Leftarrow]$$
$$\Delta \dashv \ldots \overline{@}_p \Uparrow @^{(r)} \; brg\_r[\Leftarrow] \ldots brg\_1[\Leftarrow] \; \alpha \; v \; \lambda^{(r)} w_1 \ldots w_r \dashv \ldots \vdash \ldots$$
$$\vdots$$
$$\ldots \overline{@}_p \Uparrow @^{(r)} \; crg\_r[\Leftarrow] \ldots crg\_1[\Leftarrow] \; \alpha \; v \; \lambda^{(r)} w_1 \ldots w_r \dashv \ldots \vdash \ldots \vdash$$
$$false\_expr \; [\Leftarrow] \ldots \vdash$$

where $expr[\Leftarrow]$ denotes the substitution of all free occurrences of the variables

$w_1, \ldots, w_r$ in $expr$ by the reduced arguments $m \llbracket arg\_1 \rrbracket, \ldots, m \llbracket arg\_r \rrbracket$, respectively.

Having thus substituted all free occurrences of bound variables, we can proceed to reduce all subexpressions of the remaining expression without encountering variable occurrences other than those that are free in the entire program and thus are constants. A maximum number of applications can then be reduced.

Assuming that $pred\_expr[\Leftarrow]$ reduces to TRUE, we obtain

$$\dashv \ldots \overline{@}_p \Uparrow @^{(r)} \, brg\_r[\Leftarrow] \ldots brg\_1[\Leftarrow] \alpha \; v \; \lambda^{(r)} w_1 \ldots w_r \dashv \ldots \vdash \ldots$$

$$\vdots$$

$$\ldots \overline{@}_p \Uparrow @^{(r)} \, crg\_r[\Leftarrow] \ldots crg\_1[\Leftarrow] \alpha \; v \; \lambda^{(r)} w_1 \ldots w_r \dashv \ldots \vdash \ldots \vdash$$

The control program $\widehat{EAR}$ now continues with the reduction of all pseudo-applications in pre-order, returning the skeleton expression

$$\dashv \ldots t_1 \ldots t_n \ldots \vdash$$

and creating, as side effects, slave processes for the execution of their operand expressions as they are.

We observe that potential instances for the division of labor are identified and marked by pseudo-applications of $\Uparrow$ while performing the recursion. The creation of slave processes, however, is postponed until the demand for reducing these pseudo-applications or, more precisely, for the normal forms of their operand expressions actually arises.

Following this divide-and-conquer scheme, slaves would be recursively created until in each branch of the expanding process hierarchy individually $pred\_expr[\Leftarrow]$ reduces to FALSE. From this point on, slaves would begin to synchronize in reverse order with their respective masters by returning the normal forms of their subexpressions, i.e., the hierarchy recursively collapses again.

Unfortunately, we invite considerable organizational problems when expanding in a real system with limited resources a process hierarchy without bounds. Creating processes far in excess of the available processing sites does not only inflict an unnecessary overhead for process management without a further gain in performance. Divide-and-conquer computations also have a tendency of rapidly exploding in space, claiming memory to the point of premature exhaustion and thus causing deadlocks, unless inactive segments can be swapped out.

This rather chaotic behavior can be prevented by establishing an upper limit on the number of processes (or virtual machines) which are allowed to coexist within the system at any time. To do so, we simply equip the system with a finite reservoir (or pool) of non-consumable and non-reproducible tokens which we will also refer to as tickets. These tickets represent process slots: a new process can only be created if a ticket can be allocated from the pool, and a terminating process must return its ticket to the pool. Thus, the creation of new processes is temporarily suspended whenever the ticket pool is exhausted. The important point now is that a process which unsuccessfully tries to create a slave process is not put to sleep until tickets become again available. Instead it simply ignores this and further opportunities to create slave processes and continues by reducing under its own regime the entire expression it holds in possession.

It turns out that this stabilizing measure can be elegantly combined with the solution of another problem which so far has been left open: the system must also provide unique place-holders to be inserted for executable pseudo-applications of the abstraction function $\Uparrow$. All we need to do here is to associate unique labels (or names) with the tickets since we need just as many distinct place-holders as we can have processes.

The ticket allocation mechanism thus requires that pseudo-applications be reduced as follows: let $T_0 = \{t_1, \ldots, t_q\}$ and $T \subseteq T_0$ respectively denote the initial and some actual ticket pool; likewise, let $P = \{(t_i, sub\_expr) \mid t_i \in T_0 \setminus T\}$ denote the actual set of virtual slave machines that participate in the computation of a program expression. Then we have the following reduction rules:

$$\overline{@}_p \Uparrow sub\_expr \longrightarrow \begin{cases} t_i \in T & \text{if } T \neq \emptyset \\ & \text{side effects:} \quad \begin{aligned} T &\longrightarrow T \setminus \{t_i\} \\ P &\longrightarrow P \cup \{(t_i, sub\_expr)\} \end{aligned} \\ sub\_expr & \text{else} \end{cases}$$

$$\overline{@}_p \Downarrow t_i \dashv \ldots t_i \ldots \vdash m \llbracket sub\_expr \rrbracket \longrightarrow \dashv \ldots m \llbracket sub\_expr \rrbracket \ldots \vdash$$
$$\text{side effects:} \quad \begin{aligned} T &\longrightarrow T \cup \{t_i\} \\ P &\longrightarrow P \setminus \{(t_i, m \llbracket sub\_expr \rrbracket)\} \end{aligned}$$

The incessant recycling of tickets which is implied by these reduction rules ensures that a near-maximal number of them remains committed to processes as long as the program expression yields sufficiently many instances of reducible pseudo-applications of the abstraction function $\Uparrow$.

In the worst case, we have a hierarchy of two slave processes for every master process. Hence, about half of the processes can, on average, be expected to be in a *wait* state, while the other half is either *ready* for execution or actually *executing*.

Since all reductions within a process are, under the control of a pre-order traversal scheme, performed strictly in sequence, the ticket mechanism tends to enforce, after the exhaustion of the ticket pool, lengthy periods of computations in all slave processes, provided the respective subexpressions are sufficiently complex. This property contributes significantly to a favorable ratio of useful computations vs.

the overhead required to allocate and de-allocate virtual machines and to schedule processes. Moreover, the limitation of processes in conjunction with the sequential reduction order within a process also throttles the demand for memory space quite substantially. Rather than unfolding the entire tree of a divide-and-conquer computation, a sequential process controls at any time only a single trace of recursions from the root of the tree to a leaf. Memory space consumption is thus drastically reduced from $O(n)$ to $O(\lg n)$.

7.2   A System Configuration

The dynamically expanding and collapsing hierarchy of virtual machines which may cooperate in executing a program expression non-sequentially can be readily supported by a non-hierarchically organized distributed system of real reduction machines (or processing sites). Each of them is assumed to be capable of accommodating several virtual machines (or processes).

For a conceptual outline it suffices to consider the system as a partially or fully connected graph whose set of nodes $R = \{RM_1, \ldots, RM_N\}$ represents N real reduction machines (or processing sites) and whose set of arcs $S \subseteq R \times R$ represents directed interconnections among the machines. An interconnecting line $(RM_i, RM_j) \in S$ can be used to transfer

- an expression from RM_i to RM_j in order to create in RM_j a process which reduces it;

- the normal form of the expression back from RM_j to RM_i while terminating the process in RM_j.

To facilitate a balanced allocation of processes to real machines, the system must be organized so as to feature a high degree of regularity in the following sense:

- Let $R_r = \{RM_i \mid (RM_r, RM_i) \in S\} \subseteq R \setminus \{RM_r\}$ be the subset of real machines to which RM_r may transfer expressions for execution, and let $\overline{R}_r = \{RM_i \mid (RM_i, RM_r) \in S\} \subseteq R \setminus \{RM_r\}$ be the subset of real machines from which RM_r may receive expressions for execution, then S should be configured so that

$$(\forall r \in \{1, \ldots, N\}) \left(\mid R_r \mid = \mid \overline{R}_r \mid = k \in \{1, \ldots, N-1\} \right) ;$$

i.e., each real machine is connected to the same number of input and output lines. Any of the machines $RM_r \in R$ may therefore serve as the input/output port of the entire system into which the initial program expression must be loaded, and from which the partially or completely reduced expression must be unloaded.

- Each machine RM_r incorporates a local ticket pool $T_r = \{t_1, \ldots t_q\}$ with $q = u * k, u \in \{1, 2, \ldots\}$. Tickets are withdrawn from this pool for slave processes that are created in some machine $RM_i \in R_r$ by a process executing in RM_r, while terminating slaves that synchronize with masters in RM_r also return their tickets to this pool.

- Let h_{ri} denote the number of processes which, at some time, are set up by RM_r in $RM_i \in R_r$. Then RM_r is supposed to distribute processes in a round robin manner so that

$$(\forall RM_i, RM_{j \neq i} \in R_r) \left(\mid h_{ri} - h_{rj} \mid \leq 1 \right).$$

This distribution scheme, in conjunction with the capacities of the local ticket pools, allocates to each real machine $RM_r \in R$ at most u processes from each of the machines $RM_i \in \overline{R}_r$. We thus have, after the exhaustion of all local ticket pools, $u * k$ slave processes allocated to each real machine, and a total of $u * k * N$ processes existing in the entire system. The machine which serves as input/output port must additionally accommodate the process the computation starts and terminates with and thus becomes the topmost master of the hierarchy.

The orderly creation, allocation and synchronization of processes within the system requires a unique identification scheme which reflects the hierarchical order among them. For this purpose, it is helpful to consider each real machine as being partitioned into $u * k + 1$ enumerated slots (or virtual machines which are to accommodate processes. Upon creation, a process acquires an empty slot, upon termination this slot is released.

Let p^m and p^s respectively denote a master process and an immediate slave of it. Then p^s can be uniquely identified with respect to its origin by a triple (r, v_r, t_i), of which the parameter

- $r \in \{1, \ldots, N\}$ denotes the index of the real machine RM_r in which p^m resides;

- $v_r \in \{1, \ldots, u * k + 1\}$ denotes the index of the virtual machine slot in RM_r that is occupied by p^m;

- $t_i \in T_r$ denotes the ticket which identifies, within the expression controlled by p^m, the syntactical position from which the subexpression that executes under p^s has been abstracted.

This triple contains necessary and sufficient information to synchronize a slave process with its master process.

Fig. 7.3 schematically shows four phases of a two-fold expanding hierarchy of processes in a system of four reduction machines $RM_1, \ldots, RM_4$ which are cyclically and bidirectionally interconnected. The machine RM_1 is chosen to be the

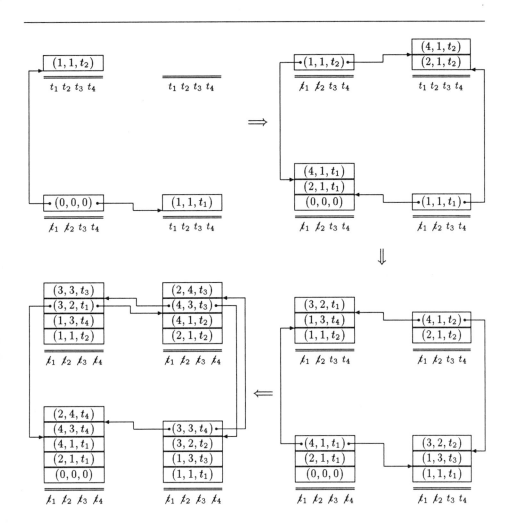

Figure 7.3: Four phases of expanding a hierarchy of virtual machines in a system
of four cooperating reduction machines

input/output location whose first virtual machine slot is occupied by the initial
process. Its identification triple is $(0, 0, 0)$, indicating that its origin is somewhere
outside. The local ticket pools are initialized with four tickets each; i.e., each real
machine is allowed to allocate two processes to each of its immediate neighbors,

occupying two virtual machine slots there. Thus, we have, after ticket exhaustion in the entire system, four slave processes set up in each real machine.

7.3   The Reduction of Pseudo-Applications

The reduction of pseudo-applications involves the transfer of expressions among virtual machines residing in different real machines. In particular, reducing a pseudo-application of

- the abstraction function $\Uparrow$ causes an expression to move from the virtual machine supporting the master process to a virtual machine in which the slave process is to be created;

- the substitution function $\Downarrow$ is preceded by the transfer of an expression from a virtual machine in which the slave process is about to be terminated to the virtual machine supporting its master process.

We have, in section 6.2, defined stack E to be the input/output location of our string reduction engine. Hence, the transfers use, in either of the above cases, stack E of the transmitting virtual machine as the source and stack E of the receiving virtual machine as the sink of the expression. As expressions are expected to reside in stack E in non-transposed form, these transfers must be carried out as two successive pre-order traversals which use an intermediate stack I. The first traversal produces in stack I the transpose of the expression occupying the topmost position in stack E of the transmitting virtual machine; the second traversal produces, as the topmost expression in stack E of the receiving virtual machine, the transpose of the expression in the intermediate stack.

The stack I may be thought of as a buffer between the transmitting and the receiving virtual machine, in which an expression may be held for any interval of time. Thus, a transmitting virtual machine may move an expression into the buffer without regard for the actual state of the receiving virtual machine and then proceed with its computations. Conversely, a receiving virtual machine may pick up from the buffer an expression destined for it after having reached a suitable state of computation.

Expressions are moved about the system as packets of the form

$$\nabla\ r\ \nabla\ v_r\ \nabla\ t_i\ expr\ .$$

The special two-place constructor ∇ is to prefix the expressions with packet headers containing the parameters of the identifier triples. These parameters are, in the course of reducing pseudo-applications of $\Uparrow$, provided by the processing sites in which the respective processes execute.

The reduction of these packets leaves the headers intact since the parameters r, v_r, t_i are constant:

$$m \left[\!\left[\mathbf{\nabla}\ r \mathbf{\nabla}\ v_r \mathbf{\nabla}\ t_i\ expr \right]\!\right] = \mathbf{\nabla}\ r \mathbf{\nabla}\ v_r \mathbf{\nabla}\ t_i\ m \left[\!\left[expr \right]\!\right] .$$

A pseudo-application of the abstraction function ⇑ is reduced by

- inspecting the ticket pool T_r for the availability of a ticket and, if one can be allocated, by

- deleting $\overline{@}_p$ and ⇑ from M and E, respectively;

- removing a ticket from the pool and by attaching a packet header to the argument expression in E;

- traversing the packet expression from E to some intermediate stack I and by pushing the ticket in its place in stack E;

- continuing with the reduction of further pseudo-applications until the skeleton expression is completely set up in stack A.

The creation and subsequent reduction of a pseudo-application of the substitution function ⇓ expects the skeleton expression to reside in stack A while the expression packet is traversed from some intermediate stack into E. A pseudo-application of it is formed by

- deleting the packet header from the expression in E, not including, however, the ticket variable;

- popping the ticket from E and pushing it into T_r;

- traversing the skeleton expression from A to E;

- copying the topmost ticket from T_r to the top of E;

- pushing the function symbol ⇓ and the pseudo-applicator $\overline{@}_p$ into E.

The pseudo-application is thus completed and can be executed by a naive β-reduction, i.e., as a literal substitution of the argument expression for the single occurrence of the ticket variable in the body of the function expression.

The respective stack control diagrams are shown in fig. 7.4. They are, in fact, extensions of the control program $\widehat{EAR}$. With respect to the creation of pseudo-applications of the substitution function ⇓ it is assumed here that the packet expression is traversed into the stack E of the receiving virtual machine under the control of an input/output process.

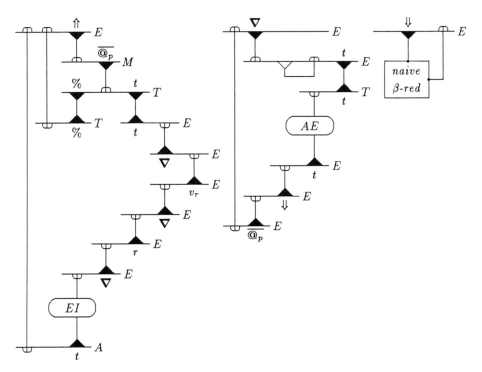

Figure 7.4: Stack control diagrams for the reduction of pseudo-applications

In order to perform $\widehat{EAR}$ otherwise correctly, the reduction of other than pseudo-applications must be inhibited as long as the expression that is being executed contains place-holder variables. This is due to the fact that, conceptually, such an expression is an λ-abstraction and thus constant.

7.4   Process Scheduling

Each of the real machines (or processing sites) of a reduction system typically comprises

- a **reduction processor** which executes the control program $\widehat{EAR}$ on OREL/0 expressions;

- some conventional **instruction processor** to support process scheduling and resource management;

- some considerable amount of directly accessible memory to accommodate the stacks of virtual reduction machines as well as operating system programs;

- input/output port facilities through which the transfer of expression packets among processing sites can be handled independently of the activities of the reduction processor;

as hardware resources.

The overall operation of each processing site is essentially governed by a small operating system kernel which we will refer to as a local process manager. It schedules the processes resident in the site, manages the allocation and deallocation of virtual machines to/from the processes, and services the ports.

The scheduling discipline realized by the local process manager is supposed to treat all processes on an equal basis in order to avoid any constraints beyond those that are imposed on the execution of a program expression by its logical structure. However, with respect to the overall performance of the system it is imperative to serve instances of creation and termination (synchronization) of slave processes by master processes with highest priority. This is to enforce a fast ticket turnaround and, thus, a high ticket commitment to processes. Moreover, once a process has created a slave by reducing at least one of two or more pseudo-applications of the function ⇑, the scheduler should convert all the remaining pseudo-applications into slave processes as well, even though due to a temporary ticket exhaustion this may not be possible in one sweep through the expression. This is to minimize the number of inactive master processes versus the number of active slave processes.

The combination of both measures yields a high utilization of the available processing capacity as it always maintains a near-maximal number of executable processes within the system.

Moreover, this scheduling discipline, in conjunction with the finiteness of the ticket reservoir, also guarantees that a program expression is partitioned into concurrently executable subexpressions only to the extent necessary to keep all processing sites busy. The job granularity is dynamically adapted by the scheduler so as to maintain a fairly balanced workload distribution regardless of the actual workload to be handled by the individual processes. Processes with a small load return their tickets early, making them available for the creation of other slave processes where the workload is heavy.

If a program expression yields sufficient computational complexity beyond the point of ticket exhaustion, then lengthy periods of sequential computations can be expected to take place in all processing sites of the system under the control of the active slave processes [SmGeHa86].

The basic operating principle of the local process manager is schematically shown in fig. 7.5. With respect to the expression packets that move in and out of the site,

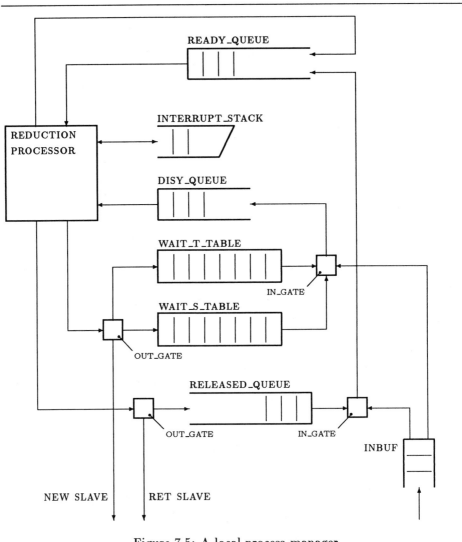

Figure 7.5: A local process manager

the manager essentially needs to distinguish

- expressions received for processing from adjacent sites for which slave processes must be created by allocating virtual machines in the site;

- reduced expressions returning from terminating slave processes in adjacent sites which must be synchronized with master processes in the site;

- expressions which by master processes executing in the site are transmitted to adjacent sites for processing;

- reduced expressions which by terminating processes must be returned to their respective master processes located in adjacent sites.

The process manager, accordingly, employs an input buffer area *inbuf* into which all incoming expression packets are taken over from the input ports of the site. This input buffer area realizes, for each expression individually, the intermediate stack that is necessary to traverse, in two steps, the expression packet from source to sink. All outgoing expression packets are, via the output ports, directly traversed into the input buffer areas of the receiving sites.

Internally, the manager distinguishes processes whose expressions contain

- no ticket variables but possibly pending pseudo-applications of ⇑ and, thus, are candidates for unrestricted processing;

- ticket variables and pending pseudo-applications of ⇑ and, hence, are in a conditional *wait* state since they are candidates for both synchronization with expression packets returning from terminating slave processes as well as for the abstraction of further subexpressions as soon as tickets become available in the local pool;

- ticket variables but no pending pseudo-applications of ⇑ and, hence, are in an unconditional *wait* state since they are candidates for the synchronization with terminating slave processes only.

The processes are managed by means of their process-context-blocks, as in principle outlined in section 2.2. In addition to the local ticket pool, the manager uses a

- *released_queue* which provides slots for as many pointers to context blocks as there are virtual machine slots available in the processing site for the creation of processes;

- *ready_queue* which, in their order of arrival, takes over pointers to context blocks of processes which are ready for unrestricted processing;

- *wait_t_table* which holds pointers to context blocks of processes which are in a conditional wait state;

- *wait_s_table* which holds pointers to context blocks of processes which are in an unconditional wait state;

- *disy_queue* into which are placed pointers to context blocks of processes from

    - the *wait_t_table* as soon as tickets become available in the local pool for the creation of further slave processes;

    - both *wait_tables* which, upon the arrival of reduced expression packets in the input buffer area, must be prepared for synchronization.

Expression packets transmitted to the site for the creation of slave processes are, after the allocation of a virtual machine and of a context block via the *released_queue*, removed from the input buffer, and a pointer to the context block is placed at the end of the *ready_queue*. Reduced expression packets returning to the site for synchronization are paired, by means of the information contained in their headers, with the respective master processes in either of the *wait_tables* and scheduled for the creation and execution of pseudo-applications of $\Downarrow$.

The manager schedules processes from the *ready_queue* and from the *disy_queue* in FIFO-order for the allocation of the reduction processor. However, the *disy_queue* is serviced with top priority: if the active process originates from the *ready_queue*, it is suspended and side lined into the *interrupt_stack* as soon as a process enters the *disy_queue*. Processes in the *interrupt_stack* may be reactivated, with priority over processes in the *ready_queue*, only if the *disy_queue* is empty.

Otherwise, an active process may release the processing unit in either of the following ways: it may

- complete the reduction of its expression which subsequently is traversed, via one of the output ports, to the processing site identified by the index r in its header, and the context block is released by returning the pointer to it to the *released_queue*;

- transfer one or more expression packets to adjacent sites for processing, whereupon the pointer to the context block is placed in either of the *wait_tables*;

- synchronize with returning expression packets, whereupon the pointers to the context blocks are put into

    - the *wait_t_table* if pseudo-applications of $\Uparrow$ are still pending;

    - the *wait_s_table* if there are only ticket variables left in the expression;

    - the *ready_queue* if the process can continue with the reduction of other than pseudo-applications.

The system configuration outlined in section 7.2, in conjunction with this local process management concept, forms what is commonly called a **distributed system**. There is no sharing of resources among processes other than processing units. Complete expressions or subexpressions are transferred between virtual machines which accommodate processes that are in a master-slave relationship. All expression transfers are carried out by special input/output port units and involve buffer areas, thus avoiding any synchronization between transmitting and receiving virtual machines. No other but a strictly local control is exercised over the processes within a site, particularly with respect to the abstraction of concurrently executable subexpressions from the program expression of the active process and their distribution over the adjacent processing sites. Thus, processing sites may freely be attached to or removed from an existing system (either logically or physically) without causing or necessitating any global changes. A processing site may be added to or taken out of the system simply by making it known or unknown to its adjacent sites. Their ticket pool capacities need to be increased or decreased accordingly. If the regularity requirements for the interconnection network can, at least to some extent, be maintained, then the processing capacity of the entire system is almost exactly upgraded or downgraded by the processing capacity of that site.

8   Some Language Issues

So far, we were primarily concerned with the mechanics of reducing λ-expressions by direct string manipulations, particularly with the implementation of a full-fledged β-reduction, and with non-sequential program execution. In doing this, we kept the machine language OREL/0 very simple, paying no attention to the problems involved in converting high-level functional programs into OREL/0 expressions, and to the space and time complexity of actually executing them.

Some of these problems relate to the concept of interactively controlled program execution which we intent to exploit to full advantage. Depending on the choice of initial reduction counter values, OREL/0 expressions may be reduced either partially or completely (i.e., to normal forms). In order to make these program transformations visible to the user in the same notation (syntax) as the original programs, conversions into OREL/0 expressions must be fully reversible. Only then can the stepwise execution of high-level programs be followed up, e.g., on a display screen, as illustrated in section 5.1.

8.1   Converting High-Level Programs into OREL/0 Expressions

A major difficulty with OREL/0 as it is arises from mutually recursive function definitions. Depending on the degree to which these definitions are nested and indeed defined in terms of each other, the time and space required to convert high-level programs into OREL/0, and even more so, to re-convert partially reduced OREL/0 expressions, may grow beyond tolerable limits.

The cause of the problem is that OREL/0 supports only the recursion operator α which binds just one variable. Mutually recursive abstractions must therefore be exhaustively substituted into each other in order to obtain equivalent OREL/0 expressions. Unfortunately, the worst case complexity of these substitutions both in time and space is $O(k^3)$, where k denotes the number of recursive functions involved. The complexity of re-converting partially reduced OREL/0 expressions into high-level programs may be even higher. This is primarily due to the need to identify and eliminate multiple occurrences of the same abstractions in different contexts, but also due to problems concerning the correct re-construction of hierarchically nested function definitions.

To overcome these complexity problems, we clearly need to support sets of mutually recursive functions at the machine language level by more direct means. The efficient implementation of an appropriate recursion construct is also imperative with respect to the complexity of program execution. The repeated literal reproduction of large nested α-constructs in the course of performing recursions would not only be extremely time-consuming but also lead to an exploding demand for memory space.

We recall from section 5.1 that the standard HLFL expressions for defining mutually recursive functions in a given scope has the form

$$\text{DEFINE}$$
$$f\_1(x\_1_1, \ldots, x\_1_{n\_1}) \; = \; expr\_1$$
$$\vdots$$
$$f\_i(x\_i_1, \ldots, x\_i_{n\_i}) \quad = \; expr\_i$$
$$\vdots$$
$$f\_k(x\_k_1, \ldots, x\_k_{n\_k}) \; = \; expr\_k$$
$$\text{IN } s\_expr \; .$$

It binds the variables (function names) $f\_1, \ldots, f\_i, \ldots, f\_k$ in s_expr on the one hand, and recursively in the function body expressions $expr\_1, \ldots, expr\_i, \ldots,$ $expr\_k$ on the other hand. An equivalent OREL/0 expressions would have the form

$$\overline{@}^{(k)} \lambda^{(k)} f\_1 \; \ldots \; f\_i \; \ldots \; f\_k \, s\_expr^B \; F\_1 \; \ldots \; F\_i \; \ldots \; F\_k \; .$$

For all $i \in \{1, \ldots, k\}$, we have

$$F\_i = \alpha f\_i \, \overline{@}^{(k)} \lambda^{(k)} f\_1 \; \ldots \; f\_i \; \ldots \; f\_k \, R\_i \, F\_1 \; \ldots \; f\_i \; \ldots \; F\_k$$

and

$$R\_i = \lambda^{(n\_i)} x\_i_1 \; \ldots \; x\_i_{n\_i} \, expr\_i^B \; ,$$

with s_expr^B, $expr\_i^B$ denoting the OREL/0 representations of s_expr, $expr\_i$, respectively.

This application can be changed into a LETREC construct of the form

$$\alpha^* <^{(k)} f\_1 \ldots f\_k > \; <^{(k)} R\_1 \ldots R\_k > \, s\_expr^B \; ,$$

in which we use a three-place recursion operator α^* to bind free occurrences of the variables from the list $<^{(k)} f\_1 \ldots f\_k >$ both in the list $<^{(k)} R\_1 \ldots R\_k >$ and in the LETREC body expression s_expr^B to the abstractions in the respective positions in $<^{(k)} R\_1 \ldots R\_k >$.

The meaning of this construct is formally defined as

$$m \left[\!\!\left[\alpha^* <^{(k)} f\_1 \ldots f\_k > \; <^{(k)} R\_1 \ldots R\_k > \, s\_expr^B \right]\!\!\right]$$
$$= m \left[\!\!\left[s\_expr^B [\ldots, f\_i \Leftarrow R\_i [\ldots, \right.\right.$$
$$f\_j \Leftarrow \alpha^* <^{(k)} f\_1 \ldots f\_k > <^{(k)} R\_1 \ldots R\_k > f\_j,$$
$$\left.\left. \ldots], \ldots] \right]\!\!\right] \; .$$

Its reduction effects in one conceptual step the substitution of all free occurrences of the variables f_i ($i \in \{1, \ldots, k\}$) in s_expr^B by the respective abstractions R_i, following the β-reduction rule of the λ-calculus. The abstractions R_i, in turn, have all their free variable occurrences f_j ($j \in \{1, \ldots, k\}$) substituted by copies of the LETREC construct whose body expressions are the variables f_j themselves. These variables, in fact, serve as selector functions for the abstractions R_j.

With the introduction of this LETREC construct, we are now ready to completely define the conversion of HLFL programs into OREL/0 expressions and vice versa. We assume that these conversions are carried out somewhere outside the reduction system itself, say, by a front-end processor supporting the user interface. Besides the conversion programs, it may include a syntax-oriented editor and library facilities for the composition of functional programs from user input and from existing components (e.g., library functions) referenced by special identifiers (names). Syntactically complete programs are transferred between the front-end and the reduction system as pre-order linearized string representations of OREL/0 expressions.

We define the **program conversion** as a function

$$\Phi : E^{HL} \rightarrow E^B$$

where

E^{HL} denotes the set of legitimate HLFL programs;

E^B denotes the set of legitimate OREL/0 expressions (or programs).

The function Φ is bijective: for all $expr^{HL} \in E^{HL}$, there exists an $expr^B \in E^B$ such that

$$\Phi \left[\!\left[expr^{HL} \right]\!\right] = expr^B \in E^B$$

with

$$\Phi^{-1} \left[\!\left[\Phi \left[\!\left[expr^{HL} \right]\!\right] \right]\!\right] = \Phi^{-1} \left[\!\left[expr^B \right]\!\right] = expr^{HL} \; .$$

In particular, the function Φ defines the following mappings:

- DEFINE constructs are converted into LETRECs:

$$\Phi \left[\!\left[\text{DEFINE} \right.\right.$$
$$\vdots$$
$$f\_i(x\_i_1, \ldots, x\_i_{n\_i}) = expr\_i$$
$$\vdots$$
$$\text{IN } s\_expr \left.\left.\right]\!\right]$$
$$= \alpha^* <^{(k)} \ldots f\_i \ldots ><^{(k)} \ldots \lambda^{(n\_i)} x\_i_1 \ldots x\_i_{n\_i} \; \Phi \left[\!\left[expr\_i \right]\!\right] \ldots >$$
$$\Phi \left[\!\left[s\_expr \right]\!\right]$$

where k is the number of functions specified under the DEFINE construct.

- nameless functions convert into λ-abstractions:

$$\Phi \left[\!\!\left[\text{SUB}(x_1, \ldots, x_n) \text{ IN } expr \right]\!\!\right]$$
$$= \lambda^{(n)} x_1 \ldots x_n \ \Phi \left[\!\!\left[expr \right]\!\!\right] .$$

- WHERE constructs are converted into applications of special λ-abstractions:

$$\Phi \left[\!\!\left[expr \text{ WHERE} \right.\right.$$
$$x\_1 = w\_expr\_1$$
$$\vdots$$
$$\left. x\_n = w\_expr\_n \right]\!\!\right]$$
$$= @^{(n)} \Phi \left[\!\!\left[w\_expr\_n \right]\!\!\right] \ldots \Phi \left[\!\!\left[w\_expr\_1 \right]\!\!\right] \overset{\vee(n)}{\lambda} x\_1 \ldots x\_n \ \Phi \left[\!\!\left[expr \right]\!\!\right] .^{19}$$

- In the case of function applications, we need to distinguish between conversion into applicative order applications as a default option and conversion into normal order applications for arguments explicitly so specified. Thus, we have respectively

$$\Phi \left[\!\!\left[func(arg\_1, \ldots, arg\_r) \right]\!\!\right]$$
$$= @^{(r)} \ \Phi \left[\!\!\left[arg\_r \right]\!\!\right] \ldots \Phi \left[\!\!\left[arg\_1 \right]\!\!\right] \ \Phi \left[\!\!\left[func \right]\!\!\right]$$

and

$$\Phi \left[\!\!\left[func(arg\_1, \ldots, \text{AS\_IS}(arg\_j), \ldots, \text{AS\_IS}(arg\_i), \ldots, arg\_r) \right]\!\!\right]$$
$$= @^{(r-(i+1))} \ \Phi \left[\!\!\left[arg\_r \right]\!\!\right] \ldots \Phi \left[\!\!\left[arg\_(r-(i+1)) \right]\!\!\right]$$
$$\overline{@}^{(i-j)} @^{(j-1)} \ \Phi \left[\!\!\left[arg\_(j-1) \right]\!\!\right] \ldots \Phi \left[\!\!\left[arg\_1 \right]\!\!\right] \ \Phi \left[\!\!\left[func \right]\!\!\right]$$
$$\Phi \left[\!\!\left[arg\_j \right]\!\!\right] \ldots \Phi \left[\!\!\left[arg\_i \right]\!\!\right]$$

where the arguments $arg\_j, \ldots, arg\_i$ (with $1 \leq j \leq i \leq r$) are destined for normal order reductions by the prefix AS_IS.

---

[19] The special binding symbol $\overset{\vee(n)}{\lambda}$ is to facilitate the re-conversion by the function Φ^{-1} of abstractions originating from WHERE clauses.

- Special binary applications in infix notation convert as

$$\Phi\left[\!\left[(arg\_2\ func\ arg\_1)\right]\!\right]$$
$$= @^{(2)}\ \Phi\left[\!\left[arg\_2\right]\!\right]\ \Phi\left[\!\left[arg\_1\right]\!\right]\ \Phi\left[\!\left[func\right]\!\right]$$

and IF-THEN-ELSE clauses convert as

$$\Phi\left[\!\left[\text{IF}\ pred\_expr\ \text{THEN}\ true\_expr\ \text{ELSE}\ false\_expr\right]\!\right]$$
$$= @^{(1)}\ \Phi\left[\!\left[pred\_expr\right]\!\right]\ \Delta\ \Phi\left[\!\left[true\_expr\right]\!\right]\ \Phi\left[\!\left[false\_expr\right]\!\right]\ .$$

- Structured objects transform as:

$$\Phi\left[\!\left[<expr\_1,\ldots,expr\_n>\right]\!\right] = <^{(n)}\Phi\left[\!\left[expr\_1\right]\!\right]\ldots\Phi\left[\!\left[expr\_n\right]\!\right]>$$

We note that due to the context-free syntax of programs from both E^{HL} and E^B all these conversions are rather straightforward transliterations.

8.2 Operations on Structured Objects

All serious computational problems involve value-transforming and structuring operations on large structured objects, especially on arrays of numerical values. The representation and efficient implementation of these operations is a considerable problem in all functional systems. Conceptually, they must create new objects rather than update existing ones in order to keep functional computations free of side effects. However, copying repeatedly large data structures in which only a few entries have been modified is extremely costly in terms of both processing time and memory space expended. Though some of these difficulties can be overcome by manipulating structured objects as conceptual entities rather than incrementally, there is no generally satisfactory remedy.

From a programmers point of view, both HLFL and OREL/0 are particularly ill-equipped in this respect, providing just the bare essentials for structuring operations on heterogeneous lists. The ensuing lack of expressive power results in awkward programs which in conjunction with the underlying string reduction machinery cause considerable run-time complexities.

A typical example is an HLFL program for the multiplication of two matrices. Since matrices must be represented as lists of lists of numbers (or of expressions that reduce to numbers) which can only be manipulated by the primitive structuring functions FIRST, REST and APPEND, this simple problem turns out to be a sophisticated piece of artful programming:

DEFINE

$ma\_prod(ma\_1, ma\_2) =$ IF $\quad$ EMPTY(x)

$\qquad$ THEN $<y>$

$\qquad$ ELSE APPEND$(<y>, ma\_prod(x, ma\_2))$

$\qquad$ WHERE $x =$ REST(ma_1)

$\qquad\qquad y = vm\_prod($FIRST$(ma\_1), ma\_2)$

$vm\_prod(vector, matrix) =$ IF $\quad$ EMPTY(x)

$\qquad$ THEN $<y>$

$\qquad$ ELSE APPEND$(<y>, vm\_prod(vector, x))$

$\qquad$ WHERE $x =$ REST$(matrix)$

$\qquad\qquad y = ip(vector,$ FIRST$(matrix))$

$ip(vec\_1, vec\_2) =$ IF $\quad$ AND$($EMPTY$(x),$ EMPTY$(y))$

$\qquad$ THEN z

$\qquad$ ELSE $(z + ip(x, y))$

$\qquad$ WHERE $x =$ REST(vec_1)

$\qquad\qquad y =$ REST(vec_2)

$\qquad\qquad z = ($FIRST$(vec\_1) *$ FIRST$(vec\_2))$

IN $ma\_prod(<< a_{11} \ \ldots \ a_{1k}>$

$\qquad\qquad\qquad \vdots$

$\qquad < a_{n1} \ \ldots \ a_{nk}>>, << b_{11} \ \ldots \ b_{k1}>$

$\qquad\qquad\qquad\qquad\qquad\quad \vdots$

$\qquad\qquad\qquad < b_{1m} \ \ldots \ b_{km}>>)$

The function

- *ma_prod* (matrix–matrix product) recursively pairs all inner lists (row vectors) of its first argument matrix with the entire second argument matrix, applies the function *vm_prod* to them and concatenates the resulting lists (which are supposed to be the rows of the product matrix);

- *vm_prod* (vector–matrix product) recursively pairs the list (vector) in its first argument position with all inner lists (column vectors) of the matrix in its second argument position, applies the function *ip* to them, and appends the resulting elements (which become the components of the row vectors of the product matrix);

- *ip* (inner product of two vectors) recursively pairs the elements of its argument lists (vectors), multiplies them and adds them up.

To transpose, if necessary, one of the argument matrices, three more function definitions must be included in the program.

This rather formidable program primarily specifies the recursive decomposition of the argument matrices into their atomic components, embedded in the recursive construction of the result matrix from other atomic components.

The multiplication of an $n * k$ matrix with a $k * m$ matrix calls n times the function ma_prod, m times the function vm_prod for each call of ma_prod, and k times the function ip for each call of vm_prod, i.e., we have altogether $n * m * k$ recursive function calls. At a first glance this computational complexity seems to be appropriate for the particular problem. It corresponds to the number of elementary multiplications and additions which need to be carried out when multiplying two matrices.

However, the inefficient and hence expensive part is due to the generation of these elementary operations by means of recursive function applications. Each function call requires the substitution of formal by actual parameters, the evaluation of an IF-THEN-ELSE clause, applications of primitive structuring functions to list structures, and the concatenation of two list structures by means of the function APPEND. The complexity of (or the time and space consumed by) these operations depends on the details of their implementation, i.e., on the workings of the underlying machine. The best we can expect is that they contribute only constant yet rather substantial coefficients to the computational complexity which is due to the recursive function calls.

Unfortunately, string reduction constitutes a worst case. This is largely due to the literal substitution of argument expressions in the course of performing β-reductions. We recall from section 6.2 that they require two traversals of the function body expressions and twice as many traversals of the argument expression as there are variable occurrences to be substituted. The complexity of these traversals grows linearly with the sizes of the expressions, which may be measured, say, in numbers of characters or nodes of the syntactical structures. Thus, the complexity of the β-reduction is roughly given by the product of the size of the function body expression, the size of the argument expression, and the number of variable occurrences that need to be substituted in the function body expression.

Representative for this computational complexity is the inner product of two vectors, as specified by the function definition ip in the above example. The complexity of applying this function to concrete argument vectors, say $<a_1, \ldots, a_n>$ and $<b_1, \ldots, b_n>$ (where a_i, b_i are assumed to be numbers), may be deduced from the following consideration: each recursive call of ip

- reproduces the entire function expression once in itself;

- literally substitutes each argument vector three times into the function expression (for occurrences of vec_1 and vec_2);

- removes the first components from each argument vector to compute their product;

- applies the new instantiation of *ip* to the remaining argument vectors.

With vectors of n components, this amounts to

- the n-fold reproduction of the function expression (which is of constant size);

- the substitution of two vectors of $(n + 1 - i)$ components in recursion step $i \in \{1, \ldots, n\}$.

We thus get a run-time complexity of $c_2 * n^2 + c_1 * n + c_0$, i.e., it roughly grows with the square of the size of the argument vectors rather than just linearly, as we assumed for the computational complexity of the matrix product. Similar considerations apply, of course, for the computation of *ma_prod* and *vm_prod* as well.

This so-called n^2-**problem** is a characteristic phenomenon of string reductions involving structured objects. It cannot be tolerated in practical reduction systems for otherwise their run-time performance would be hopelessly inferior to that of conventional computing systems.

The way out of this problem is **graph reduction**. The idea is to move at least all non-atomic component expressions of applications recursively to a **heap**, and to represent these **heap expressions** (or **heap objects**) in the remaining strings by pointers. The initial program string thus typically condenses to an application of a pointer in operator position to pointers in operand positions, with similar structures recursively extending into the heap. β-reductions can then be performed as **naive pointer substitutions** provided that name clashes are taken care of by some other means. The complexity of the above example is thus cut down from $O(n^2)$ to $O(n)$.

With suitable heap representations at hand, we may also think of enhancing the architecture of our reduction engine by more powerful and elegant operations on structured objects.

A concept supported in one way or another by almost all functional systems is **pattern matching** [HaMcQMi86, Lavi87, McQMi87, Turn86, HuWa88, PlSc90]. The basic idea is to extract substructures from a given structural context and to substitute them for names (identifiers) in another structural context. **Pattern matching functions** may in HLFL be specified as

$$\text{WHEN } pattern \; \{guard\} \text{ DO } p\_expr$$

where

pattern is either a variable, a constant or a (recursively nested) sequence whose components are variables or constants;

guard is an optional **guard expression** defined in terms of pattern variables which is
supposed to reduce to a Boolean constant;

p_expr may be any legitimate HLFL expression in which some or all pattern variables may occur free;

WHEN binds free occurrences of the pattern variables both in *guard* and *p_expr*.

The application of such a function to an argument expression *arg*, denoted as

$$(\text{WHEN } pattern \; \{guard\} \text{ DO } p\_expr \; arg) \,,$$

reduces as follows: if the syntactical structures of the pattern and of the argument
match, then all free occurrences of the pattern variables in *guard* and *p_expr* are
substituted by the respective argument substructures. If in addition the guard thus
instantiated evaluates to TRUE, then the entire application reduces to the normal
form of the instantiated *p_expr*. Otherwise the argument is considered not within
the domain of the pattern (or not of a **compatible type**), and the application remains
as it is.

Thus, the pattern in fact defines a **structured data type**. It is the set of all (nested)
sequences which match the pattern and satisfy the guard.

Several pattern matches may form a CASE expression:

$$\text{CASE} \quad \text{WHEN } pattern\_1 \; \{guard\} \text{ DO } p\_expr\_1$$
$$\vdots$$
$$\text{WHEN } pattern\_n \; \{guard\} \text{ DO } p\_expr\_n \,,$$
$$\{\text{OTHERWISE } q\_expr\}$$
$$\text{END\_CASE} \,.$$

The CASE is a unary function which, when applied to an argument, tries all pattern
matches in the order from top to bottom. The first successful match (including
a satisfiable guard) is reduced to its normal form which, by definition, is also the
normal form of the entire CASE application. If none of the pattern/guard combinations matches, then the application either reduces to the normal form of the
optional OTHERWISE expression or, if this expression is not specified, it remains as
it is.

A CASE expression defines a structured data type which is the union of all sequences (of sequences) which match the patterns *pattern_1*, ..., *pattern_n* and, if
specified, satisfy the associated guards.

It also proves useful to support a few **higher-order primitives** which in an orderly
way distribute functions about the components of structured objects (sequences).
Most prominent are

- MAP which applies a given function to all expressions of a sequence:

$$\text{MAP}(func, <>) \longmapsto <>$$
$$\text{MAP}(func, <e\_1, \ldots, e\_n>) \longmapsto <func(e\_1), \ldots, func(e\_n)> \ ;$$

- FOLD which drives a given binary function recursively into a sequence:

$$\text{FOLD}(func, \phi, <>) \longmapsto \phi$$
$$\text{FOLD}(func, \phi, <e\_1, \ldots, e\_n>)$$
$$\longmapsto func(e\_1, \text{FOLD}(func, \phi, <e\_2, \ldots, e\_n>)) \ ;$$

where ϕ denotes the neutral element of $func$.

For predominantly numerical computations it is of great advantage to support arrays (or vectors and matrices, for that matter) as machine data types, and to make available a rich set of generic value-transforming and structuring primitives as in the array programming language APL [GiGu82, Schm86, SmBlKl91a]. The former should typically include

- elementwise arithmetic and relational unary and binary operations,

- summation, multiplication, minimum, maximum, etc. over all elements of the rows or columns of arrays,

- inner and Cartesian products,

whereas the latter should include

- selecting an element or a substructure (row, column) of an array,

- rotating an array along rows or columns,

- dropping selected parts from an array.

We forgo discussing the implementation of these concepts for they are somewhat outside the scope of this monograph. However, we will simply assume that they are an integral part of the graph reduction engines to be described in the following chapters, i.e., they are included into the machine language OREL/0 as well as in the high-level language HLFL .

9 An Eager Graph Reduction Engine

We will now study another high-level interpreter for OREL/0 which performs reductions on graph representations of program expressions rather than on flat strings. It is a descendant of the string reduction engine described in chapter 6, upgraded by the language features introduced in chapter 8, of which an early version is described in [Hom82].

Following the underlying constructor syntax, OREL/0 programs may be held in memory as tree-like structures of variable arities whose

- branch nodes are (sub-)strings representing syntactically complete (sub-)terms which include as atomic components pointers to other nodes;

- leaf nodes are substrings representing atomic terms.

These structures generally include nodes that are shared among several pointers directed at them, and we also have cyclic pointer chains which depict mutually recursive dependencies. They are therefore referred to as program graphs (or graphs for short). The memory (or memory segment) in which the graph is stored is commonly called the heap.

The idea of operating on graphs is to perform reductions largely by the orderly consumption, replication and re-arrangement of pointers rather than of the complete terms they represent. The complexity of β-reductions and of many δ-reductions can thus be made independent of actual argument sizes, which significantly improves run-time performances in comparison to string reduction.

While switching to decidedly more efficient graph reduction mechanisms, it remains our objective to realize the full reduction semantics of an applied λ-calculus. In particular, we wish to support

- stepwise reductions under interactive control, including the means to inspect and modify intermediate program terms;

- full-fledged β-reductions on OREL/0 terms;

- fully transparent non-sequential program execution;

The key to efficient graph reductions is the sharing of subgraphs among several pointer occurrences. Sharing comes about due to the duplication of pointers to argument graphs in the course of performing β- (or combinator) reductions. Depending on the particular reduction order, two concepts of sharing must be distinguished.

Applicative order β-reductions require that arguments be reduced to normal forms before substitution. The idea is to evaluate an argument exactly once and then to copy its value into possibly several places in the body of a λ-abstraction. Closed terms that are in normal form can be shared without any problems: when involved in further reductions, they can only be replicated or consumed but never be replaced by anything else.

However, applicative order reductions are **eager** in the sense that they reduce arguments regardless of whether or not they actually contribute to the normal form of the entire program. The computation may thus even get trapped in non-terminating recursions although the program may have a normal form.

Normal order β-**reductions** avoid these pitfalls by substituting arguments **as they are**, i.e., they may contain redexes. The penalty that may have to be paid for this reduction order consists in repeated evaluations of several copies of the same argument terms in their places of substitution. The purpose of sharing is to avoid just that. However, rather than sharing graph representations of normal forms, we must now share **reductions to normal forms** (or to so-called **canonical forms**, i.e., to terms featuring outermost constructors other than applicators). This is to say that normal (or canonical) forms must replace the original graphs in order to make them accessible to all pointers directed at them. This reduction discipline is also referred to as **lazy evaluation**. Arguments of β-reductions are reduced at most once and only to the extent necessary to compute the normal form of the entire program.

Eager evaluation on the one hand and **lazy evaluation** on the other hand are alternative concepts of performing graph reductions. They differ significantly with respect to both the construction of the graphs and the implementation of the basic reduction mechanisms. Thus, when devising a graph reduction engine, we have to make a conscious decision in favor of either evaluation discipline. As for the engine to be described in this chapter, we will settle for eager evaluation (or applicative order reductions) since we wish to look at the simpler machinery first. Neither lazy evaluation nor ordinary normal order reductions will be (directly) supported.

Another key problem of graph reductions concerns **name clashes**. We recall from chapter 5 that these situations arise whenever argument terms containing free variables are being substituted into the scopes of binders to the same variable names. The string reduction engine of section 6.2 correctly resolves these naming conflicts by full β-reductions. However, they require complete traversals of the argument terms and of the abstraction bodies in which the substitutions are to take place in order to find out whether naming conflicts do indeed occur and how they must be dealt with (i.e., how many protection keys must be added to or subtracted from the variable occurrences that are affected). These traversals are the primary cause of the n^2-complexity of string reduction.

Graph reduction derives its efficiency essentially from the fact that in real-life programs the overwhelming majority of function applications are (or by abstracting free variables can be made to be) reducible without inflicting name clashes at all.

Thus, rather than going through the time-consuming motions of full β-reductions, argument terms can be generally passed on to functions by the naive substitution of pointers to the respective graph representations. However, some safeguards must be installed to prevent naive substitutions whenever full β-reductions may become necessary to handle conflicting names.

In the graph reducer to be described here we plan to play it safe. Before actually executing an OREL/0 program, (relatively) free variables are eliminated by systematically converting all open into closed λ-abstractions (or combinators). The theory of the λ-calculus (see section 5.3) tells us that full applications of combinators can be reduced by naive argument (pointer) substitutions. If done in one conceptual step, no name clashes can occur. As in the *SECD* machine, partial applications are transformed into closures as safeguards against naive substitutions into the scope(s) of the remaining binder(s). Closures that are left over after everything else is done are by full β-reductions reduced to weak normal forms of new λ-abstractions.

The conceptual advantages of a full-fledged λ-calculus can thus be had without actually paying the price of full β-reductions for argument substitutions that can in fact be done naively.

This concept and the ensuing machine and system architecture form the basis of a graph reduction system π-RED jointly developed at the GMD Bonn and at the University of Kiel/Germany [KlSh85, SmBlKl91a, SmBlKl91b]. It supports an interactive environment for the execution of programs written in the high-level reduction language OREL/2 [PlSc90] whose syntax resembles that of MIRANDA [Turn85, Turn86]. π-RED is implemented as a high-level interpreter written in C. It includes a sophisticated user-interface based on syntax-oriented editing facilities for OREL/2 programs.

9.1 The Basic Program Execution Cycle

The easiest way of converting open into closed λ-terms is called λ-lifting. It refers to the abstraction of all (relatively) free variable occurrences (or of minimally free subterms) to the next higher levels of λ-binders [John85, John87].

Let $h = \boldsymbol{\lambda}^{(n)} x_1 \ldots x_n \ b\_expr$ be a λ-abstraction in which the variables $w_1, \ldots, w_q$ occur free. Then h can be equivalently represented in λ-lifted form as

$$\overset{\sim (q)}{@} \ w_q \ldots w_1 \ \tilde{h} \quad \text{with} \quad \tilde{h} = \overset{\sim (q)}{\boldsymbol{\lambda}} \ w_1 \ldots w_q \ h .$$

The λ-abstraction $\tilde{h}$ thus closed is referred to as a **supercombinator** iff all occurrences of λ-abstractions in its body b_expr are closed (or supercombinators) as well (see also section 5.3), which we denote as b_expr^S. This can be guaranteed when doing the λ-lifting systematically from innermost to outermost.[20]

The special symbols $\overset{\sim(q)}{@}$ and $\overset{\sim(q)}{\lambda}$ are to distinguish the applications and binders introduced by the abstraction of free variables from those of the original OREL/0 terms. For the snake-like shape of the $\sim$, we will henceforth refer to these applications also as snake-applications, or SNAPs for short. The SNAPs are in fact pre-fabricated closures. They are to carry in flat form the complete environments (or contexts) in which the original λ-abstractions must be evaluated. When switching to de Bruijn representations of the supercombinators, the binders $\overset{\sim(q)}{\lambda} w_1 \ldots w_q$ are being replaced with nameless binding symbols $\tilde{\Lambda}_{(q)}$.

When reducing just SNAPs, full β-reductions must be employed to resolve potential name clashes. They return the original λ-abstractions

- as they are if the λ-lifted variables in the argument positions of the SNAPs are as yet uninstantiated;

- with all free variables substituted by other λ-terms if all supercombinator applications surrounding the SNAPs are being reduced (i.e., the λ-lifted variables in the SNAPs are instantiated).

At run-time, our graph reducer proceeds with reductions systematically from outermost to innermost, following a demand-driven control discipline. Supercombinator applications are then generally encountered in the form:

$$@^{(r)} \, arg\_r \ldots arg\_1 \; \overset{\sim(q)}{@} \; brg\_q \ldots brg\_1 \; \tilde{h} \, ,$$

where $\tilde{h}$ is as before, $arg\_1, \ldots, arg\_r$ are the arguments for h, and $brg\_1, \ldots, brg\_q$ are the terms substituted for $w_1, \ldots, w_q$ and thus form the actual environment of h.

Assuming that $arg\_1, \ldots, arg\_r, brg\_1, \ldots, brg\_q$ are already in normal form, full applications (i.e., whenever we have $r \geq n$) reduce in one conceptual step to

$$@^{(r-n)} \, arg\_r \ldots arg\_(n+1) \, b\_expr^S[\leftarrow]$$

where $b\_expr^S[\leftarrow]$ denotes the term obtained from b_expr^S by naively substituting $arg\_1, \ldots, arg\_n$ for free occurrences of $x_1, \ldots, x_n$ and $brg\_1, \ldots, brg\_q$ for free occurrences of $w_1, \ldots, w_q$, respectively. All substitutions can be safely carried out in this form since no other binding scopes can be penetrated inside b_expr^S.

---

[20] Another way of forming supercombinators is to abstract maximally free subterms. This approach ensures that all instances of subterms of a program, in conjunction with a lazy evaluation regime, are evaluated at most once. The ensuing evaluation strategy is referred to as being fully lazy as it is claimed to reach normal forms with the least number of reductions [Hugh82].

Partial applications (i.e., whenever we have $r < n$) transform into closures of the form

$$\overset{\sim(r+q)}{@} \quad arg\_r \ldots arg\_1 \, brg\_q \ldots brg\_1 \; \tilde{h} \; .$$

Further arguments may be added to closures by subsequent applications until we have a full application which can be reduced as above.

However, since we demand that our graph reducer supports a full λ-calculus, supercombinator reductions and the use of closures must be made completely transparent at the level of OREL/0 programs (and thus higher up at the level of HLFL programs). There we wish to see all functions (λ-abstractions) as originally defined, all closures transformed into new functions, and all name clashes among user-specified variables in an orderly manner resolved by appropriate numbers of protection keys. To accomplish this, program execution must be partitioned into three phases.

An OREL/0 expression first undergoes a pre-processing phase to convert all occurrences of (names of) open λ-abstractions into snake-applications, and to α-convert the emerging supercombinators into their de Bruijn representations so that binding levels can be uniquely identified by indices. Pre-processing also includes the recursive creation of graphs for all program terms that are constant or at least in weak normal form. They include supercombinators, the LETREC constructs they may be defined in, pattern matching functions and CASE constructs, lists of constant components, arrays of basic values and, as exceptions, conditional expressions. Whenever appropriate, we will refer to these graphs also as heap objects or heap structures.

The processing phase generally does the bulk of the work. It performs supercombinator reductions on the program graph prepared by the pre-processor, using a run-time stack which, in the form of argument (pointer) frames (or activation records), accommodates the (recursively nested) contexts in which the supercombinator bodies must be evaluated.

While traversing an instantiated supercombinator body in search for reducible applications, occurrences of de Bruijn indices are substituted by the argument pointers found in the respective index positions of the topmost run-time stack frame. δ-reductions specified as value-transforming or structuring operations on atomic or structured heap objects create graph representations of resulting objects, replacing the respective applications by pointers to them.

As before, program execution may either be halted after some user-specified number of reductions or terminate with a (weak) normal form. In either case, the resulting graph is in a subsequent post-processing phase systematically re-converted into an OREL/0 program. In particular, left-over closures (or snake-applications) are β-reduced to open λ-abstractions, and the original variable names are restored as well.

Thus a full program execution cycle on an HLFL program may be depicted as in fig. 9.1. The solid arrows show the course of program transformations and reductions along which the program execution does actually proceed, whereas the dashed arrows represent the reductions as they are conceptually performed (and may be seen) at the OREL/0 and HLFL levels. Note that the terms on the right hand sides are not necessarily the normal forms of the terms on the left hand sides. Depending on the pre-specified number of reductions, a program may pass through this cycle several times until its normal form is reached. Before starting such a cycle, any subterm of the program may be selected for reductions. Pre- and post-processing apply only to the selected subterm, while the rest of the program remains unaffected. If intermediate programs are just inspected but neither modified nor have the focus of control (reductions) moved to another subterm, pre-processing is skipped and reductions continue directly with the graphs returned by the preceding passes through the processing phase.

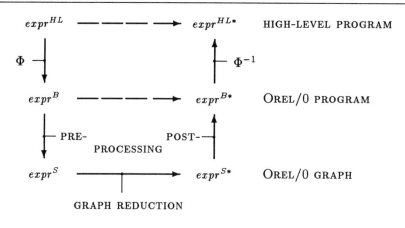

Figure 9.1: Basic program execution cycle

This graph reduction concept takes advantage of very efficient **supercombinator** reductions at run-time, while the reductions that are made visible to the user are governed by a full-fledged λ-calculus. However, this advantage comes at the expense of explicitly passing, by means of SNAPs, repeatedly the same environments (contexts) to recursive supercombinator calls. Fortunately, this redundancy reflects itself primarily in larger stack frames, whereas the net performance gains in comparison to full β-reductions generally are rather substantial.

Some of the **string reduction mechanisms** introduced in chapter 6 play a key role in the realization of the pre- and post-processing functions. Of particular importance is the availability of a full-fledged string-based β-reduction. It is required to maintain correct binding levels while converting, during the pre-processing phase, λ-abstractions into de Bruijn representations of supercombinators, and while reducing, in the post-processing phase, left-over snake-applications to λ-abstractions.

9.2   Supercombinator Reduction

Graph reductions can be readily performed by means of a kernel engine which uses the basic components and mechanisms of the **string reduction engine** described in section 6.2. This kernel primarily includes the **shunting yard** made up from the stacks E, A, M about which graph node strings are traversed in search for redexes, supplemented by a **run-time stack** R which holds the context frames for instantiated supercombinators. The traversal is governed by a modified **control program** $\widehat{(EAR_h)}$ which differs from $\widehat{(EAR)}$ of the string reduction engine mainly insofar as it must primarily deal with graph pointers.

To see how this kernel engine reduces supercombinator applications, we consider again the OREL/0 application

$$@^{(r)}\ arg\_r \ldots arg\_1\ h$$

where $h = \boldsymbol{\lambda}^{(n)}x_1 \ldots x_n\ b\_expr^S$ is assumed to be a function with free variables $w_1, \ldots, w_q$, and the arguments $arg\_1, \ldots, arg_r$ are assumed to be constant.

The **pre-processor** first converts the λ-abstraction h into a SNAP of the form

$$\overset{\sim(q)}{@}\ \#[w_q] \ldots \#[w_1]\ \tilde{\boldsymbol{\Lambda}}_{(q)}\ \boldsymbol{\Lambda}_{(n)}\ \#b\_expr^S$$

where $\#[w_1], \ldots, \#[w_q]$ are the de Bruijn indices substituted for $w_1, \ldots, w_q$, $\tilde{\boldsymbol{\Lambda}}_{(q)}$ and $\boldsymbol{\Lambda}_{(n)}$ are the **nameless binders** that replace $\overset{\sim(q)}{\boldsymbol{\lambda}}$ and $\boldsymbol{\lambda}^{(n)}$, respectively, and $\#b\_expr^S$ is the de Bruijn representation of b_expr^S.

The complete application is then transformed into the graph shown in fig. 9.2 by moving its component terms from stack E, and recursively from innermost to outermost, into **pre-allocated heap segments**. These heap locations are in fact the sink stacks of orderly traversals in which the terms build up in left-right transposed form. Each subgraph is preceded by a **descriptor** which generally includes structural and type specifications of the object it represents, and a link (or internal reference) to the subgraph itself. A supercombinator descriptor also includes a link to the list of λ-bound variables that have been extracted during the α-conversion to de Bruijn indices. This list must be carried along in order to be able to restore the variables

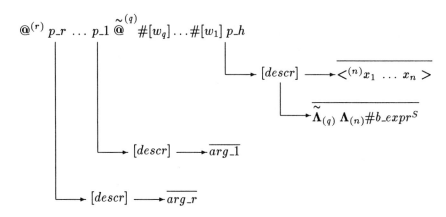

Figure 9.2: Heap representation of an application of a function-turned-supercombinator ([descr] denotes an unspecified descriptor)

if the supercombinator must be reconverted by the post-processor into the original
OREL/0 λ-abstraction.

Assuming that the entire program just consists of the above application, its top-
level string representation is what the pre-processor sets up in non-transposed form
in stack E of the shunting yard. If the application is part of a larger program,
it may be copied during the processing phase from the heap into stack E by an
orderly traversal.

The level of indirection introduced by the descriptors greatly facilitates the sharing of subgraphs as well as house-keeping operations within the heap. Graph pointers
such as $p\_1, \ldots, p\_r$ and p_h in our example always point from strings to descriptors, whereas links always point from descriptors to strings representing the topmost nodes of the subgraphs. Thus, while several pointers may be directed at a
descriptor, there is only one link to the topmost graph node.

Since all descriptors can be made to fit into the same format, they can be densely
packed in an array. Heap compactions which may become necessary from time to
time then primarily concern the relocation of the strings, i.e., the heap manager
must just walk through the descriptors to update the links, but it need not traverse
the entire program graph in search for pointers.

Fig. 9.3 exhibits by a sequence of snapshots taken from the contents of the stacks
E, A, M and R some characteristic phases of reducing the supercombinator application shown in fig. 9.2.

While traversing under the control of (EAR_h) the arguments from stack E

to stack A, the binding indices $\#[w_1], \ldots, \#[w_q]$ are substituted by pointers $p\_1'', \ldots, p\_q''$ selected from the topmost frame $p\_1', \ldots, p\_s'$ of stack R. This frame represents the context of the supercombinator application. With the components spread out over the tops of E, A, M (see fig. 9.3.c), its reduction proceeds by

- pushing a separation symbol \$ and the pointer p_h into the run-time stack R and by copying the top-level supercombinator string hidden behind p_h from the heap into the stack E (fig. 9.3.d)[21];

- moving for each applicable binder the topmost argument pointer from stack A to stack R and by subsequently decrementing the arity of the topmost applicator in stack M and the arity index of the binder $(\tilde{\Lambda}_{(q)}$ or $\Lambda_{(n)})$ on top of stack E (figs. 9.3.e–g);

- popping the snake-applicator $\overset{\sim(q)}{@}$ and the binder $\tilde{\Lambda}_{(q)}$ off stack E and stack M, respectively, after their arities have been decremented to zero (fig. 9.3.f):

- popping the topmost applicator off stack M once its arity has become equal to zero.

The reduction of the application terminates

- either by exhausting all binders $(r \geq n)$, in which case the supercombinator can be completely supplied with arguments;

- or by exhausting all arguments $(r < n)$, in which case we have a partial application.

Fig. 9.3.g shows the resulting situation for $r = n$: the application is replaced by the (top-level string of the) supercombinator body in stack E and by a complete context frame of $n + q$ entries (argument pointers) in stack R, while both the stacks A and M are left empty with respect to components of the applications.

For $r > n$, the contents of the stacks E and R are the same as in fig. 9.3.g. However, we have $r - n$ argument pointers left over in stack A, together with an applicator of arity $(r - n)$ on top of stack M.

In both cases, a separation symbol \$ is pushed in stack M, and the traversal of the supercombinator body set up in stack E may be continued in search for further instances of reductions. This expression constitutes the scope of the context frame set up on top of R. Each binding index that pops to the top of stack E during its traversal must be substituted by the argument pointer found in the corresponding

---

[21] Pushing p_h is a precautionary measure which facilitates forming a closure if the application happens to be partial (see also below).

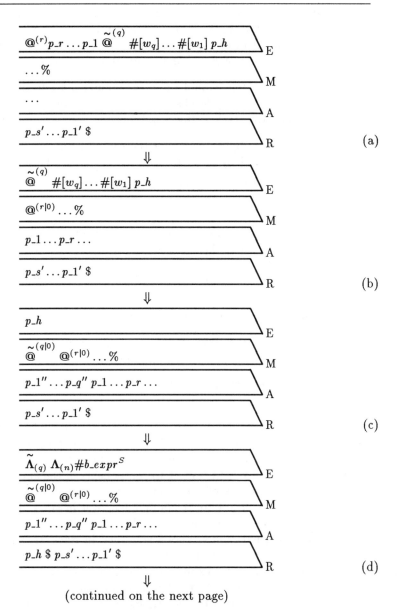

(a)

(b)

(c)

(d)

(continued on the next page)

Figure 9.3: Transformation sequence of a combinator application based on graph representations (assuming that $r = n$)

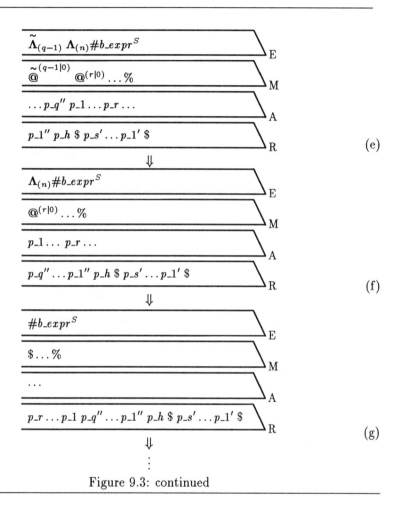

Figure 9.3: continued

index position of the stack R, counted from the actual top-of-stack position. A separation symbol $ popping to the top of stack M indicates the completion of the traversal, whereupon the associated context frame in R must be released by popping

- all entries up to and including the topmost separation symbol from stack R;

- the topmost separation symbol $ from M.

In case of a partial application (i.e., $r < n$) the engine must create a closure which in fact restores the original application. This may be accomplished by the following steps: the topmost expression is deleted from stack E (which is the λ-abstraction left over from the attempt to reduce the supercombinator application) and a snake-applicator $\overset{\sim(0|0)}{@}$ is pushed on top of stack M. Now, all entries of the incomplete frame on top of stack R are moved back to stack A. We recall that the last entry of the stack frame is the pointer p_h to the original supercombinator. For every pointer moved, the arity index of the snake-applicator on top of stack M is incremented by one. Upon popping the separation symbol \$ off stack R, the snake-applicator is moved from stack M to A with its actual arity index decremented by one, thereby completing in left-right transposed form the closure in stack A. Subsequently, a new heap object is created for this closure. In stack A, the closure is replaced by a pointer to it.

Nested supercombinator applications build up their context frames in stack R in the order of calls and release them in reverse order. Other than that, the context frames stacked up in R are totally unrelated to each other.

To prevent the run-time stack from growing unnecessarily large, tail-end recursions are made to release their current contexts before setting up the contexts for the next calls. This can be easily accomplished by earmarking tail-end recursions with special tags on the applicators. Once all argument pointers attached to such an applicator are traversed to stack A, the control program pops the actual topmost frame out of R and then moves the argument pointers from A to R in order to install the new context.

Primitive functions for value-transforming and structuring operations on atomic and structured (data) objects may be considered special combinators of fixed arities which expect typed arguments represented by pointers. Applications of these combinators constitute the hard-core δ-reduction rules. δ-reducibility is established by so-called conformity checks on the type and structure specifications included in the descriptors of the argument objects. With very few exceptions, δ-reductions generate new heap objects and replace the respective applications by their pointers, which are pushed into stack E.

The processing phase terminates with a transposed string in stack A, which may contain pointers to graph representations of subterms. As the traversal is thus completed, both the control stack M and the run-time stack R are empty. Another traversal back to stack E as the final leg of the control program $\overline{(EAR_h)}$ converts the string into its non-transposed form for post-processing. The post-processor re-transforms the actual state of the program execution into the string representation of an OREL/0 expression in which variable names and binding levels re-appear as introduced by the user.

9.3   Pre- and Post-Processing

The graph reduction engine just described receives as input from its front-end processor string representations of OREL/0 expressions which must be pre-processed in order to convert them into program graphs for processing. Conversely, graphs obtained after the termination of the processing phase must be post-processed in order to return string representations of OREL/0 expressions to the front-end as output.

Pre- and post-processing each comprise three major transformation steps which are realized as applications of complex built-in functions to the expressions residing in stack E.

Pre-processing requires

- the conversion of λ-bound variables into de Bruijn indices by a function RENAME which, by normal order application, is recursively driven into an OREL/0 expression to create applications of α-conversion functions for all λ-binders;

- the conversion of open λ-abstractions into snake-applications of supercombinators by the systematic abstraction of relatively free de Bruijn indices to the next higher level of binders by means of a function ABSTRACT, applications of which are recursively inserted into an α-converted OREL/0 expression from outermost to innermost, using a function CLOSE;

- the recursive creation of graphs (or heap objects) for all constant subexpressions by means of the functions

  CREATE which, by normal order application, prepares them from outermost to innermost for applications of

  TRANSFER which subsequently traverses these subexpressions from innermost to outermost into the heap, thereby also creating descriptors and pointers;

in this order.

Post-processing includes

- the recursive resolution of graph pointers by normal order applications of a function RESOLVE which generates in stack E a complete string representation of the resulting expression;

- the recursive normal order application of a function SUBST which, from outermost to innermost, enforces the orderly β-reduction of left-over snake-applications, thereby restoring open λ-abstractions from supercombinators and transforming closures into λ-abstractions;

- the recursive normal order application of a function RESTORE which restores
  the original names of λ-bound variables by applying, from innermost to outermost, α-conversions to nameless binders;

in this order.

The post-processing functions RESOLVE, SUBST and RESTORE are essentially in-
verse to the pre-processing functions CREATE, CLOSE and RENAME, respectively.
Applications of these functions as well as all instances of α-conversions or β-
reductions they create can only be reduced by the pre- or post-processor, using
primarily string reduction mechanisms. They are **pseudo-applications** distinguished
by special applicator symbols which merely modify the representation of OREL/0
expressions but do not belong to the language itself. Executable OREL/0 graphs
are free of these pseudo-applications.

The most formidable problem of pre-processing concerns the **conversion of LET-
REC**-defined functions (or λ-abstractions) to **supercombinators**.

Consider, as an example, the LETREC expression

$$\alpha^* \; <^{(3)} f \; g \; h> \; <^{(3)} \; \lambda x \dashv \ldots u \ldots v \ldots g \ldots h \ldots f \ldots \vdash$$
$$\lambda y \dashv \ldots w \ldots h \ldots g \ldots \vdash$$
$$\lambda z \dashv \ldots g \ldots h \ldots \vdash >$$
$$\dashv \ldots f \ldots g \ldots h \ldots \vdash$$

It specifies three mutually recursive functions f, g, h in which we have occurrences
of the relatively free variables u, v, w. To convert these open λ-abstractions (or
functions) into supercombinators, the pre-processor must

- add to each λ-abstraction snake-binders for all λ-bound variables which occur
  free in it;

- replace each occurrence of an α^*-bound variable either in one of the λ-abstrac-
  tions or in the LETREC body expression by a snake-application of it to the
  variables for which binders have been added to the respective λ-abstraction.

The problem with this abstraction scheme is that it may have to be repeatedly
applied since it may introduce new free variables which, again, have to be abstracted
[John85].

In our example, we need two passes through the LETREC to turn the functions defined in it into supercombinators. After the first pass, we get

$$\alpha^* <^{(3)} f\ g\ h> <^{(3)} \overset{\sim(2)}{\lambda}\ u\ v\ \lambda x \dashv \ldots u \ldots v \ldots \overset{\sim}{@}\ w\ g \ldots h \ldots \overset{\sim(2)}{@}\ v\ u\ f \ldots \vdash$$
$$\overset{\sim}{\lambda} w\ \lambda y \dashv \ldots w \ldots h \ldots \overset{\sim}{@}\ w\ g \ldots \vdash$$
$$\lambda z \dashv \ldots \overset{\sim}{@}\ w\ g \ldots h \ldots \vdash >$$
$$\dashv \ldots \overset{\sim(2)}{@}\ v\ u\ f \ldots \overset{\sim}{@}\ w\ g \ldots h \ldots \vdash$$

We note that these abstractions introduce w as a new free variable in f and h, requiring another pass through the LETREC which returns

$$\alpha^* <^{(3)} f\ g\ h>$$
$$<^{(3)} \overset{\sim(3)}{\lambda}\ w\ u\ v\ \lambda x \dashv \ldots u \ldots v \ldots \overset{\sim}{@}\ w\ g \ldots \overset{\sim}{@}\ w\ h \ldots \overset{\sim(3)}{@}\ v\ u\ w\ f \ldots \vdash$$
$$\overset{\sim}{\lambda} w\ \lambda y \dashv \ldots w \ldots \overset{\sim}{@}\ w\ h \ldots \overset{\sim}{@}\ w\ g \ldots \vdash$$
$$\overset{\sim}{\lambda} w\ \lambda z \dashv \ldots \overset{\sim}{@}\ w\ g \ldots \overset{\sim}{@}\ w\ h \ldots \vdash >$$
$$\dashv \ldots \overset{\sim(3)}{@}\ v\ u\ w\ f \ldots \overset{\sim}{@}\ w\ g \ldots \overset{\sim}{@}\ w\ h \ldots \vdash$$

There is a more elegant way of determining minimal sets of free variables in LETREC-defined functions based on the solution of **set equations** [John85]. It avoids repeated traversals and transformations of expressions. Nevertheless, its worst case complexity is $O(k^3)$ (with k being the number of λ-abstractions under the LETREC construct) and thus is essentially in the same complexity class as converting sets of mutually recursive function equations of a high-level program into Y-combinator terms.

However, this pre-processing complexity can be reduced to $O(k)$ at the expense of some redundancy with respect to the number of free variables that are being abstracted. In a LETREC expression of the general form

$$\alpha^* <^{(k)} \ldots f\_i \ldots > <^{(k)} \ldots R\_i \ldots > s\_expr$$

we simply need to

- determine, in a first pass through it, the union of the sets of free variables of all λ-abstractions R_i, which we assume to be $\{w_1, \ldots, w_q\}$;

- add, in a second pass, the snake-binders $\overset{\sim(q)}{\lambda}\ w_1 \ldots w_q$ to all λ-abstractions R_i and replace all occurrences of the α^*-bound variables f_i in R_i and in s_expr by SNAPs of the form $\overset{\sim(q)}{@}\ w_q \ldots w_1\ f\_i$.

In our example, we thus get

$$\alpha^* <^{(3)} f\ g\ h>$$

$$<^{(3)} \overset{\sim(3)}{\boldsymbol{\lambda}}\ w\ u\ v\ \boldsymbol{\lambda} x \dashv \ldots u \ldots v \ldots \overset{\sim(3)}{@}\ v\ u\ w\ g \ldots \overset{\sim(3)}{@}\ v\ u\ w\ h \ldots \overset{\sim(3)}{@}\ v\ u\ w\ f \ldots \vdash$$

$$\overset{\sim(3)}{\boldsymbol{\lambda}}\ w\ u\ v\ \boldsymbol{\lambda} y \dashv \ldots w \ldots \overset{\sim(3)}{@}\ v\ u\ w\ h \ldots \overset{\sim(3)}{@}\ v\ u\ w\ g \ldots \vdash$$

$$\overset{\sim(3)}{\boldsymbol{\lambda}}\ w\ u\ v\ \boldsymbol{\lambda} z \dashv \ldots \overset{\sim(3)}{@}\ v\ u\ w\ g \ldots \overset{\sim(3)}{@}\ v\ u\ w\ h \ldots \vdash >$$

$$\dashv \ldots \overset{\sim(3)}{@}\ v\ u\ w\ f \ldots \overset{\sim(3)}{@}\ v\ u\ w\ g \ldots \overset{\sim(3)}{@}\ v\ u\ w\ h \ldots \vdash$$

The redundant binders must be paid for during the processing phase in terms of larger argument frames and in terms of the additional time expended to set them up. The impact of these effects on the space and time complexity of the program execution depends in an intricate way on several factors, e.g., on the degrees to which LETRECs are nested and to which variables bound higher up occur free deeper down in a LETREC hierarchy. If relatively free (or global) variables are used carefully in mutually recursive function definitions, we may expect only a marginal linear increase of both processing time and space demand, as compared to the non-redundant (or minimal) solution described before.

Fig. 9.4 shows the graph representation of this LETREC expression as generated by the pre-processor. It roughly breaks down as follows: the topmost graph node (which is what is initially set up in the stack system before processing) is a string composed of the multiple recursion operator α^+, a pointer *p_letrec* to the graph representation of the set of function-turned-supercombinator definitions and, enclosed in the delimiters $\dashv$ and $\vdash$, the graph of the LETREC body expression. The LETREC descriptor to which *p_letrec* directly points includes the number of supercombinators defined under it and a link each to the list of function names (which must be saved for re-conversion) and to a list of pointers to the supercombinator graphs. These graphs are constructed in essentially the same way: they are preceded by FUNC descriptors which include the numbers of what were the free and bound variables of the original function definitions, and a link to the lists of bound variable names and to the graphs themselves.

Occurrences of the relatively free variables u, v, w in the LETREC body are replaced by de Bruijn indices $\#i, \#j, \#k$, respectively, which refer to binders somewhere outside this expression. All occurrences of the function names f, g, h either in the LETREC body or in the supercombinator definitions are replaced by special selector applications $\int 1\ p\_letrec$, $\int 2\ p\_letrec$, $\int 3\ p\_letrec$, respectively. The selectors $1, 2, 3$ identify the index positions of the pointers to the supercombinator graphs in the list held under the LETREC descriptor. When reducing these applications during the processing phase, the respective supercombinator graphs are copied in their places.

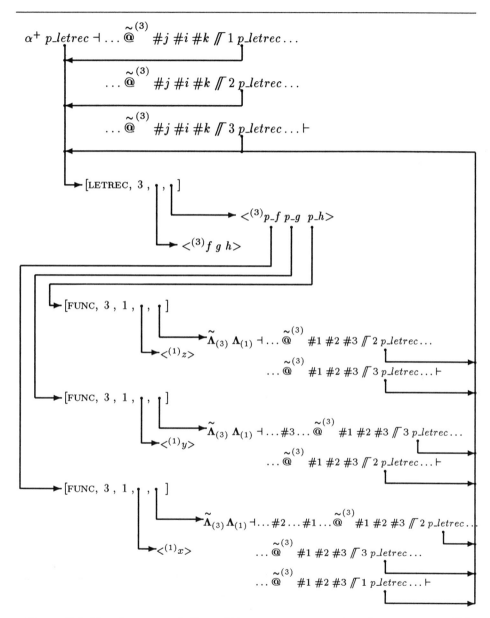

Figure 9.4: Graph representation of the LETREC expression shown on page 206

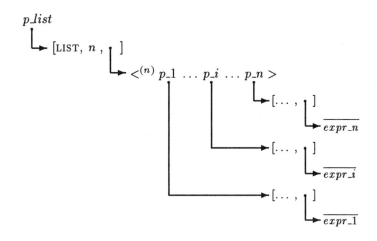

Figure 9.5: Graph representation of a list structure

The **graph** of a **list** is recursively constructed as shown in fig. 9.5. The **list** descriptor contains a link to a list of pointers to the graph representations of the subexpressions. The graph representations of **arrays** are constructed in a similar way.

In an actual system implementation, applications of all pre- and post-processing functions may be executed in one pass through the expression. All there is to be done is to modify

- the pre-processing function RENAME so that it identifies and inserts applications of the functions CLOSE and CREATE;

- the post-processing function RESOLVE so that it identifies and inserts applications of the functions SUBST and RESTORE.

9.4   The Configuration of a Hardware Machine

We are now ready to describe the basic **hardware configuration** of a reduction machine which realizes the proposed **architecture** and the underlying **graph reduction** mechanisms. It derives more or less directly from the abstract engine specified in the preceding section.

We will first consider a mono-**processor machine** supporting a virtual machine/process concept as outlined in chapter 2. To make things simple, we assume memory management in units of **regions**. Then, all static and dynamic parts of an active reduction process reside in the main memory, and all addresses (pointers) generated relative to the base of the virtual region are bound to absolute (physical) addresses at execution time.

9.4.1 The Layout of a Memory Region

The memory structures that need to be supported by the region allocated to a virtual machine/process include

- the stack system E, A, M which may be considered the **work space**, as it accommodates the part of the program expression which is actually active;

- the run-time stack R which holds the **context frames** for instantiated super-combinators;

- the **heap** which holds the program graph.

There is a **stack section** divided into two sufficiently large partitions, of which each accommodates a pair of stacks which grow towards each other. This more or less static layout creates little overhead for space management. It merely requires some monitoring of the stack top pointers to generate an interrupt if the two stacks of a partition grow into each other, i.e., we have an **overflow condition**.

The remainder of the region can be used as the **heap section**. It is expedient to divide it into two partitions as well. One is to accommodate what may be called the **static parts**, the other is to accommodate the **dynamic** (or **changeable**) **parts** of the program graph.

The static parts are basically those generated by the **pre-processor**. They typically include recursively nested LETREC constructs whose components are supercombinators. These graphs never change and generally survive the entire processing phase.

The dynamic parts include the graphs which, during the processing phase are produced and consumed, primarily in the course of performing δ-**reductions**. It also accommodates **closures** emerging from partial supercombinator applications. The pre-processor initializes this heap partition with all constant objects, other than supercombinators and LETRECs, which may occur in the body of the outermost LETREC construct of a program.

Generating and discarding graphs of varying sizes at run-time requires some space management for the dynamic heap partition which we will address in the next subsection.

The layout of a complete memory region is shown in fig. 9.6.

increasing addresses

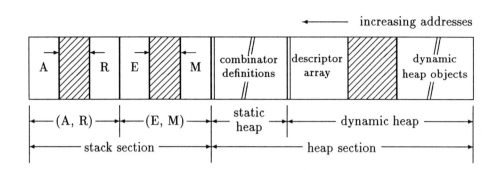

Figure 9.6: Typical layout of a memory region for a graph reduction process

If the system is equipped with a fast cache memory, then a conventional caching mechanism based on access frequencies will likely keep several of the topmost pages of all stacks permanently mapped into it.

The fact that stack accesses occur only at the stack tops suggests a slightly more sophisticated caching mechanism which tries to avoid any misses, i.e., accesses to stack pages not in the cache. This mechanism is based on a simple look-ahead scheme which works with fixed-size cache partitions of several consecutive page frames for each stack. These partitions are operated as cyclic buffers: whenever the stack-top pointer, say on a sequence of push operations, hits the lower boundary of the partition, it continues at the higher boundary, and vice versa.

Cache pages are swapped out into the main memory region from the stack bottom if only one or two empty page frames are left over in the cache partition and the stack keeps growing. Conversely, pages are swapped in at the bottom if it shrinks to just one or two cache-resident pages and the stack still extends into the main memory region.

Appropriate hardware-support provided, pages may be swapped in and out of the cache independently of and without noticeable time delay for the operations at the stack tops.

9.4.2   Heap Management

In order to manage heap space economically, its allocation and de-allocation, or at least house-keeping operations pertaining to it, must be made integral parts of reduction processes.

The most rigorous approach is based on reference counting [Col60, Knuth73]. It can be implemented so that the heap space which is actually committed is always minimized. This is done by freeing as soon as possible the space taken up by objects that are no longer needed. Since such space is referred to as **garbage**, the process of freeing it is commonly called **garbage collection**.

Conceptually, the reduction of an application consumes its components (subexpressions) and (re-)produces another expression in its place. In our graph reduction machine, the consumption and (re-)production of expressions is, to a large extent, emulated by the consumption and (re-)production of pointers to the respective graph representations. In general, a graph is shared among several pointer occurrences. The number of these pointers may be kept track of by means of an ID_COUNT field added to its descriptor. Whenever a pointer is consumed or reproduced, the contents of the ID_COUNT field are decremented or incremented accordingly.

Pointers are typically consumed in the course of performing δ-reductions and when popping run-time stack frames. They are typically reproduced when performing supercombinator reductions.

A graph can be de-allocated following the instance of pointer consumption which decrements the ID_COUNT value in its descriptor to zero. However, since substructures (or substrings) of the graph may be shared, a de-allocation procedure must in an orderly manner recursively proceed from top to bottom. Once an ID_COUNT value has become zero, only the particular descriptor and the graph representation immediately referenced by it can be safely de-allocated. Before doing this, however, all pointers to substructures contained in this level of the graph representation must be followed up to decrement the ID_COUNT values in the descriptors to which they are pointing as well. All substructures whose ID_COUNT values remain greater than zero and thus have pointers to them from somewhere else are left as they are.

When reproducing (copying) a pointer, only the ID_COUNT value in the topmost descriptor must be updated; the ID_COUNT values in the descriptors of substructures remain unchanged since no new pointers are added to them.

We remember from section 9.4.1 that the static heap partition primarily accommodates all supercombinator definitions as nested in the LETREC constructs of the initial program specification. Since these constructs can be expected to survive the larger part of the program execution, we can forgo managing the heap space in this partition at run-time, even though some of them may be actually released earlier. It also relieves us of the problem of maintaining correct reference counts in cyclic structures [Hugh82b, Bro85].

The graphs in the dynamic partition are mainly those which are consumed and reproduced during the processing phase. As is schematically shown in fig. 9.6, these graphs have their descriptors allocated in an array which dynamically grows, if necessary, from the upper address boundary of the partition downwards. Their heap segments are allocated from the lower boundary upwards. However, as the graphs are generally not produced and consumed in a LIFO-order, holes may develop in both areas. To administer them, we use a linked list each for unused descriptor entries and for holes in the heap space, and employ in both cases the segment allocation/de-allocation scheme described in section 2.3.

New graphs are in this partition primarily generated by δ-reductions of applications of primitive structuring and value-transforming functions. In most of the former cases, only a new descriptor must be allocated with a link to a new substructure of the argument object. In the latter cases, heap space for new graph representations (result structures) must be allocated as well. At least when working with formatted representations of atomic objects, the heap space demand of new graphs resulting from δ-reductions can be completely determined from the type and structural specifications contained in the descriptors of the respective arguments.

Reference counting is bound to create some overhead due to the additional memory accesses required to update the ID_COUNT entries, which happens at least twice in every reduction rule. Combining it with immediate garbage collection usually involves more effort than may be necessary. With memory capacity abundantly available, the heap space usually can be made large enough to accommodate most program runs without needing to recover too much of previously used space (in some cases even none at all). Instead, garbage may simply accumulate and only be recovered on demand, i.e., whenever no more contiguous heap space is left over to place new objects. Then the garbage collector must go in one sweep through all descriptors, searching for those whose ID_COUNT entries are down to zero and can therefore be released.

While realizing a very orderly form of house-keeping, reference counting is burdened with some implementation problems. One of them concerns a proper choice for the size (number of bits) of the ID_COUNT field. Though reference counts usually are very small (in most cases not exceeding two to three), overflow conditions may always arise in extreme situations and must be taken care of, e.g., whenever the pointer to an object is replicated many times on the run-time stack. Another problem are unpredictable time delays due to decrement operations that must be recursively propagated down through several levels of nested substructures. And finally, there is the problem of circular structures which, if not properly handled, may cause garbage to be lost forever.

To overcome these problems, we may take the argument against immediate garbage collection (i.e., generous supply of heap space) a little further and abandon reference counting altogether. Instead, we may resort to a so-called mark-and-sweep scheme which never worries about garbage until it becomes absolutely necessary to do so [McC60, Knuth73]. The idea is to allocate heap space (including descriptors) piecemeal from a contiguous chunk until it is exhausted. Then the garbage collector takes over to set in all descriptors a mark bit to zero.[22] Next the program graph and the run-time stack are searched for pointers to descriptors still in use, setting their mark bits to one. All graph structures that remain marked zero are considered garbage and in a subsequent sweep recovered as described above.

The problem with this scheme is that the computation may be suspended for considerable periods of time while collecting the garbage, and that this may happen quite frequently if heap space is in short supply. Moreover, the entire program graph and the run-time stack must be inspected to find out what is actually in use. Reference counting is more selective in this respect, touching only garbage. Also, garbage collection is more or less local and incremental, distributing the overhead rather evenly over the entire computation and thus over time.

Whichever garbage collector is employed, heap management also has to deal with the problem of steadily increasing fragmentation which from time to time may require heap compaction (see also section 2.3). The simplest form is based on a two-space copying scheme [Bak78]. It partitions the entire heap space into two equally sized sections, of which one is called the from-space, the other is called the to-space. The former is the one actually in use, the latter is the target space for compaction. Whenever fragmentation in the from-space has reached the point where no further space demands can be satisfied, all heap objects still referenced (i.e., with ID_COUNTS greater than zero or with mark bits set to one) are copied in one sweep into a contiguous area of the to-space. The objects that must be moved are identified by a so-called scavenger, and verifying that the objects have actually been moved is called scavenging. After having completely cleaned up the from-space, it is simply flipped with the to-space. Further heap space may now be allocated from the unused area of what has become the new from-space.

Two-space copying is not only rather wasteful in terms of the total heap space involved (at least half of it is always unused), but it generally causes also a considerable problem with pointers from within heap objects to others. They must all be updated to point to the new locations in the to-space. However, with the level of indirection introduced by the descriptors, the solution to this problem is rather simple in our graph reducer. Since heap compaction concerns only the space occupied by the string representations of the graph nodes but never the descriptor array (which is always densely packed), all there is to do is to go in one sweep through the descriptors and update the internal references (or links) to the subgraphs. The pointers from within the graph node strings to the descriptors need never be changed.

A more advanced form of heap compaction is life-time controlled scavenging [LiHe83]. Rather than moving all heap objects every time compaction becomes

---

[22]The mark bit replaces (or may be considered a rudimentary version of) the ID_COUNT field.

necessary, this scheme discriminates among objects of different ages. Experience shows that heap objects are likely to be discarded in the reverse order of their creation, i.e., those that come into existence early are the ones that have the best chances of survival.[23] The likelyhood that free space can be compacted in the areas occupied by objects with a long life-time is therefore very low. Thus the entire heap space may be partitioned into several sections which accommodate objects of increasing ages, and compaction generally involves only the youngest section(s). Moreover, since the majority of pointers points backwards from younger to older sections, very little pointer updating must be done. In fact, age-based scavenging is known to inflict the least overhead of all garbage collection/compaction schemes.

A detailed discussions of the pros and cons of these heap management schemes, including performance measurements, can be found in [Ung86]. For the purpose of our eager graph reducer we simply assume that it uses hardware-supported reference counting with immediate garbage collection as an integral part of performing reductions.

9.4.3 A Reduction Processor

A conceivable processing unit for our graph reducer may be implemented on the register-transfer (RT-) structure shown in fig. 9.7. Though it looks fairly conventional, function and purpose of its components are made to conform to the layout of the memory region, the heap management, and to the particularities of the internal program representation. In addition, some basic OS-kernel functions can be supported as well.

This processor includes a set of 16 word-sized general purpose registers $R0 .. R15$ and a reduction unit. No specific assumptions are made about the control unit.

The registers $R0 .. R7$ are used as temporary working registers for data, pointer and descriptor manipulations. Their contents are relevant only while actually executing reduction rules. The registers $R10 .. R15$ hold the pointers to the linked lists by which the space in the dynamic heap section is administered, and the pointers to the tops of the stacks E, A, M and R. The registers $R8$ and $R9$ respectively hold the topmost entry of the stack M and the actual reduction counter value.

The reduction unit includes the arithmetic/logic and control facilities to perform elementary register-transfer operations on the contents of the register set and to move the elements of the machine program representation in entities of words in from and out to the memory. Pragmatic design considerations pertaining to the separation of operations which serve different purposes suggest that the reduction unit be partitioned into three specialized subunits.

---

[23] Considering the highly recursive nature of functional programs, this phenomenon is not very surprising.

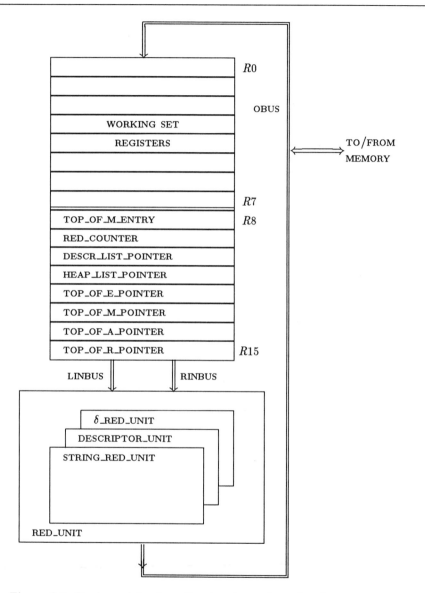

Figure 9.7: Basic register transfer structure of a reduction processor

The **string reduction unit** is to support all pre- and post-processing functions and the control program $\widehat{(EAR_h)}$ of the processing phase. It provides the controls and the integer arithmetic for fast stack pointer and general addressing/indexing operations, particularly indirect and relative addressing and index decrementation/incrementation by fixed offsets.

With these capabilities, it is also well equipped for supercombinator reductions and for structure-transforming δ-reductions, all of which primarily involve the re-arrangement of pointers, combined with relative (indexed) and indirect addressing.

The **descriptor unit** provides fast decoding and comparison logic for the identification of object types and structural specifications of graphs, and for compatibility tests on the arguments of δ-redexes. It also includes the logic circuitry which assembles new descriptors from specifications contained in the descriptors of existing objects.

The δ-**reduction unit** is designated to perform fast numerical operations on structured data objects. A minimal version should at least provide hardware support for floating point and BCD-arithmetic. A sophisticated implementation may include

- a two-stage arithmetic pipeline for the speedy computation of inner vector products;

- up to three address generators which, under complete micro-program control, traverse the graphs involved in δ-reductions.

All three subunits are linked up to two input bus systems LINBUS and RINBUS and to an output bus system OBUS, which also includes the interface to the memory.

9.5 Concurrent Processing Re-Examined

With the introduction of graph reduction mechanisms we need to take another look at non-sequential program execution and its implementation.[24] The sharing of graphs among several concurrently executable (or executing) reduction processes favors quite naturally a classical multi-processor configuration featuring a shared memory, as opposed to a distributed system of cooperating reduction machines as described in section 7.2.

9.5.1 Concurrent Graph Reduction

From chapter 7 we recall that non-sequential program execution is conceptually based on the transformation of OREL/0 expressions of the general form

$$expr = \dashv \dots sub\_expr\_1 \dots sub\_expr\_n \dots \vdash$$

---

[24] The concept and system implementation described in this section are based on thesis work by Zimmer [Zim91].

into

$$@^{(n)} sub\_expr\_n \ldots sub\_expr\_1 \; \lambda^{(n)} t_1 \ldots t_n \; \dashv \ldots t_1 \ldots t_n \ldots \vdash$$

by the abstraction of syntactically independent subexpressions which are considered suitable candidates for concurrent processing. The underlying applicative order semantics demands that the operand expressions of this application be reduced to their normal forms before the complementary β-reductions are carried out. These operand expressions may be reduced in any order and thus under the control of several processes.

In chapter 7 we introduced the notion of pseudo-applications to specify explicitly transformations by which processes are created and synchronized and to distinguish these transformations from the reduction of applications specified in the program text. In particular, we had pseudo-applications of

- an operator $\Uparrow$ which were to effect the abstraction of expressions from a given syntactical context and the subsequent creation of slave processes for their reduction;

- an operator $\Downarrow$ which were to effect the substitution of expressions for place-holders in a given syntactical context, thereby synchronizing slave processes with a master process.

In our graph reduction concept, we use these pseudo-applications in a slightly different way. We simply rewrite the above application as

$$@_p^{(n)} \; \overline{@_p} \Uparrow \; sub\_expr\_n \ldots \overline{@_p} \Uparrow \; sub\_expr\_1 \; \Downarrow^{(n)} t_1 \ldots t_n \; \dashv \ldots t_1 \ldots t_n \ldots \vdash$$

to specify process creation and synchronization operations explicitly and by means of a standardized divide-and-conquer template.

The term $\Downarrow^{(n)} t_1 \ldots t_n \; \dashv \ldots t_1 \ldots t_n \ldots \vdash$ defines a non-recursive λ-abstraction in which the symbol $\Downarrow^{(n)}$ replaces $\lambda^{(n)}$ only for syntactical reasons. In the body of this abstraction, we may have free occurrences of variables other than place-holders, in terms of which the original expression $expr$ is defined. These variables are usually bound in a larger context.

When α-converting this abstraction to its de Bruijn representation, we obtain the template

$$@_p^{(n)} \; \overline{@_p} \Uparrow \; sub\_expr\_n \ldots \overline{@_p} \Uparrow \; sub\_expr\_1 \; \ddagger_{(n)} \; \dashv \ldots \#(n-1) \ldots \#0 \ldots \vdash$$

where $\ddagger_{(n)}$ denotes a nameless binder equivalent to $\Lambda_{(n)}$. α-conversions affecting all other variable occurrences in the abstraction body generate de Bruijn indices greater than $\#(n-1)$. They are relatively free with respect to the bindings defined by $\Downarrow_{(n)}$.

We will use these **templates** as **control devices** for concurrent graph reductions. Their reduction is, again, made dependent on a system-supported **ticket alloca-tion/de-allocation mechanism** similar to the one described in chapter 7. However, its sole purpose here is to put an upper limit on the number of processes which at any given time participate in the concurrent execution of a program. The tickets will not be required to identify syntactical positions for subexpressions abstracted from expressions. This will now be accomplished by other means which merely require a ticket pool filled with a finite number of **nameless place-holders** $\square$.

A pseudo-application $\overline{@}_p \Uparrow sub\_expr\_i$ in the i-th operand position of a divide-and-conquer template now reduces to

- a place-holder symbol $\square$ if one can be taken out of the pool, creating as a side effect a slave process (i, sub_expr_i) for the computation of $m \llbracket sub\_expr\_i \rrbracket$;

- $m \llbracket sub\_expr\_i \rrbracket$ in place if the ticket pool is temporarily empty.

A terminating slave process returns $(i, m \llbracket sub\_expr\_i \rrbracket)$ to the master process. It releases its place-holder ticket to the pool upon inserting $m \llbracket sub\_expr\_i \rrbracket$ into the operand position i of the template that is under the control of the master.

Occurrences of place-holder symbols in a template represent unspecified or in-valid arguments for the abstraction $\Downarrow_{(n)} \dashv \ldots \#(n-1) \ldots \#0 \ldots \vdash$ in its opera-tor positions. The pseudo-application remains irreducible (or constant) until all place-holders are eventually substituted by legitimate OREL/0 expressions. We may therefore consider the abstraction in conjunction with the outermost pseudo-applicator of the template a **synchronization operator** which becomes activated upon the availability of legitimate arguments.

To simplify the reduction of divide-and-conquer templates and to keep the over-head for process management low, we demand that slave processes be created either for all operand expressions in **one sweep**, or for none at all. This can easily be real-ized by trying to claim from the ticket pool à priori as many tickets as are specified by the arities of the templates.

Since pseudo-applications are not supposed to appear in the high-level program representation displayed at the user interface, the transformations that are nec-essary to introduce these templates into a program need to be carried out by the **pre-processor**. Conversely, the **post-processor** must re-transform left-over divide-and-conquer templates into the original expressions.

Following the suggestions made in chapter 7 for a strictly demand-controlled uti-lization of program-inherent concurrency, the pre-processor must select for transfor-mations into divide-and-conquer templates largest possible (lists of) (sub-)expressions in which at least two concurrently executable applications of defined functions (supercombinators) can be identified.

Subexpressions which qualify for transformations into divide-and-conquer templates may be found in all body expressions of supercombinators defined under LETREC constructs and in the respective goal expressions. They are primarily characterized by occurrences of LETREC-bound variables (or supercombinator names) in operator positions of (nested) applications.

In an efficient pre-processor implementation, these transformations can neatly be integrated into the functions CLOSE and ABSTRACT which, in general terms, abstract expressions from expressions. Likewise, re-transformations of left-over divide-and-conquer templates can be integrated into the post-processing function SUBST which, again in general terms, undoes abstractions performed by the pre-processor.

Rather than giving formal specifications, we will now demonstrate by means of a small example how by the pre-processor a program is prepared for concurrent processing, how it is actually executed during the processing phase, and how it is post-processed.

To avoid unnecessary details, we use again a non-terminating and, hence, meaningless program:

DEFINE
$$f(x, y) = ((f(y, x) * g(y)) + y)$$
$$g(u) \quad = f(u, g(u))$$
IN $f(a, b)$

We immediately recognize that the applications of the defined functions f and g specified in the body expression of f can be executed concurrently. They are arguments of the application of the primitive function $*$ and thus independent of each other. In the body expression of the function g we have no concurrency since the application of f depends on the application of g.

When permitting just two concurrent reduction steps, the program conceptually transforms as follows:

DEFINE
$$f(x, y) = ((f(y, x) * g(y)) + y)$$
$$g(u) \quad = f(u, g(u))$$
IN $f(a, b)$

$$\Downarrow \qquad\qquad \text{(by reduction of } f(a, b))$$

DEFINE

$$f(x, y) = ((f(y, x) * g(y)) + y)$$
$$g(u) = f(u, g(u))$$

IN $((f(b, a) * g(b)) + b)$

$$\Downarrow \qquad\qquad \text{(by reduction of } f(b, a) \text{ and } g(b))$$

DEFINE

$$f(x, y) = ((f(y, x) * g(y)) + y)$$
$$g(u) = f(u, g(u))$$

IN $((((f(a, b) * g(a)) + a) * f(b, g(b))) + b)$

To prepare the initial program for execution in our graph reduction system, it must first be converted into the equivalent OREL/0 expression by the front-end processor:

$$\alpha^* \; <^{(2)}f \; g><^{(2)}\lambda^{(2)}x \; y \; @^{(2)}y \; @^{(2)}@^{(1)}y \; g \; @^{(2)}x \; y \; f \; * \; +$$
$$\lambda^{(1)}u \; @^{(2)}@^{(1)}u \; g \; u \; f>$$
$$@^{(2)}b \; a \; f \; .$$

The pre-processor transforms this expression into the concurrently executable program graph shown in fig. 9.8.

We note that the body of the function f is transformed into a divide-and-conquer template. In the operand positions of this template we find pseudo-applications of the operator $\Uparrow$ to the de Bruijn representations of the abstracted applications $@^{(2)}x \; y \; f$ and $@^{(1)}y \; g$. Its operator position is taken up by a pointer p_abs to the abstraction

$$\sharp_{(2)}@^{(2)}\#2 \; @^{(2)}\#1 \; \#0 \; * \; + \; .$$

The indices $\#0$ and $\#1$ bound by $\sharp_{(2)}$ identify the place-holder positions for the abstracted applications. The relatively free index $\#2$ appears in the place of the formal parameter y of the function f.

The pre-processor need not transform this abstraction into a supercombinator. Since it is not recursive, it can be invoked only once inside an instantiated function (combinator) f. Thus, if the respective run-time stack frames are directly pushed on top of each other (i.e., without a separation symbol in between), all de Bruijn indices within the abstraction body specify correct displacements relative to the stack-top.

We now consider the non-sequential execution of this program as seen by the initial process (or virtual machine). The sequence of reductions performed by this process on the divide-and-conquer template applies recursively to all subprocesses which reduce applications of the function f.

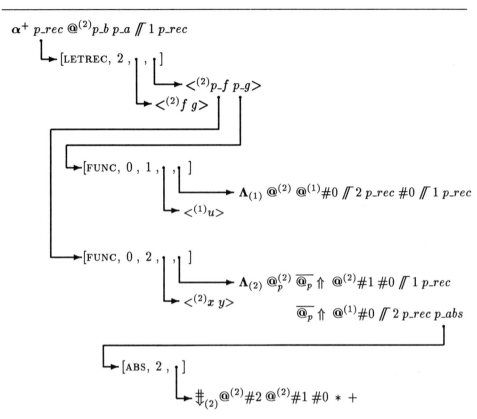

Figure 9.8: Concurrently executable graph representation of the program

DEFINE
$$f(x, y) = ((f(y, x) * g(y)) + y)$$
$$g(u) \quad = f(u, g(u))$$
IN $f(a, b)$

Some characteristic phases of this reduction sequence are illustrated in fig. 9.9. It sets out, in fig. 9.9.a, with the situation following the reduction of the combinator application $@^{(2)}p\_b\ p\_a\ /\!\!/ 1\ p\_rec$. The divide-and-conquer template which makes up the body expression of f is copied into stack E, and the stack frame specifying its context is set up in R (this stack is dropped from the phases shown in figs. 9.9.b to 9.9.f during which it remains unchanged).

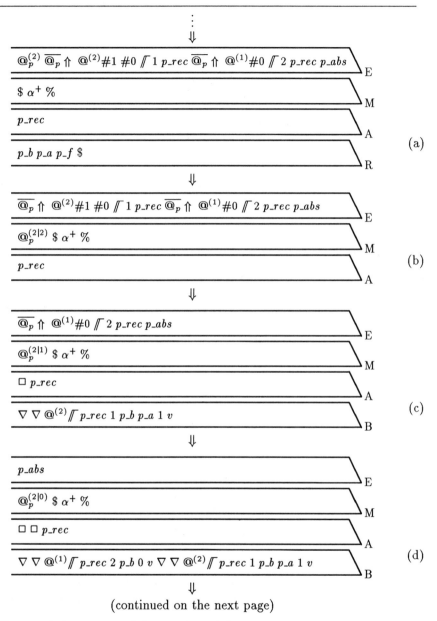

Figure 9.9: Non-sequential execution of the program shown in fig. 9.8

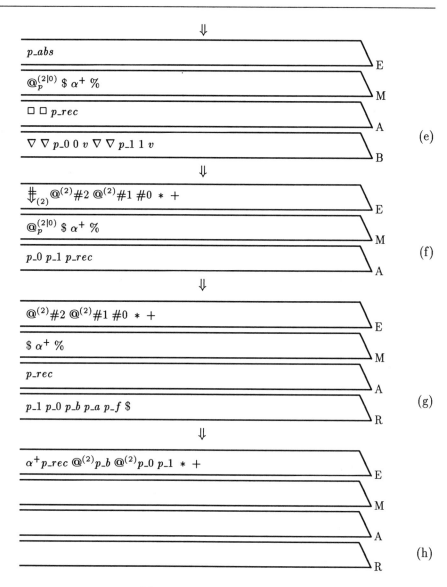

Figure 9.9: continued

Having pushed the topmost pseudo-applicator $@_p^{(2)}$ into stack M (fig. 9.9.b), the control program $\widehat{EAR_h}$ now encounters in succession two normal-order pseudo-applications of the operator $\Uparrow$. They reduce to place-holder symbols $\square$ and, as side effects, embed their operand expressions into **packet constructs** of the form $\nabla v\ \nabla i\ sub\_expr\_i$. These packets are traversed into a buffer area B, from where they are picked up for the creation of slave processes (fig. 9.9.c/d). The packet parameter v identifies the current process as the master. The index i identifies the place-holder position relative to the top of stack A into which the pointer of the expression returned by the slave process must be inserted. This index is taken from the actual arity count index of the pseudo-applicator that is on top of M. The process suspends itself on having decremented this index to zero. At this point, we have the identifier p_abs of the abstraction on top of stack E, forming together with the pseudo-applicator on top of M a **synchronization operator** which is not yet enabled.

It is important to note that the expressions prepared by the pre-processor for concurrent execution are supercombinator applications. The emerging slave processes therefore always start (and terminate) their virtual machines with empty run-time stacks. No stack entries in the run-time stacks of the respective master processes need be accessed. Sharing is restricted to graphs.

Each packet returned to the suspended process via the buffer B (fig. 9.9.e) is disassembled, and the identifier p_i of the resulting expression replaces the respective place-holder symbol in stack A. The synchronization operator and hence the process is reactivated once both place-holders are substituted (fig. 9.9.f). It now continues with the reduction of the pseudo-application of the abstraction identified by p_abs which moves the topmost two identifiers from stack A to R (fig. 9.9.g). Thus, the de Bruijn indices in the abstraction body refer to the correct index positions of the argument pointers in stack R.

Assuming that the reduction counter allows each process to perform just one supercombinator reduction, the processing phase terminates with the expression shown in fig. 9.9.h. The pointers p_0 and p_1 returned by the slave processes represent the expressions

$$@^{(2)}@^{(1)}p\_b \parallel 2\ p\_rec\ p\_b \parallel 1\ p\_rec$$

and

$$@_p^{(2)}\ \overline{@_p} \Uparrow @^{(2)}p\_b\ p\_a \parallel 1\ p\_rec$$
$$\overline{@_p} \Uparrow @^{(1)}p\_a \parallel 2\ p\_rec$$
$$\sharp_{(2)}\ @^{(2)}p\_a\ @^{(2)}\#1\ \#0\ *\ +\ ,$$

respectively.

The post-processor re-transforms this expression into the string representation

$$\alpha^* \;<^{(2)}f\;g>\;<^{(2)}\lambda^{(2)}x\;y\;@^{(2)}y\;@^{(2)}@^{(1)}y\;g\;@^{(2)}x\;y\;f\;*\;+$$
$$\lambda^{(1)}u\;@^{(2)}@^{(1)}u\;g\;u\;f>$$
$$@^{(2)}b\;@^{(2)}@^{(2)}@^{(1)}b\;g\;b\;f\;@^{(2)}a\;@^{(2)}@^{(1)}a\;g\;@^{(2)}b\;a\;f\;*\;+\;*\;+\;,$$

thereby also reducing the left-over divide-and-conquer template.

Re-converting this OREL/0 expression into a high-level program finally yields, as expected,

DEFINE
$$f(x,y) = ((f(y,x)*g(y))+y)$$
$$g(u) \;\;= f(u,g(u))$$
IN $((((f(a,b)*g(a))+a)*f(b,g(b)))+b)$.

9.5.2 A Multi-Processor Graph Reduction System

Fig. 9.10 schematically shows how concurrent graph reduction can be supported on a multi-processor system configuration. It includes

- a set of some $k \leq 16$ reduction processors RP_1..RP_k which are equipped with fast local memories LM_1..LM_k of medium capacities of, say, up to 4 MBytes;

- a large global memory MEM of ≥ 16 MBytes capacity, to which all processing units have shared access via

- a fast memory bus MEMBUS which by a hard-wired arbitration scheme is allocated to processors competing for memory access cycles.

A separate operating system (OS-) machine (not shown in fig. 9.10) equipped with its own processing unit and working memory controls the peripheral devices and provides the usual OS-services. In particular, it realizes the front-end processor which supports the interactive functional programming environment and converts HLFL program specifications into OREL/0 expressions and vice versa.

The multi-processor system is assumed to be operated by the OS-machine in a batch-processing mode: OREL/0 expressions are processed one at a time. The OS-machine creates an initial master process in the multi-processor system by submitting an OREL/0 expression to it, and it terminates this process upon receiving a partially or completely reduced expression from it. To do so, the OS-machine has privileged access to the global memory MEM via a special bus interface.

The process hierarchies that dynamically evolve inside the multi-processor system are managed by a small OS-kernel which in identical copies is installed at the upper

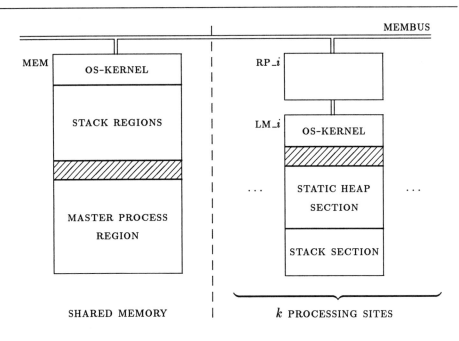

Figure 9.10: A multi-processor configuration

ends of the local memories. All data structures that need to be shared among these local process managers are held in a region at the upper end of the global memory. The remaining address space of the global memory and of the local memories is available for program execution.

The os-machine claims a fairly large region for the initial master process at the low end of the global memory, which is partitioned into sections as schematically shown in fig. 9.6. The static and dynamic parts of the heap section are shared with the emerging hierarchy of slave processes. The contents of the stack section, however, are process-specific: they completely define the state of computation of the master process. To accommodate the process-specific stacks of the slave processes, the os-machine also establishes in the global memory a set of some $u * k$ stack regions. The sizes of the master process region and of the stack regions may be specified by the user according to the expected space demands of the program.

All local memories may accommodate a stack section and a static heap section under the same absolute addresses as in the region of the master process. As a final step of the pre-processing phase, the static heap of the master process is downloaded into all local memories. A slave process that becomes active on a particular reduction processor instantiates the stack section in the respective local memory with the contents of its stack region. Conversely, a terminated or suspended process copies its actual stack contents back into its region. Thus, all accesses performed by a process to its stacks and to the static heap can be serviced by the local memories. Only the dynamic heap must be shared in the global memory.

Process scheduling follows the scheme illustrated in fig. 9.11. To allocate the processing units RP_1..RP_k to executable processes and to represent global process states, the schedulers incorporated into the local os-kernels employ the usual queues and tables. In addition, there is a **buffer area** to communicate expressions among the processes. These data structures are shared among all local os-kernels and therefore held in the os-region of the global memory. Access to them may be controlled by

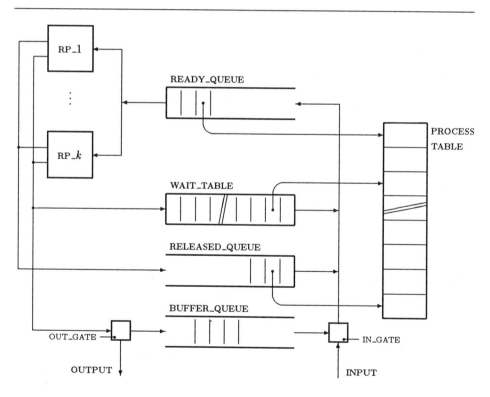

Figure 9.11: Process scheduling scheme

means of semaphores or of a monitor.

The process table is implemented as an array of some $u * k + 1$ context block frames whose indices are from the interval $[0 .. u * k]$. The frame with index 0 is always allocated to the initial master process. All other frames may be allocated in any order to the processes of the hierarchy. Pointers to unused context block frames are held in the *released_queue* which in fact constitutes the ticket pool. The *ready_queue* and the *wait_table* respectively hold the frame pointers of executable processes and of processes waiting for the synchronization with slaves.

Since we may have up to $u * k$ slave processes circulating about the system in addition to the initial master process, we also need as many regions to accommodate their stack sections. In order to facilitate the creation and termination of processes, it is expedient to bind context block frames from the interval $[1 .. u * k]$ to the same stack regions at least for the duration of a particular program run. The frame with index 0 remains bound to the region allocated to the master process.

A good choice for the total number of processes may be derived from the following consideration: a process hierarchy branches at least two-fold, i.e., we get two slave processes for every master process temporarily suspending itself. This amounts to $m - 1$ processes in the *wait* state for m executable processes.

To keep all k processing units of the system busy, we therefore need to expand process hierarchies to at least $2 * k$ processes, of which at most k are executable. This, however, leaves us with an empty *ready_queue*, i.e., with no processes by which a terminating process could be immediately replaced. Experience shows that idling processors can be avoided if the process capacity is raised to some value $\geq 3 * k$, in which case a sufficient number of executable processes fills the *ready_queue*.

A free processing unit is by its local scheduler allocated as quickly as possible to the process held in the first position of the *ready_queue*. Simultaneous requests for executable processes by several schedulers are serviced in an arbitrary order. A processing unit stays idle only if the *ready_queue* is (temporarily) exhausted.

An active process releases the processing unit it holds in possession

- either by suspending itself temporarily upon creating slave processes;

- or by terminating itself either upon exhausting its reduction counter value or upon having computed a normal form.

Before the processor is released in the former case, it instantiates the context block frames allocated to the emerging processes, traverses the expressions to be executed by them from the buffer area into the respective stack regions, and finally appends the pointers to the context blocks to the *ready_queue*.

In the latter case, the processor returns the pointer of the resulting expression to the suspended master process and inserts it into the proper place-holder position.

In doing this, the processor uses the parameters of the packet header attached to the identifier. The process thus synchronized with a slave remains in the *wait* state if synchronizations with further slaves are still pending, and returns to the *ready* state otherwise.

10 A Lazy Graph Reduction Engine

We will now look at another high-level interpreter for OREL/0 which performs lazy graph reductions. The basic concept of this engine, particularly the realization of full β-reductions, was first published by Berkling in 1986 [Berk86]. An architecture for Berkling's engine (based on a language called THORPE) and a formal derivation for it are described by Hilton [Hil87, Hil90]. For reasons of consistency we have taken the liberty to adapt this concept to the machinery and graph representations introduced in the preceding chapter.

Lazy evaluation is a clever implementation technique for normal order reductions which produces normal forms without engaging in redundant computations. It was introduced by Wadsworth [Wads71] and Vuillemin [Vui74], and first applied to functional versions of LISP [HeMo76, FrWi76]. The basic idea is to avoid repeated evaluations of argument expressions that are being duplicated in the course of performing normal order β- (or combinator) reductions. This is accomplished by substituting pointers to graph representations of unevaluated arguments and by sharing their reductions among possibly several pointer occurrences. These reductions are carried out only to the extent absolutely necessary, and at most once. Thus, we can expect to arrive at normal forms with the shortest possible reduction sequences, provided the programs are irredundantly specified.

Lazy evaluation requires that, in addition to constant expressions, all applications are converted into graph nodes as well. Program graphs are reduced to their normal forms by systematically overwriting reducible application nodes with semantically equivalent graphs.

The call-by-need regime of lazy evaluation requires that the arguments of applications be reduced only as far as is necessary to make the particular functions applicable. This implies that the reduction of the arguments be controlled by the functions themselves rather than by specific applicators. Thus, we need only one applicator for lazy languages.

All defined functions (internally represented as λ-abstractions or supercombinators) are applied to their arguments as they are, i.e., without reducing them.

Primitive functions generally require that their arguments be reduced to so-called canonical forms, i.e., to terms which are either constant or whose outermost syntactical nodes are constructors other than applicators. In particular,

- value-transforming functions and conditionals must have their arguments reduced to normal forms in order to be able to decide about type compatibilities and to perform the respective δ-reductions. These functions are therefore said to be strict with respect to their arguments.

• primitive **structure-transforming functions** such as SELECT or APPEND are strict in their structuring parameters but **non-strict** with respect to the structured argument. This is to say that these arguments must only be reduced to the extent that outermost applicators disappear.

If the expressions thus obtained are structured objects, i.e., arrays or lists, then the respective δ-reductions can actually be carried out, provided that the objects conform to the values of the structuring parameters. Otherwise the functions are not applicable.

Arrays are rather tedious canonical forms since they are constant objects by definition and thus in normal form. The interesting canonical forms are lists whose component expressions need not be in normal form before they can be re-structured. This simple fact gives rise to a special semantics of **lazy lists** which is advocated to entail an elegant way of programming finite problems using infinite structures.

To give an idea of how this works, we consider again a program which computes the product of all integers from the interval $[m \ldots n]$ with $m \leq n$ (of which another version has been extensively discussed in section 5.1). It has the form[25]

DEFINE
$$f(u, v) \quad\quad = \;<u, v, f((u + 1), (u * v))>$$
$$prod(m, n) = \text{DEFINE}$$
$$\qquad g(y) = \text{IF} \quad\quad (\text{SELECT}(1, y) = (n + 1))$$
$$\qquad\qquad\qquad \text{THEN} \;\; \text{SELECT}(2, y)$$
$$\qquad\qquad\qquad \text{ELSE} \;\; g(\text{SELECT}(3, y))$$
$$\qquad \text{IN} \; g(f(m, 1))$$
$$\text{IN} \; prod(2, 7) \,.$$

This program admittedly looks a little complicated, but it exhibits the basic construction scheme in a nutshell. It is specified in terms of two recursive functions, of which $f(u, v)$ obviously does not contain a termination condition, i.e., it is a **free-running generator** (or **producer**) for a list. If this function would be applied, say, to the arguments $u = 2$, $v = 1$ and reduced in **applicative order**, it would generate the infinite list structure

$$<2, 1, <3, 2, <4, 6, <5, 24, <6, 120, < \ldots \,.$$

However, the recursive subfunction $g(y)$ of $prod(m, n)$, in conjunction with a lazy evaluation (or call-by-need) regime, controls step-by-step the construction and subsequent decomposition of this list, and eventually enforces termination.

---

[25] For convenience, we use here a primitive selector function SELECT(i, y) which returns the i-th component of an n-ary list substituted for y, provided that $n \geq i$.

The trick that is being played here is that the controlling (or consumer) function g recursively receives as arguments (applications of the function SELECT to) applications of the function f which have the form $f(a, b)$, where a and b denote unevaluated arithmetic expressions. These arguments are, after the substitution of pointers to them for free occurrences of the variable y in the body of the function g, reduced to the point where they have the canonical form $<a, b, f((a+1), (a*b))>$. Such list structures emerge as by-products of forcing the reduction of the predicate expressions of the IF-THEN-ELSE clauses to normal forms. They are shared among all other pointer occurrences, i.e., among all places originally held by occurrences of the variable y.

As long as the predicate reduces to FALSE, the reduction continues with applications of the form

$$g(\text{SELECT}(3, <a, b, f((a+b), (a*b))>))$$

in the alternative; otherwise it terminates with the normal form (value) of the expression b as a result of reducing the consequence.

Non-termination of the list-generating function f is prevented solely by the fact that under lazy evaluation the function SELECT does not force the reduction of its argument beyond having reached the canonical form of a list structure.

The lazy evaluation of the above program is in fig. 10.1 illustrated as it may be observed at the user interface of a lazy graph reduction system which is capable of restoring HLFL representations (the DEFINE constructs are in all but one case omitted). We note that all reductions are delayed until they become absolutely necessary, and that reductions are shared among all occurrences of applications that are being duplicated by argument pointer substitutions.

Programming with infinite structures, though widely considered to be an attractive feature of functional languages, is a somewhat controversial issue whose benefits are in many cases arguable. For instance, our example can be decidedly more concisely specified as

DEFINE
$$prod(m, n) = \text{IF} \quad (m \text{ LE } n)$$
$$\text{THEN} \ (n * prod(m, (n - 1)))$$
$$\text{ELSE} \ 1$$
IN $prod(2, 7)$,

and more efficiently be executed as well. The same applies to many other problems praised as good examples in kind. However, there are also a variety of convincing application problems which have been discussed in the literature [HuAn88, BiWa88]. Careful consideration must in each case be given to the particular problem at hand and to the language constructs that are available to formulate it as a program.

$$prod(2,7)$$
$$\Downarrow$$

DEFINE
$$g(y) \;=\; \text{IF} \quad (\text{SELECT}(1,y) = 8)$$
$$\text{THEN } \text{SELECT}(2,y)$$
$$\text{ELSE } g(\text{SELECT}(3,y))$$
IN $g(f(2,1))$

$$\Downarrow$$

IF $\quad (\text{SELECT}(1, f(2,1)) = 8)$
THEN $\text{SELECT}(2, f(2,1))$
ELSE $g(\text{SELECT}(3, f(2,1)))$

$$\Downarrow$$

IF $\quad (\text{SELECT}(1, <2, 1, f((2+1),(2*1))>) = 8)$
THEN $\text{SELECT}(2, <2, 1, f((2+1),(2*1))>)$
ELSE $g(\text{SELECT}(3, <2, 1, f((2+1),(2*1))>))$

$$\Downarrow$$

IF $\quad (2 = 8)$
THEN $\text{SELECT}(2, <2, 1, f((2+1),(2*1))>)$
ELSE $g(\text{SELECT}(3, <2, 1, f((2+1),(2*1))>))$

$$\Downarrow$$

$g(\text{SELECT}(3, <2, 1, f((2+1),(2*1))>))$

$$\Downarrow$$

IF $\quad (\text{SELECT}(1, \text{SELECT}(3, <2, 1, f((2+1),(2*1))>)) = 8)$
THEN $\text{SELECT}(2, \text{SELECT}(3, <2, 1, f((2+1),(2*1))>))$
ELSE $g(\text{SELECT}(3, \text{SELECT}(3, <2, 1, f((2+1),(2*1))>)))$

$$\Downarrow$$

IF $\quad (\text{SELECT}(1, f((2+1),(2*1))) = 8)$
THEN $\text{SELECT}(2, f((2+1),(2*1)))$
ELSE $g(\text{SELECT}(3, f((2+1),(2*1))))$

$$\Downarrow$$

(continued on the next page)

Figure 10.1: Lazy evaluation of the function application $prod(2,7)$

$$\Downarrow$$

IF   (SELECT$(1, <(2+1),(2*1),f(((2+1)+1),((2+1)*(2*1)))>) = 8)$
THEN SELECT$(2, <(2+1),(2*1),f(((2+1)+1),((2+1)*(2*1)))>)$
ELSE $g($SELECT$(3, <(2+1),(2*1),f(((2+1)+1),((2+1)*(2*1)))>))$

$$\Downarrow$$

IF $((2+1) = 8)$
THEN SELECT$(2, <(2+1),(2*1),f(((2+1)+1),((2+1)*(2*1)))>)$
ELSE $g($SELECT$(3, <(2+1),(2*1),f(((2+1)+1),((2+1)*(2*1)))>))$

$$\Downarrow$$

IF $(3 = 8)$
THEN SELECT$(2, <3,(2*1),f((3+1),(3*(2*1)))>)$
ELSE $g($SELECT$(3, <3,(2*1),f((3+1),(3*(2*1)))>))$

$$\Downarrow$$

$g($SELECT$(3, <3,(2*1),f((3+1),(3*(2*1)))>))$

$$\Downarrow$$

$$\vdots$$

$$\Downarrow$$

$g($SELECT$(3, <8,(7*(6*(5*(4*(3*(2*1)))))),f(\ldots)>))$

$$\Downarrow$$

$$\vdots$$

$$\Downarrow$$

SELECT$(2, <8,(7*(6*(5*(4*(3*(2*1)))))),f(\ldots)>)$

$$\Downarrow$$

$(7*(6*(5*(4*(3*(2*1))))))$

$$\Downarrow$$

$$\vdots$$

$$\Downarrow$$

5040

Figure 10.1: continued

We will not engage in a detailed discussion of this issue since it is outside the scope of this monograph. The point to be made here is that this programming style can be had in graph reduction systems which are based on a lazy evaluation regime.

10.1   The Implementation of Lazy Graph Reductions

When designing a lazy graph reduction engine for OREL/0 expressions, we can adopt in slightly modified form the machinery of the eager graph reducer described in chapter 9. Other than needing to transform applications into graph nodes as well, we can basically use the same internal program representations and, in slightly modified form, most of the pre- and post-processing functions. The stack-based shunting yard mechanisms may also be employed more or less as they are to traverse program expressions in search for instances of reductions and to actually execute them.

However, the data structures for the representation of (recursively nested) function instantiations, i.e., the run-time environment, must be changed to the extent that supporting full-fledged β-reductions on open λ-abstractions becomes decidedly more rational and effective than abiding by supercombinator reductions.

We remember that the purpose of using supercombinators is to eliminate the potential for name clashes altogether rather than dealing with them dynamically at run-time. Our eager graph reduction engine shows that supercombinator reductions are fairly easy to implement in conjunction with an applicative order reduction discipline. Representing a complete supercombinator instantiation requires a single run-time stack frame containing pointers to graphs which are in normal form. Stack frames specifying different supercombinator instantiations are totally unrelated to each other. No references need ever be made to another but the actual topmost stack frame.

The lazy graph reducer to be discussed in the sequel works with a more sophisticated run-time structure for the following reason. Functions are generally applied to unreduced argument expressions represented as recursively nested graphs. When delaying the substitution of de Bruijn indices in these argument graphs until it becomes absolutely necessary to compute their canonical forms, they must inevitably carry with them the complete environments in which they are instantiated. This can be readily accomplished by pairing the pointers to these graphs with pointers to the respective argument frames. Since this applies recursively to the entries in the frames as well, they are in fact connected by pointer chains.

A run-time environment which mimics β-reductions of open λ-abstractions must be implemented in essentially the same way. Its frames accommodate only the instantiations of the variables (de Bruijn indices) bound in (or local to) λ-abstractions. Frames which form coherent environments are connected by pointer chains realized as additional frame entries. Instantiations of the local variables within the body of a λ-abstraction that is about to be reduced can be directly accessed in the most recent frame. Instantiations of global (or relatively free) variables must be accessed indirectly in frames located deeper down in the environment via pointer chains.

Thus, in a lazy graph reduction engine with delayed substitution we can directly support full-fledged β-reductions with negligible additional costs. The advantages are two-fold. We avoid

- the redundancy caused by supercombinator reductions due to the repeated copying and stacking of pointers to non-local arguments;

- the conversion of open λ-abstractions into (snake-applications of) supercombinators by the pre-processor and their re-conversion by the post-processor.

In the following, we separate, for reasons of clarity, the description of the basic lazy graph reduction mechanisms from the implementation of the run-time environment necessary to support full β-reductions. In the remainder of this section, we will outline the transformations to be performed by a lazy graph reducer on graph representations of OREL/0 expressions, and how these graph transformations can be mechanized using our familiar shunting yard technique.

10.1.1 Lazy Graph Representations of OREL/0 Expressions

To prepare string representations of OREL/0 expressions for lazy graph reductions, we simply need to include in the pre-processor the transformation of applications to graphs. This must, of course, be complemented by including into the post-processor their re-conversion into strings. Instead, we can drop the pre-processing functions CLOSE and ABSTRACT together with the post-processing function SUBST for our lazy graph reduction engine performs full-fledged β-reductions on λ-abstractions as they are.

The reduction of argument expressions is under lazy evaluation solely controlled by the functions that are applied to them. We therefore need only applications of the form

$$\phi^{(r)} \, arg\_r \ldots arg\_1 \, func \,,$$

where $\phi^{(r)}$ denotes an applicator which has no bearing on reduction orders.

When creating graphs, we must pay attention to an important detail. A lazy graph reducer overwrites application nodes by graphs representing the respective normal or canonical forms. These nodes are in our particular graphs represented

by application descriptors (or AP-descriptors for short). The functional character
of reductions implies that instances of application graphs are overwritten at most
once. When reducing applications of λ-abstractions we can therefore generally not
overwrite the λ-abstraction graphs directly since the program may produce several
instances of them in different environments (or with different sets of arguments).
Instead, we must work with copies of the original graphs which use their own sets of
AP-descriptors for reductions. These new descriptors may be allocated dynamically
while copying λ-abstraction graphs. Their contents are taken over from the original
descriptors.

To distinguish AP-descriptors that can be overwritten from those that cannot,
we must introduce special markings which may be included as flag bits into the tag
fields of the respective pointers. Application graphs specified inside the bodies of
λ-abstractions have the pointers to them marked, applications specified elsewhere
remain unmarked. Unmarked pointers to applications may be directly overwritten.
Marked pointers need to be replaced with unmarked pointers to new AP-descriptor
instances.

10.1.2   Rewriting Graphs

To illustrate how a lazy graph reducer must rewrite a program graph, we consider as
a simple example the application of a non-recursive λ-abstraction to an unevaluated
argument. In the syntax of OREL/0 it has the form

$$ \phi^{(1)}\phi^{(2)}3\ 2\ +\ \lambda^{(1)}x\ \phi^{(2)}\phi^{(2)}1\ x\ -\ x\ * \ . $$

The graph of this application is shown in fig. 10.2.a. All AP-descriptor nodes are
annotated with indices which make it easier to follow up on what is overwritten by
what in the course of performing reductions. All pointers to AP-descriptors in the
λ-abstraction graph are marked by a $\square$, indicating that new AP-descriptors must be
allocated when invoking it. These markings are included here to cover the general
case even though the λ-abstraction is applied only once in the particular example
and could therefore be directly overwritten. Note also that all numerical values are
represented as pointers to SCALAR descriptors which contain a type specification
and an internal reference to the value itself.

The lazy graph reducer sets out with the pointer p_expr to the topmost application node (1), demanding its reduction. Since λ-abstractions are applied to
their arguments as they are, this application must be overwritten by a copy of the
λ-abstraction body. As is shown in fig. 10.2.b, this copy has

- all pointers marked by a $\square$ replaced with unmarked pointers to instances of
  new AP-descriptors with the original contents;

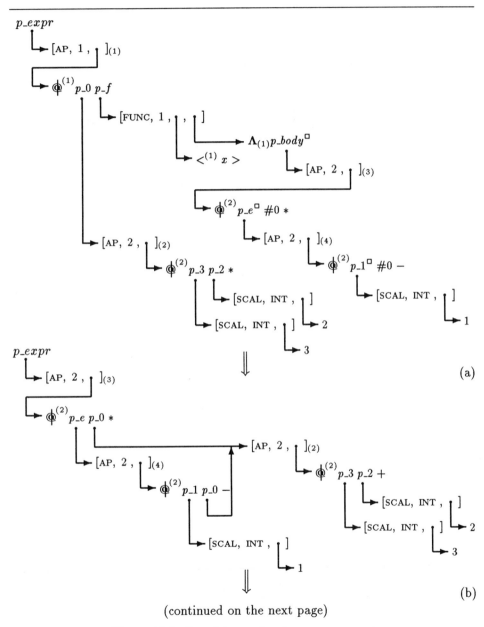

(a)

(b)

(continued on the next page)

Figure 10.2: Rewriting a simple program graph

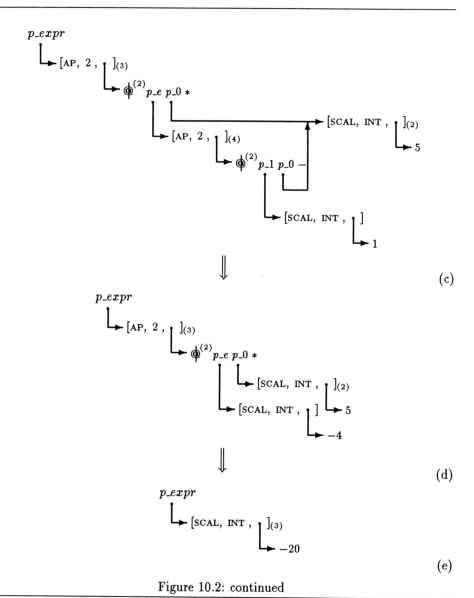

Figure 10.2: continued

- all occurrences of the de Bruijn index #0 substituted by pointers p_0 to the unreduced argument graph.

The AP-descriptor (1) to which p_expr was originally pointing is now overwritten with the contents of the topmost AP-descriptor (3) of the λ-abstraction's body.

The following reduction steps are rather straightforward for the new graph contains only unmarked pointers to AP-descriptors.

The lazy regime forces again the reduction of the application to which p_expr is pointing. Since multiplications are strict, it recursively forces the reduction of both arguments from innermost to outermost, i.e., first p_0 and then p_e. The reduction of the application node (2) produces the value 5 in its place (see fig. 10.2.c), which is shared between both occurrences of p_0. This, in turn, enables the reduction of the application nodes (4) and (3) in this sequence, overwriting the node (4) with the value -4 (see fig. 10.2.d) and the node (3) to which p_expr is pointing with the result value -20 of the entire application (see fig. 10.2.e). The SCALAR-descriptors by which the AP-descriptors are overwritten are being created in the course of performing the respective δ-reductions.

To motivate the need for the allocation of new descriptors for different instances of λ-abstractions, we consider, as another example, the computation of the factorial number of 10 by the OREL/0 program

$$\phi^{(1)} 10 \; fac \quad \text{with} \quad fac = \lambda^{(1)} n \; \phi^{(1)} \phi^{(2)} n \; 0 \; \text{GT} \; \Delta \phi^{(2)} n \; \phi^{(1)} \phi^{(2)} n \; 1 \; - \; fac * 1 \, .$$

To avoid unnecessary details in the program graph shown in fig. 10.3.a, we skip the LETREC construct in terms of which the recursive function (λ-abstraction) fac would have to be correctly defined, and install a direct **feedback pointer** instead. Moreover, we represent scalar values as contents of boxes in application strings rather than as complete descriptor graphs.

The reduction of this program graph reproduces recursively the encircled subgraph to construct as an intermediate structure the graph shown in fig. 10.3.b. It specifies the nested multiplication of all integer values from the interval $[10 .. 1]$. This graph is composed of 10 distinct instantiations of the AP-descriptor (3) and of the applications to which the internal links are pointing.

In general, overwriting application nodes is a little more complicated than in these simple examples. The application of a λ-abstraction of arity n to some r arguments may be specified in OREL/0 notation as

$$\phi^{(r)} arg\_r \ldots arg\_1 \; \lambda^{(n)} x_1 \ldots x_n \; b\_expr$$

at one extreme, or as

$$\phi^{(1)} arg\_r \; \phi^{(1)} arg\_(r-1) \ldots \phi^{(1)} arg\_1 \; \lambda^{(n)} x_1 \ldots x_n \; b\_expr$$

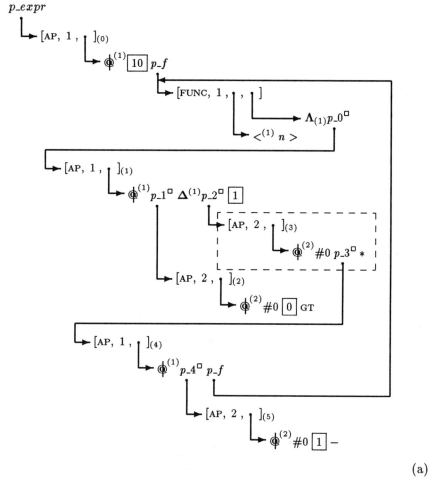

(a)

Figure 10.3: Graph representation for the computation of factorial numbers (a)

at the other extreme. In the former case we are lucky since we need to overwrite only one application node. In the latter case, however, we would have to overwrite up to r application nodes in succession to perform all β-reductions that are possible. Unless we have to deal with the rather unusual case that the normal forms of the intermediate applications (which are λ-abstractions of decreasing arities) must be

p_expr

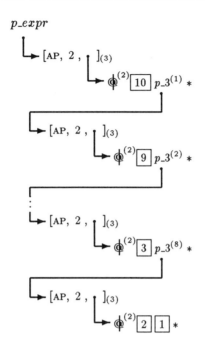

(b)

Figure 10.3: Intermediate graph of nested multiplications built up by the factorial function (b)

shared with other parts of the program, overwriting the intermediate application nodes should be avoided. Whether or not an intermediate application node is shared and must therefore be overwritten can be decided by inspecting the reference count field in the respective AP-descriptor (not shown in figs. 10.2 and 10.3).

Irrespective of the particular construction of the application, the lazy graph reducer must produce

- a new graph for a λ-abstraction of arity $n - r$ if $r < n$, which derives from the original one in that all occurrences of the variables $x_1, \ldots, x_r$ (or of the respective de Bruijn indices) are substituted by the respective arguments;

- the application of some new expression graph in its function position to the $r - n$ remaining arguments (which subsequently may or may not have to be reduced) if $r > n$.

10.1.3   The Mechanization of Lazy Graph Reductions

We will now investigate to which extent our stack-based shunting-yard mechanism can be employed to rewrite graph representations of OREL/0 expressions, as described in the preceding subsection. We are here primarily interested in the sequences of stack operations and descriptor manipulations that are necessary to overwrite application nodes. For this purpose, the details of constructing and manipulating the correct run-time environment for full-fledged β-reductions can be largely ignored. This subject will be treated at full length in section 10.2.

The basic principle of overwriting application nodes in the stack system E, A, M is illustrated in fig. 10.4 by a sequence of representative snapshots. Stack operations are indicated by dashed arrows; overwriting application nodes is depicted by solid arrows.

We set out with an initial situation in which we have on top of stack E a marked pointer $p\_e^\square$ to the outermost application node (AP-descriptor) of an expression *expr* (see fig. 10.4.a). The objective now is to reduce this expression lazily and to overwrite a new instantiation of the application node referenced by an unmarked pointer p_e with the resulting expression. The pointer p_e is then moved to stack A.

The first steps consist in creating a new context (or a new virtual machine) in which *expr* can be reduced. This can be accomplished by

- allocating a new AP-descriptor with the unmarked pointer p_e into which the contents of the original descriptor identified by the pointer $p\_e^\square$ are copied (this step is skipped if the original pointer is unmarked).

- pushing a special separation symbol $\|$ followed by a copy of the pointer p_e into stack M;

- pushing the same items in reverse order into stack A;

- replacing the pointer p_e in stack E with a copy of *expr* taken from the respective heap location.[26]

The resulting situation is depicted in fig. 10.4.b. What is above the separators $\|$ in the stacks A and M belongs to the new context (or virtual machine), what is underneath constitutes the context in which the reduction of the application identified by p_e is required. We note that the pointer p_e occurs in both contexts (virtual machines) which obviously are in a master-slave relationship to each other.

---

[26] This is a somewhat idealized picture. What is really copied is the outermost application to which p_e is directly pointing. Further components of this application (which, again, are generally applications) are in the same way recursively copied into stack E as demand arises.

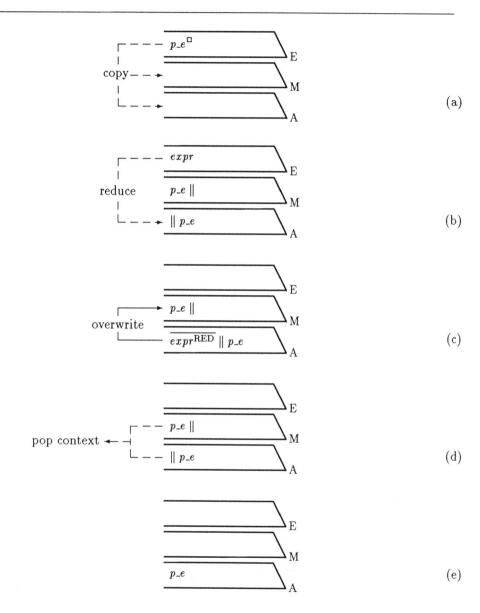

Figure 10.4: Basic principle of stack-supported lazy graph reduction

In what has now become the current (or active) context, a control program $\boxed{EAR_g}$ takes over to perform lazy reductions on *expr* while traversing it from stack E to A. In between, other contexts may be recursively created in order to reduce subterms, and applicators may pile up in stack M. Once the reduced expression, denoted as $expr^{\text{RED}}$, is set up in transposed form in stack A, we still have the pointer p_e left on top of the separation symbol $\|$ in stack M, i.e., in the current context (see fig. 10.4.c).

This pointer can now be used to overwrite the application node with $expr^{\text{RED}}$ This is done in three steps, of which

- the first allocates a new heap segment for $expr^{\text{RED}}$ whose base address replaces the contents of the internal reference field of the descriptor to which p_e points;

- the next overwrites the remainder of the descriptor with the type and structural specification (or whatever applies) of $expr^{\text{RED}}$;

- the last transfers the contents of stack A from the top down to the separation symbol $\|$ (which happens to be the transpose of $expr^{\text{RED}}$) directly into the new heap location.

This leaves in the current context only the pointer p_e on top of stack M (see fig. 10.4.d). The graph for $expr^{\text{RED}}$ is, however, shared with the occurrence of p_e underneath the separation symbol $\|$ in stack A and thus returned to the context in which it is required. The current context can therefore be released by cleaning the stacks M and A up to and including the separation symbols $\|$. Thus we get, as expected, p_e instantiated with the graph for $expr^{\text{RED}}$ in stack A (see fig. 10.4.e).

Now that we have established the mechanics for it, we have to find out just how we can identify, in the course of executing the control program $\boxed{EAR_g}$, the application nodes which must be overwritten and thus are candidates for the creation of new contexts.

The answer to this question is quite simple: creating a new context for the reduction of an application node depends on its syntactical position in a constructor expression. A new context is required whenever, in the course of traversing an expression from stack E to A, we encounter a pointer to an application node

- as the topmost pointer of the entire program expression;

- as a component of another but an application node (which for all practical purposes can only be a pointer to the body of a LETREC construct or to a subexpression of a list structure);

- in the operand position of a primitive function application which requires the canonical form(s) of its argument(s);

- in the function position of an application which is shared (i.e., the reference count in the respective AP-descriptor is greater than one).

These situations can be easily identified by inspecting the topmost entry of stack M (including the descriptor that may be associated with it) or the topmost entry in stack E.

As an example we consider the reduction of an arithmetic expression in which a subterm is shared. For this purpose, we return to the graph in fig. 10.2.b, which we show again below (the scalar values are abbreviated here as boxes).

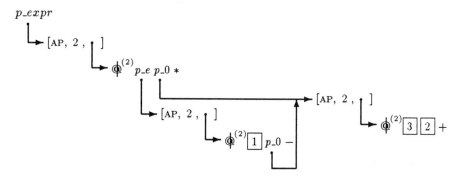

Its reduction in our stack system may be followed up in fig. 10.5. Starting with the topmost pointer p_expr in stack E (fig. 10.5.a), a new context must be created to reduce the outermost application it represents. This application is copied from its heap location (fig. 10.5.b) and subsequently traversed from stack E to A until the function symbol $*$ appears on top of E (fig. 10.5.c). The primitive function $*$ is strict in both arguments. The descriptors referred to by the argument pointers p_0 and p_e on top of stack A must therefore be inspected to determine whether or not the arguments must be reduced.

Since the first argument is found to be an application, its pointer p_0 is copied on top of stack E to set up a new context for its reduction (fig. 10.5.d). Here we have an application of the primitive function $+$ to two arguments which are already in normal form (the numerical values 2 and 3) and of a compatible type (fig. 10.5.e). Its δ-reduction produces in stack A the pointer p_res to the graph representation of the value 5 (fig. 10.5.f). This intermediate result overwrites, in the next step, the application node identified by the pointer p_0 that is on top of stack M, whereupon the graph to which p_res is pointing disappears. The context for computing the

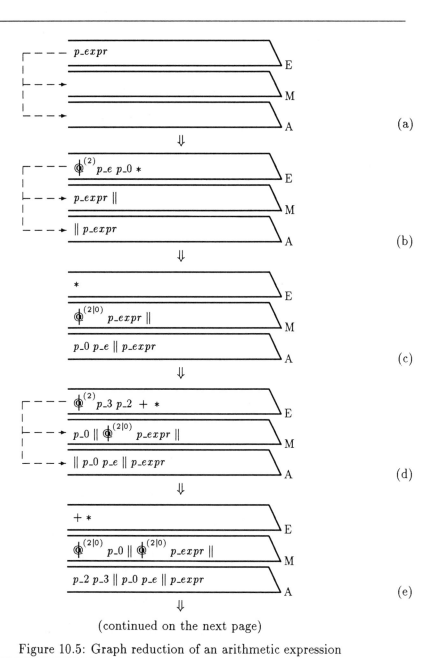

(continued on the next page)

Figure 10.5: Graph reduction of an arithmetic expression

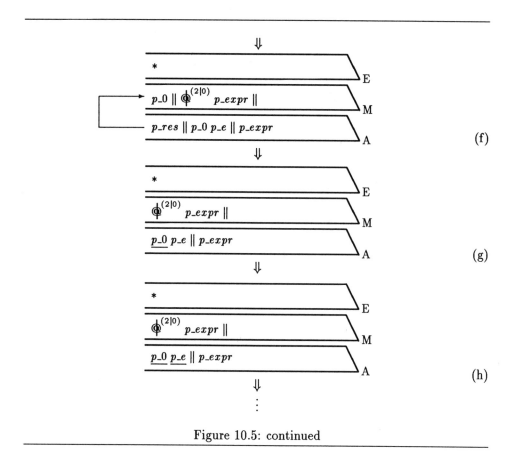

Figure 10.5: continued

value 5 can now be released (see fig. 10.5.g, in which p_0 is to indicate that the node identified by p_0 is in normal form).

The function $*$ that re-appears on top of stack E inspects the descriptors of its arguments again. It now finds the first argument in normal form and thus proceeds to force the reduction of the second argument hidden behind the pointer p_e. Following the same course of actions as for the first argument, we eventually get the situation shown in fig. 10.5.h, in which the node identified by p_e has assumed the value -4 and thus is also in normal form. This finally enables the δ-reduction of the outermost application which overwrites the node to which p_expr is pointing with the result value -20.

When comparing the mechanics of performing lazy graph reductions to the one for eager graph reductions, we note that the main difference lies in the creation of contexts as a means to overwrite application nodes in a uniform way. The idea of using different contexts separated by special stack entries is born out of the necessity that under a lazy evaluation regime the focus of control (or activity) must be moved rather irregularly about the program graph.

The control path basically follows a normal order reduction course. In compliance with the particular syntax chosen for the graph representation of applications, this course is realized as a pre-order traversal which treats pointers in operand positions of applicators as atoms, i.e., it skips the reduction of the argument graphs hidden behind them while moving on to the operator position. The expression in this position decides whether and to which extent the arguments must be reduced. Whenever a primitive function symbol is encountered there, control may be forced off the pre-order traversal path. It may have to jump back to operand positions it has already passed through in order to reduce them to canonical forms. Eventually, control must return to the stack constellation (or state) it has left. While reducing the argument graphs, these transfers of control may occur recursively.

Thus, the primary purpose of introducing contexts is to provide a standardized mechanism which recursively transfers the focus of control back and forth between graph nodes that must be traversed in an order deviating from the pre-order traversal. As an important side effect, this mechanism also overwrites the application nodes to which control is transferred and shares them with the contexts to which control eventually returns. It can therefore generally be applied to overwrite application nodes even though control need not necessarily leave the pre-order traversal path.

10.2   Run-Time Support for Full-Fledged β-Reductions

At the beginning of section 10.1 we argued that it may be more expedient for a lazy graph reduction engine to support full-fledged β-reductions on open λ-abstractions rather than going through the trouble of converting them into supercombinators in order to avoid name clashes at run-time. Lazy graph reduction is generally based on a normal order reduction discipline which applies operators to operands as they are, i.e., without reducing them. Under lazy evaluation, we even wish to delay the substitution of formal by actual parameters in operand expressions until it becomes absolutely necessary to reduce them to their canonical forms. Thus, we need to make provisions for all expressions specified in terms of de Bruijn indices (i.e., free occurrences of bound variables) to carry with them the environments in which they must be executed. Since delayed substitutions may be recursively nested, we have inevitably a recursively nested environment as well. Its construction essentially follows the recursive nesting of function definitions in the original program expression and may therefore also be used to reduce applications of the respective λ-abstractions directly, i.e., without prior conversion into supercombinators [27].

We will now investigate how exactly the environment for full-fledged β-reductions with delayed substitutions (or lazy β-reductions for short) must be implemented and manipulated. For this purpose it suffices to consider only the subset of OREL/0 expressions which realize the pure λ-calculus. This clean setting has the advantage that we need to deal only with variables (de Bruijn indices), λ-abstractions and applications. In particular, control follows without deviations a normal order reduction path since no other functions but λ-abstractions can appear in operator positions of applications.

10.2.1 Head Forms and Head-Order Reductions

To understand the concept of an environment for lazy β-reductions, it is very helpful to look at the construction of expressions of the pure λ-calculus in a particular way. They all have a so-called head form in the sense that they are composed of

- a sequence of some $n \geq 0$ binders, followed by

- a sequence of (nested) applications of a head expression H to some $r \geq 0$ tail expressions T.

Head and tail expressions are recursively constructed in the same way, i.e., they all have head forms as well. There is one exception though: a head expression cannot be an application but only a variable or a λ-abstraction. Otherwise it would simply lengthen the sequence of applications in the head form. If the head expression is a variable, then we have the special case of a head normal form in compliance with the definition given section 5.3.5.

In the syntax of OREL/0 expressions, and using de Bruijn indices in places of bound variable occurrences, the construction of head forms may thus be formally specified

- either as

$$ H \mid T := \#i \mid \underbrace{\Lambda \ldots \Lambda}_{n} \, \phi \, \underbrace{T \ldots \phi \, T}_{r} \, H $$

when using only one-place binders and one-operand applicators;

---

[27]Lazy supercombinator reduction requires that new graph instances be created for unevaluated expressions before they can be passed on to other contexts. They must have all occurrences of de Bruijn indices directly replaced by argument pointers retrieved from the curerent context. An interpreting graph reducer generally would have to do this while copying an uninstantiated graph template into another heap location.

- or as

$$H \mid T := \#i \mid \Lambda_{(n)} \, \Phi^{(r)} \, \underbrace{T \ldots T}_{r} \, H$$

when using the most compact representation with r-ary applicators and n-ary binders.

Since both representations are semantically equivalent, we use in the following only the former for it is easier and more instructive to depict them graphically.

We note immediately that the head and tail expressions are in fact the **operators** and **operands**, respectively, of r-ary applications. Since we consider λ-abstractions which may contain relatively free variables, there are no restrictions on the de Bruijn indices $\#i$ that may occur in the terminal head positions other than that they must be smaller than the number of binders encountered along the paths from the root node of the expression to them.

On a path from the root to a terminal head position we find alternatingly only **sequences of binders** Λ and **sequences of applicators** Φ. We refer to these sequences as *lambdas* and as *apps*, respectively. The path to the terminal head position of the outermost head form is said to be its **spine**. All tail expressions of the spine have recursively spines of their own.

The spines play an important role in lazy β-reductions which, as stated before, derive from a normal order reduction discipline. Following its definition given in subsection 5.3.3, we must in fact systematically **reduce head forms to head normal forms** from outermost to innermost. Put another way, redexes which may recursively occur in a head position must be reduced without ever looking at the tail expressions until a head normal form is reached. Thus, we need only be concerned with what is going on along the spine of a head form and refer to this either as **spine reduction** or as **head-order reduction**.

Head-order reductions can neatly be illustrated using meander-shaped graphical representations of spines as shown in fig. 10.6. Here we have *apps* and *lambdas* represented as horizontal lines oriented to the right and to the left, respectively. Vertical lines on the left connect *lambdas* with succeeding *apps* and vertical lines on the right connect *apps* with succeeding *lambdas*. We will alternatively refer to these connections as **left-hand** and **right-hand corners**, respectively.

The interesting parts of these meanders are the *apps-lambdas* (or right-hand) corners. They pair applications with binders to form β-redexes. When reducing them, the corners shift step-by-step to the left, exposing the next redexes. Thus, β-reductions may proceed in these corners until either the applicators or the binders are exhausted.

Performing these β-reduction lazily is conceptually equivalent to

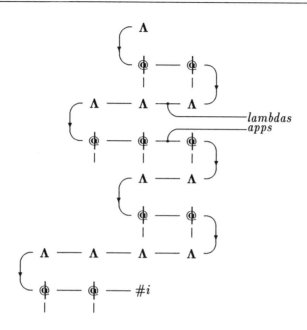

Figure 10.6: Meander representation of a spine

- cutting the largest possible number of β-redexes off an *apps-lambdas* corner;

- pushing this cut down into the succeeding *apps* where it must be copied in front of all tail expressions and of the head expression.

We call this operation a (lazy) β-**reduction-in-the-large** for it does all β-reductions that belong to the cut in one conceptual step.

The cut thus inserted into an *apps* constitutes the environment in which the head and tail expressions must be reduced.

Just how the cut must be sliced depends on the relative lengths of the *apps* and *lambdas* that form a right-hand corner. The two situations that must be distinguished are shown in fig. 10.7. If the length of the *apps* equals or exceeds the length of the *lambdas*, then we have a **full application**: the cut includes as many redexes as there are Λ-binders. The left-over *apps* remains as it is (see fig. 10.7.a). If the *lambdas* is longer than the *apps* (see fig. 10.7.b), then we have a **partial application**. In this case the cut would have to be pushed across the remaining *lambdas*,

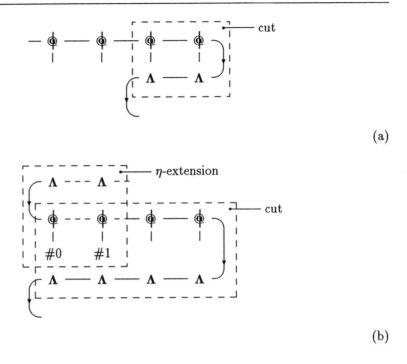

(a)

(b)

Figure 10.7: Taking cuts off *apps-lambdas* corners

i.e., all occurrences of relatively free de Bruijn indices in the cut would have to be incremented accordingly.

However, this is conceptually the same as a so-called η-extension. A λ-term M is known to be **extensionally equivalent** to $\lambda x \, \phi \, x \, M$ or, using the de Bruijn notation, to $\Lambda \, \phi \, \#0 \, M$ (which derives straightforwardly from the semantic equivalence of the applications $\phi \, NM$ and $\phi \, N \, \Lambda \, \phi \, \#0 \, M$). When adding a Λ, all free occurrences of de Bruijn indices in M must be incremented by one, as above. The trick now consists in η-extending the preceding *lambdas-apps* corner by as many applications as are necessary to saturate all Λ-binders in the succeeding *lambdas* (see the dashed extension in fig. 10.7.b).

In fact, the purpose of η-extension is to leave occurrences of de Bruijn indices from the interval $[\#0 .. \#(n - r - 1)]$ (with r being the number of extensions) in the abstraction body as they are or, put another way, to substitute them by themselves. This is exactly what is accomplished by the η-extended spine of fig. 10.7.b: the redexes formed by the two innermost pairs of $\boldsymbol{\Lambda}$'s and added applications are to substitute occurrences of #0 and #1 in the succeeding *apps* by #0 and #1, respectively.

Fig. 10.8 shows in a sequence of three steps how the spine of fig. 10.6 β-reduces lazily when systematically pushing the topmost cut down into the branches of the succeeding *apps*. The cuts are labeled by capital letters, and both the applicators and the binders are enumerated from top to bottom in order to be able to follow up on what is being inserted where.[28] The cut C preceding the head in the spine obtained after the third β-reduction-in-the-large (see fig. 10.8.d) is recursively expanded in fig. 10.9.a. Here we have an interesting situation with respect to the remaining *apps-lambdas* corner. All β-redexes of the original spine are now collected in one cut, namely C, which is recursively specified in terms of the cuts B and A. The *lambdas* of this cut is just followed by the de Bruijn index #i. Thus, the general form of the spine is

$$\underbrace{\boldsymbol{\Lambda}\ldots\boldsymbol{\Lambda}}_{m} \, \phi \, T_r \ldots \phi \, T_n \ldots \phi \, T_i \ldots \phi \, \underbrace{T_1 \, \boldsymbol{\Lambda}\ldots\boldsymbol{\Lambda}}_{n} \, \#i$$

$$\underbrace{\hspace{5cm}}_{\text{cut}}$$

with $r \geq n$ and $i < n + m$. When performing the remaining β-reduction-in-the-large, we have to distinguish two cases:

- if $i < n$, then we get

$$\underbrace{\boldsymbol{\Lambda}\ldots\boldsymbol{\Lambda}}_{m} \, \phi \, T_r \ldots \phi \, T_{n+1} \, T_{n-i} \, ,$$

  i.e., the λ-abstraction in the head is, in fact, a **selector** for the i-th tail expression T_i;

- if $i \geq n$, then we get

$$\underbrace{\boldsymbol{\Lambda}\ldots\boldsymbol{\Lambda}}_{m} \, \phi \, T_r \ldots \phi \, T_{n+1} \, \#(i - n) \, ,$$

  i.e., the λ-abstraction in the head consumes the innermost n tails and produces #$(i - n)$ in its place.

This can be given the following interpretation: what is marked as the cut in the above spine expression constitutes an **environment** of n consecutive entries for the

---

[28] $\boldsymbol{\Lambda}$'s and ϕ 's added due to η-extensions receive no indices.

head index $\#i$. The spine preceding this cut is of no relevance for $\#i$. If this index is within the range of the environment, it can be substituted by the respective entry. In general, this entry is another spine (head form) containing redexes with which the computation must continue in the head of the outermost spine (in the spine

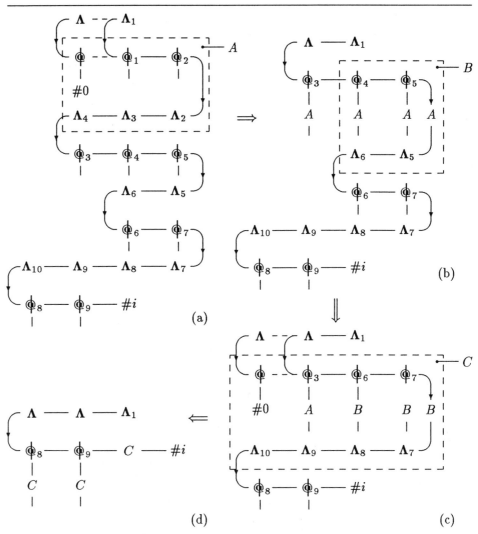

Figure 10.8: β-reductions-in-the-large on the spine shown in fig. 10.6

of fig. 10.9.a we have indicated such a selection for $\#i = \#2$, as a result of which we obtain the spine of fig. 10.9.b). A head index reaching beyond the environment is considered undefined: we have arrived at a head normal form and, for the time being, are done (see fig. 10.9.b). In either case, the cut disappears from the spine but not necessarily from the head (normal) form. At least parts of it (if not the complete environment) continue to exist in the tails of a left-over *apps*-sequence (see, for instance, the cuts C and B in figs. 10.9.b and 10.9.c).

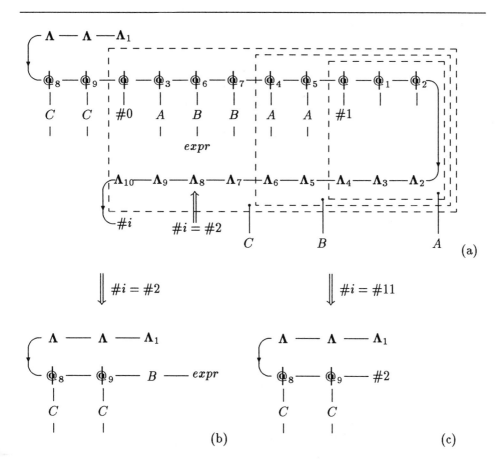

Figure 10.9: Continuation of the spine reduction of fig. 10.8

The recursively nested cuts through the spine in fig. 10.9.a and the way they have built up may insinuate that the environment forms a continuous structure which grows and shrinks in a LIFO-manner. This would suggest a straightforward implementation as a run-time stack. However, things are not that simple for two reasons. Both have to do with the sharing of the environments among their various occurrences in the representation of an expression.

Firstly, the environment grows continuously only to the point where it is conceptually pushed down to the terminal head position of a spine, i.e., to a de Bruijn index. As illustrated in fig. 10.9.a and 10.9.b, this index may select from the actual environment a tail expression embedded in an earlier environment with which reductions in the head of the spine are to continue. However, the intervening part of the environment cannot be released since it may be required to perform reductions in the tails of the preceding *apps* with which it is shared. Thus, the continuation of the environment for the spine reductions that are taking place in the extended head expression must be pushed on top of the existing one, and the intervening environment part must be bridged. A discontinuous environment, however, considerably complicates indexed accesses to it. Rather than using de Bruijn indices straightforwardly as offsets relative to the top of the environment structure, several consecutive within-range tests may have to be performed in order to determine how many bridges must be crossed to arrive at the correct environment position.

Secondly, unless all components of a head (normal) form that refer to a particular part of the environment are reduced to normal forms, this part cannot be released. Once reductions along a spine have produced a head normal form, the tail expressions along the left-over *apps* may be reduced in any order since they are completely independent of each other and do not any more affect the shape of the spine. The question is just which way to proceed in order to release environment parts as early as possible. Unfortunately, traversing and thereby reducing the tail expressions form the head backwards to the root, though straightforward, may not be optimal in this sense. The tails are usually embedded in different environments not necessarily contained in each other. Tails that share the same environment may not necessarily be adjacent to each other, and the largest environments may not necessarily be associated with the tails closest to the head and thus cut back first. Transferring control about the *apps* so that the tail expressions are reduced in an order determined by the lengths of the respective environments is bound to create a considerable overhead. Thus, the problems that we have at hand with respect to controlling and accessing the environment seem to be rather formidable.

In the real world of an applied λ-calculus, i.e., of OREL/0 expressions which include δ-redexes, the problem of finding a proper sequence for the reduction of the tail expressions more or less disappears. In addition to variables (de Bruijn indices) we have then primarily primitive functions in terminal head positions of spines. They force the reduction of their arguments (i.e., of tail expressions) to canonical forms in the order from innermost to outermost (or from the head towards the root), as described in subsection 10.1.3. These reductions are usually shared with other parts (spines) of the expression. Thus, we can expect many of the tails along a spine to be in normal (canonical) form before the spine itself is reduced to head normal form. This is to say that the order of reducing the tails of a spine is predominantly dictated by the primitive functions.

No special consideration must be given to **recursions** which in OREL/0 expressions are specified by LETREC-constructs. Including them in the pure λ-calculus simply means that we have head forms with free occurrences of LETREC-bound variables in head positions. These variable occurrences are nothing but place-holders for LETREC-defined λ-abstractions, i.e., for head forms. Replacing these variable occurrences by the head forms they represent is exactly the same as extending the spines by the environment entries (tail expressions) selected via de Bruijn indices.

10.2.2 Representing Binding Levels by Index Tuples

We indicated in the preceding subsection that one of the major problems in implementing a **run-time** environment for lazy β-reductions consists in bridging gaps. While these gaps cannot be avoided, we have to find at least an elegant and efficient way of bridging them. Unfortunately, we face great difficulties accomplishing this with de Bruijn indices.

The cause of the problem is that **de Bruijn indices** represent **binding levels** of **variable occurrences** as distances to the Λ's that bind them. These distances are measured in numbers of intervening Λ's encountered along the paths (spines) to them, irrespective of the *lambdas*, i.e., of the **sequences** of contiguous Λ's, that are in between. The *lambdas*, however, dictate the structure of the environment. They define largest possible contiguous segments (or frames) of it which represent instantiations of variables (de Bruijn indices) bound in λ-abstractions. Environment gaps are due to λ-abstractions (or head forms) substituted into head positions of spines, i.e., due to *lambdas* separated by *apps*.

We may have de Bruijn indices bound by Λ's in *lambdas* higher up along the paths to the root. Unfortunately, the indices themselves dò not directly specify which *lambdas* these are and, hence, which frame of a possibly non-contiguous environment they refer to. Instead it must be dynamically figured out at runtime in which frame the environment entry is locáted and how to get there if the environment is non-continuous.

However, there is a rather straightforward remedy to this problem. All we need to do is to represent binding levels of variable occurrences by index tuples $[\#i, \#j]^\lambda$ rather than by simple de Bruijn indices. They are to specify the distances from variable occurrences to their Λ-binders by

- the indices i in terms of the intervening *lambdas*;

- the indices j in terms of the intervening Λ's within the *lambdas* in which the binders occur.

We therefore refer to the components i and j also as the *lambdas*-binding levels and the Λ-binding levels, respectively. As an example that may help to illustrate this concept, we consider the λ-term

$$\lambda^{(2)}u\ v\ \dashv\ldots u\ldots v\ldots$$
$$\lambda^{(2)}w\ x\ \dashv\ldots w\ldots u\ldots v\ldots x\ldots$$
$$\lambda^{(2)}y\ z\ \dashv\ldots y\ldots x\ldots v\ldots w\ldots u\ldots z\ldots\vdash\ldots\vdash\ldots\vdash\ .$$

The equivalent de Bruijn representation is

$$\Lambda_{(2)}\ \dashv\ldots\#1\ldots\#0\ldots$$
$$\Lambda_{(2)}\ \dashv\ldots\#1\ldots\#3\ldots\#2\ldots\#0\ldots$$
$$\Lambda_{(2)}\ \dashv\ldots\#1\ldots\#2\ldots\#4\ldots\#3\ldots\#5\ldots\#0\ldots\vdash\ldots\vdash\ldots\vdash\ .$$

Using the index tuples, we get

$$\Lambda_{(2)}\ \dashv\ldots[\#0,\#1]^{\lambda}\ldots[\#0,\#0]^{\lambda}\ldots$$
$$\Lambda_{(2)}\ \dashv\ldots[\#0,\#1]^{\lambda}\ldots[\#1,\#1]^{\lambda}\ldots[\#1,\#0]^{\lambda}\ldots[\#0,\#0]^{\lambda}\ldots$$
$$\Lambda_{(2)}\ \dashv\ldots[\#0,\#1]^{\lambda}\ldots[\#1,\#0]^{\lambda}\ldots[\#2,\#0]^{\lambda}\ldots[\#1,\#1]^{\lambda}\ldots$$
$$\ldots[\#2,\#1]^{\lambda}\ldots[\#0,\#0]^{\lambda}\ldots\vdash\ldots\vdash\ldots\vdash\ .$$

The interesting part about these index tuples is that we need only be concerned with the *lambdas*-binding levels when performing β-reductions-in-the-large. They conceptually effect the consumption of entire *lambdas* and the substitution of (tail) expressions that may contain free variable occurrences into the scopes of entire *lambdas*.

We can therefore define *lambdas*-binding levels in a form equivalent to the λ-binding levels as defined in subsection 5.3.1.

With respect to a *lambdas* that is a distance of $k \geq 0$ intervening *lambdas* away on the path (spine) to the root of the expression, the occurrence of an index tuple $[\#i, \#j]^{\lambda}$ is said to be

- *lambdas*-protected if $i > k$;

- *lambdas*-free if $i = k$;

- *lambdas*-bound if $i < k$.

Likewise, β-reductions-in-the-large of redexes of the general form

$$\oint T_n \ldots \oint T_1 \underbrace{\boldsymbol{\Lambda} \ldots \boldsymbol{\Lambda}}_{n} b\_expr$$

can now be defined as follows: occurrences of index tuples $[\#i, \#j]^\lambda$ in

- the λ-abstraction $\boldsymbol{\Lambda}_{(n)} b\_expr$

    - decrement their *lambdas*-binding indices i by one if they are *lambdas*-protected;
    - are substituted by the respective operand (tail) expressions $T_1, \ldots, T_n$ if they are *lambdas*-free;
    - remain as they are if they are *lambdas*-bound;

- the operand terms $T_1, \ldots, T_n$

    - increment their *lambdas*-binding indices by l if they are *lambdas*-free or *lambdas*-protected;
    - remain as they are if they are *lambdas*-bound;

    when substituting them into the scopes of some $l > 0$ nested *lambdas* in b_expr.

The $\boldsymbol{\Lambda}$-binding levels, i.e., the components $\#j$ of the index tuples, remain unaffected.

When performing β-reductions-in-the-large strictly in **head order**, we have no free occurrences of index tuples left over in operand (tail) expressions other than in the case of **partial applications** which are conceptually handled by η-extensions. To comply with the above definition of β-reductions-in-the-large, a head form

$$\ldots \underbrace{\boldsymbol{\Lambda} \ldots \boldsymbol{\Lambda}}_{k} \oint T_r \ldots \oint T_1 \underbrace{\boldsymbol{\Lambda} \ldots \boldsymbol{\Lambda}}_{n} b\_expr \quad \text{with} \quad n > r$$

must be η-extended to

$$\underbrace{\boldsymbol{\Lambda} \ldots \boldsymbol{\Lambda}}_{k} | \underbrace{\boldsymbol{\Lambda} \ldots \boldsymbol{\Lambda}}_{n-r} \oint [\#0, \#0]^\lambda \ldots \oint [\#0, \#(n-r-1)]^\lambda \oint T'_r \ldots T'_1 \underbrace{\boldsymbol{\Lambda} \ldots \boldsymbol{\Lambda}}_{n} b\_expr'$$

where the terms $T'_1, \ldots, T'_r$ and $expr'$ derive from $T_1, \ldots, T_r$ and $expr$, respectively, in that all *lambdas*-**protected occurrences** of index tuples have their *lambdas*-binding levels incremented by one. This is in fact equivalent to

- substituting the tails $T_1, \ldots, T_r$ into the scope of the *lambdas* of length $n - r$ that remains after β-reducing the partial application;

- leaving unchanged the index tuples bound by the remaining *lambdas*.

It is important to note here that the *lambdas* appended to each other by η-extensions must be conceptually kept separated, as is indicated by the symbol |. This is to maintain correct *lambdas*-binding levels with respect to the nesting of λ-abstractions in the original expression.

As a simple example, we consider the λ-term

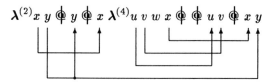

which β-reduces to

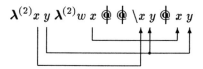

(the arrows underneath depict the binding structure).

Transforming this term into the index tuple representation yields

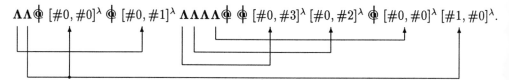

When η-extending the partial application, we get

$$\boldsymbol{\Lambda\Lambda} \mid \boldsymbol{\Lambda\Lambda} \ \, \widehat{\phi} \ [\#0, \#0]^\lambda \ \widehat{\phi} \ [\#0, \#1]^\lambda \ \widehat{\phi} \ [\#1, \#0]^\lambda \ \widehat{\phi} \ [\#1, \#1]^\lambda$$
$$\boldsymbol{\Lambda\Lambda\Lambda\Lambda}\widehat{\phi} \ \widehat{\phi} \ [\#0, \#3]^\lambda \ [\#0, \#2]^\lambda \ \widehat{\phi} \ [\#0, \#0]^\lambda \ [\#2, \#0]^\lambda \ ,$$

whereupon a β-reduction-in-the-large can be performed which yields

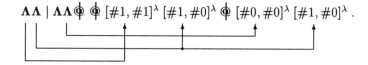

A comparison of the binding structures shows that we obtain the same λ-expression as above.

The index tuple representation of a λ-term may be derived by systematically applying from outermost to innermost a modified α-conversion to it. It directly relates to a run-time environment structure in which

- each instance of a λ-abstraction is specified by a frame of as many entries as there are λ-bound variables;

- the ordering of frames reflects the order of nesting of the respective λ-abstractions in the initial λ-term.

The entries in the frames represent the operand terms with which the λ-abstractions are actually instantiated. They are either pointers to their graph (heap) representations (including pointers to the environments in which they, in turn, are invoked) or, as a consequence of partial applications, dummy symbols or left-over index tuples. Environment entries can now be straightforwardly accessed using the *lambdas*-binding indices $\#i$ of index tuple occurrences as selectors for frames and the Λ-binding indices $\#j$ as offsets relative to the tops of these frames. Since the order of creating and releasing frames does not necessarily conform to a LIFO-discipline with respect to their *lambdas* indices, the environment must be implemented as a linked structure rather than as a stack. We will therefore use the term run-time structure with the understanding that its frames need to be linked up to each other by pointers in order to represent continuous environments. This structure may even develop holes when releasing frames as soon as possible.

10.2.3 Binding Levels of LETREC-Bound Variable Occurrences

In OREL/0 expressions we have, in addition to λ-bound variables, also LETREC-bound variables. Occurrences of the latter in head positions of spines are placeholders for (recursively defined) λ-abstractions. At run-time, these λ-abstractions are generally associated with environments specifying the actual instantiations of their relatively free variables, i.e., of the index tuples with *lambdas*-binding indices greater than zero.

In contrast to index tuples which are selectors for environment entries, LETREC-bound variable occurrences are, in fact, selectors for templates of λ-abstractions in LETREC structures. The difference which matters here is that expressions selected from environments are, in turn, directly associated with their respective environments, whereas λ-abstractions selected from LETRECs as new head terms are not. So, the question that we must answer is: where do we find the actual environments for LETREC-defined λ-abstractions, particularly if LETRECs are recursively nested?

We discuss this problem by means of the following example program:

DEFINE
$f(u, v)$ = DEFINE
$g(w, x)$ = DEFINE
$h(y, z)$ = ⊣ ... $g(z, w)$ ... $f(v, y)$ ... ⊢
IN ⊣ ... $h(u, w)$ ... $f(x, v)$ ... ⊢
IN ⊣ ... $g(u, u)$ ... $f(v, v)$ ... ⊢
IN ⊣ ... $f(a, b)$ ... $f(b, a)$ ... ⊢ .

In this program, we have three recursively nested function definitions. All functions recursively refer to themselves, and also from lower nesting levels to functions higher up. Likewise, the actual parameters are chosen so as to include all possible binding levels.

The conversion of this program into an OREL/0 expression yields:

$$\alpha^* <f><\lambda^{(2)}u\ v> \dashv \ldots \phi^{(2)} b\ a\ f \ldots \phi^{(2)} a\ b\ f \ldots \vdash$$
$$\alpha^* <g><\lambda^{(2)}w\ x> \dashv \ldots \phi^{(2)} u\ u\ g \ldots \phi^{(2)} v\ v\ f \ldots \vdash$$
$$\alpha^* <h><\lambda^{(2)}y\ z> \dashv \ldots \phi^{(2)} w\ u\ h \ldots \phi^{(2)} v\ x\ f \ldots \vdash$$
$$\dashv \ldots \phi^{(2)} w\ z\ g \ldots \phi^{(2)} y\ v\ f \ldots \vdash$$

(the horizontal brackets depict the recursive nesting of LETREC expressions).[29]

The *lambdas* in this expression apparently are nested in the same way as are the LETREC-binders to which they belong: the variables

- u, v are *lambdas*-free in the body of the abstraction f but *lambdas*-protected in g and hence in h;

- w, x are *lambdas*-free in the body of g but *lambdas*-protected in h;

- y, z are *lambdas*-free in the body of h.

This would suggest that we assign so-called *alphas*-binding levels to all α^*-(LETREC-)bound variables in the same way as *lambdas*-binding levels to λ-bound variables: *alphas*-binding levels would then count the number of intervening α^*s

---

[29] In this expression we have, for reasons of clarity, not changed the ordering of applications within the body expressions, even though this may be necessary if they themselves are arguments of applications.

on the paths from occurrences of LETREC-bound variables upwards to the α^*'s by which they are bound. All variables bound by the same α^* thus receive the same *alphas*-binding levels in the same α^*-contexts.

Denoting an *alphas*-binding index k attached to an α^*-bound variable (function name) f as a tuple $[\#k, f]^\alpha$, our example expression would transform to:

$$\alpha^* <f><\Lambda_{(2)}> \dashv \ldots \phi^{(2)} b\, a\, [\#0, f]^\alpha \ldots \phi^{(2)} a\, b\, [\#0, f]^\alpha \ldots \vdash$$

$$\alpha^* <g><\Lambda_{(2)}> \dashv \ldots \phi^{(2)}[\#0, \#1]^\lambda\, [\#0, \#1]^\lambda\, [\#0, g]^\alpha \ldots$$

$$\ldots \phi^{(2)}[\#0, \#0]^\lambda\, [\#0, \#0]^\lambda\, [\#1, f]^\alpha \ldots \vdash$$

$$\alpha^* <h><\Lambda_{(2)}> \dashv \ldots \phi^{(2)}[\#0, \#1]^\lambda\, [\#1, \#1]^\lambda\, [\#0, h]^\alpha \ldots$$

$$\ldots \phi^{(2)}[\#1, \#0]^\lambda\, [\#0, \#0]^\lambda\, [\#2, f]^\alpha \ldots \vdash$$

$$\dashv \ldots \phi^{(2)}[\#1, \#1]^\lambda\, [\#0, \#0]^\lambda\, [\#1, g]^\alpha \ldots \phi^{(2)}[\#0, \#1]^\lambda\, [\#2, \#0]^\lambda\, [\#2, f]^\alpha \ldots \vdash$$

In this particular example, we seem to have a simple indexing rule: in the same α^*-scope, the *alphas*-binding levels of the (LETREC-defined) λ-abstractions seem to be greater by one than the *lambdas*-binding levels of their λ-bound variables. Put another way: the *alphas*-binding levels seem to refer to the environments in which the λ-abstractions (or, more precisely, their relatively free variable occurrences) are instantiated, i.e., we seem to have exactly what we want. However, this is not generally the case. We note already a deviation with respect to the *alphas*-binding indices for occurrences of f and g in the body of the innermost function definition (which is the function h); according to this rule, they should be one higher than they actually are. While this problem could be remedied by putting dummy α^*s in front of the innermost defining expressions, the rule does also not apply in cases of

- parameterless LETREC-defined functions, where we have α^*s without *lambdas* and thus no environment frames for them;

- nameless λ-abstractions directly specified as components (operators) of applications, where we have *lambdas* and thus environment frames without there being α^*s.

Since it is the *apps-lambdas'*, not the α^*s, which specify the construction of an environment, we must re-define *alphas*-binding levels as follows: they count the number of intervening *lambdas* on the paths from occurrences of LETREC-defined function names to the α^*s that bind them. These *alphas*-binding levels (or indices) now identify the environments in which the actual applications of LETREC-defined functions must be reduced.

Another example program shows how this works:

DEFINE

$f(u, v) =$ DEFINE

$g(\ ) =$ DEFINE

$h(y, z) = \dashv \ldots \text{SUB}(w) \text{ IN } \dashv \ldots$

$\text{SUB}(x) \text{ IN } \dashv \ldots g(z, w) \ldots \vdash$

$\ldots f(v, y) \ldots \vdash \ldots \vdash$

IN $\dashv \ldots h(u, v) \ldots \text{SUB}(x, w) \text{ IN } \dashv \ldots f(x, w) \ldots \vdash \ldots \vdash$

IN $\dashv \ldots g \ldots \text{SUB}(x) \text{ IN } \dashv \ldots f(v, v) \ldots \vdash \ldots \vdash$

IN $\dashv \ldots f(a, b) \ldots \text{SUB}(x) \text{ IN } \dashv \ldots f(b, a) \ldots \vdash \ldots \vdash$.

This program expression features the parameterless function g and various nameless functions of the form SUB...IN.... It converts into the OREL/0 expression:

$$\alpha^* <f><\lambda^{(2)}u\,v> \dashv \ldots \phi^{(2)}b\,a\,f \ldots \lambda x \dashv \ldots \phi^{(2)}a\,b\,f \ldots \vdash \ldots \vdash$$

$$\alpha^* <g><> \dashv \ldots g \ldots \lambda x \dashv \ldots \phi^{(2)}v\,v\,f \ldots \vdash \ldots \vdash$$

$$\alpha^* <h><\lambda^{(2)}y\,z> \dashv \ldots \phi^{(2)}v\,u\,h \ldots \lambda^{(2)}x\,w \dashv \ldots \phi^{(2)}w\,x\,f \ldots \vdash \ldots \vdash$$

$$\dashv \ldots \lambda w \dashv \ldots \lambda x \dashv \ldots \phi^{(2)}w\,z\,g \ldots \vdash \ldots \phi^{(2)}y\,v\,f \ldots \vdash \ldots \vdash$$

Counting *lambdas-* and *alphas-*binding levels as specified, we obtain:

$$\alpha^* <f><\Lambda_{(2)}> \dashv \ldots \phi^{(2)}b\,a\,[\#0, f]^\alpha \ldots \Lambda_{(1)} \dashv \ldots \phi^{(2)}a\,b\,[\#1, f]^\alpha \ldots \vdash \ldots \vdash$$

$$\alpha^* <g><> \dashv \ldots [\#0, g]^\alpha \ldots$$

$$\ldots \Lambda_{(1)} \dashv \ldots \phi^{(2)}[\#1, \#0]^\lambda\,[\#1, \#0]^\lambda\,[\#2, f]^\alpha \ldots \vdash \ldots \vdash$$

$$\alpha^* <h><\Lambda_{(2)}> \dashv \ldots \phi^{(2)}[\#0, \#0]^\lambda\,[\#0, \#1]^\lambda\,[\#0, h]^\alpha \ldots$$

$$\ldots \Lambda_{(2)} \dashv \ldots \phi^{(2)}[\#0, \#0]^\lambda\,[\#0, \#1]^\lambda\,[\#2, f]^\alpha \ldots \vdash \ldots \vdash$$

$$\dashv \ldots \Lambda_{(1)} \dashv \ldots \Lambda_{(1)} \dashv \ldots \phi^{(2)}[\#1, \#0]^\lambda\,[\#2, \#0]^\lambda\,[\#3, g]^\alpha \ldots \vdash \ldots$$

$$\ldots \phi^{(2)}[\#2, \#1]^\lambda\,[\#2, \#0]^\lambda\,[\#3, f]^\alpha \ldots \vdash \ldots \vdash$$

Here all *lambdas-* and *alphas-*binding indices identify correct binding levels with respect to the environment frames in which they are instantiated.

10.2.4   Outline of an Implementation

Implementing the run-time structure for full-fledged β-reductions-in-the-large as just described obviously encompasses two things.

Firstly, we must adapt the **pre-** and **post-processor** to the modified internal representations of bound variable occurrences. This concerns

- the pre-processing function RENAME which now must convert occurrences of λ-bound variables into index tuples $[\#i, \#j]^\lambda$ rather than into plain de Bruijn indices, and must attach *alphas-*binding levels to occurrences of LETREC-bound variables;

- the post-processing function RESTORE which now must substitute in a partially or completely processed expression the original variable names for occurrences of index tuple representations of λ-bound variables, and must eliminate α^*-binding levels.

Secondly, we have to specify a **suitable representation of the run-time structure** itself and of its manipulation. This includes the representation and manipulation of **closures**, i.e., of instances of expressions in given environments.

The run-time structure that dynamically grows and shrinks during the execution of program expressions, as variously pointed out, is made up from

- frames created by β-reductions-in-the-large whose entries, in general, represent

- closures composed of argument (operand) expressions and of the environments which specify the instantiations of their relatively free variable occurrences.

The frames that are to form continuous environments may be piled up non-contiguously, requiring special pointer chains to link them in the correct order of nesting. To accommodate these pointer chains and other data pertaining to the construction and management of the run-time structure, it is expedient to attach so-called **frame control blocks** (or **frame descriptors**) to all frames of the run-time structure. Each frame control block includes

- a LINK entry for the pointer to the preceding frame in the particular environment (or for a $\triangle$ if no further frame exists);

- an ID_COUNT entry which keeps track of the number of environment pointers referring to the frame;

- a NO_OF_ARGS entry specifying the number of closure entries in the frame;

- a PAR_AP entry indicating whether or not the frame results from the partial application of a λ-abstraction, in which case we have dummy symbols $\otimes$ in one or several of the uppermost frame entry positions.

These items can be conveniently packed into a double-word format, of which the LINK pointer occupies, say, the first word.

A closure must be represented as a pair of **pointers**, of which one identifies the graph of an **argument expression**, whereas the other points to its **environment**. This would suggest that all frame entries have double-word format to accommodate two pointers of word-format. However, this approach may not be very economical in terms of the stack space expended. On the one hand, many argument expressions do not include relatively free variable occurrences, in which case the environments are empty. On the other hand, it is imperative for the indexed addressing mode that all frame entries be of equal size. Thus, whenever an argument object has no environment, a memory word is wasted.

We could simply tolerate this waste as being rather minor if we wouldn't have an easy way of avoiding it. We remember that our program graphs include descriptors specifying type and structure of subgraphs (or heap objects). They can be made large enough to make available a complete word for an environment pointer entry PTR_TO_ENV in each of the relevant descriptor formats.

Thus, the entries into the frames of the run-time structure remain pointers to argument expressions whose descriptors now contain the pointers to the respective environments. Empty environments are depicted as $\triangle$ symbols.

Without specifying the program expression whose reduction brings it about, we show in fig. 10.10 a typical run-time structure R constructed from the described components. It features several frames set up in their order of creation by β-reductions-in-the-large, with the creation of the topmost frame just in progress. The structure is controlled by two registers TOP_OF_ENV and CURR_ENV_PTR, of which

- the former holds the pointer to the actual top position into which the next entry is to be placed;

- the latter holds the pointer to the environment in which the current β-reduction-in-the-large (i.e., the one creating the topmost frame) takes place.

The control blocks on top of the frames hold the pointers by which the frames belonging to a particular environment are linked up in the order of increasing *lambdas*-binding levels. The frame entries point to descriptors of argument expressions (graphs) which, in turn, contain the pointers to the environments in which the arguments must be reduced.

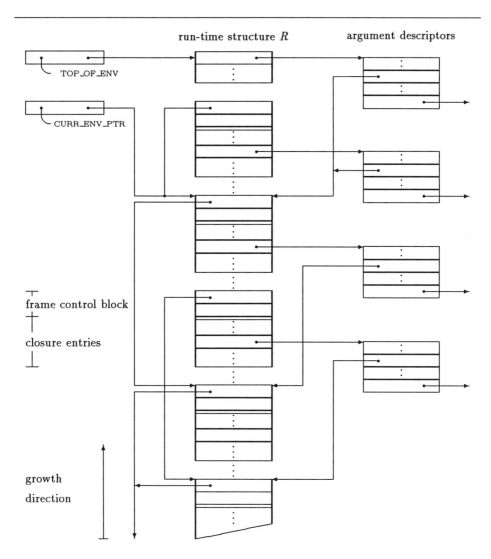

run-time structure R argument descriptors

TOP_OF_ENV

CURR_ENV_PTR

frame control block

closure entries

growth
direction

Figure 10.10: A typical run-time structure for lazy β-reductions-in-the-large

Accesses to the run-time structure are effected by occurrences of tuples $[\#i, \#j]^\lambda$ or $[\#k, f\_i]^\alpha$ in the program expression. Their *lambdas-*(or *alphas-*)binding indices in fact specify the number of link pointers (or levels of indirection) that have to be followed up along the pointer chain originating in the CURR_ENV_PTR register, in order to arrive at the frames that have to be accessed. The index #0 specifies the frame referred to by the pointer in the CURR_ENV_PTR register.

In particular, the following operations involving the **run-time structure** R need to be carried out while traversing a program expression in search for reducible applications: whenever we encounter in the head position of a spine (or in the operator position of an applicator)

- an index tuple $[\#i, \#j]^{\lambda}$, the i-th frame of the current environment is accessed with the index j as offset relative to its top. The argument expression (graph) referred to by the pointer found in this frame entry is copied into the head position of the spine (i.e., on top of stack E), and the CURR_ENV_PTR register is overwritten with the environment pointer found in the argument descriptor in order to set up the environment in which further reductions at the head are to take place.

- an index tuple $[\#k, f\_i]^{\alpha}$, the λ-abstraction represented by f_i is copied into the head position of the spine, and the control block of the k-th frame of the current environment is accessed to copy its ENV_PTR entry into the CURR_ENV_PTR register as the new environment pointer.

- a pointer, it is replaced with a copy of the expression identified by it, and the CURR_ENV_PTR register is overwritten with the environment pointer found in its descriptor.

- an instance of a β-reduction-in-the-large, it is reduced in essentially the same way as supercombinator applications: pointers to tail expressions (arguments) are taken from stack A and pushed into the run-time structure R as part of a new frame. When pushing a pointer to an argument which contains free variables, the current environment pointer (i.e., the contents of the CURR_ENV_PTR register) is copied into the PTR_TO_ENV entry of its descriptor if this entry is not yet instantiated. When completing a frame, a control block is put on top. It receives its ENV_LINK entry from the contents of the CURR_ENV_PTR register, has its NO_OF_ARGS entry set to the arity of the λ-abstraction, and its ID_COUNT entry set to one.

Occurrences of index tuples $[\#i, \#j]^{\lambda}$ in tail (or operand) positions are replaced with the argument pointers found in the respective environment frame entries. The ENV_PTR entries in the descriptors of these argument expressions are left as they are.

The occurrence of an index tuple $[\#k, f\_i]^{\alpha}$ in a tail position must be replaced with a pointer to the instantiation of the function definition (λ-abstraction) f_i in the environment identified by the *alphas*-binding level $\#k$. To do so, the contents of the descriptor template for f_i are copied into a new descriptor. The PTR_TO_ENV entry of this descriptor is overwritten with the ENV_LINK entry of the frame control block found $\#k$ levels of indirection down from the CURR_ENV_PTR register entry. Finally, the pointer to the new descriptor is substituted for the tuple $[\#k, f\_i]^{\alpha}$.

Whenever an environment pointer is copied, the ID_COUNT entry in the frame control block must be incremented by one. The consumption of environment pointers in the course of deleting frames or graphs, or in the course of reducing graphs to normal forms, decrements the respective ID_COUNT entries by one. A frame whose ID_COUNT entry is thus decremented to zero may be released.

A severe handicap of these rather complex run-time structures concerns the time required to access its entries. It grows linearly with the *lambdas*-binding levels which, in fact, denote the number of indirect accesses (or the number of bridges established by the link pointers that must be crossed) in order to arrive at the specified environment frames. If the program makes frequent use of global parameters, the overall run-time performance may thus be considerably degraded.

However, there is a well-known remedy to this problem based on so-called **displays**. Whenever a new environment must be configured from the existing run-time structure, all pointers along the chain connecting its frames are in the order of increasing *lambdas*-binding indices collected in an **array** (the **display**). The pointer to the base of this display (rather than the pointer to the topmost frame of the environment) is loaded into the CURR_ENV_PTR register.

Accesses to all environment entries can now be accomplished in the same time, involving just one level of indirection: the *lambdas*-binding index of an index tuple is used as an offset relative to the base of the display to locate the pointer to the selected frame, and the Λ's binding index, as before, is used as an offset relative to the top of this frame.

Another problem concerns the management of the memory space taken up by the run-time structure.

Economy in space requires that the frames whose ID_COUNT values have decremented to zero be released immediately. Since creating and in this way releasing frames does not necessarily follow a LIFO-order, the run-time structure may develop holes, i.e., it behaves like a heap. The holes have to be administered by a linked list, and new frames have to be placed into fitting holes.

Efficiency in time, however, requires a less elaborate space management scheme by which frames are released only from the top of the run-time structure if and to the extent possible. This approach may waste memory space in that it holds on to frames that are no longer needed, but it expands and contracts the space occupied by the run-time structure strictly in LIFO-order, thus operating it truly as a stack. Whenever the entire space (segment) allocated to the stack is about to be exhausted, the stack may be compacted by

- releasing in one sweep all frames which have their ID_COUNT values set to zero;

- moving the remaining frames towards the stack bottom until all holes have disappeared.

Since run-time efficiency is generally considered more important than the efficient utilization of memory space (which can be generously supplied), preference will in almost all systems be given to the latter solution.

10.3 A Critical Assessment

In comparison to applicative order (or eager) supercombinator reductions, lazy β-reductions-in-the-large obviously require a decidedly more sophisticated run-time environment.

In the former case, the run-time structure expands and contracts strictly in LIFO-order and thus can be implemented as a stack. Otherwise its frames are totally unrelated to each other: they represent supercombinator instances whose entries are pointers to argument expressions which are in normal form. New frames are pushed into the stack on instances of supercombinator reductions; frames are popped off the top of the stack whenever control returns from the reduction of the respective body terms. All accesses are made to the actual topmost stack frame only.

Moreover, since all graph structures are in normal form, they can be shared without any problems. Once they are created, they are only copied and eventually consumed, but never overwritten.

However, in the latter case we have to deal with rather complex run-time structures. Their frames must be linked together in an intricate way by pointer chains in order to configure complete environments in which to reduce the various subterms of a program. Accessing these frames may require indirect addressing over several levels, unless special displays are generated for the active environments. The frame entries represent operand expressions in which the substitution of free variable occurrences is delayed until it becomes absolutely necessary to reduce them to canonical forms. They must therefore, in the form of closures, carry their complete environments with them. Since these closures can be rather freely substituted anywhere else, the frames of the run-time structure cannot be released in a clear-cut LIFO-order. Instead, the states of computation in which this can be done must be determined by carefully counting the number of environment pointers directed at them.

Executing instances of β- and δ-reductions becomes more complicated as well. Lazy evaluation entails overwriting application nodes in order to share reductions to normal forms among possibly several pointer occurrences. Special contexts must be created to do this in an orderly way.

All this adds up to the hard fact that our lazy graph reduction engine, considering a comparable hardware configuration, bandwidth, clock frequency and other performance-relevant physical parameters, is bound to accomplish less reductions per unit time than our eager graph reduction engine. On average, the performance degradation can be expected to considerably outweigh the gains made by avoiding a few redundant reductions.

Another problem with lazy graph reduction in general concerns non-sequential program execution.

If laziness is to be fully sustained, application nodes that are shared among several concurrently executing processes must be protected against multiple attempts to evaluate them. This may not only inflict a substantial communication overhead, but processes that are temporarily blocked while waiting for the evaluation of a shared subgraph ought to be re-scheduled in order to avoid idling processing capacity. Blocking may also serialize potentially concurrent processes to the extent that little is gained in comparison to a strictly sequential execution mode.

The constraints of laziness may be relaxed by a less rigorous approach called eager beaver evaluation. The idea is to have a master process work its way down the spine of a (sub-)graph, and to have the tails picked up for concurrent evaluation by slave processes as long as processing capacity can be made available. In order to cut down on synchronization and communication overhead, the slave processes reduce the tails eagerly (or on a speculative basis), with the effect that more reduction steps than necessary may be performed, regardless of whether or not multiple evaluations of shared (sub-)graphs are tolerated. However, at least some of this redundancy can be avoided by a careful selection and ordering of the tails that benefit most from concurrent evaluation, e.g., based on program annotations introduced by the pre-processor (or a compiler) as part of a strictness analysis. For all practical purposes we thus end up performing non-sequential computations in essentially the same way as under an applicative order regime.

Thus, a lazy evaluation regime does not appear to be the best choice with respect to non-sequential program execution. Even a sequential execution mode is not competitive, in terms of raw run-time performance, with applicative order reduction. As pointed out before, the overhead necessary to avoid a few superfluous reduction steps generally more than outweighs the processing time that can be saved.

Lazy evaluation derives its merits primarily from its semantics and from the ensuing programming style. On the one hand, it guarantees program termination with a normal form if one exists (i.e., if the program is at all meaningful). On the other hand, it opens up new ways of elegantly and concisely formulating finite application problems based on the composition and de-composition of infinite structures.

However, using this programming technique effectively requires a rather intimate knowledge of the details of lazy program execution, which seems to contradict to some extent the purely declarative character of a functional programming style.

The controversy surrounding the issue of lazy vs. eager evaluation reflects itself in the existence of functional languages and (reduction) systems supporting them that are applicative, e.g., Standard ML, HOPE and SCHEME [HaMiTo88, BuMQSa80, Dyb87, AbSus85], lazy, e.g., SASL, LML, MIRANDA and HASKELL [Turn76, Aug84, Turn85, HuWa88], or partly lazy where explicitly so specified in the program text, such as HOPE, SML and Henderson's LISPKIT [Hend80, HeJoJo83]. With the eager graph reduction engine on the one hand and the lazy graph reduction engine on the other hand, we have presented two conceivable architectures for reduction systems that cover both ends of this spectrum with respect to

- the form in which operands (arguments) are passed on to operators (functions), and

- the way non-local (or relatively free) variables and the ensuing potential for naming conflicts are dealt with.

11 Compiling Functional Languages

Reduction relates to a purely functional programming paradigm which is free of all elements pertaining to the organizational details of program execution. The semantics of reduction language programs is directly and completely defined by the rewrite rules of a formal (functional) calculus. Application problems are specified merely in terms of recursive function definitions and function applications. They prescribe little more than partially ordered meaning-preserving program transformations which generally are expected to terminate with problem solutions eventually. It is entirely left to the system to deduce from a given program a plan (or a schedule) for its execution. This plan includes the sequencing of transformation steps in compliance with their logical dependencies on the one hand, and the allocation of the system's resources on the other hand. In short: a program ideally specifies just what is to be computed, whereas the system must figure out how the computation is to be organized.

The reduction systems described so far in this monograph are high-level interpreters for OREL/0 which do all the program-internal scheduling dynamically at run-time. This is largely a consequence of supporting a full-fledged untyped λ-calculus which accepts as arguments of β-reductions all legitimate OREL/0 expressions. Functions are truly treated as first class objects: they may be applied to other functions or to themselves, and functions may be returned as results, e.g., of partial applications. The component expressions of lists, IF-THEN-ELSE clauses and CASEs need not be of the same type, and almost all primitive functions are generic (or overloaded), i.e., they are applicable to objects of different types and shapes.

The ensuing freedom of program design renders it difficult, if not impossible, to deduce à priori complete run-time schedules by means of a static program analysis. To do so, a pre-processor or a compiler would have to infer from a given program text

- if and to which extent applications can be actually reduced with respect to compatible types and arities of their component expressions;

- types and shapes of the expressions consumed and (re-)produced in the course of performing reductions, which in turn determines

- how much memory space either in the heap or in the environment structure can be released or must be claimed upon each instance of a reduction.

The crucial issue here is static type inference. With untyped languages such as HLFL (or OREL/0) we face the problem that the types of IF-THEN-ELSE clauses, CASEs or selector operations on heterogeneous lists can only be narrowed down to the union of the respective component types. Further difficulties arise from applications of primitive generic functions to untyped variables which may eventually become instantiated with objects of different types, depending on the actual program parameters.

Uncertainties about types also foreclose the static preparation of complete schedules for the allocation/de-allocation of memory space since different types generally require different formats. For the same reason it is generally not possible to decide à priori whether and to which extent applications specified in the source program text can be actually reduced.

Taking care of all these things at run-time, as we have seen, creates a considerable overhead. In addition to dynamic type checking and heap space management, it consists in searching the actual program expression for executable instances of reductions, matching the arities of functions against the arities of applicators, creating environment frames, etc. When running non-trivial programs, a substantial part of this overhead is inflicted by recursive function calls and thus highly repetitive. This is particularly annoying if the functions are in fact tail-end recursive, in which case the same heap segments and environment structures, once configured and allocated, could be used repeatedly.

This overhead may simply be accepted as the price that must be paid for the freedom of programming provided by an untyped λ-calculus. Distinguishing different instances of a general operational scheme quite obviously is more expensive to implement and more time-consuming to execute than dedicated operations on objects of specific types.

However, it is perfectly justified to challenge the generality of a full-fledged λ-calculus when it comes to writing useful application programs and to executing them efficiently. There are good reasons to argue that full support for higher-order functions (including self-applications), heterogeneously typed conditionals or lists, etc., are luxuries which are rarely used, and that stepwise program execution under interactive control is not a very practical means to validate large programs. Intermediate programs may easily become too complex to be comprehensible.

Instead, more confidence in the **correctness** of **programs** may be established by a rigorous **typing discipline**. A polymorphic or monomorphic type system which requires that all legitimate programs be **well-typed** does not only facilitate the static detection of a variety of programming errors. It also renders it possible to compile **high-level programs into low-level machine code** in which the sequencing of operations, the types of operators and operands, and the configuration of the memory are largely worked out à priori. This can of course only be done to the extent to which types can be inferred from (or are explicitly specified in) the original program text, and to which the objects of a particular type can be represented by the same format or by a scheme for the systematic construction of composite formats.

Compiled versions of well-typed programs can be efficiently executed on fairly simple machinery. Operands are represented as bit strings of type-specific formats placed into pre-assigned memory (environment frame) locations. These formatted strings have no meaningful interpretation of their own. Operators simply take the contents of the memory (frame) locations they refer to as formatted operand representations, perform type-specific operations on them, and put formatted representations of result values into pre-assigned memory locations.

This primitive operator/operand concept is used in almost all computing systems that are commercially available today. In these systems, the responsibility for the correct execution of high-level language programs by equivalent machine code rests entirely with the compiler. It must work out a detailed and complete plan for the sequencing of machine-level operators (or instructions), for the configuration of the memory space (environment frames) and, most importantly, for the coordinated interaction of the machine code with the memory contents. Since all operators, loosely speaking, expect the right things to be in the right places at the right time, this plan (or schedule) must be strictly obeyed at run-time in order to guarantee correct results. Unless explicitly incorporated in the plan, alternative courses of action are not permitted. In particular, the plan itself cannot be changed dynamically, i.e., machine-level programs must be treated as constant objects.

A widely accepted concept of executing high-level functional programs in this way is compiled graph reduction. It constitutes a significant departure from reduction concepts described thus far which has repercussions on both the expressive power of the high-level languages and on the appearance of the system to the user.

What is usually done is to compile the set of (recursively nested) function definitions of a program into intermediate code of some suitably defined abstract machine. This abstract machine code, which is subsequently compiled to code of a conventional target machine, essentially manipulates the graph representation of the outermost goal expression whose normal form is to be computed.

Representing defined functions internally as procedural code implies that

- functions of n formal parameters (λ-bound variables) must be applied to n actual parameters (arguments), possibly of specific types, in order to execute the code correctly;

- programs must be executed to completion in order to transform the graph into a legitimate successor graph;

- we have a separation of functions from the objects (or operands), in this particular case the components of the graph, they operate on.

As a consequence, we must abandon the concept of higher-order functions as supported by a full-fledged untyped λ-calculus. Whereas functions may still be passed

as actual parameters and partial function applications may be internally represented
as closures, there is no way of returning in a high-level representation functions as
values (or normal forms). Moreover, the possibilities of inspecting partially reduced
programs are at least severely limited due to the fact that intermediate machine
states cannot be re-transformed in a straightforward way into equivalent high-level
program expressions. Machine states suited for re-transformations are usually those
following the completion of top-level function applications, i.e., when returning from
code sequences that perform full rewrite operations on the graph.

The overwhelming majority of functional computing systems proposed or implemented to date are based on compiled graph reduction. The most prominent
example in kind is the so-called G-machine [John83] which has become more or less
a standard vehicle for the implementation of lazy functional languages. Recursively
nested function definitions are transformed into a flat set of supercombinators using
λ-lifting techniques, and the supercombinators are subsequently compiled into abstract G-machine code which generates and manipulates a graph. The emphasis of
this concept is almost exclusively on high run-time performance without concern
for the advantages that come with full reductions. It is carefully tuned to compute
with utmost speed (sequences of) elementary values, taking short-cuts through sequences of δ-reductions whenever possible, rather than transforming expressions in
a more general sense.

SKI combinator reduction systems [Turn79, ClGl80] which implement functional
languages in yet another way suffer, for different reasons, from essentially the same
limitations. High-level programs are here converted into expressions composed of
standardized combinators by the systematic abstraction of bound variables. Each
combinator passes an argument just from one syntactical node to the next by
re-arranging a few pointers within a very narrow scope. Since each combinator
reduction step produces another combinator expression, we have a full reduction
semantics, i.e., the system could be made to perform reductions in a stepwise manner.

However, the conversion into SKI combinator expressions is a one-way affair
which alienates even simple high-level programs to the extent that both representations can hardly be related to each other. With all variables gone, a systematic
re-conversion is not possible either. Thus, even though functions can be computed
as normal forms of programs, they cannot be made visible to the user other than
as unintelligible SKI combinator expressions.

We will briefly outline these two graph reduction concepts in the following sections.

11.1   The G-Machine

The G-machine was proposed by Johnson in 1984 [John83, John84, John85, John87] as an intermediate level of code generation for the compilation of lazy ML [Aug84] to conventional target machines featuring a VAX-like architecture (see chapter 12). It defines an abstract lazy evaluator for compiled supercombinator terms.

The G-machine compiler accepts as source programs flat sets of (mutually recursive) supercombinator definitions followed by goal expressions. They have the following simple syntax:

$$program = f\ x\_1 \ldots x\_n = f\_expr$$
$$\vdots$$
$$g\ y\_1 \ldots y\_m = g\_expr$$
$$s\_expr\ .$$

The supercombinator names $f, g, \ldots$ may occur free in all body expressions on the right hand sides of the definitions and in the goal expression s_expr; other variables in f_expr and g_expr may only be from the formal parameter sets $\{x\_1, \ldots, x\_n\}$ and $\{y\_1, \ldots, y\_m\}$, respectively.

Expressions may be

- variables (including supercombinator names) or constants;

- curried applications, denoted as

$$expr\_0\ expr\_1\ \ldots\ expr\_n$$

  (where $expr\_0$ is taken as the function and $expr\_1, \ldots, expr\_n$ are taken as the arguments);

- local variable definitions which may be non-recursive, denoted as LET D IN s_expr, or recursive, denoted as LETREC D IN s_expr, where D $\equiv$ $x\_1 =$ $expr\_1, \ldots, x\_n = expr\_n$.

Note that expressions do not include local supercombinator definitions. The LETREC expressions, in contrast to their semantics in OREL/0, merely serve to define local cycles within supercombinator bodies. In conjunction with the lazy evaluation regime of the G-machine, these cycles are very useful for generating infinite structures. The LET expressions are semantically equivalent to the WHERE clauses of HLFL .

Programs specified, say, in HLFL or in another functional language such as MIRANDA or ML, which may have nested function definitions containing relatively free variables, can be readily converted into this form. All there is to be done is to

- first transliterate these programs into terms of an applied λ-calculus;

- then transform all open λ-abstractions into supercombinators by systematically abstracting free variables out to the next higher levels of binders;

- finally lift all supercombinator definitions thus obtained to the top level.

For an outline of the first two conversion steps, the reader is referred to section 8.1 which defines the transliteration of HLFL programs into the applied λ-calculus OREL/0, and to section 9.3 which describes the conversion of recursively defined OREL/0 λ-abstractions into supercombinators. The third step can be added as a matter of convenience: there is no need to define supercombinators local to others unless the original nesting levels of function definitions must be re-constructed.

The G-machine too employs **supercombinators** to eliminate name clashes when substituting (pointers to) arguments for formal function parameters. As we learned earlier, this requires that supercombinators be applied to full argument sets and that all substitutions be carried out **in one conceptual step**. Partial applications must remain as they are and be treated as closures. Supercombinators can therefore be expected to compile to fairly simple and hence efficiently executable static code.

11.1.1   The Run-Time Environment

Very much like the *SECD* machine introduced in section 5.3.8, the G-machine essentially works with four data structures which define the complete machine state. They are

- a **control structure** C which holds the G-machine code;

- a **run-time stack** S which holds the **contexts** in which supercombinator reductions are to be carried out;

- the **graph** G of the expression to be reduced by the code held in the control structure C;

- a **dump** D which handles recursively nested reductions.

All G-machine instructions may be defined in terms of a **state transition function**

$$\tau_G : (S, G, C, D) \rightarrow (S', G', C', D')$$

which maps a current state into a next state. In order to specify τ_G in detail, we first have to develop some informal understanding of how these data structures interact with each other.

The basic mechanism of the G-machine concerns the evaluation of function-turned-supercombinator applications and primarily involves the graph and the stack. The graph may be considered the actual focus of control of a program in execution. The code held in C repeatedly constructs new parts of the graph representing instantiated supercombinator bodies and subsequently reduces them by overwriting application nodes with graphs of the respective canonical forms. The stack essentially accommodates the activation records (argument frames) of supercombinator instances, together with some dynamically expanding and collapsing local work spaces for temporaries.

To see how this works, we consider an application

$$func \; arg\_1 \; arg\_2 \; arg\_3 \; arg\_4 \; ,$$

assuming that $func$ is a supercombinator of arity 3. The graph for this application features a two-place constructor syntax, using explicit normal order applicators @ as introduced in section 6.1 to form inner graph nodes. Thus, the pre-order linearized version of the graph is

$$\overline{@} \; \overline{@} \; \overline{@} \; \overline{@} \; \$func \; arg\_1 \; arg\_2 \; arg\_3 \; arg\_4$$

where $\$func$ denotes the code for executing the instantiated body of $func$.

Fig. 11.1 illustrates the two major transformation steps necessary to set up the G-machine for the execution of the code sequence $\$func$ which is expected to return the canonical form of a full application of $func$. These transformations are carried out by the control instruction UNWIND. It is the most complex instruction of the G-machine which in fact realizes an interpreter for application graphs. It sets out with a pointer to the topmost application node of the graph in the stack (fig. 11.1.a), traverses the spine of the graph, and thereby pushes into the stack all graph pointers in the order in which they are encountered (with the stack growing downwards). This continues until the code $\$func$ in the head of the spine is reached[30] (see fig. 11.1.b). Upon inspecting an arity tag associated with $\$func$, UNWIND dereferences, as a prelude to entering the code sequence $\$func$, the topmost three application node pointers on the stack to retrieve the respective argument pointers. They are pushed on top of the pointer to the outermost node of the full supercombinator application (the node referenced by the pointer is the one to be overwritten by the canonical form). The frame thus constructed, together with items that may be temporarily pushed onto and popped off the stack while executing the code, forms the context in which the supercombinator body is to be actually reduced (see fig. 11.1.c).

---

[30]Note that, in difference to the lazy graph reducer described in chapter 9, the spines are here left-right transposed.

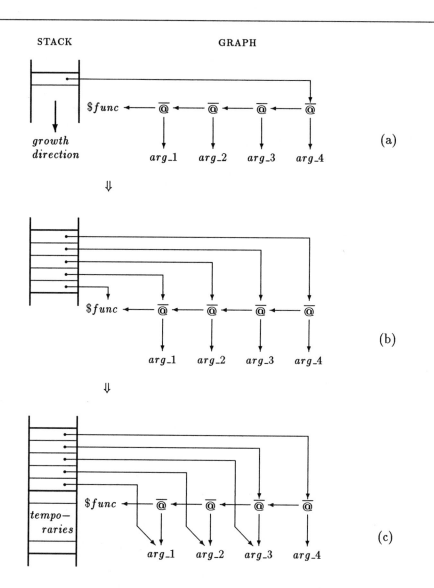

Figure 11.1: Unwinding a spine on the stack

It is important to note that the instruction UNWIND in fact interprets the actual graph: it analyses the structure of the spine and, upon inspecting the arity of the function, constructs an argument frame from its components.

The G-machine code accesses stack entries with fixed offsets relative to the actual stack top, and only within the topmost context. To figure out what these offsets are, the compiler uses two parameters ρ and d with the following conventions: assuming that all entries are **pointers** of unit length (say one memory word),

- d measures the depth of the actual context in multiples of these units;

- ρ is a mapping which assigns indices $i \in \{0, \ldots, d-1\}$ to all entries of the actual context in monotonically ascending order, starting with $i = 0$ at the lowermost entry (which is the pointer to the topmost application node);

- $(d-1-i)$ is the actual offset of the i-th entry relative to the top of the stack (assuming that the stack top pointer always points to the topmost entry).

For the formal parameters of a supercombinator

$$f\ x\_1 \ldots x\_n = f\_expr$$

we thus have a mapping ρ with

$$\rho(x\_i) = (n+1) - i \quad \text{for all } i \in \{1, \ldots, n\}\,,$$

i.e., the argument pointers to be substituted for the parameters x_i can be found in the index positions $(d-1-\rho(x\_i))$ relative to the actual stack top. Though not very significant, we note that the order induced by ρ is reverse to the one in which the argument pointers must be stacked up when using de Bruijn indices as offsets relative to the stack top (compare section 9.2).

11.1.2 Compiling Supercombinators to G-Machine Code

To keep the specification of the G-compiler simple, we focus only on the basic syntactical constructs of the source language as given at the beginning of this chapter, and abstract completely from the particularities of various primitive functions and type instantiations. We also assume that **type checking** is performed as an integral part of the **semantic analysis** of the source programs. G-code is produced only for **well-typed programs**. G-machine instructions will be introduced and explained as we proceed.

The G-compiler uses three major **compilation schemes** F, R and C.[31] The top-level scheme F applies to complete supercombinator definitions, transforming them

---

[31] We use here the compilation schemes introduced by Peyton-Jones in [Peyt87] rather than those that can be found in the original work of Johnson [John84, John87].

thus:

$$F[\![\, f \; x\_1 \ldots x\_n = f\_expr \,]\!] = \text{GLABEL}\, f, n; R[\![\, f\_expr \,]\!][x\_1 = n, \ldots, x\_n = 1]n+1;$$

where

$$R[\![\, f\_expr \,]\!]\, \rho\, d = C[\![\, f\_expr \,]\!]\, \rho\, d; \text{UPDATE}\; (d+1); \text{POP}\; d; \text{UNWIND}\,.$$

The code specified on the right-hand sides of F and R breaks down as follows:

GLABEL f, n is a pseudo-instruction which assigns to the code sequence a global entry label $\$f$ and the number of arguments needed;

$R[\![\, f\_expr \,]\!]\, \rho\, d$ defines a compilation scheme for supercombinator bodies of which we consider, for the time being, only the general case;

$C[\![\, f\_expr \,]\!]$ generates the code for f_expr which upon completion leaves on the stack a pointer to some resulting graph, thus increasing the depth of the actual context by one;

UPDATE $(d+1)$ overwrites the root node pointer of the application of f with a copy of the pointer pushed by $C[\![\, f\_expr \,]\!]$, and subsequently pops it;

POP d pops the topmost d entries, i.e., the complete argument frame, leaving only the pointer to the new graph on the stack;

UNWIND   unwinds the new graph along its spine to continue with further reductions (or to terminate if this graph is a canonical form other than a supercombinator or a primitive function).

The compilation scheme C applies only to expressions. It sets up code for the construction of instantiated graphs, using the parameters ρ and d to determine the offsets to the frame entries by which the variables $x\_1, \ldots, x\_n$ must be replaced. All code sequences generated by C terminate by pushing a pointer to the instantiated graph on the stack.

In defining C, we first consider the cases that are rather straightforward:

$$C[\![\, expr \,]\!]\, \rho\, d = \begin{cases} \text{PUSHVAL } val & \text{if} \quad expr = val \\ & \text{and } val \text{ is a constant value} \\ \text{PUSHFUN } \$func & \text{if} \quad expr = func \\ & \text{and } func \text{ is a supercombinator value} \\ \text{PUSHVAR } (d-1-\rho(x)) & \text{if} \quad expr = x \\ & \text{and } x \text{ is a formal parameter} \\ C[\![\, expr\_2 \,]\!]\, \rho\, d; C[\![\, expr\_1 \,]\!]\, \rho\, (d+1); \text{MKAP} \\ & \text{if} \quad expr = expr\_1 \; expr\_2 \end{cases}$$

(the various PUSH instructions push onto the stack whatever item follows as a parameter).

The last case is the one which builds new application nodes in the graph. The instruction MKAP creates a cell of the form

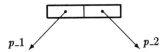

where p_1 and p_2 are copies of the pointers pushed on the stack by the codes $C[\![expr\_1]\!]$ and $C[\![expr\_2]\!]$, respectively. Having done so, MKAP pops these pointers and pushes the pointer p to this cell.

As for the compilation of the local variable declarations, let us first consider the non-recursive version

$$\text{LET } x\_1 = expr\_1, \ldots, x\_n = expr\_n \text{ IN } s\_expr .$$

When applying the compilation scheme C to all subexpressions from left to right, the resulting code pushes pointers to the respective graphs in the same order, creating in fact a frame for the instantiation of the variables $x\_1, \ldots, x\_n$ on the stack. The layout of this frame must simply be passed on, by means of the parameters ρ and d, to the compilation of s_expr in order to have all its variable occurrences replaced by the proper offsets into the stack. Upon completing the execution of the code for s_expr, the entire frame can be dropped, leaving on the stack only the pointer to the graph of s_expr. We thus get the following compilation rule:

$$C[\![\text{LET } x\_1 = expr\_1, \ldots, x\_n = expr\_n \text{ IN } s\_expr]\!] \, \rho \, d =$$
$$C[\![expr\_1]\!] \, \rho \, d, \ldots, C[\![expr\_n]\!] \, \rho \, d; C[\![s\_expr]\!] \, \rho' \, d'; \text{SLIDE } n$$

where $\rho' = \rho[x\_1 = d, \ldots, x\_n = d + n - 1]$ and $d' = d + n$, and the instruction SLIDE n 'squeezes' n consecutive entries from underneath the topmost entry out of the stack. Note that the LET-frame simply extends the current context.

The compilation of a LETREC expression is a little trickier for here we have to construct cyclic structures. To illustrate what the compiled code is supposed to do, we consider, as a simple example, the expression

$$\text{LETREC } x = (f \, y), y = (g \, x) \text{ IN } \dashv \ldots x \ldots y \ldots \vdash .$$

It defines two mutually recursive variables with which the body must be instantiated.

Fig. 11.2 shows what is supposed to happen on the stack and to the graph in the various phases of executing the code for this LETREC. For each variable definition it first pushes (a pointer to) an empty cell, called a hole, thus setting up a frame with dummy instantiations of x and y. Next the code creates a graph for $(f\ y)$, replacing y with the pointer retrieved from the corresponding position in the frame, and pushes the pointer to this graph (see fig. 11.2.b). To instantiate x with this graph, its frame entry is overwritten with the pointer just pushed, whereupon this pointer is popped (fig. 11.2.c). Repeating the same for the expression $(g\ x)$ brings about the situation shown in fig. 11.2.d, in which we find both frame entries instantiated with the respective graphs. Finally, the code constructs the graph for s_expr (fig. 11.2.e), and subsequently squeezes the frame out from underneath the graph pointer (fig. 11.2.f).

To generate such code, the compilation scheme C must be defined thus:

$$C \llbracket \text{LETREC } x\_1 = expr\_1, \ldots, x\_n = expr\_n \text{ IN } s\_expr \rrbracket\ \rho\ d =$$
$$\text{ALLOC } n;\ C \llbracket expr\_1 \rrbracket\ \rho'\ d'; \text{UPDATE } n;$$
$$\vdots$$
$$C \llbracket expr\_n \rrbracket\ \rho'\ d'; \text{UPDATE } 1;$$
$$C \llbracket s\_expr \rrbracket\ \rho'\ d'; \text{SLIDE } (d' - d)$$

where ALLOC n creates a dummy frame of n hole entries, and $d' = d + n$, $\rho' = \rho[x\_1 = d, \ldots, x\_n = d + (n - 1)]$. Note again that the frame for the LETREC variables just extends the context in which the expression is to be executed.

Compiling a complete program includes the compilation of its **goal expression** s_expr to code which constructs and reduces its graph. To do this in a way that is consistent with the compilation of the definition part, this expression simply needs to be considered as a supercombinator of arity zero, i.e., it has no formal parameters. Thus we can use again the scheme R (and recursively C) to compile it.[32]

The context in which the graph for s_expr is to be executed contains, as its lowermost entry, the pointer to its code rather than to an application node. This, however, is exactly what eventually needs to be overwritten by the canonical form of the graph as the result of the program execution.

A compiled program thus typically includes

- some piece of code which sets up the run-time environment (e.g., the pointers to the stack, the graph and the dump, all of which are initially empty) and exercises top-level control over the program execution;

---

[32] A supercombinator of arity zero is also referred to, somewhat misleadingly though, as a constant expression (or constant application form) for it cannot be applied to anything.

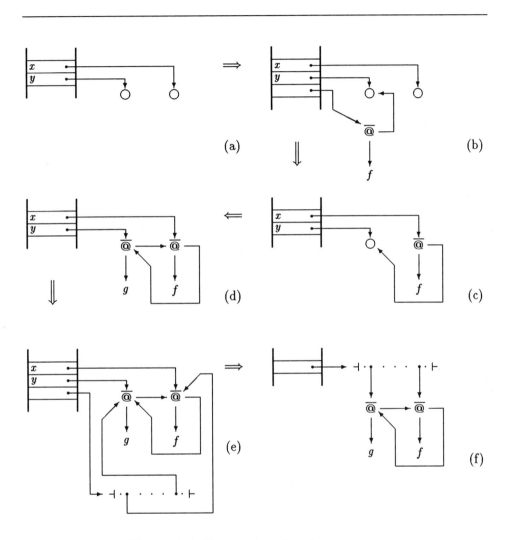

Figure 11.2: Phases of constructing a LETREC

- the *G*-code sequence for the goal expression (whose entry label is assumed to be $\$s$) which contains references to

- the *G*-code sequences for the supercombinator definitions, all of which have unique entry labels by which they may be referenced from within the goal expression graph and may cross-reference each other;

- a run-time library of G-code sequences which evaluate applications of primitive functions (or perform δ-reductions).

The G-code for the top-level initialization and control sequence looks like this:

BEGIN	(∗ of program execution, initialize the run-time environment ∗)
PUSHGLABEL $s	(∗ pushes the pointer to the goal expression code ∗)
EVAL	(∗ forces the evaluation (reduction) of the code referenced by the top-of-stack pointer which returns a graph in canonical form ∗)
PRINT	(∗ forces the evaluation of the graph referenced by the top-of-stack pointer to normal form and prints it on the output medium ∗)
END	(∗ of program execution ∗)

The instructions EVAL and PRINT play a key role in executing G-code programs. They recursively appear in all code sequences to control the reduction of selected parts of the graph in compliance with the lazy evaluation regime. We will see more of this when discussing, in the next section, some typical G-code sequences for δ-reductions. A precise definition of what these instructions effect follows in section 11.1.4.

11.1.3 G-Code for Primitive Functions

As just indicated, applications of primitive functions are reduced by means of code sequences contained in a run-time library which is attached to every executable program. Primitive functions are nothing but 'wired-in' supercombinators whose names are used as global entry labels into this library. Occurrences of primitive function symbols in the source program are compiled as $C [\![p\_func]\!] = \$p\_func$. Setting up the code $\$p\_func$ for δ-reductions follows the same path as depicted in fig. 11.1: prior to entering the code, the application is unwound on the stack, i.e., the argument pointers are pushed from outermost to innermost, and the pointer to the topmost application node is underneath.

Let us now consider three typical examples.

The application graph

$$\overline{@}\ \overline{@}\ \$\text{ADD}\ arg\_2\ arg\_1$$

specifies the addition of two arguments which generally are not in normal form and thus non-trivial graphs themselves. Since addition is strict, the code for $\$$ADD must force the evaluation of these graphs first. This can be accomplished by the following instruction sequence:

PUSH 1	(* pushes (the pointer to) *arg_1* on top of the stack *)
EVAL	(* forces the evaluation of *arg_1* and overwrites its root node with the resulting graph *)
PUSH 1	(* pushes (the pointer to) *arg_2* *)
EVAL	(* evaluates *arg_2* *)
ADD	(* adds the two topmost values on the stack, pops them, and pushes the result *)
UPDATE 3	(* overwrites the application node with this value and pops it *)
POP 2	(* pops the arguments of the application *)
RETURN	(* continues with the calling sequence *)

Applications of the binary function CONS just form a binary list node (or a CONS node) from two arguments without reducing them. The node is realized by means of a cell which looks exactly like the one for an application node, except that it is tagged as CONS rather than as AP. Thus the graph

$$\overline{@} \; \overline{@} \; \$CONS \; arg\_2 \; arg\_1$$

transforms to

$$\circ \; arg\_2 \; arg\_1$$

(where ∘ denotes the CONS node), using the trivial code sequence

MKCONS	(* forms a CONS cell from the two topmost pointers on the stack, pops them, and pushes the pointer to the node *)
UPDATE 0	(* overwrites the application node with the CONS node *)
RETURN	(* returns to the calling sequence *).

A conditional is represented by the graph

$$\overline{@} \; \overline{@} \; \overline{@} \; \$IF \; pred\_expr \; true\_expr \; false\_expr \; .$$

The function $IF is strict in its first argument (the predicate), and evaluates to canonical form the argument selected by the predicate value. We thus have the following code for $IF:

PUSH 0	(* pushes the (pointer to) the predicate expression *)
EVAL	(* evaluates it *)
JUMPFALSE LF	(* control jumps conditionally to label LF upon the predicate value FALSE *)
PUSH 1	(* pushes (the pointer to) *true_expr* *)
JUMP LT	(* jumps unconditionally to the label LT *)
LABEL LF	(* is a pseudo-instruction defining a local label LF *)
PUSH 2	(* pushes (the pointer to) *false_expr* *)
LABEL LT	(* defines a local label LT *)
EVAL	(* evaluates the expression actually referenced by the stack top *)
UPDATE 4	(* overwrites the application node with the canonical form *)
POP 3	(* pops the arguments *)
UNWIND	(* continues with further reductions *)

At this point, we have to become more specific as to what the instruction EVAL must effect and why we use in some cases the instruction UNWIND and in others the instruction RETURN to terminate a code sequence. Also, we have to explain how, by means of the instruction PRINT, the *G*-machine finally produces normal forms from graphs returned by EVAL. These graphs are generally in canonical form, i.e., all but the top-level nodes may be reducible applications.

11.1.4   A Formal Definition of the Control Instructions

The instruction EVAL is the sole enactor of reductions in the *G*-machine and thus the most important means of exercising control over the sequencing of actions. It appears in the code wherever the lazy evaluation regime demands that the canonical form of a (sub-)graph in the tail of a spine be computed. This is the case with all subgraphs in argument positions of strict function applications, and trivially so with the graph generated for the goal expression of a program (which for this purpose may be considered the tail of an application node which exists somewhere outside the program under consideration). Hence we have two EVALs in the code for $ADD, one EVAL in the top-level control sequence, but none in the code for $CONS.

Reducing a graph to canonical form involves unwinding its spine, executing the code referenced in the head of the spine, (which recursively may have to unwind the spines of tails for further reductions) and finally overwriting the root node of the graph. By convention, the pointer to this graph is always taken from the top of the stack.

Thus, EVAL in fact realizes a standardized **subroutine call** which uses a pre-defined location as the source of a reference parameter. The subroutine starts off with the instruction UNWIND to set up an argument frame for the code sequence entered at the head of the spine. Having completed the execution of this code, control

- either returns to the calling sequence by means of the instruction RETURN,

- or takes a short cut to continue with further reductions along the spine, using the instruction UNWIND as the last instruction of the sequence.

The choice of the terminating instruction depends on what the particular code sequence is computing. If it is bound to return a canonical form other than a primitive function or a supercombinator, as is the case with $ADD and $CONS, then RETURN is being used, for nothing else can be done. The situation is quite different with applications of supercombinators and with conditionals. Here we can expect to get the head of a spine expanded by a new function or by a partial application which enables further reductions along the same spine. Hence, the G-machine must continue to unwind this spine within the current call of EVAL, using the instruction UNWIND. However, UNWIND must include a RETURN to cover the case that the code produces a canonical form other than a primitive function or a reference to a supercombinator.

EVAL trivially returns its actual parameter if it is a constant value, a CONS node, or a function (supercombinator) which, by definition, are already in canonical form. Likewise, UNWIND does nothing to a constant value or a CONS node since they are already trivially unwound.

Calling a subroutine generally requires that the current state of the machine be saved, and that this state be restored when returning from it. The state of the G-machine is essentially defined by the stack, the current focus of control in executing the code, and by the dump which serves as the save area for suspended machine states. Entering a new machine state upon a subroutine call conceptually requires pushing the current state into the dump and setting up a new stack and a new code sequence. When returning from the subroutine, the old state must be retrieved from the dump and subsequently popped.

With this in mind, we are now ready to define the **state transition function**

$$\tau_G : (S, G, C, D) \rightarrow (S', G', C', D')$$

for the control instructions EVAL, UNWIND and RETURN. In doing this, we use the notation introduced in section 5.3.8 for the *SECD* machine, including the following syntax for graph nodes:

val for a constant value

∘ $p\_1\ p\_2$ for a CONS node

$\overline{@}$ $p\_1\ p\_2$ for an application node

▷ $k\ c$ for a function (supercombinator) node,

where p_1, p_2 are pointers to subgraphs, k specifies the arity of a supercombinator and c is its code sequence. Furthermore, we use $G[p\| = \ldots]$ to denote the graph node obtained by dereferencing the pointers p.

We thus get

- for the instruction EVAL:

$$(< p, S >, G[p\| = \overline{@}\ v\ n], < \text{EVAL}, C >, D) \longrightarrow$$
$$(< p >, G, < \text{UNWIND} >, < (S, C), D >) \ ;$$

$$(< p, S >, G[p\| = ▷\ 0\ c], < \text{EVAL}, C >, D) \longrightarrow (< p >, G, c, < (S, C), D >) \ ;$$

$$(< p, S >, G \begin{bmatrix} p\| = val \\ ∘\ p\_1\ p\_2 \\ ▷\ k\ c \end{bmatrix}, < \text{EVAL}, C >, D) \longrightarrow (< p, S >, G, C, D) \ ;$$

- for the instruction UNWIND:

$$(< p, S >, G[p = \overline{@}\ v\ n], < \text{UNWIND} >, D) \longrightarrow$$
$$(< v, < p, S >>, G, < \text{UNWIND} >, D) \ ;$$

$$(< p\_0, < p\_1, < \ldots < p\_k, S > \ldots >, G \begin{bmatrix} p\_0 = ▷\ k\ c \\ \text{and } \forall i \in \{1, \ldots, k\} \\ p\_i = \overline{@}\ p\_(i-1)\ n\_i \end{bmatrix},$$
$$< \text{UNWIND} >, D) \longrightarrow$$
$$(< n\_1, < n\_2, < \ldots < n\_k, < p\_k, S > \ldots >, G, C, D) \ ;$$

$$(< p\_0, < \ldots < p\_k', S > \ldots >, G[p\_0 = \overline{@}\ k\ c \text{ and } k' < k],$$
$$< \text{UNWIND} >, < (S, C), D >) \longrightarrow (< p\_k', S >, G, C, D) \ ;$$

$$(< p >, G \begin{bmatrix} p\| = val \\ ∘\ p\_1\ p\_2 \end{bmatrix}, < \text{UNWIND} >, < (S, C), D >) \longrightarrow$$
$$(< p, S >, G, C, D) \ ;$$

- and for the instruction RETURN

$$(< p\_0, < \ldots < p\_k >>, G, < \text{RETURN} >, < (S, C), D >) \longrightarrow$$
$$(< p\_k, S >, G, C, D) \,.$$

The transformation rules that deserve some special attention are

- the second one for EVAL by which control is passed directly to the code of a supercombinator with arity zero (which applies when evaluating the goal expression of a program);

- the third one for UNWIND which returns the spine as it is if the arity of the supercombinator exceeds the number of arguments (tails), i.e., we have a partial application.

Implementing the state changes effected by these instructions is actually much simpler than the definitions may suggest. What is to be saved on and unsaved from the dump conceptually are complete tuples (S, C). However, when taking a close look at the transformation rules for EVAL and RETURN, we observe that the graph pointer p in the topmost position of the old stack becomes the lowermost entry of the new stack and vice versa. Thus, rather than saving the old stack somewhere else, it may simply be extended, and the contexts of the calling and the called code sequences may be overlapped with respect to this entry – a very convenient and efficient way of passing the graph pointer as a reference parameter back and form between the two. This leaves the actual state of execution of the calling code sequence, represented by the pointer to the instruction immediately following EVAL, as the only item to be saved and unsaved. Thus, in a G-machine implementation the dump is in fact reduced to a stack for return addresses.

The last control instruction that we need to define is PRINT. It is applied to the graphs returned by the topmost EVAL as the canonical forms of the goal expressions, reduces the remaining applications, if any, and prints the resulting normal forms on the output medium, e.g., a display screen. PRINT produces legitimate output only for (CONSed graphs of) atomic values, not however for normal forms which, for instance, contain partial supercombinator applications. The obvious reason is that compiled code, particularly after it has undergone certain optimizations, cannot be printed in an intelligible form that can be readily related to the functions defined in a high-level language program.

In order to include the output into the definition of PRINT, we simply extend the quadruple specifying the state of the G-machine to $(\emptyset, S, G, C, D)$, where $\emptyset$ denotes the output medium:

$$(\emptyset, <p, S>, G[p = val], <\text{PRINT}, C>, D) \longrightarrow (<\emptyset, val>, S, G, C, D)$$
$$(\emptyset, <p, S>, G[p = \circ\ p\_1\ p\_2], <\text{PRINT}, C>, D) \longrightarrow$$
$$(\emptyset, <p\_1, <p\_2, S>>, G, <\text{EVAL}, <\text{PRINT}, <\text{EVAL}, <\text{PRINT}, C>>>>, D)\ .$$

In all other cases, the output either remains unchanged or produces some error message.

Note that in this form PRINT does not even preserve structures. Consider, as an example, the graph

$$\circ\ \circ\ a\_1\ \circ\ a\_2\ a\_3\ \circ\ a\_4\ a\_5\ .$$

Rather than printing it, say, as

$$<<a\_1 <a\_2\ a\_3>> <a\_4\ a\_5>>\ ,$$

it simply produces the flat sequence

$$a\_1\ a\_2\ a\_3\ a\_4\ a\_5\ .$$

However, this is a minor problem which can be easily rectified.

11.1.5   Some *G*-Code Optimizations

When executing compiled functional programs, the *G*-machine seems to go through essentially the same motions as the interpreting graph reducers described in chapter 9 and 10. This is not at all surprising since in either case graph representations of constructor expressions (terms) must be traversed in search for instances of reductions which subsequently must be replaced by other terms that have the same meanings. The particular reduction regime (eager or lazy) determines the traversal order and the extent to which (the components of) applications must be evaluated. Different implementations of the same basic mechanisms are primarily due to different internal program representations.

The *G*-machine constructs and reduces graphs by executing compiled code. Reductions are controlled by the instruction EVAL which subsequently unwinds the outermost spine of a graph to set up a context for the supercombinator code referenced in its head, and then executes the code in this context. The compilation schemes defined in section 11.1.2 produce code which faithfully constructs from the bottom up curried graph nodes for all applications specified in the source programs, and it does this repeatedly for recursive function (supercombinator) calls.

The interpreting graph reducers have complete program graphs laid out in the heap when entering the execution phase. In terms of application nodes, these graphs

correspond one-to-one to the respective source programs. Reductions are governed
by the appropriate version of the **control program** $\widehat{(EAR)}$ which recursively copies
application nodes (spines) into a shunting yard made up from three stacks E, A, M.
There they are traversed to create in a run-time stack R the contexts for whatever
terms are referenced in their head (function) positions, and finally the (copies of
the) head terms thus instantiated are reduced.

Thus, when running the same source program, the G-machine and the lazy interpreting graph reducer must process the same number of application nodes in
essentially the same way. With respect to elementary abstract machine operations
that need to be performed, there is no significant difference, apart from implementation details, between

- constructing a piece of graph from code vs. copying it from the heap;

- setting up a context by unwinding the spine of a graph vs. traversing an
  equivalent string of pointers about stacks;

and thus between executing an EVAL subroutine call vs. executing, say, the control
program $\widehat{(EAR_h)}$.

So far, very little, if anything at all, seems to have been gained by compilation to
G-machine code. However, the G-compiler leaves lots of room for rather straightforward optimizations which, when consequently applied, enhance the raw run-time
performance of the code significantly.

Profitable targets for optimizations are code sequences which construct superfluous application nodes and, as an immediate consequence of this, may include
redundant UNWINDs, UPDATEs, or even EVALs. They come about due to the fact
that the compilation scheme R, as it is defined in section 11.1.2, compiles supercombinators of the general form

$$f\ x\_1 \ldots x\_n = g\ expr\_1 \ldots expr\_m$$

into the standard code sequences

$$R \llbracket g\ expr\_1 \ldots expr\_m \rrbracket\ \rho\ d =$$
$$C \llbracket expr\_m \rrbracket\ \rho\ d; \ldots; C \llbracket expr\_1 \rrbracket\ \rho\ (d+m-1); C \llbracket g \rrbracket\ \rho\ (d+m);$$
$$\text{MKAP}; \ldots; \text{MKAP}; \text{UPDATE}\ (d+1); \text{POP}\ d; \text{UNWIND}$$

without regard for what the function g actually is. Thus, we obtain code which
routinely

- constructs an instantiated graph in a given context (or, more precisely, from
  entries of the current argument pointer frame);

- updates the root node of the original graph and pops the argument frame;

- then unwinds the spine of the new graph, thereby often again pushing what was already (or still is) on the stack;

- and finally executes the code $\$g$ (provided the spine holds sufficiently many arguments).

However, there are many cases in which the entire computation, if more cleverly organized, could be conveniently carried out without constructing and unwinding new spines at all. To do so, we simply redefine the compilation scheme R so as to set up dedicated code sequences for these cases.

Consider, as typical examples, applications of the primitive functions CONS, ADD, and IF to just the right number of arguments. Optimized code can then be compiled thus:

$$R \left[\!\left[\text{CONS } expr\_1 \; expr\_2 \right]\!\right] \rho \; d =$$
$$\quad C \left[\!\left[expr\_2 \right]\!\right] \rho \; d; C \left[\!\left[expr\_1 \right]\!\right] \rho \; (d+1); \text{CONS}; \text{UPDATE } (d+1); \text{POP } d; \text{RETURN}$$

$$R \left[\!\left[\text{ADD } expr\_1 \; expr\_2 \right]\!\right] \rho \; d =$$
$$\quad C \left[\!\left[expr\_2 \right]\!\right] \rho \; d; \text{EVAL}; C \left[\!\left[expr\_1 \right]\!\right] \rho \; (d+1); \text{EVAL}; \text{ADD};$$
$$\quad \text{UPDATE } (d+1); \text{POP } d; \text{RETURN}$$

$$R \left[\!\left[\text{IF } pred\_expr \; true\_expr \; false\_expr \right]\!\right] \rho \; d =$$
$$\quad C \left[\!\left[pred\_expr \right]\!\right] \rho \; d; \text{EVAL}; \text{JUMPFALSE LF}; R \left[\!\left[true\_expr \right]\!\right] \rho \; d;$$
$$\quad \text{LABEL LF}; R \left[\!\left[false\_expr \right]\!\right] \rho \; d;$$

We note that all three code sequences are free of costly MKAPs. The UNWINDS are replaced by RETURNs in the former two cases, for they do not return functions, whereas the proper completion of the code in the latter case will be set up by the recursive applications of the compilation scheme R to both alternatives of the IF-THEN-ELSE clause. The respective code sequences therefore need not even be joined by a JUMP instruction. The library code sequences which a non-optimizing R-scheme would have 'linked in' for CONS and ADD are now replaced by the G-machine instructions CONS and ADD, respectively; explicit code for the function IF has completely disappeared.

These code sequences may be further optimized by replacing all occurrences of $C \left[\!\left[expr \right]\!\right] \rho \; d; \text{EVAL};$ with a compilation scheme $E \left[\!\left[expr \right]\!\right] \rho \; d$. It generates code which evaluates $expr$ directly rather than first constructing the graph and then reducing it.

Another important optimization of the compilation scheme R concerns tail-end function calls. They are characterized by supercombinator bodies of the above general form, in which g denotes some other supercombinator of arity m.

When reducing a full application of f, say f $arg\_1 \ldots arg\_n$, the code $\$f$ first creates a new context by pushing the argument pointers, and then executes the subsequences $C [\![expr\_m]\!], \ldots, C [\![expr\_1]\!], C [\![g]\!]$ in this order, whereupon the context is extended by the pointers to the respective graphs. This situation is shown in fig. 11.3.a. Up to here, the optimized and the non-optimized code sequences are exactly the same.

The non-optimized code would now step through the sequence of m MKAPs to construct the complete graph for $\$g$ $expr\_1 \ldots expr\_m$. UPDATE $(d+1)$ and POP d would overwrite the root node of the application of f and clear the argument frame off the stack, respectively, and UNWIND would bring about the situation depicted in fig. 11.3.b.

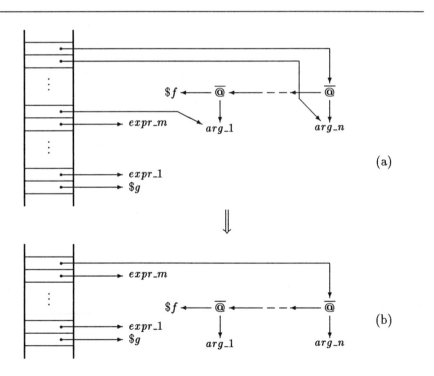

Figure 11.3: Handling tail-end recursions

We immediately recognize that we had already exactly the same argument frame as part of the old context. Moreover, updating the root node of the application $f\ arg\_1 \ldots arg\_n$ at the end of the code sequence $\$f$ can obviously be spared: the resulting graph is in fact constructed by the code $\$g$ which updates the same node. So, we may take a shortcut in getting from the context shown in fig. 11.3.a to the one of fig. 11.3.b: having pushed the pointer to the code sequence $\$g$, we must simply squeeze out the argument frame for f by sliding the topmost $(m + 1)$ stack entries down by n positions, and then jump directly to the code $\$g$. Thus, the optimized code looks like this:

$$R \llbracket g\ expr\_1 \ldots expr\_m \rrbracket\ \rho\ d =$$
$$C \llbracket expr\_m \rrbracket\ \rho\ d; \ldots; C \llbracket expr\_1 \rrbracket\ \rho\ (d + m - 1);$$
$$\text{PUSHLABEL } \$g; \text{SQUEEZE } (m + 1)\ n; \text{JFUN};$$

(JFUN takes the topmost stack entry as pointer to the code). This code passes the arguments for $\$g$ directly, i.e., without going through the redundant motions of constructing a graph from a stack frame, just to have the same frame immediately restored by unwinding this graph again.

Since R is recursively driven into the components of conditionals, we obtain code optimized in this way also for **tail-end recursive functions** of the general form

$$f\ x\_1 \ldots x\_n = \text{IF } pred\_expr\ (f\ expr\_1 \ldots expr\_n)\ false\_expr.$$

The JFUN instruction placed by R at the end of the code sequence for the THEN clause in fact turns the recursive function into an **iteration loop**.

There are a number of other code optimizations which we will not discuss here. For a complete picture on this subject the interested reader is referred to the original papers by Johnson and to the book by Peyton-Jones [John83, Peyt87]. May it suffice to say here that these optimizations, in conjunction with a clever code generator, improve the run-time performance of G-machine code by up to one order of magnitude, depending on the application programs. This makes executing functional programs almost competitive in this department with equivalent imperative programs. However, the price that must be paid for this 'advantage' in terms of the conceptual sacrifices outlined at the beginning of this chapter appears to be rather substantial.

11.1.6   What Is Given Up

The G-machine, though in some way transforming graphs, is far from realizing a full reduction semantics, let alone a full-fledged λ-calculus. On the one hand, compilation to efficient machine code imposes a number of constraints on the semantics of the functional source language, most of which are due to typing and concern higher-order functions. On the other hand, it is extremely difficult, if not impossible, to relate intermediate G-machine states uniquely to reduction steps performed on source language terms.

The primary cause of the latter problem is that the G-machine, in sharp contrast to the interpreting graph reducers, derives much of its efficiency from performing reductions within reductions. This is more or less an inescapable consequence of including, in the form of nested EVALs, the control over the graph manipulations to a large extent into pre-fabricated code, rather than inferring it from the graph itself.

In executing an EVAL, the G-machine transfers control to a subroutine which generally constructs a new spine of the graph from the components of an existing one, with most of the information distributed over the stack, the dump and the code while in the process of doing it. Nesting EVALs means that there is never a complete graph, only partially assembled pieces of it, unless the machine returns from the top-level EVAL. Eliminating many explicit EVALs by means of the compilation rule E does not basically change anything on this situation, it just shifts even more responsibilities to the code. Moreover, the code is statically type-checked and thus expects everything to be at the right time in the right place, e.g., on the stack, and of the required type and format. Thus there can be no notion of performing within a code sequence just some limited number of EVALs and of skipping the remaining ones, say by executing them as no-operations (NOPs). Correct and intelligible output can only be produced if a compiled code sequence runs to completion, or at least to the point where a canonical form can be returned, without taking shortcuts. For all practical purposes, this rules out stepwise reductions under interactive control, including the orderly termination of unending recursions, as supported by the interpreting graph reducers.

11.2 *SKI* Combinator Reduction

Another interesting concept of compiled lazy graph reduction was proposed by Turner as early as 1979 [Turn79]. The idea is to use as a target language for (intermediate) code generation a fixed set of standard combinators. It includes the *SKI* combinators introduced by Schoenfinkel and Curry as a basis for combinatory logic [Scho24, Curr29, Curr34, Curr36] (see also section 5.3), supplemented by a few others which help to reduce the size of the compiled code and hence execution times. These combinators are to distribute arguments about function bodies. The complete combinator set also includes the usual primitive value-transforming and list-structuring functions.

Compiling to and reducing *SKI* combinator terms has several conceptual and pragmatic advantages:

- the compilation follows simple rules of recursive variable abstractions from source programs of an applied λ-calculus;

- the *SKI* combinators constitute the axiomatic basis of a formal calculus with a full reduction semantics; i.e., program execution truly is a sequence of meaning-preserving combinator term transformations;

- combinator reduction is inherently free of naming conflicts and also self-optimizing;[33]

- since the compiler abstracts all bound variables individually and systematically from innermost to outermost, the combinator code for defined n-ary functions is in fact curried, i.e., partial function applications can be reduced;

- the set of combinators is simple enough to be directly taken as the specification of an *SKI* reduction machine architecture (or as the set of hard-wired reduction rules of such a machine).

The reduction of *SKI* combinator terms, as we will see in section 11.2.3, can be directly implemented on a *G*-machine. All there is to do is to include into the run-time library, in addition to the code for primitive functions, also the code for the combinators S, K, I and for some supplementary combinators. An implementation of an *SKI* reduction machine, so far as basic mechanisms are concerned, does not significantly differ from the *G*-machine [Turn79].

11.2.1   Compilation to *SKI* Combinator Terms

As the source language for compilation to *SKI* combinator terms we consider an applied λ-calculus with the following simple syntax:

$$expr = var \mid const \mid (expr\ expr) \mid \lambda var.expr \mid \text{DEFINE} \ldots f = expr \ldots \text{IN}\ expr$$

Programs of any high-level functional language, as we know, can be brought into this syntactical form more or less by straightforward transliteration.

---

[33] Combinator reductions systematically proceed in the head of the outermost spine of the graph and are shared with all pointers directed at them. All functions are therefore reduced to weak normal forms only when needed and at most once before being applied to arguments, i.e., combinator reductions are in fact fully lazy.

In order to define the rules by which these λ-terms can be compiled to combinator terms, it is helpful to look at the *SKI* reduction rules in a particular way:

$$\underline{S\,f\,g}\,a \quad\longrightarrow\quad (f a)\,(g a)$$
$$\underline{K\,c}\,a \quad\longrightarrow\quad c$$
$$\underline{I}\,a \quad\longrightarrow\quad a\,.$$

The applications on the left-hand sides of these rules supply the respective combinators with just the right number of arguments, three for S, two for K, and one for I. The underlined terms are then in fact unary functions which accomplish the following:

- $S\,f\,g$ maps its argument a into both components of an application $(f\,g)$, thereby creating another level of applications $(f\,a)$ and $(g\,a)$;

- $K\,c$ returns the term c irrespective of its argument a;

- I maps the argument a into itself.

Thus we have a combinator each to duplicate, consume and reproduce argument terms.

With this in mind, we can now consider the compilation of an abstraction $f = \lambda x.expr$ into a combinator term. Assuming that $expr$ does not contain further binders λx, we simply need to apply the following compilation scheme:

- $\lambda x.(expr\_1\ expr\_2) \quad\Rightarrow\quad S\ \lambda x.expr\_1\ \lambda x.expr\_2$
- $\lambda x.const \quad\Rightarrow\quad K\ const$
- $\lambda x.x \quad\Rightarrow\quad I$

The equivalence of the terms on both sides of $\Rightarrow$ can be easily verified by application to some argument term arg. We then get

- for the first rule

$$(\lambda x.(expr\_1\ expr\_2)\ arg) = (expr\_1[x \Leftarrow arg]\ expr\_2[x \Leftarrow arg])$$

  and

$$S\ \lambda x.expr\_1\ \lambda x.expr\_2\ arg$$
$$= (\lambda x.expr\_1\ arg)\ (\lambda x.expr\_2\ arg) = (expr\_1[x \Leftarrow arg]\ expr\_2[x \Leftarrow arg])$$

- for the second rule

$$(\lambda x.const\ arg) = (K\ const\ arg) = const$$

- and for the third rule

$$(\lambda x.x \; arg) = (I \; arg) = arg.$$

The combinators themselves are treated as constant terms: they cannot be transformed into anything else.

Let us now see how compilation to combinator terms works for a simple example, the abstraction $f = \lambda x.(op \; x \; x)$, where op denotes some primitive function (or combinator):

$$\lambda x.(op \; x \; x) \Rightarrow \lambda x.((op \; x) \; x) \Rightarrow S \; \lambda x.(op \; x) \; \lambda x.x$$
$$\Rightarrow S \; (S\lambda x.op \; \lambda x.x) \; \lambda x.x \Rightarrow S \; (S \; (K \; op) \; I) \; I \; .$$

When substituting for op the arithmetic function $+$, the application $(f \; 5) = (S \; (S \; (K+) \; I) \; I \; 5)$ reduces as follows:

$$(S \; (S \; (K+) \; I) \; I \; 5) \longrightarrow S \; (K+) \; I \; 5 \; (I \; 5) \longrightarrow K + 5 \; (I \; 5) \; (I \; 5) \longrightarrow + 5 \; 5 \longrightarrow 10 \; .$$

Things become decidedly more complex if we have abstractions of two or more variables, in which case the compilation rules have to be applied to all variables individually and systematically from innermost to outermost. To illustrate this we consider the slightly modified function $f = \lambda x \lambda y.(op \; x \; y)$. Starting with the innermost abstraction $\lambda y.\; \dashv \ldots \vdash$ we get:

$$\lambda x \lambda y.(op \; x \; y) \Rightarrow \lambda x.(\lambda y.((op \; x) \; y)) \Rightarrow \lambda x.(S \; \lambda y.(op \; x)\lambda y.y)$$
$$\Rightarrow \lambda x.(S \; (S \; \lambda y.op \; \lambda y.x) \; \lambda y.y) \Rightarrow \lambda x.(S \; (S \; (K \; op) \; (K \; x)) \; I) \; .$$

At this point we have eliminated the variable y and can now proceed in the same way with the abstraction $\lambda x.\; \dashv \ldots \vdash$, eliminating x:

$$\lambda x.(S \; (S \; (K \; op) \; (K \; x)) \; I) \Rightarrow$$
$$(S \; \lambda x.(S \; (S \; (K \; op) \; (K \; x))) \; \lambda x.I) \Rightarrow$$
$$(S \; (S \; \lambda x.S \; \lambda x.(S \; (K \; op) \; (K \; x))) \; (K \; I)) \Rightarrow$$
$$(S \; (S \; (K \; S) \; (S \; \lambda x.(S \; (K \; op)) \; \lambda x.(K \; x))) \; (K \; I)) \Rightarrow$$
$$(S \; (S \; (K \; S) \; (S \; (S \; \lambda x.S \; \lambda x.(K \; op)) \; (S \; \lambda x.K \; \lambda x.x))) \; (K \; I)) \Rightarrow$$
$$(S \; (S \; (K \; S) \; (S \; (S \; (K \; S) \; (S \; \lambda x.K \; \lambda x.op)) \; (S \; (K \; K) \; I))) \; (K \; I)) \Rightarrow$$
$$(S \; (S \; (K \; S) \; (S \; (S \; (K \; S) \; (S \; (K \; K) \; (K \; op))) \; (S \; (K \; K) \; I))) \; (K \; I)) \; .$$

We note that what originally was a rather simple λ-abstraction of two variables has now become a combinator term of considerable complexity. It effects 18 combinator reduction steps to accomplish the equivalent of two β-reductions. Moreover, the term is completely unintelligible, bearing no resemblance to the λ-abstraction from which we started. The only way to convince ourselves that both are semantically equivalent is to apply them to the same arguments, and to reduce these applications to normal forms.

We will do this for the above combinator term by applying it to x, the variable just eliminated:

$$((S \ (S \ (K \ S) \ (S \ (S \ (K \ S) \ (S \ (K \ K) \ (K \ op))) \ (S \ (K \ K) \ I))) \ (K \ I)) \ x) \longrightarrow$$
$$(((S \ (K \ S) \ (S \ (S \ (K \ S) \ (S \ (K \ K) \ (K \ op))) \ (S \ (K \ K) \ I))) \ x) \ (K \ I \ x)) \longrightarrow$$
$$((K \ S \ x) \ ((S \ (S \ (K \ S) \ (S \ (K \ K) \ (K \ op))) \ (S \ (K \ K) \ I)) \ x) \ I) \longrightarrow$$
$$(S \ ((S \ (K \ S) \ (S \ (K \ K) \ (K \ op))) \ x) \ (S \ (K \ K) \ I \ x) \ I) \longrightarrow$$
$$(S \ ((K \ S \ x) \ (S \ (K \ K) \ (K \ op) \ x) \ (K \ x)) \ I) \longrightarrow$$
$$(S \ (S \ (K \ op) \ (K \ x)) \ I) \ .$$

This term denotes a unary function equivalent to what we obtain when β-reducing $(\lambda x.(S \ (S \ (K \ op) \ (K \ x)) \ I) \ x)$. The abstraction in operator position of this application is the one we got by eliminating y from $\lambda x.\lambda y.(op \ x \ y)$, i.e., we have established the equivalence between the original λ-abstraction and the combinator term with respect to a partial application.

When applying the above combinator term, say to y, we can continue with further reductions:

$$((S \ (S \ (K \ op) \ (K \ x)) \ I) \ y) \longrightarrow$$
$$((S \ (K \ op) \ (K \ x) \ y) \ (I \ y)) \longrightarrow$$
$$(K \ op \ y \ (K \ x \ y) \ (I \ y)) \longrightarrow$$
$$(op \ x \ y) \ ;$$

thus getting the same normal form as for the application

$$(\lambda x.\lambda y.(op \ x \ y) \ x \ y) \ ,$$

which was to be demonstrated.

11.2.2   Some Obvious Code Optimizations

From what we saw just now, the concept of SKI combinator reduction appears to be totally unacceptable for complexity reasons. Even simple λ-abstractions blow up to combinator terms of enormous size. Every occurrence in the body of a λ-abstraction of

- a curried application translates into an S-combinator term;

- a constant expression translates into a K-combinator term;

- the variable to be eliminated is replaced by an I-combinator.

They effect as many very elementary reduction steps to instantiate the abstraction body with arguments. The complexity problem is not so much caused by the granularity of the SKI combinators as it is by the fact that they are not too well suited for what they are expected to accomplish.

So far, we have available only the S-combinator to distribute an argument over a function body expression. It does so by mapping the argument term into both the operator and operand position of an application, irrespective of whether or not it is actually needed there. In many applications that are made up from constant subterms in either or both branches, the effect of S-combinators must therefore be offset by additional K-combinators which consume superfluous argument copies. This extremely wasteful way of passing arguments manifests itself in SKI combinator terms which typically contain about as many K-combinators as S-combinators; the combinator term of the preceding section being a perfect example in kind.

However, there is a rather obvious remedy to this problem: all we need to do is to introduce another two combinators

$$B \ f \ g \ x = f \ (g \ x) \ ;$$
$$C \ f \ g \ x = (f \ x) \ g \ ;$$

of which $B \ f \ g$ pairs an argument substituted for x only with the operand subterm of $(f \ g)$, whereas $C \ f \ g$ pairs it only with the operator subterm. With these additional combinators at hand, we can define four compilation rules which remove redundant SK combinations from SKI combinator terms:

$$
\begin{array}{lcl}
S \ (K \ expr\_1) \ expr\_2 & \Rightarrow & B \ expr\_1 \ expr\_2 \\
S \ expr\_1 \ (K \ expr\_2) & \Rightarrow & C \ expr\_1 \ expr\_2 \\
S \ (K \ expr\_1) \ (K \ expr\_2) & \Rightarrow & K \ (expr\_1 \ expr\_2) \\
S \ (K \ expr) \ I & \Rightarrow & expr \ .
\end{array}
$$

(The reader may convince himself that the left- and right-hand sides of these rules are semantically equivalent)

These term optimizations have a particularly impressive effect on the abstraction $\lambda x.\lambda y.(op \ x \ y)$. We get:

$$\lambda x \lambda y.(op \ x \ y) \Rightarrow \lambda x.(S \ (S \ (K \ op) \ (K \ x)) \ I) \Rightarrow \lambda x.(S \ (K \ (op \ x)) \ I)$$
$$\Rightarrow \lambda x.(op \ x) \Rightarrow (S \ \lambda x.op \ \lambda x.x) \Rightarrow (S \ (K \ op) \ I) \Rightarrow op$$

i.e., we have reduced the number of combinators from 18 to just one, the operator op, as compared with the respective SKI combinator term.

Eliminating superfluous SK combinations from more complex terms shows similar results. Take, as an example, the factorial function, which in λ-notation may have the form

$$fac =_s \lambda n.\text{IF} (= 0\ n)\ 1\ (*\ n\ (fac\ (-\ 1\ n)))\ ^{34}$$

Since there is only the variable n to be eliminated, it is fairly easy to see that in the equivalent SKI combinator expression

$$fac \;=\; S\ (S\ (S\ (K\ \text{IF})\ (S\ (S\ (K\ =)\ (K\ 0))\ I))\ (K\ 1))$$
$$(S\ (S\ (K\ *)\ I)\ (S\ (K\ fac)\ (S\ (S\ (K\ -)\ (K\ 1))\ I)))$$

we have an S-combinator for every binary application, a K-combinator preceding every constant symbol, and the combinator I in place of every occurrence of n.

In the optimized version

$$fac = S\ (C\ (B\ \text{IF}\ (=\ 0))\ 1)\ (S\ *\ (B\ fac\ (-\ 1)))$$

the number of combinators is reduced from 21 to 5, and all K-combinators have disappeared.

11.2.3 An SKI Graph Reduction Engine

As indicated before, the G-machine is perfectly suited to reduce SKI combinator terms as well. The combinators S, K, I, B, C are nothing but special supercombinators: they are atomic in the sense that they do not effect reductions within reductions. Instances of S, B, C combinator reductions re-arrange three application nodes, whereas the combinators K, I just return argument pointers. The appropriate G-code sequences become part of the run-time library, which otherwise contains the same G-code for primitive functions as introduced in section 11.1.3.

However, in contrast to compiled supercombinator reduction the G-machine now sets out with the complete graph representation of the SKI (BC) combinator expression to which the high-level functional program is compiled. The top-level code sequence remains the same except for the fact that it pushes the pointer to the root node of this graph rather than a code pointer.

Fig. 11.4 shows the initial G-machine state for computing the factorial of 5, using the graph of the optimized combinator expression given at the end of the preceding subsection.

Fig. 11.5 illustrates three phases of reducing a full S-combinator application. Starting with a pointer to the topmost application node on the stack (fig. 11.5.a),

---

[34]Note that we have omitted the Y-combinator here. In the SKI graph reducer it can be realized by means of a direct feedback pointer.

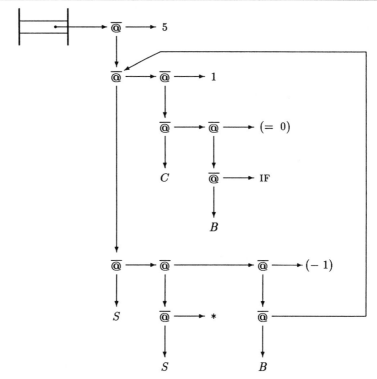

Figure 11.4: Combinator graph for the factorial function

the spine of the graph is unwound as part of an EVAL subroutine (fig. 11.5.b). From there the code sequence for the S-combinator takes over to form the new graph, to update the root of the original graph, to pop the argument pointers (fig. 11.5.c), and then to continue unwinding the spine, as usual. Thus, the code for S must be as follows:

        PUSH 2[2)]   (* pushes the third argument *)
        PUSH 2   (* pushes the second argument *)
        MKAP[2)]   (* forms an application node from both and pushes the pointer to it *)
        PUSH 3[1)]   (* pushes the third argument again *)
        PUSH 1   (* pushes the first argument *)
        MKAP[1)]   (* forms an application node from both and pushes the pointer to it *)

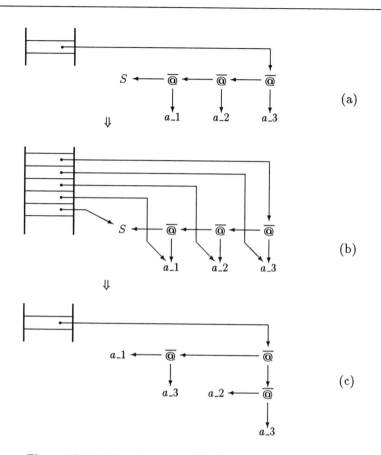

Figure 11.5: Reducing an application of the combinator S

MKAP	(* forms another application node from the topmost two pointers and pushes its pointer *)
UPDATE 4	(* overwrites the original root node *)
POP 3	(* pops the arguments *)
UNWIND	(* unwinds the new spine *).

The code sequences for the combinators B, C are very similar. All there is to be changed is to drop the instructions earmarked [1] from the B-code, and those earmarked [2] from the C-code.

We note that neither of these sequences contains further EVALs, i.e., they perform reductions just in the head of the actual spine and return complete graphs (or sub-graphs). Only the G-code sequences for primitive functions which are strict in at least one of their arguments include EVALs to force reductions within the tails of spines and thus reductions within reductions.

To avoid the ensuing problems with partially completed graphs, applications of primitive functions could be implemented in an SKI reduction machine as δ-reduction rules in essentially the same way as in our interpreting graph reducers. Before entering into the reduction of such an application, the machine first checks whether the arguments are in canonical form. If not, it leaves the application nodes untouched, forces the reduction of their tails, overwrites in an orderly form the respective root nodes, and then tries again. We thus have a complete graph after each $SKI\,(BC)$ or δ-reduction step, i.e., the machine realizes a full combinator reduction semantics.

Unfortunately, this property is not very useful from a pragmatic point of view. Partially reduced combinator terms cannot be generally re-converted into equivalent λ-terms and thus represented in an intelligible form. A major conceptual problem arises from the fine granularity of SKI combinator reductions which cannot be related one-to-one to β- or supercombinator reductions. For many intermediate combinator terms there are simply no equivalent λ-terms that would have much resemblance to the original function definitions. Another problem concerns the restoration of the original variable names. We saw that this can be basically done by applying a combinator term to the variables abstracted from it, which for this purpose would have to be saved in a descriptor. However, since combinator reductions perform naive substitutions, it cannot be done correctly in the presence of left-over partial function applications, unless there is a full β-reduction available to resolve potential name clashes.

11.2.4 SKI Combinators vs. Compiled Supercombinators

It may appear somewhat difficult to draw a clear-cut line between graph reduction based on $SKI\,(BC)$ combinators on the one hand and on compiled supercombinators on the other hand. Since the former are just special cases of the latter, the underlying formal concept seems to be essentially the same, and we can even use the same basic machinery to execute the respective internal program representations.

Yet there is a significant difference whose consequences have already been discussed: supercombinators are used as source language for the compilation to target code of some abstract evaluator, whereas SKI combinators are used as a target language for the compilation of λ-expressions, thus defining themselves an abstract engine.

The G-machine is an abstract control flow architecture which, in the form of instructions like EVAL, PRINT, UNWIND, MKAP etc., merely provides some essential mechanisms for graph transformations, but it is not in itself a reduction engine. Instead, the G-compiler synthesizes code sequences for this machine which may be considered **program-specific graph reducers**. They specify **composite reduction rules** which transform high-level programs more or less in one conceptual step first to canonical forms, and then in several subsequent steps, triggered by PRINT instructions, recursively to normal forms. Only canonical forms are internally represented as complete graphs, otherwise the states of a computation are in an intricate way distributed over the code, the stack, the dump and (pieces of) the graph. No intelligible and coherent output which in a meaningful way can be related to identifiable reduction steps of, say, an applied λ-calculus can be produced from these states. Thus, the G-machine, when used as a target for supercombinator compilation as described in section 11.1, does not support a reduction semantics. This problem is largely of a conceptual nature.

In emulating the **combinators** $S, K, I, B, C, \ldots$ by self-contained G-code sequences, we simply introduce into the G-machine another level of **code abstraction** which realizes a full-fledged SKI reduction machine.[35] The compiler constructs from source programs of an applied λ-calculus complete SKI combinator graphs in which all combinator occurrences are replaced by pointers to the respective code sequences. Since each of these code sequences performs an atomic graph transformation, the machine generally moves through a sequence of many complete intermediate graphs when reducing a large program, and thus realizes a full **combinator reduction semantics**.

Using a modified PRINT routine, all intermediate graphs could be easily converted into coherent combinator terms as output. This output could be inspected, possibly modified or extended, and then returned to the machine for further reductions, i.e., we could have basically the same amenities of **stepwise reductions** under interactive control as with our interpreting graph reducers. However, implementing this feature in an SKI graph reducer is of limited use for a simple pragmatic reason: even an experienced programmer would encounter considerable problems in correctly interpreting only moderately complex combinator terms, and in relating them to the original high-level programs. Intelligible output is again confined, as in the case of compiled supercombinator reductions, to (sequences of) basic values. If the result of a computation is, say, a function, then the user is merely notified of this fact, but the function itself is not printed since it is only available as a combinator term. Thus, the low-level reduction semantics of SKI combinators is of little practical value as far as the appearance of the system to the user is concerned.

---

[35] The same ends can, of course, be achieved by implementing the combinators as microcode of a dedicated SKI reduction machine which otherwise uses the same data structures as the G-machine.

Considering implementation aspects, SKI combinators on the whole appear to be inferior to compiled supercombinators. While fairly simple to emulate by G-code or by dedicated microcode, it generally takes too many reduction steps to instantiate a function body with arguments, as compared with supercombinator reductions. The combinators S, B, C pass single arguments just one syntactical level down within a term, thereby creating new application nodes which almost instantly are discarded in the next reduction steps. This rather unproductive work places a considerable burden on heap space management as well. Moreover, compilation to SKI combinators is more complex than supercombinator compilation, and so are the resulting codes. Whereas the former requires as many passages through partially compiled terms as there are variables to be abstracted, the latter can be typically done in one sweep. For source language terms of size n, we have worst case space and time complexities of $o(n^2)$, and $o(n \lg n)$, and typically complexities of $o(n \lg n)$ and $o(n)$, respectively.

11.3   Other Abstract Machines for Compiled Functional Languages

The G-machine and the SKI reduction machine are the two most prominent examples of lazy evaluators for functional languages which are based on compiled graph reduction. The former is primarily used as an intermediate code generation level for the compilation of lazy ML [Aug84], but there has also been work going on to develop a RISC hardware architecture for it [Kieb88]. The latter has been used as a target for the compilation of SASL and MIRANDA [Turn76, Turn85]. The description of an SKI reduction machine called $SKIM$ can be found in [ClGl80]. The development of a commercial graph reduction machine based on SKI combinators, Burrough's $NORMA$ project [Schee86], despite considerable support by dedicated hardware, fell short of expectations in terms of its performance and was abandoned.

Other abstract machines include the Three Instruction Machine (TIM) proposed by Fairbairn and Wrag [FaWr88], a lazy supercombinator-based engine, and Curien's Categorial Abstract Machine (CAM) [CoCuMa87, Cur86]. The latter uses categorial combinators to distribute environments over λ-terms converted to de Bruijn notation, and the de Bruijn indices to access the environments. The CAM may be used both as a lazy and as an eager evaluator.

There is also a number of concepts and implementations for non-sequential compiled graph reductions, among them the multi-processor version of a modified G-machine [AuJo89], the Parallel Abstract Machine (PAM) proposed by Loogen [LoKu89], the GRIP parallel graph reduction machine of Peyton-Jones [PeClSaHa87], and the Applicative Language Idealized Computing Engine (ALICE) of Darlington and Reeve [DaRe81, HaRe86] and its descendant, the FLAGSHIP reduction system [GrWo89] (another product-oriented pilot project which failed), to mention only a few.

More traditional abstract machines for compiled functional languages are direct descendants of the *SECD* machine (section 5.3.8) which support an applicative order (or eager) evaluation regime.

One of the first is Henderson's LISPKIT implementation [HeJoJo83, Hend80] which differs from the original *SECD* machine mainly insofar as the *C*-structure is made up from compiled abstract code rather than from (the components of) λ-terms. Lazy evaluation can be had on this machine by including into the source programs DELAY and FORCE instructions which respectively protect and unprotect terms from being evaluated.

Another version of the *SECD* machine is Cardelli's Functional Abstract Machine (FAM) [Card83]. Much like the *G*-machine, it is adapted to the needs of generating executable machine code for VAX-like run-time environments. Function calls are in the FAM essentially supported by a stack *AS* for argument frames (including local variables and temporaries) and by a return stack *RS* (the dump) to save and unsave machine states. Functions are represented as closures composed of (a pointer to) the function code and (a pointer to) the environment in which the code is to be executed. The environment is a flat structure of as many entries as the function has (relatively) free variables. FAM-code is subject to several optimizations, the most important being the usual conversion of tail-end recursions into code iterations. The FAM is, for instance, used as an intermediate level of code generation in compiling standard ML.

12 Data Flow Systems

The data flow concept was first proposed by Dennis [Denn69, Denn74, DeMi75] as a radically new way of organizing on a large scale non-sequential computations. Dennis' original approach was based on a rather simple static execution model. Since then, various more advanced dynamic models and architectures have emerged, of which several led to successful experimental or prototype implementations [Dav78, SyCoHi77, YoNaNa84, Yub84, GuKiWa85, ArNi87, HiSeShi89, PaCu90, PaTr91].

We recall from chapter 4 that data flow is a functional model of computation which is characterized by

- a control discipline based on the availability of operand objects, as opposed to the demand for result objects (or normal forms) in reduction systems;

- an operational discipline based on the orderly consumption and (re-)production of operand objects, which is a common feature of all functional systems;

- the realization of primitive and defined functions as constant operator objects, which it has in common with compiled graph reduction.

It is generally based on an applicative order semantics, though lazy evaluation may be realized as well [AmHa84, PiAr85, Pi88, Hell88].

Data flow programs are usually compiled versions of high-level functional programs. Both the primitive and composite operators of such a machine-level program remain partially ordered, merely reflecting their data (operand) dependencies. A schedule for the execution of operators develops dynamically at run-time, depending on their activation by operand tokens on the one hand, and on the availability of processing sites on the other hand. There is no control mechanism which would force the execution of enabled operators in a particular order. The objective here is to fully utilize the potential for concurrent computations at the level of primitive operations.

A well-known representation for data flow programs are directed graphs as, for example, shown in fig. 12.1. In contrast to the PrT-net models introduced in chapter 4, these data flow graphs depict only operators as nodes whereas operands are shown as tokens on the arcs that connect them. Otherwise, we have essentially the same token game as in PrT-nets. The occurrence of an operator consumes a token from each of its input arcs and produces a token on each of its output arcs.

Data flow graphs represent defined functions (abstractions) as constant objects which may be used repeatedly for different operand (argument) token sets. Data flow therefore does not give full support to higher-order functions. Functions may receive functions as actual parameters, and partial function applications may be

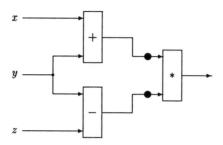

Figure 12.1: Data flow graph for the computation of $(x + y) * (y - z)$

internally represented in the form of closures, but there is no way of computing new functions.

Data flow must primarily be seen as a model for fine-grain concurrent computations. It is expected to satisfy a growing demand for more computational speed that is claimed necessary to run complex scientific and real-time application programs within acceptable time bounds. There is no doubt that substantial performance enhancements beyond the gains regularly made by advancing hardware technologies and improved fine-tuning techniques can only be achieved when consequently exploiting problem-inherent concurrency. The advocates of data flow suggest that this be done on a very large scale [Denn80, ArCu85, ArCuMa], i.e., with the finest possible granularity of concurrent operations and involving large numbers of processing sites. It is quite evident that the complexity of coordinating large quantities of concurrent operations cannot be managed by the programmer but must be dynamically dealt with by the system. To do so, concurrency must inevitably be expressed in a functional form in order to abstract completely from the particularities of the system configuration, from the mechanics of program execution, and from the details of resource scheduling. The Church-Rosser property of the functional programming paradigm guarantees the determinacy of results irrespective of execution orders.

The fine-grain concurrency exposed in data flow graphs is bound to cause a considerable run-time overhead. Data flow operators in fact synchronize their operands: they may occur iff all their input operand positions are instantiated with legitimate argument objects. For many primitive operators the time spent on synchronization may exceed the time necessary to actually execute them. Thus, with primitive operators far outnumbering composite operators (or abstractions) in a data flow program, the system has to deal with a fairly high ratio of synchronization overhead vs. useful computations.

Moreover, since there is no **sequencing scheme** for enabled operators, we have a considerable scheduling problem at hand as well. All operators must be treated as **atomic processes** which may assume the states *waiting* (for synchronization with operands), *ready-to-execute, executing* and *terminated*; i.e., we need to implement a scheduling scheme similar to the ones described in chapter 7 and section 9.5. The problem with the data flow concept is that the scheduler must be able to handle very large (potentially unbounded) numbers of atomic processes that perform only primitive operations rather than a limited number of larger processes that perform fairly complex computations.

12.1 Basic Language Issues

High-level programs for data flow systems may be specified in basically the same functional notation as introduced in section 5.1. They are **expressions** composed of **recursively nested function definitions** and function applications which may come in various syntactical forms [ArGoPl78, AcDe79, Ack82, AmHaOn84, Nikh88].

Noteworthy syntactic and semantic differences relate to the introduction of

- voluntary or mandatory **type specifications** which enable the compiler to generate efficiently executable, well-typed code;

- **block structures** in conjunction with the concept of **assignment statements** as an alternative way of defining and instantiating local variables with values (and types);

- special constructs for **tail-end recursions** (iteration loops) by means of which the programmer may for instance explicitly specify the traversal of and operations on the components of structured objects in a more conventional style;

- **special arrays**, in the literature referred to as I-structures [ArTh80], which allow for concurrent read/write operations on their components in compliance with a functional semantics;

- **streams**, i.e., potentially infinite sequences of objects of the same monomorphic or polymorphic type, as a means to specify **communication channels** between **producer** and **consumer processes** which may operate independently of each other, possibly within the margins set by finite synchronic distances.

The notions of block structures, assignments, iteration loops etc. are clearly inherited from high-level **imperative programming languages**. The functional character is solely maintained by a constraint on the use of variables within block structures which is commonly known as the **single assignment rule**. We will see that this rule straightforwardly derives from the substitution concept of the λ-calculus. The special I-structures are to realize the single assignment rule for all components of structured data objects (i.e., for individual array entries) independently.

Streams are devices which may legally introduce non-determinism into data flow programs. This is due to merge operations which channel the tokens of two or more input streams non-deterministically into one output stream, without changing the order of tokens originating from the same input stream.

Instead of WHERE (or LET) clauses, most high-level data flow languages use block structures to specify instantiations of local variables. They generally define in flat form nested acyclic binding structures.

We recall from section 5.1 that a WHERE clause

$$(\; expr \; \text{WHERE}$$
$$x\_1 \; = \; x\_expr\_1$$
$$\vdots$$
$$x\_n \; = \; x\_expr\_n \;)$$

defines the substitution of free occurrences of the variables $x\_1, \ldots, x\_n$ in $expr$ with the normal forms of the argument expressions $x\_expr\_1, \ldots, x\_expr\_n$, which must be computed in the environment of the clause. The applicative order semantics also requires that this be done for all arguments to complete the context in which the abstraction body $expr$ must be evaluated, i.e., in the scope of binders surrounding it. The ordering of the equations in a WHERE clause is irrelevant iff the variable names defined on their left-hand sides are unique.

Let us now consider a nested WHERE clause of the form

$$(\; expr \; \text{WHERE}$$
$$x\_1 \; = \; (\; x\_expr\_1 \; \text{WHERE}$$
$$y\_11 \; = \; y\_expr\_11$$
$$\vdots$$
$$y\_1m \; = \; y\_expr\_1m \;)$$
$$\vdots$$
$$x\_n \; = \; (\; x\_expr\_n \; \text{WHERE}$$
$$y\_n1 \; = \; y\_expr\_n1$$
$$\vdots$$
$$y\_np \; = \; y\_expr\_np \;)) \; .$$

The nesting of binding structures in conjunction with the applicative order regime defines the partial order in which the components of this expression must be evaluated to obtain its normal form.

Since the variables that appear on the left-hand sides of the defining expressions are unique throughout all nesting levels, the binding structures are in fact uniquely defined in terms of occurrences of these variables in the expressions on the right-hand sides. Thus, nesting and ordering of the defining equations become irrelevant, i.e., the above WHERE clause may be specified in the flat form of a block structure (or a block for short), say as:

$$\{ \; y\_n1 \;\; = \; y\_expr\_n1,$$

$$\vdots$$

$$y\_np \; = \; y\_expr\_np$$

$$\vdots$$

$$x\_1 \;\;\; = \; x\_expr\_1,$$

$$\vdots$$

$$x\_n \;\;\; = \; x\_expr\_n,$$

$$\vdots$$

$$y\_11 \;\; = \; y\_expr\_11,$$

$$\vdots$$

$$y\_1m \; = \; y\_expr\_1m,$$
$$\text{IN } expr \; \}$$

The partial order of computing these equations can be uniquely inferred since in this particular example it is assumed that the expressions

- $y\_expr\_11, \ldots, y\_expr\_np$ are specified in terms of variables bound outside the block,

- $x\_expr\_1, \ldots, x\_expr\_n$ are specified in terms of variables bound outside the block and in terms of the variables $y\_11, \ldots, y\_np$,

- $expr$ is specified in terms of variables bound inside and outside the block.

Blocks with multiple occurrences of the same variable name on the left-hand sides of the defining equations must be rejected by the compiler.

The defining equations of a block are also called **assignment statements** (or **assignments** for short): they assign the values (normal forms) of the expressions on the right-hand sides to the variables on the left-hand sides, which are called the **block variables**. All block variables are assigned values at most once in every instantiated block (**single assignment rule**). Blocks may be recursively nested: every expression inside a block may be replaced with another block.

Expressions of the form DEFINE ... IN ... may be considered **block structures** as well. They define mutually recursive functions as assignments of λ-abstractions to identifiers (names). These DEFINE blocks may also include as 0-ary functions cyclic **variable definitions**. A block of the form

$$
\{
$$

$$
\vdots
$$

$$
x = x\_expr,
$$

$$
\vdots
$$

$$
y = y\_expr,
$$

$$
\vdots
$$

$$
\text{IN} \quad \text{DEFINE}
$$

$$
\vdots
$$

$$
f(u\_1, \ldots, u\_n) = f\_expr
$$

$$
\vdots
$$

$$
\text{IN } expr \, \} \, ,
$$

specifies local variables and (recursive) functions, similar to the block conventions used in imperative languages.

The entire block expression enclosed in a pair of parentheses $\{\,\}$ is commonly considered the **scope** of the block variables. This perception is somewhat misleading for it obviously does not comply with the scoping rule of the λ-calculus, according to which we may have several nested scopes within a block. What this view really reflects is the way blocks and block instances may be implemented. Notwithstanding the particularities of different data flow execution models which we will discuss in detail in the next section, we may think of a block as a piece of data flow code and of a **block instance** as the pairing of this code with an **activation record** (or frame) for actual instantiations of the block variables.

The opening parenthesis { defines the **entry point** into a block at which a frame is to be allocated. It contains as yet uninstantiated block variable entries whose formats are by the compiler inferred from the variable types. These entries are step-by-step instantiated with (pointers to) values as the execution of the respective assignment statements proceeds. Since there is at most one assignment per entry, instantiated entries are never overwritten. The closing parenthesis } defines the **exit point** of the block where the frame is released again.

Blocks are in data flow languages primarily used in conjunction with **loop con-structs**. They realize tail-end recursions as iterations which may use the variable entries in the respective block frames repeatedly.

The general construct for the specification of tail-end recursions is a so-called WHILE expression (or loop). It denotes a tail-end recursive function application of the form

$$
\begin{aligned}
&\text{DEFINE}\\
&\quad f(x\_1, \ldots, x\_n) = \text{IF} \quad pred\_expr\\
&\qquad\qquad\qquad\quad\; \text{THEN } f(expr\_1, \ldots, expr\_n)\\
&\qquad\qquad\qquad\quad\; \text{ELSE } res\_expr\\
&\quad \text{IN } f(arg\_1, \ldots, arg\_n)
\end{aligned}
$$

as

$$
\begin{aligned}
&\{\; x\_1 = arg\_1, \ldots, x\_n = arg\_n\\
&\quad \text{IN } \{\; \text{WHILE } pred\_expr \text{ DO}\\
&\qquad\qquad new\ x\_1\ =\ expr\_1\\
&\qquad\qquad\qquad \vdots\\
&\qquad\qquad new\ x\_n\ =\ expr\_n\\
&\qquad\qquad \text{RETURNS } res\_expr\;\}\;\}\;.
\end{aligned}
$$

The outer block structure defines and initializes the formal loop parameters $x\_1, \ldots, x\_n$ with the values of the argument expressions $arg\_1, \ldots, arg\_n$, respectively, and then executes the inner block which includes the WHILE expression itself. The outer block is thus equivalent to the function call $f(arg\_1, \ldots, arg\_n)$, whereas the inner block corresponds to the IF-THEN-ELSE clause in the function body of f. It is also referred to as the loop body.

When evaluating $pred\_expr$ to TRUE, the loop body computes new instantiations of the loop parameters in $new\ x\_1, \ldots, new\ x\_n$. When returning from the inner block, they overwrite the respective loop parameters $x\_1, \ldots, x\_n$ of the outer block for another call of the WHILE expression. This corresponds to executing the application $f(expr\_1, \ldots, expr\_n)$ in the body of the function f.

If $pred\_expr$ evaluates to FALSE, the inner block computes the value of res_expr and returns it as the result of the WHILE loop instance.

It is important to note that only what is defined as loop parameters in the outer block may be annotated with the prefix new in the inner block (or loop body). In particular, the new parameters of the inner block may only be a subset of the loop parameters defined in the outer block. In addition, there may be other local variable definitions in the loop body in terms of which the defining expressions for the new loop variables may be specified. However, $pred\_expr$ and res_expr may only use the loop variables of the outer block and variables bound outside the entire WHILE construct.

For index-controlled traversals of structured data objects (I-arrays), data flow languages usually include FOR loops as well. They have the form

$$\{ \; x\_1 = arg\_1, \ldots, x\_n = arg\_n$$
$$\text{IN} \; \{ \; \text{FOR} \; i = index\_expr \; \text{DO}$$
$$new \; x\_1 \; = \; expr\_1$$
$$\vdots$$
$$new \; x\_n \; = \; expr\_n$$
$$\text{RETURNS} \; expr \; \} \; \} \; .$$

The expression *index_expr* is of the form *l_expr* UPTO *u_expr* or *u_expr* DOWNTO *l_expr*. It defines an interval through which the index i must be stepped in increments or decrements of one, respectively. The expressions *l_expr* and *u_expr* must be of type *integer* and respectively denote the lower and upper bounds of the interval.

Some of the loop parameters are usually of an **array type**, and assignments to these parameters in the loop bodies are made to individual array entries selected by index tuples.

Structured data objects are in data flow programs preferably specified as I-arrays and operated on by WHILE or FOR loops. They allow for read and write operations to be carried out concurrently on several array entries. In particular, an I-array may be passed on between a producing and a consuming FOR loop (or between any other pair of composite operators, for that matter) before all entries are instantiated with valid data. The system may thus interleave the elementary operations within both loops.

Annotating a variable with the type *I_array* has the effect that at run-time an array of the specified size and entry type is allocated as part of the respective activation record frame. Its entries, as all other frame locations, are as yet uninstantiated (or empty). They get filled with valid data items as assignments to the individual array positions are being performed, say, in the course of executing a loop. Only array entries that are filled may be read by subsequent operators, thus synchronizing producers and consumers.

Selecting an entry in an I-array which is declared as

$$x : I\_array[dim\_1, \ldots, dim\_k] \; of \; \alpha$$

must be specified as

$$x[expr\_1, \ldots, expr\_k] \; ,$$

where [...] denotes a k-tuple of indices, i.e., *expr_1*, ..., *expr_k* must be of type *integer* and from the intervals $[1 \,.\, dim\_1], \ldots, [1 \,.\, dim\_k]$, respectively.[36]

---

[36] The assignment $x = [value]$ will be used as a short-hand notation for initializing all entries of the I-array x with *value*.

We will now consider, as an example, two expressions for the computation of the matrix product, based on I-arrays as matrix representations, which illustrate the difference between using WHILE and FOR loops with respect to this particular problem. The operand matrices a and b are assumed to be defined somewhere outside the loop constructs under consideration as

$$a : I\_array[n, k] \text{ of } dec\_number \text{ and } b : I\_array[k, m] \text{ of } dec\_number,$$

respectively, and properly instantiated with values. With nested WHILE loops we get

```
{ r : I_array[n, m] of dec_number = [0],
  i : int = 1
IN { WHILE (i LE n) DO
        new i = (i + 1),
        { j : int = 1
        IN { WHILE (j LE m) DO
                new j = (j + 1),
                { h : int = 1
                IN { WHILE (h LE k) DO
                        new h = (h + 1),
                        new r[i, j] = (r[i, j] + (a[i, h] * b[h, j]))
                     RETURNS r }
                RETURNS r } }
        RETURNS r } } }
```

Using FOR loops, the expression becomes more concise since fewer nesting levels are necessary. We get

```
{ r : I_array[n, m] of dec_number = [0]
IN { FOR i = 1 UPTO n DO
        { FOR j = 1 UPTO m DO
            { FOR h = 1 UPTO k DO
                new r[i, j] = (r[i, j] + (a[i, h] * b[h, j]))
             RETURNS r }
          RETURNS r }
       RETURNS r } }.
```

In the sequel, we will refer to the language HLFL enriched by blocks, iteration loops, I-arrays, type declarations, etc. as a high-level data flow language, or as HLDFL for short.

12.2   Data Flow Execution Models

In section 4.3 we briefly discussed three basic execution models for data flow which conceptually differ with respect to the realization of recursions [Denn84]. To study these models in more detail, we switch to the data flow graph representations commonly used in the literature, of which a simple example was shown in fig. 12.1.

The major difference to PrT-nets is that data flow graphs depict as nodes only operators (also referred to as actors). The directed edges connecting the nodes represent channels or links via which operators communicate operand objects. The presence (or availability) of an operand on a link is shown as a token on the respective edge of the graph. Tokens represent values (or constant expressions) since data flow generally realizes an applicative order evaluation regime.

Just dropping places (predicate schemes) from data flow graphs does not pose a major problem when it comes to defining an operational semantics. In general, a data flow operator is enabled iff all its input links carry at least one token, and all its output links can absorb at least one token. Whether or not the links may carry more than one token depends on the particular execution model. In any case, the occurrence of an enabled operator consumes one token from each of its input links and produces one token on each of its output links. The values represented by the output tokens may be specified in terms of the input token values by predicates inscribed in the operators, i.e., in the same way as in PrT-nets.

One of the problems with data flow operators is that there are exceptions to the general firing rule. There are operators which are enabled without having all their input links instantiated with tokens, and there are operators which do not consume tokens from all its input links or do not produce tokens on all its output links. Moreover, we have operators with non-deterministic behavior. Token duplication operations are simply represented by branching links. However, an operational semantics can be defined for all data flow operators in terms of equivalent PrT-nets.

These equivalences are shown in fig. 12.2 for the basic data flow operators (or operator schemes). Here we have

- a primitive n-ary operator representing the application of an n-ary primitive function to n argument values which produces one result value (fig. 12.2.a);

- a branching link realizing the n-fold reproduction of a value (constant expression), which (in PrT-net notation) is equivalent to a one-input substitution scheme (fig. 12.2.b);

- the conditional branching of a value under the control of a Boolean constant, which is equivalent to a one-input/one-output-per-branch conditional substitution scheme (fig. 12.2.c).

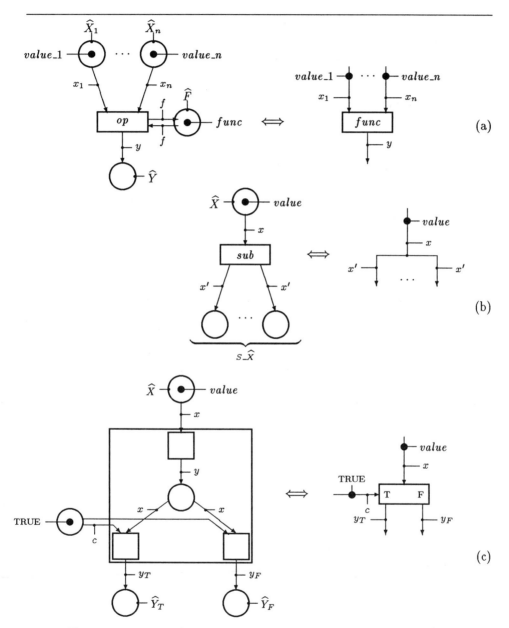

Figure 12.2: Equivalence between PrT-nets and data flow operators

The conditional merging of two branches may be accomplished by an operator which is complementary to conditional branching, i.e., with the directions of all arcs other than the control input reversed. Unconditional merging simply requires joining two or more data flow arcs.

Applications of defined functions may either be realized in the same way as applications of primitive functions, i.e., as operators inscribed with function names (identifiers), or as operator schemes which must be explicitly instantiated with function tokens arriving on designated input links, as in the PrT-net models discussed in chapter 4.

The reproduction of tokens is modeled by branching links, meaning that these operations are in fact integrated into the outputs of the operators from which the tokens emerge. The substitutions thus realized are naive, i.e., they are not equivalent to full β-reductions. To sustain a static scoping rule, naming conflicts must therefore be consequently avoided by

- prohibiting variables that are free in the entire program;

- converting all defined functions which contain relatively free variables into supercombinators (or by using equivalent internal representations, e.g., closures);

- evaluating only complete supercombinator applications.

These constraints render it possible to use simple branching links for the substitution of formal parameter occurrences by actual argument values in function (supercombinator) body expressions. Multiple parameter substitutions via individual branching links need neither be ordered nor must they be synchronized. Since no name clashes can occur, they may be carried out in any order, provided all of them take place eventually.

The same applies, of course, to conditional substitutions realized by individual one-input conditional branching operators as well. These operators are also referred to as TF-gates (for TRUE/FALSE). A control token on the input c routes a value token from the input x to the output link y_T if it is TRUE, and to the output link y_F if it is FALSE. Degenerate forms of it are so-called T-gates and F-gates. They differ from TF-gates in that the output link y_F is missing from the former and the output link y_T is missing from the latter. Thus, the T-gate passes its input token on to the output link if the control token carries the value TRUE, otherwise it consumes the input token without producing a token on the output link. The F-gate realizes the complementary operation.

The conditional merge operator complements the conditional branch. Depending on the Boolean value of a control token on input c, a value token is routed from either of the inputs x_T or x_F to the output link y, if one is present. We will see later that conditional merging is required in only one of the execution models to maintain order among token sets passing successively through either of the component graphs of an IF-THEN-ELSE clause. The other two models merge alternative branches of a data flow computation unconditionally. An unconditional merge operator has no control input link, and the predicate scheme that is shared between the two input transitions is missing from the equivalent PrT-net.

In the course of discussing the execution models in the following subsections, we will add to these basic data flow operators a few others which primarily perform model-specific control operations pertaining to the realization of (recursive) function calls and to loop iterations.

Data flow graph implementations are based on two syntactical entities:

- operators (actors) of the general form

$$rator \ (contr) \ (const) \ (\{rand\}^n) \ \{dest\}^m$$

  where

$rator$	specifies the operation to be performed,
$(contr)$	denotes optional operator-specific control information,
$(const)$	is an optional constant operand,
$(\{rand\}^n)$	optionally specifies some n operands to which the operator must be applied,
$\{dest\}^m$	specifies some m destination operators, possibly including their environments, to which the result value must be distributed;

- tokens of the general form

$$< dest\_tag \ value >$$

  where

$dest\_tag$	specifies the destination operator (or operator instance) in a form identical to or including $dest$,
$value$	denotes the constant expression (value) carried by the token.

The operator components $\{dest\}^m$ are in fact the link specifications (with m-fold branching) of the data flow graphs.

Finer details of the syntax of the operator and token components depend on the execution model on the one hand, and to some extent on the particular operators on the other hand. Some of the components may not be required at all, e.g., explicit operand specifications in the tagged token model or control information.

12.2.1   Recursive Program Graphs

This execution model is equivalent to the basic data flow model developed in section 4.3. It is a dynamic model supporting a general recursion concept [Denn84]. Special CALL operators are recursively expanded with copies of data flow graphs which specify the computation of function values. Alternatively, universal operators may be expanded when instantiated with explicit function tokens. The emerging graphs are in either case acyclic, and at most one token passes through each link. Neither iterations nor the pipelining of tokens on successive links are permitted. There is no special treatment of tail-end recursions either.

To illustrate the compilation to recursion graphs, we consider two versions of a program for the inner product of two vectors. For the time being, we forgo using I-arrays and assume that the vectors are represented as lists of numerical values, and that we have only some basic list functions such as FIRST, REST, EMPTY available. We can then use, as one version, the recursive definition of the function ip from section 8.2 more or less as it is. Just replacing the WHERE clause with an equivalent block structure, we get:

$$
\begin{aligned}
res = \text{ DEFINE} \\
ip(vec\_1, vec\_2 : list\_of\ int) = \{\ & x = \text{REST}(vec\_1), \\
& y = \text{REST}(vec\_2), \\
& z = (\text{FIRST}(vec\_1) * \text{FIRST}(vec\_2)) \\
& \text{IN IF}\quad \text{AND}(\text{EMPTY}(x), \text{EMPTY}(y)) \\
& \text{THEN } z \\
& \text{ELSE}\ (z + ip(x, y))\ \} \\
\text{IN}\ ip(< a_1 \ldots a_n >, < b_1 \ldots b_n >)\,.
\end{aligned}
$$

This program translates into the data flow graph shown in fig. 12.3.

We note that some of the links in this recursion graph can be directly associated with formal function parameters or with local block variables, while all the other links are introduced by the compiler. These links may simply be thought of as temporaries used at the machine language level which are not visible to the programmer.

The operator CALL ip expands dynamically by a copy of the entire graph for ip when activated by argument tokens on its input links x_1, x_2. The input/output links vec_1, vec_2 and res of the graph then connect directly to the links x_1, x_2, y, respectively, of the CALL operator, and pass the tokens along.

In this respect, the execution of recursive data flow graphs closely resembles the expansion of function/supercombinator applications by instantiated body expressions in our interpreting reduction systems. However, whereas the reduction systems systematically rewrite these expressions until they have reached a normal form, thereby repeatedly expanding and shrinking them in size, recursive data flow

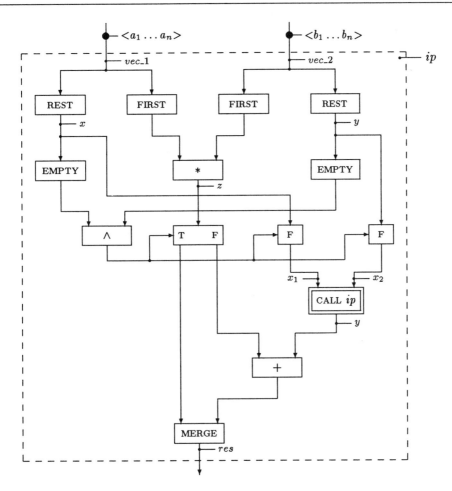

Figure 12.3: Recursion graph for the recursive computation of the inner vector product

graphs conceptually just keep growing. This is due to the fact that they are constant objects which specify acyclic pathways for tokens.[37]

This problem has particularly painful consequences in terms of memory space

---

[37]In an actual implementation, copies of expanded function body graphs would, of course, be collapsed upon completing their computations.

consumption when using equivalent tail-end recursive programs. We then get as another version for our inner product computation:

$$res = \text{DEFINE}$$
$$ip(prod : int, vec\_1, vec\_2 : list\_of\ int) =$$
$$\{\ x = \text{REST}(vec\_1),$$
$$y = \text{REST}(vec\_2),$$
$$v = (prod + z),$$
$$z = (\text{FIRST}(vec\_1) * \text{FIRST}(vec\_2))$$
$$\text{IN IF}\quad \text{AND}\big(\text{EMPTY}(x), \text{EMPTY}(y)\big)$$
$$\text{THEN}\ v$$
$$\text{ELSE}\ \ ip(v, x, y)\ \}$$
$$\text{IN}\ ip(0, < a_1 \ldots a_n >, < b_1 \ldots b_n >)\ .$$

The recursive data flow graph shown in fig. 12.4 to which this program can be compiled again creates a memory space demand of $O(n)$ due to the recursive expansion over the vector size n. However, this graph module also points the way out of the problem. It is easy to see that whenever the CALL operator is activated by input tokens, there are no other tokens left anywhere else in the graph that would have to be combined with the result token of the function call. So, rather than expanding the CALL operator with a new copy of the graph, we can alternatively drop this operator altogether and feed its input links x_1, x_2, x_3 directly back to the graph inputs $prod, vec\_1, vec\_2$, respectively. This establishes a cyclic graph structure (or an iteration loop) through which tokens may pass repeatedly.

The space consumption problem is serious enough to equip practical data flow systems with the means to represent tail-end recursions in this cyclic form, i.e., to abandon the concept of recursion graphs.

12.2.2   Static Data Flow Graphs

This simple execution model, which was the first one to be proposed [Denn74, DeMi75], avoids the problems of recursively expanding program graphs by outlawing general recursions altogether. Defined functions may only be tail-end recursive, and tail-end recursion is realized by means of iteration loops, i.e., by cyclic data flow graphs. The entire program graph remains as constructed by the compiler while executing it with actual argument token sets. A high-level program may be written in terms of defined functions and loop constructs. Applications of tail-end recursive functions, WHILE and FOR expressions are compiled to iteration loops which are inserted in place. All other recursive functions are rejected by the compiler. There is no notion of higher-order functions.

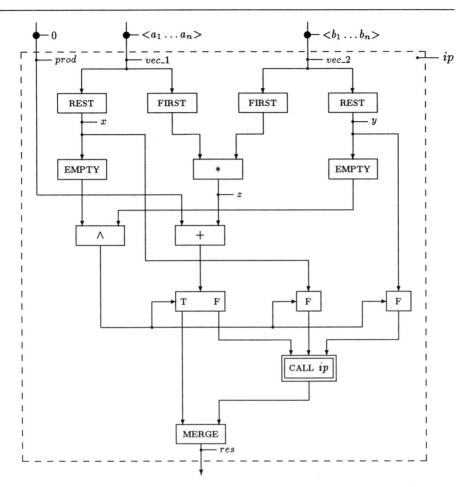

Figure 12.4: Recursion graph for the tail-end recursive computation of the inner vector product

Cyclic graph structures may be used repeatedly and several token sets may be pipelined in acyclic parts of a graph. Order among different operator occurrences is solely maintained by limiting the capacities of all links (or link branches) to just one token. This enforces the firing rule of condition-event (CE-)nets (see section 3.1). An operator is enabled to take place iff there is exactly one token on each of its input links, and no token is on any of the branches of the output link.

To specify, say, the computation of the inner vector product in a form suitable for compilation into a static data flow graph, we may use either the tail-end recursive function defined in the previous subsection or a WHILE expression, in which case we get:

$res =$ DEFINE
$$ip(vec\_1, vec\_2 : list\_of\ int) =$$
$$\{\ prod = 0, x = vec\_1, y = vec\_2$$
IN $\{$ WHILE NOT(AND(EMPTY(x), EMPTY(y))) DO
$$new\ x = \text{REST}(x),$$
$$new\ y = \text{REST}(y),$$
$$new\ prod = (prod + (\text{FIRST}(x) * \text{FIRST}(y)))$$
RETURNS $prod\ \}\ \}$
IN $ip(< a_1 \ldots a_n >, < b_1 \ldots b_n >)$.

This program translates into the data flow graph depicted in fig. 12.5. We note that the loop body is enclosed in a set of entry gates (conditional merges) and a set of exit gates (TF- and T-gates). They govern the cyclic passage of tokens which represent instantiations of the loop variables $prod, x, y$. All gates are in a particular loop cycle controlled by copies of the Boolean value token emerging from the computation of the predicate expression. When initializing the loop, the entry gates must be instantiated with FALSE-tokens on their control inputs (as shown in the figure) in order to let the initial values enter the loop. For all loop cycles in which the predicate evaluates to TRUE, the exit gates route tokens for $new\ prod, new\ x, new\ y$ back to the T-inputs of the entry gates through which they enter the loop body again as new instantiations of $prod, x, y$, respectively. If the predicate evaluates to FALSE, the exit gates return the actual value of $prod$ to the calling environment and consume the actual tokens for $new\ x$ and $new\ y$. Thus, no tokens return to the entry gates which at the control inputs remain instantiated with FALSE-tokens, ready to accept tokens for another loop instance.

This strict loop control via entry and exit gates obviously permits only one token set to cycle within a loop, i.e., it can not be instantiated simultaneously by several token sets that are pipelined. Pipelining is only possible in acyclic parts of a static data flow graph.

The static data flow model can be most successfully employed in application areas requiring highly repetitive and performance-intensive computations such as image and speech processing, but it also suffers from obvious conceptual deficiencies. For one, the absence of a general recursion concept and of the notion of higher-order functions severely limits the use of elegant and concise programming techniques which have become standard in functional languages. For another, the particular loop control mechanisms are somewhat counter-productive to the idea of data flow

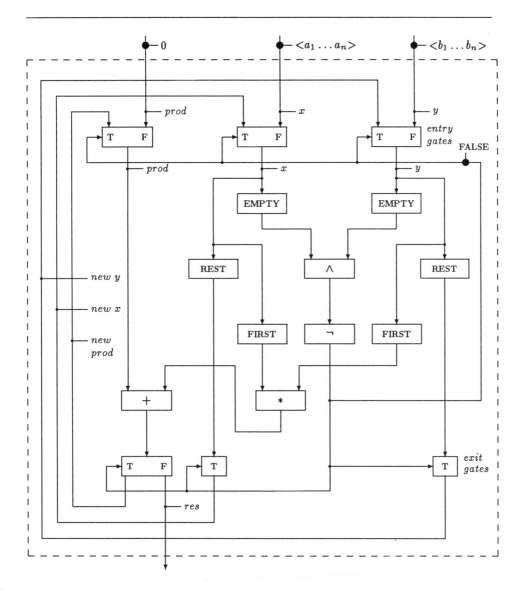

Figure 12.5: Static data flow graph for the iterative computation of inner vector products

computations. They tend to throttle the potential for concurrently executable computations inherent in iteration loops, rather than setting it free.

12.2.3   The Tagged Token Model

This dynamic execution model supports

- general recursions and to some extent higher-order functions (partial applications),

- loop constructs in which several iteration cycles may be overlapped (or pipelined);

- contexts representing instances of defined functions, blocks, or iteration loops.[38]

For the time being, we may think of contexts as activation records (or frames) specifying the instantiation of data flow operators with operand tokens. We will loosely refer to the set of contexts associated with the actual state of a data flow computation as its environment.

With all dynamic components held in the environment, the program graphs can be kept completely static at run-time. Tokens belonging to different function and loop instances are distinguished by tags. They uniquely identify operator instances, i.e., operator occurrences in particular contexts, as token destinations. All tokens with identical tags are input tokens of the same operator instance. This instance is enabled to take place iff all input links carry tokens with the same tag. Exceptions are unconditional merge gates which may fire with tokens of any identity (tag) on either of its input links. Thus, we may have unbounded numbers of unique tokens on all links of the graph.

To determine just what information must be included in the token tags, we have to discuss some basic implementation issues first.

Since a program graph under the tagged token model remains constant when actually executing it, all operators can be located in its code representation under fixed logical or real addresses, e.g., relative to the base of a code segment. The code segments for all defined functions and iteration loops exist in only one copy each, i.e., they must be shared among possibly several instances.[39]

As said before, function and loop instances are uniquely defined by their contexts. In the case of iteration loops, distinct contexts must be created for all loop cycles that execute concurrently.

---

[38] The material contained in this subsection is adopted from [ArGoPl78, ArNi87].

[39] When referring to defined functions, we will always assume that they are converted into supercombinators, if necessary.

Thus a tag which completely specifies an operator instance or an activity (i.e., an operator occurrence in a given environment) as a token destination must be of the form

$$tag = < env \; op\_id >$$

where

$$env = \triangle \; | < ff \; env > | < bf[i] \; env >$$

and

$\triangle$ denotes the empty environment;

ff denotes a context for an instantiated function;

bf defines a context for an instantiated loop;

i denotes an iteration count index for loops;

$bf[i]$ with $i \geq 1$ denotes the context for the i-th loop instance;

op_id identifies an operator in the program code.

This tag must be augmented by an index specifying the input link (or port) via which the operator must receive the token:

$$dest\_tag = < tag \; port >$$

where $port \in [1..n]$ and n is the arity of the operator.

These destination tags may be thought of as token descriptors whose components ff and $bf[i]$ are pointers to context frames and whose components op_id are pointers into the program code, possibly split up into code block base addresses and displacements relative to them.

Thus, besides the operators which manipulate the token values, we also need some control operators. They are to modify the tags when calling and returning from defined function applications, when entering or exiting from iteration loops, and when cycling within loops.

We will now define the operational semantics of these various operators in terms of the tagged tokens they consume and (re-)produce, starting with primitive value-transforming or structuring operations. They are at the machine level specified as

$$prim\_op \; n < s\_1 \; p\_1 > \ldots < s\_m \; p\_m >$$

where $prim\_op \; n$ denotes an n-place operator and $< s\_j \; p\_j > | j \in [1..m]$ denotes the j-th result token destination by means of the identifier s_j and the input port number $p_{-}j$ of the receiving operator. The explicit specification of the operands is omitted here since they are uniquely identifiable as sets of n tokens with identical tags, and port indices ranging over the interval $[1 \ldots n]$.

Taking s as the operator address (identifier) and using

$$y_1 \ldots y_m = prim\_func^{(n)} \ x_1 \ldots x_n$$

to define the semantics of **primitive operators** that are followed by an m-fold branching link, we get for all outputs $j \in [1 \ldots m]$ tokens of the form

$$y_j \ = \ <<< env \ s\_j > p\_j > prim\_func(a\_1, \ldots, a\_n) >$$

$$\begin{array}{ll} \text{iff for all } k \in [1 \ldots n] & x_k = << tag\_k \ k > a_k > \\ \text{and} & tag\_k = < env \ s > \ . \end{array}$$

Conditional branching is represented as a machine level operator of the form

$$\text{IF } m_t \ m_f \ <u\_1 \ p\_1> \ldots <u\_m_t \ p\_m_t> <v\_1 \ q\_1> \ldots <v\_m_f \ q\_m_f>$$

and may be semantically defined as

$$y_{T1} \ldots y_{Tm_t} \mid y_{F1} \ldots y_{Fm_f} = \text{IF } pred \ x$$

where for all $j \in [1 \ldots m_t]$

$$y_{Tj} = \begin{cases} <<< env \ u\_j > p\_j > a > & \text{iff } pred = << tag\_pred \ 1 > \text{TRUE} > \\ \emptyset & \text{else} \end{cases}$$

and for all $j \in [1 \ldots m_f]$

$$y_{Fj} = \begin{cases} <<< env \ v\_j > q\_j > a > & \text{iff } pred = << tag\_pred \ 1 > \text{FALSE} > \\ \emptyset & \text{else} \end{cases}$$

and in addition we have

$$x = << tag\_x \ 2 > a > \quad \text{and} \ tag\_x = tag\_pred = < env \ s > \ .$$

(The symbol $\emptyset$ denotes the fact that no token is emitted on this output link.)

A complementary definition holds for **merging**. If it is unconditional, we simply have to drop the predicate for the control input 1 of the operator.

All these operators have in common that they pass the environment specifications of their input token tags on to the output token tags. What changes in the tags are merely the specifications of the destination operators.

Control operators are inserted into data flow graphs by the compiler in order to change the environment specifications in the token tags. They are pseudo-operators completely transparent to the user. Their sole purpose is to make tokens that belong to different operator instances distinguishable. They do never change token values and there are no equivalent operators in a high-level data flow program, i.e., they serve only organizational purposes.

At the machine language level, control operators have the syntactical form

$$contr\_op < s\_1 \ p\_1 > \ldots < s\_m \ p\_m > \ .$$

It defines the m-fold replication of one input token, thereby modifying its environment specification in the same way on all output tokens. Its semantics may be specified as

$$y_1 \ldots y_m = contr\_op \ x.$$

In the following definitions we again assume that s is the address of the control operator under consideration.

Iteration loops are in fact special nameless functions which can be used only in the places in which they are specified. There are no references to them from somewhere else. Thus, their interfaces to the surrounding data flow graphs are fixed.

Passing argument tokens in and result tokens out of a loop requires two complementary control operators LOOP and LOOP^{-1} which are defined as follows:

for all $j \in [1 \ldots m]$

- $y_j \quad = \quad <<< new\_env \ s\_j > p\_j > arg >$

  where $\quad new\_env = < new\_bf[1] \ env >$

  iff $\qquad x = <<< env \ s > 1 > arg >$ and $contr_op = $ LOOP

  ($new\_bf[1]$ is the new context frame allocated for the loop);

- $y_j \quad = \quad <<< env \ s\_j > p\_j > res >$

  iff $\quad x = <<<< new\_bf[i] \ env > s > 1 > res >$

  and $\quad contr_op = $ LOOP^{-1}.

Loop cycles are followed up by means of the control operator INCR which increments the loop index i:

for all $j \in [1 \ldots m]$, we have

$$y_j = <<<< bf[i + 1] \ env > s\_j > p\_j > arg >$$

iff $x = <<<< bf[i] \ env > s > 1 > arg >$ and $contr_op = $ INCR .

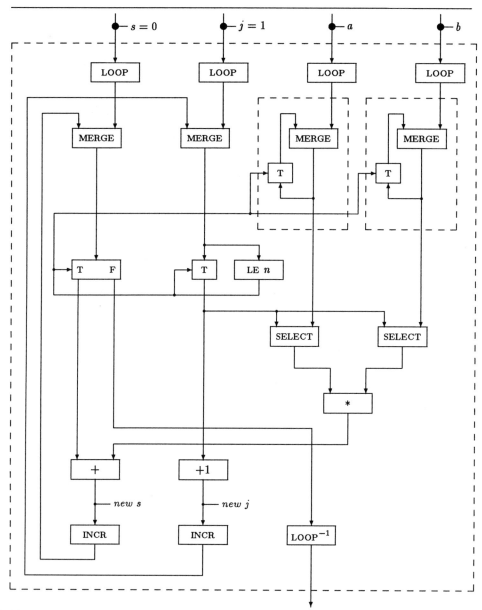

Figure 12.6: Tagged token graph for an iteration loop which computes the inner vector product

The use of these control operators may be illustrated by means of the simple FOR-loop construct

$$\{ \ s : dec\_number = 0$$
$$\text{IN} \ \{ \ \text{FOR} \ j = 1 \ \text{UPTO} \ n \ \text{DO}$$
$$new \ s = (s + (a[j] * b[j])) \ \} \ \} \ .$$

It computes the inner product of two vectors declared outside the loop as

$$a, b : I\_array[n] \ of \ dec\_number \ .$$

This loop compiles to the graph shown in fig. 12.6. Here the LOOP operators assign the same environment to all tokens entering the loop, and LOOP^{-1} returns the resulting token to the calling environment. The cycles within the boxes drawn by the dashed lines are to represent copies of the I-arrays a, b as side conditions for the SELECT operators, i.e., they are not consumed until the loop terminates. In a real system implementation, these cycles do not exist since the I-arrays are represented as constant objects in the environment in which they are declared and instantiated.

The application of defined functions to some n arguments is in the tagged token model realized by means of a special *apply*-operator AP. The machine level representation of an application has the syntactical form

$$\text{AP} \ n \ (func) < s\_1 \ p\_1 > \ldots < s\_m \ p\_m > \ .$$

The explicit specification of the function is optional. It is not required if the model demands that it be supplied to the *apply*-operator as a token via a special function link, as in the PrT-net models described in chapter 4.

The important point here is that functions, in contrast to loops, can be called in many places of a data flow graph where they must be interfaced with the input and output links of the respective *apply*-operators. As is schematically shown in fig. 12.7, this can be accomplished by means of n input control operators LINK which alter the tags of the argument tokens while injecting them into possibly several places of the function body graph, and by an output control operator LINK^{-1} which returns the result token to and distributes it within the calling data flow graph. Conceptually, we consider these control operators parts of the function graphs, as indicated in the figure.

To establish an orderly call-return linkage, the LINK-operators must be made known to the calling graph as destinations for the argument tokens, and the set of destinations for the result token specified in the *apply*-operator, which is commonly referred to as the return-continuation, must be made known to the LINK^{-1} operator of the function graph.

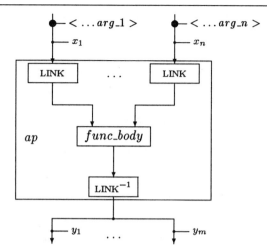

Figure 12.7: Control schema for defined function calls

Input interfacing is straightforward since a function graph is known to the calling graph by the function name, i.e., the input links of an *apply*-operator can be directly connected to the input links of the LINK-operators. However, output interfacing requires that the return-continuation be passed on to the called function, e.g., as part of the environment specification.

Thus, when defining the semantics of a function application as

$$y_1 \ldots y_m = @^{(n)} func\ x_1 \ldots x_n \ ,$$

and again using s as the address of the *apply*-operator, we get for a set of n input tokens with identical tags:

- for the k-th input control operator LINK:
  for all $j' \in [1 \ldots m_k]$

$$y_{kj'} = {<}{<}{<}\ new\_env\ s\_j' > p\_j' > \grave{a}rg\_k >$$

  where $new\_env = {<}{<}\ new\_ff\ ret\_cont > env >$
  and $\quad ret\_cont = {<}{<}\ s\_1\ p\_1 > \ldots < s\_m\ p\_m >>$
  iff $\quad x = {<}{<}{<}\ env\ s > 1 > arg\_k >$

(here *new_ff* denotes the context of the function call, the tuples $< s\_j'\ p\_j' >|$ $j' \in [1 \ldots m_k]$ denote m_k token destinations within the function body, and *ret_cont* denotes the return-continuation);

- for the output control operator LINK^{-1}:
  for all $j \in [1 .. m]$

$$y_j = <<< env \ s\_j > p\_j > func(arg\_1, \ldots, arg\_n) >$$

$$\text{iff} \quad x = <<< new\_env \ s > 1 > func(arg\_1, \ldots, arg\_n) >$$
$$\text{where } new\_env = << new\_ff \ ret\_cont > env >$$
$$\text{and} \quad ret\_cont = << s\_1 \ p\_1 > \ldots < s\_m \ p\_m >> .$$

Control over the entry of argument tokens into loops and function graphs actually is a little more complicated than just described. In order to have the operators LOOP and LINK change the argument token tags as specified, the respective new context frames must be made available first. This can be modeled by an additional control operator GET_FRAME which receives as argument token the required frame size (as figured out by the compiler), and produces a result token which includes a pointer to the allocated frame. This pointer is used as an additional trigger token for LOOP and LINK operators, as shown in fig. 12.8.

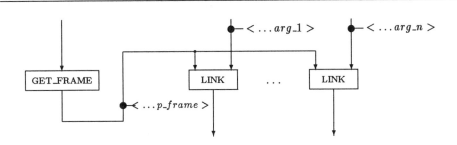

Figure 12.8: Allocation of a context frame to entry control operators

The complementary exit operators LOOP^{-1} and LINK^{-1} must either produce additional output tokens specifying the frame sizes to be returned which must be fed as inputs to REL_FRAME operators, or LOOP^{-1} and LINK^{-1} include the frame release operations.

The details of implementing function and loop instances, particularly the internal structure of the control operators, will be extensively discussed in the next section.

12.3 A Tagged Token Data Flow System

We will now outline in a case study a system implementation of the tagged token data flow model. It has many characteristic features in common with reduction systems based on supercombinators compiled to conventional machine code (see section 11.1). Many of the ideas presented here are adopted from the MIT tagged token architecture [ArNi87]. They can also be found, in more or less the same form, in the Manchester data flow machine [WaGu79, WaGu82, GuKiWa85] and in the SIGMA_1 system developed at ETL in Japan [Yub84, HiSeShi89, SaYaHiKoYu89a, SaYaHiKoYu89b]. The latter exists as a prototype hardware configuration comprising 128 processing sites which is operational since 1988. An advanced version of the MIT architecture which works with control flow threads, the MONSOON, is described in [PaCu90, PaTr91].

Our emphasis in this section will be primarily on the implementation of the contexts for instantiated functions and iteration loops, on the identification of token sets that activate operator instances, and on techniques of exploiting the potential for fine-grain concurrent operations beyond what can be directly deduced from the logical structures of data flow graphs. We will also explore a conceivable system configuration and the ensuing problems of workload distribution and throttling.

All tagged token systems center around two memory concepts which differ in function and purpose from ordinary random access memories. They play a key role in representing structured data in a form compatible with the fine-grain concurrent operations that are characteristic for data flow systems and in realizing the data flow token game itself. One is the so-called I-structure memory which supports concurrent operations on the components of structured data objects, following the single assignment rule. It is used to hold the I-arrays explicitly specified in high-level data flow programs but also to accommodate environment structures. The other is a so-called matching memory which is to synchronize the tagged tokens belonging to the same operator instances.

We set out with an informal explanation of these memory concepts for they largely determine the mechanization of operations on tagged tokens. In doing this, we assume that the value entries of the tokens are either atomic data values or pointers to complex constant objects such as the data flow graphs of defined functions, context frames, I-arrays etc. The heap representations of these objects may be preceded by descriptors, if necessary.

12.3.1   Memory Concepts

As pointed out in section 12.1, structured data objects are in data flow programs primarily declared as I-arrays. Their entries may either be atomic data values of a particular type or pointers to substructures of a particular shape and element type. I-arrays require a special internal representation which helps to realize the single assignment rule for all array entries individually in order to be able to perform concurrent operations on them.

To do so, the entries of I-arrays must be augmented by **flags** which distinguish the states *empty* (or uninstantiated), *filled* (or instantiated with valid data items), and *deferred_read* (indicating read operations that must be kept pending until the respective entries become *filled*). Annotating in a high-level program a variable with the type *I_array* has the effect that at run-time an array of the specified size and entry type is allocated, say, as a part of the respective context. Its entries are initially all flagged out as being *empty*. Whenever a read (copy) operation is attempted on an empty entry, the flag changes to *deferred_read*. In addition, the read request creates the first element of an entry-specific *deferred_read* list which specifies the operator instance (or tag) from which the request actually originates. Further elements are appended to this list on subsequent attempts to read the entry. Whenever a write (store) operation is performed on an entry whose state is either *empty* or *deferred_read*, the flag changes to *filled*. In the latter case, all pending requests are serviced subsequently, i.e., a token is produced for every element of the *deferred_read* list. All read operations on a filled entry are serviced immediately. An attempt to write into an entry that is already filled should not occur in a correctly constructed and compiled program. It must cause an error condition.

Thus, with $< flag\ entry >$ and $<< tag\ port > chain\_pointer >$ respectively denoting the elements of I-arrays and of *deferred_read* lists, we typically have I-structures of the form schematically shown in fig. 12.9. They may be readily mapped to formatted memory representations in which I-array elements can be accommodated, say, in consecutive word locations. Elements of several *deferred_read* lists may be placed in consecutive double word locations in their order of creation. The

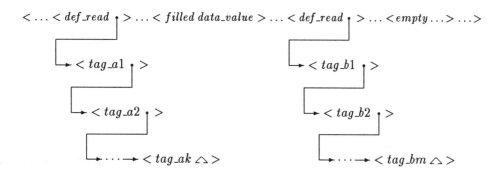

Figure 12.9: Typical I-array with *deferred_read* lists ($\triangle$ denotes an empty pointer)

elements belonging to the same list are linked up by chain-pointer entries.

We now have to explain why and how we get deferred read operations in the first place.

As pointed out in section 12.1, operations on I-array entries must be specified as applications of selector functions which have the general form

$$x[expr\_1, \ldots, expr\_k] \,,$$

where x is the identifier of a k-dimensional I-array and $expr\_1, \ldots, expr\_k$ denote expressions of type *integer* whose values specify index positions along the array coordinates. The occurrence of such a selector operation on the left- or right-hand side of an assignment statement respectively defines a write or read operation. It is activated iff there are tokens for x and for all index positions available on the input links of the particular SELECT operator. The important point now is that the data value carried by the token for x merely is a pointer to the base of an array in the I-structure memory. It just represents the fact that the I-array exists (is allocated) but not whether and to which extent it is actually filled with valid data items.

Read-select operations on I-arrays are therefore not atomic. They must be implemented in a split-phase mode, as depicted in fig. 12.10.a for the simple read-select operation $x[i]$. The READ_SEL operator internally splits into four. The operator ADDR computes from the base address of the I-array carried by the token x and from the value entry of the index token the I-structure memory address under which the array entry is located. Using this address, the FETCH operator then sends a token of the general form $<$ READ , *address* , *tag* $>$ off to the access control operator AC (which is realized by means of a control unit attached to the memory). Eventually, AC returns a token of the form $<< tag\ 1 > value >$ to the operator DISTR which finally generates output tokens to be sent to the destination operator instances. The token returning from AC is delayed until the addressed array location becomes filled. While read accesses are thus in progress, other enabled data flow operators may be executed, including more split-phase read operations on I-arrays.

Write-select (or assignment) operations on I-array entries may be implemented in a similar way. As is shown in fig. 12.10.b for the assignment $x[i] = expr$, the operator WRITE_SEL internally produces by means of ADDR and STORE a token of the form $<$ WRITE , *address* , *value* $>$ which is sent off to the access control operator AC. It has no explicit data output links for its sole purpose is to store its input data value in an I-structure memory location. However, the completion of the write operation may be signaled by an acknowledge token fed back from AC to DISTR which replicates it for consumption elsewhere. These tokens may be used to control resource management operations, but they have no part in executing the data flow graph of an application program.

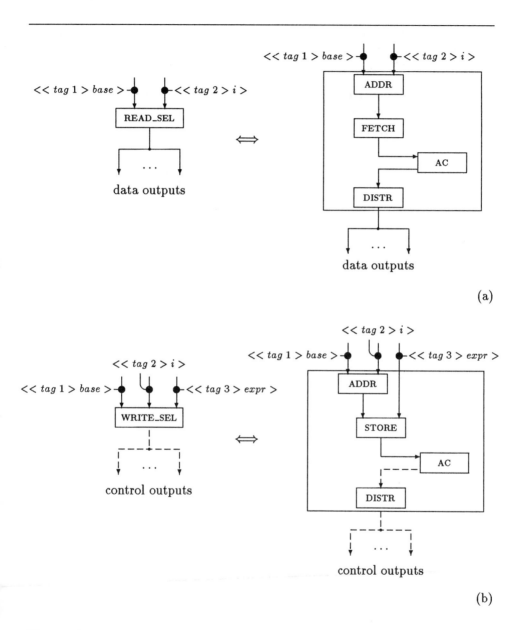

Figure 12.10: Internal structure of a read_select (a) and a write_select (b) operator

A write-select operation on an I-array entry, say $x[i]$, is generally followed by several read-select operations on $x[i]$. The combination of these operators in fact constitutes a branching link named $x[i]$ via which a token is propagated from a source operator to several sink operators. The I-structure memory location identified by the selector operation $x[i]$ merely serves as a buffer through which the token must pass. This equivalence is schematically illustrated in fig. 12.11.

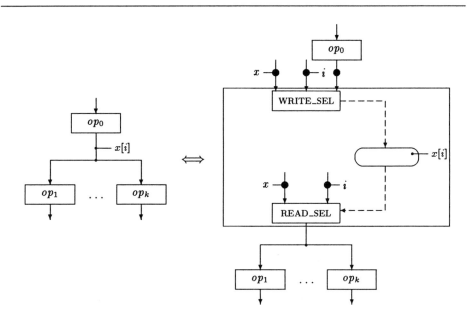

Figure 12.11: Establishing a token link via write-select and read-select operations on an I-array

It is important to note at this point that combinations of write/read operations on I-arrays have a very interesting property which may be elegantly utilized to change environments. A token written to an I-array loses its tag and thus is stripped off the environment it originates from, since I-array entries contain only (pointers to) values. When subsequently reading an entry, a new tag is attached to the value which includes the environment specification carried by the I-array token (and, of course, the selector token). This environment may or may not be the same as the one originally associated with the value.

Another token buffer which realizes the direct operator links is the matching memory. It holds tokens waiting for the synchronization with others having the same tag in order to complete token sets which constitute operator instantiations. To do so, the matching memory supports **token set structures** of the general form

$$[tag \; k \; ptr]$$

$$\llcorner \!\!\rightarrow <^{(n)} \ldots value\_i \ldots >$$

where [...] may be considered a **token set descriptor**. Its entry

- *tag* denotes the tag which the members of the token set have in common;

- *k* denotes the number of tokens still missing from the complete set;

- *ptr* points to the list of values carried by the members of the token set.

The tag of a token $<< tag \; i > value\_i >$ sent out by an operator is compared against the tags of all token set descriptors resident in the matching memory. If no match occurs, a new token set structure is allocated with an as yet empty value list. Its size n derives from the number of input operands specified in the destination operator of the token. Its port index i is taken as a selector for the list position to which $value\_i$ must be written as the first valid element. The count index k in the descriptor is initialized with $(n-1)$.

Further tokens with the same tag now match against an existing descriptor. Their values are simply written to the list positions selected by their port indices. When adding a new token value, the count index k is decremented by one. If it is down to zero, the token set is complete, i.e., the operator instance specified by it is enabled. After its execution, the token set structure can be released.

Token matching via these structures is used in conjunction with the activation of primitive data flow operators, and in a degenerate form also for the various control operators. They require that all input tokens be present before they can actually take place.[40]

Both the l-structure memory and the matching memory can be implemented using conventional random access memory devices.

The single assignment semantics and the treatment of deferred read accesses is taken care of by a dedicated access control unit which realizes the various AC operator instances. It inspects the flags of I-array locations prior to performing

---

[40]Most data flow systems use a degenerate matching scheme by permitting only unary or binary operators. In the former case, the single token is directly passed on to the destination operator instance. In the latter case, there is at most one token of a pair in the matching memory. It is removed whenever the second token with which it matches arrives, and both are passed on as a packet to the operator instance specified by their common tag. Tokens may thus be stored in the matching memory directly as they are, avoiding the more complex token set structures.

read or write operations on them, constructs *deferred_read* lists, if necessary, and processes them as soon as the respective locations are instantiated with valid data items.

Matching the tags of new tokens against existing descriptors and subsequent update operations on specific elements of token set structures are of an associative nature. However, they can also be implemented with reasonable efficiency in addressable memories using hashing techniques.

The code representations of the data flow graphs and of all other constant objects are held in memories requiring just conventional random addressing modes.

12.3.2   Function Invocations

We pointed out earlier that data flow employs naive substitutions of formal by actual parameters and thus requires the conversion of open into closed functions (or supercombinators) in order to avoid naming conflicts. In the tagged token model, functions must be closed for yet another reason: legitimate operator instantiations are defined by operand tokens that carry identical tags, i.e., they must belong to the same contexts. If relatively free variables would be permitted, then we would have to deal with operators which become instantiated with operands from different contexts.

Complete contexts for function-turned-supercombinators include the collection of all token set structures necessary to execute the respective data flow graphs. Since we have chosen to create and release these structures dynamically at run-time, space may be allocated (and de-allocated) piecemeal anywhere in the matching memory. Thus, we generally have no contiguous frames that could be stacked nor unique frame pointers that could be used as context identifiers in the token tags in order to represent complete environments.

To overcome this problem in a way that is consistent with the environments of the supercombinator-based reduction systems described in chapters 9 and 11, we represent instances of defined functions (turned into supercombinators) by argument frames (or linear arrays) of some $(n_f + n_b)$ entries, where n_f and n_b respectively denote the numbers of relatively free and bound variables of the original functions. These frames are taken as the contexts in which the function bodies are to be executed.

Function applications are in data flow computations merely governed by the partial ordering of the respective *apply*-operators in the graph. Every application creates a complete context of its own. Thus, the environment structure of the entire program execution is a dynamically evolving and collapsing hierarchy of context frames. No special pointer structures are required to interconnect these frames. The partial ordering among them is solely maintained by means of the token tags.

Since there is no particular order in which the arguments of function applications are being computed and no synchronization of them is required either, the argument frames may be realized as I-arrays whose entries can be filled in any order. To do so, complete frames with all locations in the state *empty* must be allocated. This complies with the argument substitution scheme depicted in fig. 12.8. It shows the availability of context frames as pre-conditions for occurrences of the control operators LINK which substitute argument tokens in function bodies, and thereby also change their tags.

These and all other control operators introduced in subsection 12.2.3 can be realized as specific instances of a **control operator scheme** CS which has the general form depicted in fig. 12.12. This scheme is a special version of the buffered token link shown in fig. 12.11. It is characterized by a frozen (or constant) selector index j for both the WRITE_SEL and READ_SEL operators (whose addresses are assumed to be a and b, respectively). Tokens on the respective control links c_a and c_b activate these select operators for the passage of some **value token** from the input link IN to the output branching link OUT via the I-array location with index j. These

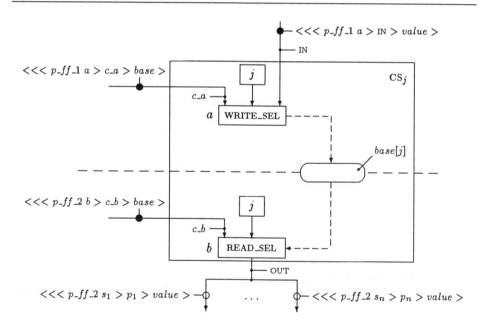

Figure 12.12: General control operator scheme

tokens must carry as values the **base addresses** of the same I-array (or **argument frame**) but may differ with respect to their **environment specifications**. For the time being, we simply assume that environments can be represented as pointers p_ff_1, p_ff_2 to the bases of the actual frames. To illustrate the operational behavior of this operator scheme in one figure, pre-conditions are represented as black tokens, and the post-conditions eventually resulting from the operator occurrence are blank tokens.

With the **control operator scheme** CS at hand, we can now discuss the details of implementing function applications. The functions are realized as **static data flow graphs** of fixed arities which must be instantiated with complete sets of **argument tokens** in order to execute them correctly and to return **result tokens** eventually. This requires that partial and complete function applications be implemented in different ways since execution in the former case must be delayed until it is certain that all input links receive argument tokens.

To handle **partial applications**, the system must form **closure tokens** that can be moved about the data flow graph through several *apply*-operators to collect all arguments. The degenerate case of a closure token represents a function in its original form.

The values carried by closure tokens are pointers to descriptors, of which each includes

- an internal link pointer to the code representation of the data flow graph that realizes the function body expression;

- an arity entry specifying the total number of argument tokens required;

- the actual number of arguments collected and

- a pointer to the data structure in which these arguments are held.

For reasons of uniformity, all *apply*-operators within a data flow graph are assumed to be equipped with input links for closure tokens. However, only partial applications make use of and modify data items or substructures represented by them. Complete applications use degenerate closure tokens merely as triggers for the allocation of argument frames. The compiler expands these applications directly, i.e., **in place**, by call-return structures as shown in fig. 12.7.

Fig. 12.13 depicts the **in-place expansion** of complete function applications in greater detail. This data flow graph uses CS operators to realize the **input** and **output control operators** LINK and LINK^{-1}. In addition we have an operator

- GET_FRAME which extracts from the closure token on its input link the arity n of the function, allocates an I-array frame of size $(n + 1)$ for n argument

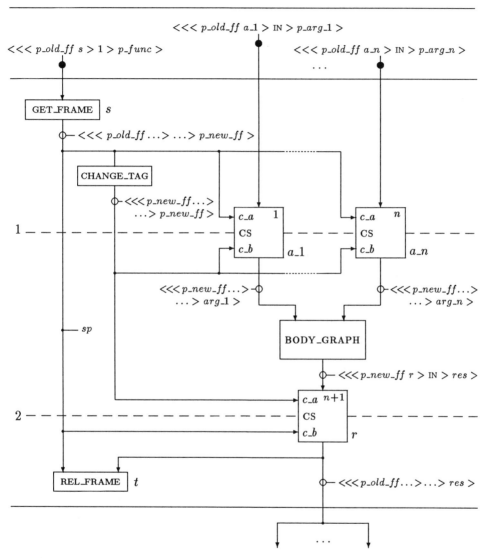

Figure 12.13: In-place expansion of complete supercombinator applications

values (or pointers) and one result value (or pointer),[41] and returns the pointer p_new_ff to its base as value of the output token;

- REL_FRAME which releases the argument frame identified by the pointer value of the token on its first input link when triggered by a result token on its second input link;

- CHANGE_TAG which takes the pointer value of its input token as the environment specification of its output token without changing the pointer in value positions.

For illustration purposes we use again in this graph black and blank tokens to represent pre-conditions and successively emerging post-conditions, respectively. Irrelevant token components are depicted as dots.

The entire **call-return structure** which replaces the original *apply*-operator partitions into three parts separated by the dashed horizontal lines 1 and 2. They respectively run through the upper set of CS operators which realize the LINKs and through the lower CS operator which realizes the LINK^{-1}, thus defining the interfaces between what is commonly referred to as the **caller** and the **callee**. Within the CS operators, these interfaces are realized by means of the I-array locations (or buffers) of the context frame that separate the WRITE_SEL operators from the READ_SEL operators. All operators above line 1 and below line 2 become part of the caller's code, i.e., of the compiled version of the data flow graph in which the original *apply*-operator occurs. This code must be executed in the **calling environment** identified by the frame pointer p_old_ff. All operators between the interface lines belong to the callee's code, i.e., to the compiled version of the data flow graph which includes the function body expression. This code exists in only one copy which must be executed in the **callee's (or new) environment** identified by the frame pointer p_new_ff. The pointer is produced by the operator GET_FRAME which in fact installs the new context. Its last copy is consumed by the REL_FRAME operator when returning from this context. Thus, the evaluation of a complete function application may start as soon as a token becomes available at the closure input link. It may even proceed to some extent within the body expression graph without injecting a single argument token.

When comparing this implementation of the call-return structure with the formal definitions given in subsection 12.2.3 for the control operators LINK and LINK^{-1}, we note that it suffices to represent an environment just by a pointer to the base of what is its actual context frame. The stacking and unstacking of frames specified

---

[41] Depending on implementation and compilation details, context frames for function instances may contain more entries, e.g., for local variables, context information, etc.

by the tag modifications

$$env \Rightarrow < new\_ff\ env >\quad \text{in LINK}$$

$$< new\_ff\ env > \Rightarrow env \quad \text{in LINK}^{-1}$$

is in fact realized by means of the link labeled sp in fig. 12.13. It passes the token
whose tag specifies the context frame directly from the input interface to the output
interface where they effect the orderly return from the called to the calling contexts.
If the functions are recursive, many of these tokens may pile up in the matching
store, waiting for synchronization with the respective result tokens.

We also observe that, contrary to the formal definitions, the token tags do not
carry return-continuations with them for they are directly generated by the compiler
as part of the call-return structure.

In-place expansion by call-return structures will likely be possible for the overwhelming majority of defined function calls specified in high-level data flow programs. However, a more general implementation of the *apply*-operator must be
supported as well in order to deal dynamically with partial applications. It must
be capable of forming and manipulating closures and of transforming closures into
complete function applications whenever sufficiently many arguments are collected.

The general scheme for applying a closure to an argument, as a result of which
we get another closure, is illustrated in fig. 12.14. Here the left input link of an
apply-operator is instantiated with a token representing a closure. It is composed of
a function of arity n and of a binary list of some $r < n$ arguments which have been
collected so far. The right input link carries the argument token $arg\_(r + 1)$. The
occurrence of the operator returns a closure token whose argument list is augmented
by the new argument, and the argument count index r in the token descriptor is
incremented by one. The tail of what is now the new argument list may be shared
with other closure tokens occurring somewhere else in the graph.[42]

By convention, *apply*-operators do not require synchronization with argument
tokens, i.e., they may fire with just a closure token present. However, this pre-
supposes the implementation of the argument lists as I-structures in order to be
able to construct them without there being argument tokens available to fill their
entries. In fact, argument lists which have accumulated as many empty or filled
entries as are necessary to saturate the arities of the respective supercombinators

---

[42] At this point, the reader may convince himself that these closures are only good for the
internal representation of partial function applications which eventually receive all arguments.
Since the functions exist only as compiled machine code, they cannot be transformed into new
functions for the code does not execute correctly unless it receives all arguments. There is also no
straightforward way of returning closures to the user in an intelligible form. Thus, while higher-
order functions are supported internally, this feature is in data flow systems for all practical
purposes not available at the user interface.

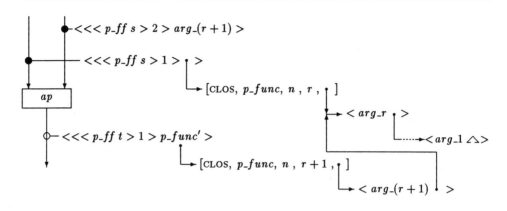

Figure 12.14: Partial application of a closure

are fully consistent with the context frames of complete function applications which are implemented as I-arrays.

The *apply*-operator which completes the argument list of a closure to $r = n$ entries appends another entry for the result and dynamically installs a call-return structure similar to the one shown in fig. 12.13. However, rather than allocating a new frame, the argument list is directly taken as the interface between the caller and the callee (line 1). The list pointer entry in the closure descriptor is used as the new context pointer p_new_ff. As a consequence, the callee-side of this interface must be modified insofar as the read-select operations on I-arrays must be replaced with read-select operations on the equivalent components of a binary list linked by pointers. Likewise, the return-interface (line 2) must be implemented as a write/read operation on the $(n + 1)$-st entry of a binary list. Thus, if a function is in a given program applied both partially and completely, it must be compiled into data flow code which includes both interface versions.

Instances of iteration loops may be realized in essentially the same way as in-place expanded function calls. Context frames for all loop variables may be allocated when entering and de-allocated when leaving loops. The entries may be filled in any order by performing within the loops assignments to the variables they represent. Nested loops require their own blocks to separate inner and outer loop instances.

Instantiating ordinary block structures which usually define the body expressions of functions does not require new contexts. The variables used in these blocks specify token links which in fact can be realized directly through the matching store, using in the token tags the context pointers of the respective function instances.

The block structures specified in a HLDFL program need not necessarily correspond one-to-one to those of the machine-level data flow code. The compiler may perform certain optimizations aimed at accommodating several block or loop instances in one large contiguous frame rather than in several non-contiguous frames that must be claimed and released piecemeal. One such optimization would consist in flattening nested block structures using λ-lifting techniques, another would consist in allocating in one piece an array of frames for instantiated loops. At the maximum, one could have as many frames as are necessary to execute all loop iterations concurrently.

Of course, it is of little use invoking loop iterations far in excess of the resources (processing sites) that can be made available to execute them. Allocating to a loop with an index interval of size n just some $k < n$ frames is therefore advocated as a means to throttle its unfolding. Only k out of n iterations can then be active at any time.

Unfortunately, this concept does not have any stabilizing effect at all on the overall system behavior.

For one, throttling iteration loops solves only part of the problem. There can be no similar bounds on general recursions since they could deadlock by exhausting pre-allocated environment frames before termination.[43] Thus, the system may get flooded with concurrently executable function calls which do not differ from loop instances in any way relevant to this problem.

For another, an upper bound on instantiated loops has only a local throttling effect. Even if such bounds would either be specified by the user or fixed by the compiler for all loops of a program, the system may still get flooded with unbounded numbers of loop instances. The problem may be partly caused by the absence of bounds on the nesting of loops, but to a larger extent by iteration loops contained in recursive function definitions.

The conceptual shortcomings of the loop throttling approach can best be exposed when comparing it with the ticket concept used to stabilize systems of cooperating reduction processes (compare chapter 7 and section 9.5). There, a finite ticket reservoir establishes a ceiling on the number of processes that can co-exist system-wide at any time. We thus have a global invariance property as opposed to many unrelated local invariants due to k-bounded loops. The most important point, however, is that in our reduction systems we have also a separation of processes from instances of recursive functions. A process may support unbounded numbers of recursions (which includes iterations). Keeping an upper bound on the number of processes does therefore only limit the degree to which concurrency can be exploited but it

---

[43] As a matter of fact, deadlocks may also occur in k-bounded loops, e.g., if the loop unfolds towards increasing indices but there are data dependencies towards decreasing indices which reach beyond k.

does not throttle the computation itself. Thus, there can be no deadlocks due to the exhaustion of tickets (or of opportunities to create more processes).

In contrast to this, data flow suffers from the fundamental problem that each function or loop instance is in fact treated as an individual process, i.e., process creation (and termination) is directly tied to recursion (iteration) steps. This leaves us with a rather unpleasant choice when it comes to exercising control over concurrent computations in a way that is supposed to bring about an orderly system behavior. We can either limit the number of processes (which inevitably implies a limit on recursions) and thus invite deadlocks, or we can avoid these deadlocks at the expense of allowing unbounded numbers of processes. In either case, there is no way of establishing under these circumstances any form of invariance property that holds system-wide. Stated more drastically: dynamic data flow systems are inherently unstable.

For most practical purposes, this may not have any dramatic consequences since the majority of application programs can be expected to behave reasonably well. However, the point is that we have only the choice of risking deadlocks or chaos.

Moreover, the absence of invariance properties renders it impossible to implement organizational measures which guarantee a reasonably balanced dynamic work load distribution. This deficiency is particularly painfully felt in distributed system where all processing sites maintain their own local pools of processes but have no explicit knowledge of the workload in other sites. Exchanging messages to this effect is known to create a lot of unproductive traffic which impairs the overall system performance significantly.

12.3.3   A System Configuration

Before discussing the machinery for the execution of tagged token data flow programs, we have to develop a reasonably clear picture of what we mean by a data flow process. Indeed, this concept is a little difficult to explain for, which ever way we are trying to do it, it is somewhat at odds with the definition given in section 2.1. There we said that '... *processes* ... *are considered units of activity which execute programs or parts thereof in a strictly sequential manner, requiring exactly one processing unit...* ', and '... *a process comprises both the executable representation of a program and a virtual machine in which the program can actually run...* '. Furthermore, we said that processes are completely characterized by process contexts which, besides the virtual machines, specify global process states, actual states of the computations to be performed, and interruptibility.

Unfortunately, these characteristics can not be easily related to data flow computations. The difficulties largely arise from the underlying control discipline.

In the introduction to this chapter we pointed out that there are good reasons to consider all occurrences of primitive operators as atomic processes. They clearly are units of activity which may assume the states *waiting* (for the arrival of their operand tokens), *executable* (having synchronized with all operands), *executing* and *terminated* (having consumed their operand tokens and produced result tokens instead). Since there is no explicit sequential control, all operator instances must undergo a full scheduling cycle. Also, the tags of the operand tokens undoubtedly specify contexts in which the operators are to be executed, though there is only a very trivial notion of a program.

Instantiated function and loop bodies, as mentioned at the end of the preceding subsection, seem to realize a decidedly more useful process concept. Here we have non-trivial program code composed of many partially ordered primitive operators, all of which must be executed in the same context. We also have a non-trivial virtual machine which is generally distributed over distinct physical memory modules. The code segment and other constant objects are held in a conventional random access memory, I-arrays and environment structures are stored in an I-structure memory, and tokens waiting for synchronization are buffered in a matching memory.

The problem here is that within an instantiated function or loop we may not only have operators in various states of activation, but executable operators also may be distributed over more than just one processing unit. Thus, we have neither a sequential execution order nor a well-defined state of the computation.

However, what may appear to be a serious deficiency with respect to process management has no harmful practical consequences at all. Data flow computations activate and execute under a given set of input parameter values only those parts of a program which contribute to the actual result. There are generally no speculative evaluations which eventually must be aborted. All processes, once started, may run to completion without temporary suspension. Error conditions must be propagated along as bottom tokens in order to terminate the computation in an orderly form, i.e., without any tokens left over in the data flow graph. There can be no abortion of the process. Process synchronization is solely accomplished by means of token matching.

All this adds up to the fact that data flow does not require an interrupt concept. Without interrupts, there is no context switching either, i.e., an intermediate state of the computation must never be saved and thus need not be known. It suffices to characterize a data flow process by the code segment to be executed, by the virtual machine assigned to it, and by a global state. This state is solely determined by the flow of tokens in and out of the code segment: a process becomes *executable* and immediately starts *executing* as soon as it is triggered by a closure (or control) token to allocate a context frame. It *terminates* when producing a result token and releasing the frame. There is no explicit process scheduling at this level. This is entirely done at the level of primitive operator occurrences. Also, there is no need to support in the traditional sense process context blocks.[44]

With this notion of data flow processes at hand, we can now proceed to study in some detail the configuration of a tagged token data flow system, setting out with a single processing site (or a physical data flow domain), of which fig. 12.15 shows the basic components. They form a cyclic pipeline comprising three major stages which are interconnected via queues. The inscriptions on the interconnecting arcs specify the structures of the tokens that are carried along. The *operand_match_unit* receives at its input operand tokens whose tags are by means of hashing techniques compared against the tags of the token sets resident in the *matching_memory*. If there is no match, a new token set structure with one valid entry is created, otherwise the token value is simply written to the token set structure with the matching tag.[45] The entry is selected by the port specification of the token. When completing a token set structure, it is put to the back-end of the *operand_set_queue* and deleted in the *matching_memory*. The *operator_fetch_unit* takes one-by-one token set structures from the front-end of the *rand_set_queue*, uses the *op_id* specifications of their tags to fetch the destination operators from the code segments stored in the *program_memory*, and forms complete operation packets comprising the operators, the operand sets and the result destination sets. These packets are via the *operator_packet_queue* transmitted to the *processing_unit* for execution. Read-select and write-select operations on I-structures are sent off to the *access_control_unit* of the *I-structure-memory*. The *processing_unit* and the *access_control_unit* generate, by means of the destination lists contained in the operation packets and by the *deferred_read* lists hung up in I-array entries, sequences of result value tokens. The context frame pointers in their tags are usually taken from the tags of the operand token sets. Only the control operators CHANGE_ENV extract new context pointers from the value entries of their input tokens. Depending on their destinations, these tokens are either recycled to the *operand_match_unit* or leave the processing site via the *out_gate*. New tokens may enter the site via the *in_gate*.

A single processing site of this kind constitutes a full-fledged data flow machine. Any of its components may be replicated to meet certain bandwidth requirements which ensure a steady and balanced token flow through the cyclic pipeline. This machine must be connected via the input and output ports to an operating system (OS-)machine which provides the usual OS-services. The *program_memory* may be loaded from the OS-machine through another interface not shown in the picture. A data flow computation may be started by sending a trigger token via the *in_gate* to the outermost block or function application of the loaded program code, followed by argument tokens if necessary. The computation terminates by sending a result

---

[44] These context blocks must not be confused with activation records.

[45] If the destination operator has arity one (as in the case of all control operators), the token is simply passed on to the *operator_fetch_unit*.

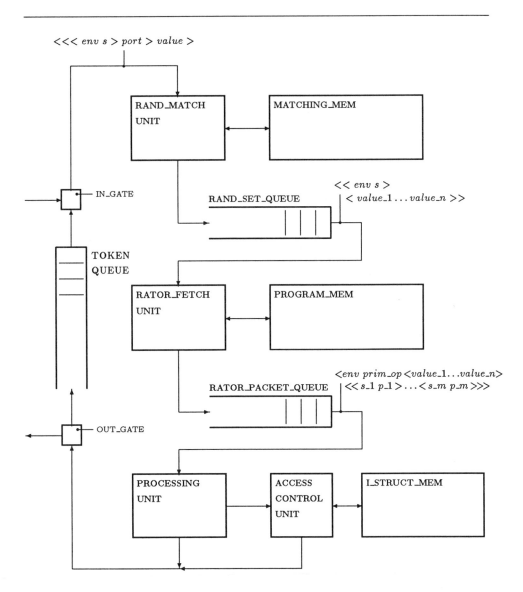

Figure 12.15: Configuration of a data flow processing site

token back to the OS-machine via the *out_gate*. The entire program execution may be considered a single data flow process created and terminated by the OS-machine.

To exploit program-inherent concurrency on a large scale, data flow systems are expected to be configured as arrays of fairly large numbers, say from 64 to 256, of such processing sites. They are typically interconnected by a network each

- to route tokens from source to destination sites;

- to configure the local I-structure memory modules as a memory bank which forms a globally uniform address space that is accessible from all sites, with fastest access for the respective local processing unit(s) and larger memory latencies for remote sites;

- to load program code segments down to the local program memories.

We thus get a system configuration as schematically depicted in fig. 12.16.

The local program memories may be operated in either of two ways. If they are small, they may be used as caches to which active parts of the program code may be downloaded upon demand. This may be done in units of variable-length code segments, in which case the code must be made relocatable, or in units of pages, in which case the real or virtual pages of the program code are directly mapped to cache pages by hardware. Inactive parts of the program code resident in the caches may be overwritten. If sufficient space is available, the entire program code may be copied under identical addresses into all local program memories prior to executing it.

Without loss of generality, we assume the latter to be the case in order to liberate the following discussion from irrelevant details. We also assume that a local I-structure memory module realizes the I-address interval $A_r = [r * size .. (r+1) * size - 1]$, where $r \in [0 .. N-1]$ denotes the index of the processing site, and $size = 2^k$ denotes the capacity, say in bytes, of each module.

Based on these assumptions, we can develop a very simple scheme for the allocation of data flow processes to particular processing sites. All we need to do is to place the context (argument) frame of a process that is supposed to execute in site r in the I-address interval A_r and to route the tokens belonging to this process by means of the frame base address $p\_ff \mid p\_bf \in A_r$ which is part of the token tags. These addresses decompose into

$$p\_ff \mid p\_bf = r * size + offset \quad \text{where} \quad 0 \leq offset < size \; ;$$

i.e., the site indices r can be directly extracted from the tags to control the routing switches *out_gate* within the processing sites as well as the switches in the *token_routing_network* connecting the sites. A token produced in some site r whose token tag carries a site index p remains in that site if $p = r$, and leaves the site through the output port into the routing network otherwise. Thus, the entire token flow of a particular function or loop instance is bound to the site in which the

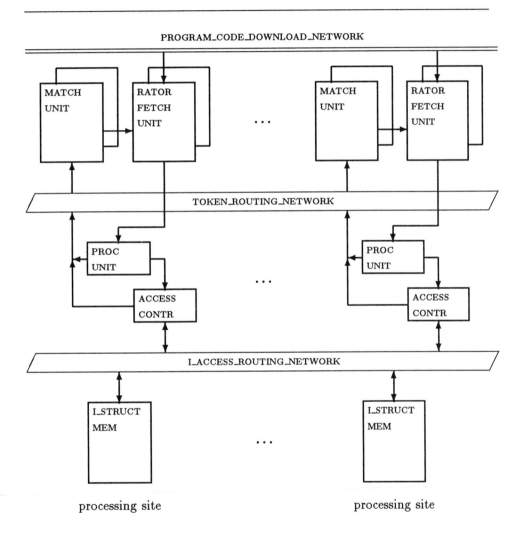

Figure 12.16: Configuration of a tagged token data flow system comprising several processing sites

context frame is located. Stated in another form: the processing site selected as the location of the context frame is the site in which the process associated with an instantiated function or loop executes, i.e., the I-structure memory manager in fact governs the workload distribution within the system.

To study this in more detail, let us return to fig. 12.13 which depicts a complete call-return structure for a function. Suppose the caller's code is executing in site r, i.e., we have a frame pointer $p\_old\_ff \in A_r$, and the GET_FRAME operator returns a new frame pointer $p\_new\_ff \in A_p$, with $p \neq r$ specifying another site. Then the WRITE_SELECT operators of the caller/callee interface (line 1) execute in site r but write the argument values to the frame located in site p. The CHANGE_TAG operator generates a sequence of tokens with tags p_new_ff that are routed to site p. There they activate the READ_SELECT operators of the caller/callee interface (line 1) and the WRITE_SELECT operator of the callee/caller interface (line 2), thus creating a new process. All tokens injected into the body graph carry frame pointers p_new_ff and thus bind its execution to the site p (further function or loop calls within the body may be placed somewhere else). The callee/caller interface (line 2) eventually performs the reverse operation, i.e., it returns the result token back to site r where the calling process executes, thereby terminating the process in site p. Also, the frame p_new_ff is released from this site by the REL_FRAME operator.

As for a suitable placement strategy for processes over the processing sites, we can basically use a similar scheme as the one described in subsection 7.2 for cooperating reduction machines. However, with large numbers of processing sites in the system, it is definitely advisable to establish some form of locality of interconnections in order to keep the complexity of the token routing and I-memory access networks within reasonable bounds, possibly permitting only a few direct interconnections among adjacent sites. A good choice for the number of these links would be in the same order as the number of loop iterations that can be instantiated concurrently. Thus, the I-memory manager may allocate frames for some k loop instances in k processing sites adjacent to the site in which the loop is called. I-memory space (and thus process allocation) may be managed locally in order to minimize the number of conflicting allocation/de-allocation requests that must be serviced per manager.

We could employ the ticket allocation concept described in chapter 7 to limit the number of processes that can be created by a site r in another site $p \neq r$ to which it is directly connected. However, this measure cannot have any noteworthy stabilizing effect, as in cooperating reduction machines. This is essentially for the same reasons as discussed at the end of the preceding section. All the excess work which after ticket exhaustion cannot anymore be distributed somewhere else must be handled in the processing site in which it comes about, i.e., it must nevertheless be possible to create unbounded numbers of processes within a site. On a first glance, it may be argued that, as far as I-memory consumption for argument frames is concerned, it does not really matter whether every function or loop instance is considered another data flow process, or whether we have just a limited number of processes with unbounded recursions (or iterations), as in reduction systems. But this line of reasoning misses an important point.

Reductions within a process are strictly sequential, governed by a pre-order traversal of the program expression. Thus, when performing divide-and-conquer recursions (which constitute the main source of concurrency in reduction systems) under the control of one process, there can be only function calls along a single trace of the entire recursion tree, i.e., a tree expanding over time to a total of $O(n)$ calls demands at any time space for only $O(\lg n)$ calls.

This contrasts with data flow systems which have no sequential control mechanisms whatsoever. Here the entire tree may unfold concurrently, demanding space for $O(n)$ function calls to accommodate the argument frames in the I-structure memory modules and the tokens in the matching memories, even if all of them are contained in one processing site.

Similar considerations apply to tail-end recursions vs. data flow iterations as well.

Thus, even with a ticket distribution scheme little can be done to prevent data flow computations from exploding in space, whereas the space demand for the equivalent reduction processes can be kept decidedly lower for many applications.

12.4 Streams

The concept of **streams** comes as a natural extension of data flow [ArGoPl78], but may generally be used in functional systems (see [Bur75]), and also in control flow systems. Streams are **ordered sequences of object tokens**, possibly of the same monomorphic or polymorphic type, which may be unending. They are to establish communication links between **producer** and **consumer processes** which are supposed to operate concurrently, at least within the margins set by finite synchronic distances.[46]

Streams may be defined as

$$\underline{x} : stream\_of \; \alpha = stream\_expr$$

where *stream_expr* denotes a generator (or producer) expression for a sequence

$$\underline{x} = x_1 \; x_2 \ldots x_i \ldots$$

---

[46] A synchronic distance generally defines the number of occurrences by which one of two or more concurrent events can go ahead of the others before they must be synchronized, i.e., the others must catch up. In the particular case, it simply measures the number of elements which the stream may contain at the maximum.

of stream elements, of which each is uniquely identified by its stream position $i \in \{1, 2, \ldots\}$. If the stream is of finite length, it terminates with an implicit *end_of_stream* symbol $\lhd$.

The **generator expression** *stream_expr* may itself be defined in terms of other streams which it consumes. In particular, it may be recursively defined by the stream it produces, i.e., streams may form **feedback loops** and thus introduce history sensitivity.

Operations on streams may be defined in the same way as those on binary lists. The primitives usually refer to their first elements, called the **heads**, or to the remaining streams, called the **tails**. We have

$$\text{EMPTY}(\underline{x}) = \begin{cases} \text{TRUE} & \text{if } \underline{x} = \lhd \\ \text{FALSE} & \text{otherwise} \end{cases}$$

$$\text{HEAD}(\underline{x}) = \begin{cases} \perp \text{ (undefined)} & \text{if } \text{EMPTY}(\underline{x}) = \text{TRUE} \\ x_1 & \text{otherwise} \end{cases}$$

$$\text{TAIL}(\underline{x}) = \begin{cases} \perp & \text{if } \text{EMPTY}(\underline{x}) = \text{TRUE} \\ x_2 \ldots x_i \ldots & \text{otherwise} \end{cases}$$

$$\text{CONS}(\text{HEAD}(\underline{x}), \text{TAIL}(\underline{x})) = \underline{x} \,,$$

where $\underline{x}$ is a stream as defined above.

These stream operations are **non-strict**: the actual streams must contain only the head elements in order to render them executable, i.e., they basically follow the semantics of infinite lists under a **lazy evaluation regime** (compare the introduction to chapter 10).

To illustrate the construction of more complex stream operations, we consider as an example the **prime sieve of Eratosthenes**, which realizes the following algorithm to determine prime numbers: from an input stream of integer numbers in monotonically increasing order, starting at 2,

- take the first element as prime number;
- filter out multiples of this prime from the remaining stream;
- continue recursively with the filtered stream.

Taking $\underline{x}$ as an unending input stream of integers and $\underline{y}$ as the output stream of primes, this algorithm may be specified as follows:

$$\underline{y} : stream\_of\ integer =$$
DEFINE
$$filter(p, \underline{u}) = \text{IF} \quad ((\text{HEAD}(\underline{u})\ \text{MOD}\ p) = 0)$$
$$\text{THEN}\ filter(p, \text{TAIL}(\underline{u}))$$
$$\text{ELSE}\ \text{CONS}(\text{HEAD}(\underline{u}), filter(p, \text{TAIL}(\underline{u})))$$
$$sieve(\underline{v}) \quad = \text{CONS}(\text{HEAD}(\underline{v}), sieve(filter(\text{HEAD}(\underline{v}), \text{TAIL}(\underline{v}))))$$
IN $sieve(\underline{x})$

In this stream expression the function *filter* receives an integer value p and a stream of integers $\underline{u}$ as arguments, and returns a stream from which all elements u_i with $(u_i\ \text{MOD}\ p) = 0$ are removed. The function *sieve* receives as argument a stream of integers $\underline{v}$ and produces a stream that is recursively constructed from the head element of $\underline{v}$ and from the application of *sieve* to the stream tail filtered by means of the head element.

The generation of an infinite input stream $\underline{x}$ for the prime sieve may be specified as

$$\underline{x} : stream\_of\ integer = \text{DEFINE}$$
$$gen(n) = \text{CONS}(n, gen((n + 1)))$$
$$\text{IN}\ gen(2)\ .$$

This prime sieve program would have to be written in exactly the same form for a lazy evaluator (see chapter 10). Each recursive call of the consumer/producer function *sieve* (and subsequently of its subfunction *filter*) would then trigger the producer function *gen* to deliver just the actual first element of the stream, whereupon *gen* would go to rest until triggered again by the demand for the next element. Producer and consumer activities are thus very tightly coupled with a synchronic distance of just one, which leaves no room for concurrent computations. Instead we have only alternation at the expense of a considerable synchronization overhead.

However, the idea of streams is to establish larger synchronic distances (or possibly no synchronization at all) between consumer and producer, i.e., to have their computations controlled by different processes.

The effects of using streams are for the prime sieve program illustrated in fig. 12.17. Similar to recursion graphs, we have here expanded two recursive calls of the function *sieve* in order to exhibit the pipelining of stream tokens more clearly than would be possible in the equivalent tagged token graph.

This graph depicts a situation in which all links specified as streams carry several tokens in the order of descending values. The outermost instance of *sieve* receives the input stream generated by the producer process *gen*. This stream is split up by the operator HT (for Head/Tail) into the head token which leaves through the

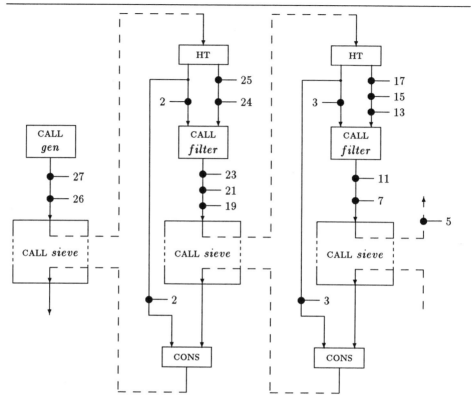

Figure 12.17: Stream-supported computation of the *prime sieve*

left output and into the entire tail stream which leaves through the right output. One copy of the head token is propagated to the outermost CONS operator, the other controls the passage of the tail stream through the subsequent *filter* operator, removing all tokens with an even value. The resulting stream is passed on to the next instance of *sieve*, where multiples of the value 3 are sorted out, and so on.

The pipelining of many tokens on the various stream segments uncouples at least to some extent the operators that are connected by them, i.e., they can be executed concurrently. That this concurrency can indeed be exploited to advantage, may be concluded from the following consideration.

Suppose the function *gen* generates only a finite sequence of n integers. They all have to pass through the first instance of *sieve*. The second instance of *sieve* becomes active as soon as the first output token is produced by the first instance, and so on. Since the stream becomes shorter with every sifting step, many instance of *sieve* can be expected to process consecutive segments of the stream concurrently. The time required to execute the *i*-th instance of *sieve* is $O(n_i)$, where n_i is the number of tokens still in the stream. Due to the cascading of the *sieve* instances, the total time to perform the prime sieve for all *n* integers roughly equals the time it takes to process all integers by the first *sieve* instance, which is $O(n)$. This contrasts quite favorably with the time required to execute this program under a lazy evaluation regime which performs all *sieves* more or less in sequence. This time is given as $O(\sum_{i=1}^{m} n_i)$, where *m* is the number of primes within the interval $[2 \mathinner{\ldotp\ldotp} n]$.

Conceptually, there are no differences between streams and objects represented by single tokens (or **simple objects** for short). Operations on streams apply uniformly to all stream elements. We basically have to distinguish the two cases illustrated in fig. 12.18 for binary operators.

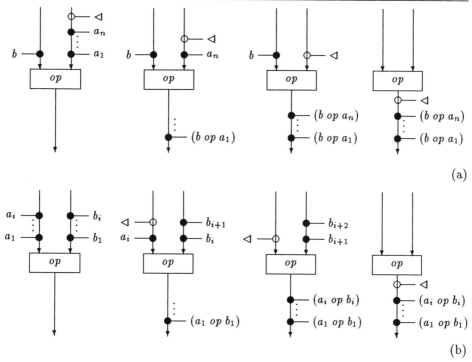

Figure 12.18: Execution rules for data flow operations on streams

If one of the operands, say the one on the left input link, is a simple object and the other is a stream (see fig. 12.18.a), then the operator pairs the former with all elements of the latter. The single token on the left input is sustained as a pre-condition for the operator until all stream elements have passed through the right input. The operator is enabled iff in addition to the token on the left input there is at least one token available in the stream on the right input. The occurrence of the operator consumes the head token from the stream and, if this token carries the end-of-stream symbol ◁, the token from the left input as well.

If both operands are streams (see fig. 12.18.b), then the operator pairs elements with identical indices from both input streams. The occurrence of an end-of-stream symbol in one of the input streams terminates the output stream and consumes the remaining tokens, if any, from the other stream.

These execution rules apply equivalently to n-ary operators with arbitrary subsets of inputs for single tokens and for streams.

In the tagged token data flow model, the rules for manipulating the tags remain the same for streams as for single object tokens. All tokens of a stream are identically tagged. They maintain their tags when passing through a value-transforming or structuring operator, and change them uniformly when passing through a control operator.

In addition to stream expressions based on recursive function definitions, as we used them in the prime sieve example, we have in data flow languages also iterative constructs. They have either of the general forms

$$\underline{u} : stream\_of\ \alpha\ =\ \{\ x_1 = arg\_1, \ldots, x_n = arg\_n$$
$$\text{IN}\ \{\ \text{WHILE}\ pred\_expr\ \text{DO}$$
$$new\ x_1 = \ldots$$
$$\vdots$$
$$new\ x_n = \ldots$$
$$\text{RETURNS\_ALL}\ res\_expr\ \text{BUT}\cdot e\_expr\ \}\}$$

or

$$\underline{v} : stream\_of\ \alpha\ =\ \{\ x_1 = arg\_1, \ldots, x_n = arg\_n$$
$$\text{IN}\ \{\ \text{FOR\_EACH}\ z_1, \ldots, z_m\ \text{IN}\ \underline{z_1}, \ldots, \underline{z_m}\ \text{DO}$$
$$\{\ \text{WHILE}\ pred\_expr\ \text{DO}$$
$$new\ x_1 = \ldots$$
$$\vdots$$
$$new\ x_n = \ldots$$
$$\text{RETURNS\_ALL}\ res\_expr\ \text{BUT}\ e\_expr\ \}\}\}\ .$$

Both WHILE expressions produce new values of *res_expr* on every iteration and place all except those equal to the values of e_expr as tokens into their output streams. An end_of_stream symbol is implicitly generated upon termination of the loop. When generating unending streams, the construct WHILE $pred\_expr$ DO ... may either be replaced with DO_FOREVER or omitted.

In the former expression, the stream values for $\underline{u}$ are computed merely from the initial and subsequent values of the loop variables $x_1, \ldots, x_n$, i.e., we have a pure stream generator. In the latter case, the output stream $\underline{v}$ is also a function of the input streams $\underline{z_1}, \ldots, \underline{z_m}$ which are being consumed. The FOR_EACH ... IN ... construct is to compute the values of the output tokens from the values of the tokens which in every loop iteration are at the heads of all input streams. It also prescribes the subsequent annihilation of these tokens.

Note that the high-level constructs used in both WHILE expressions render the primitive functions HEAD, TAIL and CONS largely superfluous when it comes to specifying how streams must be recursively generated and consumed.

With these iterative expressions at hand, we can alternatively program the prime sieve algorithm as follows:

$$\underline{x} = \text{DEFINE}$$
$$sieve(\underline{v}) = \{ \text{ WHILE NOT(EMPTY}(\underline{v})) \text{ DO}$$
$$prime = \text{FIRST}(\underline{v});$$
$$new \; \underline{v} = \{ \text{ FOR\_EACH } v \text{ IN } \underline{v} \text{ DO}$$
$$s = \text{IF} \quad ((v \text{ MOD } prime) = 0)$$
$$\text{THEN } 0$$
$$\text{ELSE } v$$
$$\text{RETURNS\_ALL } s \text{ BUT } 0 \}$$
$$\text{RETURNS\_ALL } prime \}$$
$$\text{IN } sieve(\{ x = 2$$
$$\text{IN } \{ \text{DO\_FOREVER}$$
$$new \; x = (x + 1)$$
$$\text{RETURNS\_ALL } x \}\}) \; .$$

When unfolding the $sieve$ function of this program, we obtain essentially the same data flow graph as in fig. 12.17.

With the stream operations introduced so far, we can only specify systems of communicating data flow processes featuring a **deterministic behavior**. The data flow graphs into which these specifications translate are pure **synchronization graphs**. However, in all systems in which processes share resources, e.g., communication channels, we also have conflicts. In order to be able to include conflicts into process communication structures, at least one **non-deterministic operation**, the **merging** of two or more input streams into one output stream is required. This must be done so that all tokens of the former eventually occur in the latter without changing the order of tokens originating from the same input streams. Binary merge operations may be defined thus: let $\underline{u} = u_1 \ldots u_i \ldots$, $\underline{v} = v_1 \ldots v_j \ldots$, $\underline{x} = x_1 \ldots x_k \ldots$ denote streams, then $\underline{x} = \text{MERGE}(\underline{u}, \underline{v})$ denotes the merging of streams $\underline{u}$ and $\underline{v}$ into stream $\underline{x}$ such that

for all stream positions k, k' in $\underline{x}$, i, i' in $\underline{u}$ and j, j' in $\underline{v}$ we have

$$((x_k \leftarrow u_i) \wedge (x'_k \leftarrow u'_i) \wedge (k < k') \Rightarrow (i < i'))$$

and likewise

$$((x_k \leftarrow v_j) \wedge (x'_k \leftarrow v'_j) \wedge (k < k') \Rightarrow (j < j')) \,,$$

where $(x_k \leftarrow u_i)$ denotes the placement of input stream element u_i into the output stream element x_k.

Merging is conceptually based on the resolution of successive **backward conflicts** among the actual head tokens of the input streams, and thus introduces the desired non-determinacy. The availability of the MERGE operator lifts the expressive power of data flow languages (and of other functional languages as well) to a level at which operating systems, data base systems, communication protocols etc. can be specified within an otherwise purely functional world.

Synchronic distances between producers and consumers may be established by finite **stream capacities**. They may be defined by annotating stream variables or stream-generating expressions as $\underline{x}^{[k]}$ or $stream\_expr^{[k]}$, respectively, meaning that the stream $\underline{x}$ (or the stream produced by $stream\_expr^{[k]}$) may contain at most k tokens at any time. It is in many cases important to introduce finite capacities at least for some streams of a program in order to prevent the system from being flooded with tokens by free-running producer processes.

One such stream would be the one connecting in the above prime sieve programs the generator function *gen* for integer tokens with the consumer function *sieve*. Here the former must be expected to produce tokens at a decidedly faster rate than can be consumed by the latter, i.e., the token generator must be slowed down by synchronization with the consumer in order to stabilize the system. Other capacity limitations may not be necessary in this program since the various *sieve* instances can be assumed to process tokens at about the same rate.

12.5   Some Complementary Remarks

In concluding this chapter, two problems concerning the tagged token architecture just described should be addressed.

We chose to implement function (turned supercombinator) calls by means of activation records (argument frames). This approach is more or less in line with the implementation of function calls in our various graph reducers. Pointers to these frames (which are held in the I-structure memory) are used as context identifiers in the token tags. Moreover, we chose to create dynamically the token set structures which in the matching memory represent operator instances, and to use hashing techniques for the matching of token tags.

However, this implementation is not very efficient in terms of time and space consumption, and in terms of memory management overhead. When using I-array-based argument frames, it takes a WRITE_SELect operation followed by a (deferred) READ_SELect operation to pass an argument (result) token between a caller and a callee. This requires two cycles through the pipeline of the data flow processor to complete it. I-structure memory space for argument frames must be allocated and de-allocated dynamically. It follows a partial ordering of calls, i.e., the space occupied by argument frames is generally non-contiguous. At a faster rate and usually with finer granularity, the same allocation problem arises with the placement of token set structures in the matching memory. However, these things can be had in a much simpler form as well [ArNi87].

For one, the call-return structure for complete function applications can be realized without using argument frames at all. Instead, the control operators LINK (LOOP) and LINK^{-1} (LOOP^{-1}) which interface callers with callees can be implemented so that argument and result tokens are passed on directly (or in one step). This does not only save considerable space in the I-structure memory and management overhead, but it also reduces from two to one the number of pipeline cycles required to perform the control operations.

For another, the matching memory space necessary to accommodate all token set structures that are generated when executing instantiated functions or blocks may be allocated as contiguous segments rather than piecemeal. These segments are in fact the local work space frames. As a pleasant consequence, the compiler can now generate decidedly faster code which refers to token locations that are fixed relative to the bases of the frames, rather than using expensive hashing techniques. Moreover, the pointers to these work space frames can now be used as context identifiers within the token tags, replacing the pointers to the argument/result frames which have completely disappeared.

Notwithstanding these modifications, the call-return structure depicted in fig. 12.11 remains basically the same. The GET_FRAME and REL_FRAME operators now respectively allocate and release work space frames rather than argument/result frames, and the CS operators at the caller/callee interfaces are replaced with direct LINK and LINK^{-1} (LOOP and LOOP^{-1}) operators.

Another problem concerns the overhead of synchronizing operators with their operands, which somehow must be hidden. The technique employed by the tagged token architecture is based on the supposition that data flow systems are generally flooded with executable operator packets to the extent that operand token synchronizations by the matching units can be completely overlapped with useful computations in the processing units [ArIa85].

However, for this to be the case, there must be a carefully tuned balance within the pipeline (see fig. 12.15) between the rates at which on average

- the processing unit consumes executable operator packets and produces new tokens;

- these tokens can be processed and complete token set structures can be set free by the matching unit(s);

- token set structures can be completed to operator packets by the operator fetch unit(s);

- accesses to the I-structure memory can be performed.

Of course, the application program must also yield sufficiently many concurrently executable operations to keep all active units permanently busy.

The crucial issue here is overcoming memory latencies, i.e., the time that elapses between generating an access request and receiving a response. This problem concerns all memory units within the pipeline. It is partly of a physical nature (memory word sizes, signal propagation delays, reloading cycles for the memory cells etc.) and partly of an organizational nature (representation of data, accessing techniques and data validation, resolution of access conflicts and, in the case of I-structure memories, delays due to deferred read operations, which may be considerable).

In terms of physical parameters, the memory bandwidth problem must primarily be overcome by physical means which, of course, may have to be supplemented by organizational and architectural measures. The remedies include fast cache memories, very large processor-internal register sets and load/store architectures, very long memory word sizes, banks of independently accessible memory modules etc. They all help either to reduce the number of memory accesses or to raise the overall memory bandwidth, measured, say, in numbers of bytes which at the maximum can be moved in or out of the memory per unit time.

Insufficient bandwidth clearly constitutes a bottleneck for the circulation of computational objects between the memories and the processing unit(s). Among other things, this bottleneck limits the rate at which operators can be fed with operands and thus throttles the supply of executable operator packets. Put another way: since memory bandwidth dictates the degree to which concurrent operations can be sustained, the physical part of the latency problem cannot be overcome by trying to exploit concurrency.

Large numbers of concurrently executable operations are primarily a remedy to the latency problem caused by read operations deferred in the I-structure memory, i.e., to a problem that comes about due to the particularities of organizing data flow computations in the first place. While individual read accesses may require considerable, even widely varying intervals of time to complete, many deferred read accesses may coexist (or be overlapped) within the I-structure memory, waiting for the arrival of the respective data tokens. Thus, the I-memory is in fact a large buffer for read operations in progress which is capable of receiving read/write access requests and of returning data tokens in response to earlier read requests at a rate determined only by physical parameters. Exploiting fine-grain concurrency to a largest possible extent is not only necessary to sustain a continuous flow of tokens in and out of this buffer, but also to prevent busy-wait situations in the remaining pipeline.

However, fine-grain concurrency also creates a considerable overhead that is necessary to synchronize operand tokens and to prepare executable operator packets. Thus, even when separating in three different stages of a pipeline token matching, the preparation of operator packets and packet execution in an attempt to overlap these activities, we may have to cope with the problem that the processing unit on average consumes operator packets faster than the other units can deliver.

Switching from individual token set structures to large contiguous work space frames is an important step towards decidedly faster matching operations: hashing techniques can now be replaced with fast direct addressing methods since the memory locations into which operand values must be placed can be fixed à priori by the compiler relative to the frame bases.

Even if this measure has the desired effect of balancing the pipeline, the synchronization overhead is only hidden at the expense of a rather sophisticated machinery, but it has not disappeared. In fact, overlapping the synchronization of operand tokens with useful computations is the main purpose of using a pipeline configuration in the first place.

The synchronization overhead has been well recognized as the single most serious obstacle in the way towards high-performance data flow computations. Curing the disease rather than (with considerable effort) its symptoms appears to be an inescapable consequence, particularly if this can be had much cheaper. This cure consists in abandoning the fine-grain data flow concept in favor of what is called multi-threading, which comes in two forms.

Large-grain (or macro) data flow exploits concurrency only at the level of larger units of computation, say defined function (supercombinator) applications or loop iterations. The respective expressions are compiled to sequential control flow threads of which several can be executed simultaneously. There are no tokens propagated and synchronized along the threads: operand values are directly read from and result values are directly written to pre-assigned work space (or register) locations, and the sequencing of operators is controlled by means of conventional instruction counters. The full data flow mechanics applies only to function calls, loop iterations etc., i.e., to the activation of entire control flow threads rather than to primitive operators, thus reducing significantly the synchronization overhead relative to useful computations.

A similar concept is multi-threaded data flow, as exemplified by MIT's more advanced MONSOON architecture [PaCu90, PaTr91]. It is based on experience with conventional instruction pipelining, according to which concurrency at the level of primitive operations can be more efficiently exploited by overlapping several phases of pre-specified sequential execution rather than adhering to the traditional data flow approach of enabling all operators by token synchronization and of scheduling enabled operators more or less at random. The basic idea is to organize the flow of tokens in a pipelined processing site so that operators are enabled along sequential threads laid over the program graphs and in this order follow each other through the pipeline. Many intermediate results can thus be temporarily stored in processor-internal registers and directly fetched from there by subsequent operators rather than passing them along by tokens. Reducing the number of tokens that are floating about the processing sites also reduces the overhead for their synchronization. This can be had either with pipeline multiplexing among several threads, i.e., with one operation of each thread occupying a pipeline stage, or with consecutive operations of a single thread filling consecutive pipeline stages.

Another important aspect of multi-threading relates to the stability problem of data flow computations. As with non-sequential reductions, the number of threads that are active at any given time can be readily limited by a ticket allocation scheme or by equivalent means. Since recursive function calls may develop along a thread without bounds, there is no risk of deadlocks on the one hand, and the entire computation remains reasonably well contained in space on the other hand.

13   Control Flow Systems

It may look a little strange to find the traditional control flow concept as the last item on our agenda though it dominates almost exclusively the computing scene both commercially and also intellectually.

However, the PrT-net models developed in chapter 4 characterize control flow as a degenerate form of functional computations, which introduces an explicit notion of history sensitivity (or of an environment) into programming. Control flow works with

- an operational discipline which treats the presence of operand objects as side conditions in the sense that they are neither consumed nor (re-)produced but only copied or modified, as a consequence of which there must be

- a control discipline based on the orderly consumption and reproduction of explicit control tokens.

The idea is to share the same channel (or box) for the direct passage of possibly several object values among different subsets of operators (or operator occurrences) rather than providing individual channels. Different channel instantiations must be distinguished by unique states of control in order to maintain the determinacy of program execution. Of course, this precludes the unrestricted sharing of channels (boxes) among operators belonging to concurrent control flow threads. Since these operators may occur in arbitrary order, the Church-Rosser property would be violated due to the non-deterministic sequencing of copy (read) and update (write) operations. Thus, control flow is basically a sequential execution model.

The ensuing imperative (or procedural) programming style differs from functional programming in that

- the variable concept and the static scoping rule of the λ-calculus are replaced by the notion of box variables as identifiers of object values which can be copied and updated (overwritten) without restrictions, based on a multiple assignment rule;

- as a generalization of simple assignments which realize primitive operations, we have abstractions in the form of procedures which update one or several box variables specified in the respective calling environments;

- assignment statements, simple or composite , must be fully ordered along a control flow thread;

- a program (or a procedure) specifies explicitly the interaction with a state representation (or an environment structure) made up from instantiated box variables.

Thus, a major problem of imperative programming consists in scheduling the use of the box variables for the transfer of several operand objects.

Most high-level imperative languages have a call-by-value (or applicative order) semantics which requires that expressions in parameter positions of function or procedure calls be evaluated before substitution. Typical examples are FORTRAN, PASCAL, C etc. [JeWi75, KeRi78]. Only a few languages (ALGOL being the most prominent example [Nau60, vWi69, RaRu64]) use a call-by-name (or normal order) semantics which substitutes actual for formal parameters as they are. Since control flow machines generally do not provide built-in mechanisms for the manipulation of environment structures, it is up to the compiler to generate appropriate code sequences as integral parts of the machine-level programs.

Control flow too distinguishes between a static and a dynamic execution model. The former relates to older language concepts such as FORTRAN IV [AN66] which allows for iterations but outlaws recursive procedures. Thus, under sequential execution there can be only one instance of a procedure at a time, i.e., the environment can be completely included in the machine-level program code. However, all modern imperative languages support recursive procedures or functions and thus follow a dynamic execution model which works with an expanding environment that needs to be accommodated by a run-time stack.

The IBM/370 instruction set [Stru75, Rudd76, IBM78] and its descendants favor the implementation of the static model and are therefore often referred to as typical FORTRAN architectures. There are no addressing modes available that would effectively support stacks. Recursive subroutine (procedure) calls are in these architectures commonly realized by means of so-called save areas which may be dynamically placed anywhere in the program's memory region, using special space allocation (de-allocation) routines as outlined in section 2.3.

The VAX architecture [Stre78, LeEc80, KeBa84] and its micro-processor descendants MC 68000 [Mot88, Mot84, Wil85], INTEL 8086 [ReAl80] etc. are designed to support a dynamic execution model. They provide special registers and a rich variety of addressing modes for operations on run-time environments realized as stacks. Since the static execution model is merely a special case of the dynamic model, it can be implemented on these architectures without any difficulties.

In the sequel we will therefore concentrate on the description of a VAX-like dynamic architecture and its implementation. The configuration of the run-time environment, which is of primary interest here, will be based on a call-by-value semantics. The high-level language which serves as our point of reference will be a kernel of PASCAL [JeWi75]. This kernel includes assignments, functions, procedures, WHILE-expressions etc. which can be easily related to equivalent functional language constructs. Pointer structures, files, input/output statements etc. will not be considered.

13.1 An Imperative Kernel Language

Other than predominantly using procedures instead of functions, programs of high-level imperative languages are basically constructed in the same way as functional programs. In fact, they have many syntactical components in common with the high-level data flow language introduced in section 12.1. The majority of imperative languages requires that all box variables have monomorphic types assigned to them, i.e., they are strongly typed. This typing discipline considerably facilitates the compilation into machine code, particularly the layout of the context frames for procedure and function calls.

A high-level PASCAL program essentially consists of a block preceded by a standardized program heading. The block partitions into

- a declarations part for labels, constants, types, box variables, procedures and functions used throughout the program;

- a statement part, usually enclosed in a pair of BEGIN/END labels, which specifies as a sequence of assignment statements (including procedure and function calls) the computation to be performed.

Procedures and functions are recursively constructed in the same way. In fact, the main program is itself a procedure. Procedure and function headings define names (or identifiers) followed by lists of formal parameters.

The scope of all variable and type declarations that appear in the heading or in the declarations part of a function or procedure extends over the entire block, including local function or procedure definitions within the block. With respect to these declarations, we have essentially the same scoping rules as in the λ-calculus: the scope of a variable or type declared in an outer heading or block includes recursively all inner blocks, but it does not penetrate the scope of an identically named variable declared in an inner block.

The statement part constitutes the body of a procedure or function. Within a body, we may have multiple assignments to any local box variable defined in the procedure (function) itself or to any global box variable defined in an enclosing procedure (function). Procedures must return results to their calling environments by assignments to global variables, whereas functions return their values by assigning them to the function identifiers. Assignments to global variables in function bodies, though syntactically possible, are strongly discouraged for they cause **side effects** which conflict with the notion of functions.

There are two different ways of making assignments to global box variables in a procedure body. These variables can either be referenced directly, in which case assignments will be made for all procedure calls to the same boxes in the calling environment. Alternatively, the global variables may be explicitly passed on to a procedure via so-called **reference parameters**, in which case the results of different procedure calls may be passed on to different global variables.

Calling a parameter **by reference** means that the procedure receives a **pointer** to the actual argument value (or object), calling a parameter **by value** means that the procedure receives the value of the actual parameter directly. In a procedure call, **value parameter** positions may therefore be replaced with all legitimate expressions (including variables), whereas **reference parameter** positions may only be replaced with variables defined in the calling procedure (or function). Since a procedure call copies into its argument frame

- a **pointer** to an object for a variable in a reference parameter position, but

- the object value itself for a variable in a value parameter position,

it is highly advisable for performance reasons to pass all non-atomic objects (arrays, records etc.) by reference, even if these objects are not changed by the procedure. The difference in run-time complexity may be exemplified, say, by an $n * m$ matrix: when passing it by reference, it takes one unit of time to copy the pointer, but when passing it by value, it takes $n * m$ units of time and of memory space to copy all its elements.[47]

For the same reasons, function values must be of so-called **simple data types** which fit into one or two memory words since they are directly returned to the calling procedure or function via pre-defined register or memory locations. Values of a **structured data type** (e.g., arrays) must be computed by procedures.

Most of the constructs which form the kernel of PASCAL occur in the procedure shown in figure 13.1. It realizes an in-place **quicksort** on a linear array of integer numbers. The underlying idea is to partition a list of arbitrarily ordered numbers recursively into two segments. All numbers smaller than a so-called **pivot number** selected from the list are sorted into the first segment, and all numbers greater than or equal to the pivot number are sorted into the second segment of the array. The recursive partitioning terminates with one (or several copies of the same) number left in each segment, in which case we have the entire list sorted in monotonically increasing order.

---

[47] Many compilers generate code which implements value-parameters as reference parameters as well, in which case this problem does not occur.

```
PROCEDURE quicksort(i, j : integer; REF list : array[1 .. maxsize] of integer);
  VAR pivot, pivot_pos, k : integer;
  FUNCTION piv(i, j : integer) : integer;
    VAR k : integer;
      BEGIN
        k := i;
        WHILE (k LT j) AND (list[k] EQ list[k + 1]) DO k := k + 1;
        IF     k EQ j
        THEN piv := 0;
        ELSE IF     list[k] LT list[k + 1]
                THEN piv := k + 1;
                ELSE piv := k;
      END
  FUNCTION part(i_min, j_max, pivot : integer) : integer;
    VAR i, j, h : integer;
      BEGIN
        i := i_min; j := j_max;
        REPEAT
          h := list[i];
          list[i] := list[j];
          list[j] := h;
          WHILE list[i] LT pivot DO i := i + 1;
          WHILE list[j] GE pivot DO j := j - 1;
        UNTIL i GT j;
        part := i;
      END
  BEGIN
    IF     i LT j
    THEN BEGIN
            pivot_pos := piv(i, j);
            IF     pivot_pos NE 0
            THEN BEGIN
                    pivot := list[pivot_pos];
                    k := part(i, j, pivot);
                    quicksort(i, k - 1, list);
                    quicksort(k, j, list);
                 END
         END
  END
```

Figure 13.1: A PASCAL program for quicksorting

To do so, the procedure *quicksort* is defined in terms of the formal parameters
i, j and *list*, of which

- the latter specifies by means of the keyword REF as a reference parameter the
  linear array whose elements are to be sorted;

- the former two specify as value parameters the lower and upper boundaries,
  respectively, of an index interval in *list* within which the sorting actually takes
  place.

This procedure uses two subfunctions *piv* and *part* in which *list* occurs as a
global variable. The function *piv* selects from an index interval $[i..j]$ within the
array *list* a pivot number and returns its index position as a value. The pivot
number is the larger of the leftmost pair of numbers within the specified interval
which are different. If all numbers are equal, the function returns 0, and no sorting
takes place. Otherwise, the pivot number is taken by the function *part* to sort the
elements within the interval $[i..j]$, and to return as a value the index position k, to
the left of which $(p < k)$ all elements are smaller, and to the right of which $(p \geq k)$
all elements are equal to or greater than the pivot number. Subsequently, *quicksort*
is recursively applied to the array intervals $[i..k-1]$ and $[k..j]$.

An application of *quicksort* to an array defined in some enclosing procedure, say,
as

$$\text{VAR } unsorted\_list : array[1..1000] \text{ } of \text{ } integer$$

takes the form

$$quicksort(1, 1000, unsorted\_list) \; .$$

Since this list is passed either as a reference parameter (to *quicksort* itself) or as
a global variable to its subfunctions, all sorting actions take place in the original
unsorted_list, i.e., entirely in the calling environment. No copying of this array is
necessary, as would be the case in an equivalent functional program. We also note
that we have applied a rather dirty trick here in order to perform the sorting in
place: in violation of the concept of functions, we have chosen the function *part* to
swap, as a side effect, the elements of the global variable *list*.

Syntactically, the differences between imperative and functional programs are
not very significant. Procedure (function) definitions of the former resemble the
DEFINE constructs of the latter: we have a set of local procedure (function) declarations followed by a statement part which takes the place of the goal expression
whose normal form is to be computed. Defining the local box variables of a block
explicitly **before** the statement part rather than taking the first assignments to them
as defining occurrences (as for instance in HLDᶠL) is a convenience which renders
it possible to compile a program in one pass. Firstly, the context (or activation

record) of a procedure or function can be completely laid out before compiling the statement part; secondly, these variables can be easily recognized as being global to the local procedure or function declarations.

Since one-pass compilation generally requires that everything must be declared before it is being used, PASCAL also includes the notion of forward declarations for mutually recursive procedures (functions). They merely define the names (identifiers) and the formal parameter lists of procedures (functions) in order to enable the compiler to generate the appropriate call-return structures for them in other procedures (functions). To illustrate this concept, we consider three mutually recursive procedures which must be declared as follows:

> PROCEDURE $name\_1(formalparamlist)$; FORWARD;
> PROCEDURE $name\_2(formalparamlist)$; FORWARD;
> PROCEDURE $name\_3(formalparamlist)$;
>   VAR ...
>   PROCEDURE ...
>   FUNCTION ...
>   BEGIN
>
>   ⋮
>
> $name\_1(actualparamlist)$;
>
>   ⋮
>
> $name\_2(actualparamlist)$;
>
>   ⋮
>
>   END
> PROCEDURE $name\_1$;
>   VAR ...
>   PROCEDURE ...
>   FUNCTION ...
>   BEGIN
>
>   ⋮
>
> $name\_2(actualparamlist)$;
>
>   ⋮
>
> $name\_3(actualparamlist)$;
>
>   ⋮
>
>   END

(continued on the next page)

PROCEDURE *name_2*;

$\vdots$

BEGIN

$\vdots$

name_3(*actualparamlist*);

$\vdots$

name_1(*actualparamlist*);

$\vdots$

END

The procedures *name_1* and *name_2* are declared forward so that they can be called in the body of the procedure *name_3* which is fully specified right away. The full procedure declarations for *name_1* and *name_2* may now follow in any sequence. However, since the parameter lists are already part of the forward declarations, they need not be repeated here. The order of forward declarations is irrelevant.

Procedures (functions) may also be applied to other procedures or functions as actual parameters. A procedure which uses another procedure as a parameter must be defined as

PROCEDURE *name_1*(. . . ; PROCEDURE *formal_name*(*formalparamlist*); . . .);

$\vdots$

BEGIN

$\vdots$

formal_name(*actualparamlist*);

$\vdots$

END

where *formal_name* is treated as a formal parameter. The idea is to call *name_1* with one of several actual procedures declared somewhere else whose list of formal parameters must fully conform to the specifications given in *formalparamlist*. The procedure *name_1* may then be called with

name_1(. . . ; *name_2*; . . .);

where *name_2* is the identifier of the procedure actually used.

Likewise, function parameters may be declared as

PROCEDURE $name\_1(\ldots;$ FUNCTION $formal\_name(formalparamlist) : type; \ldots);$

$\vdots$

VAR $x : type;$

$\vdots$

BEGIN

$\quad \vdots$

$\quad x := formal\_name(actualparamlist);$

$\quad \vdots$

END ,

and instantiated with a concrete function identified by the name $name\_2$ as

$$name\_1(\ldots; name\_2; \ldots); .$$

Though functions and procedures may thus be used as parameters, we neverthe-less have in imperative languages no full notion of higher-order functions or proce-dures. New functions or procedures cannot be computed by others since we have a strict separation of the world of functions or procedures from the world of the objects that can be actually transformed by them.

13.2 Basic Organization of a Control Flow Engine

The basic principles of organizing dynamic control flow computations follow more or less directly from the concept of recursive procedures as outlined in the preceding section. At the machine language level, an instantiated procedure is essentially defined by a sequence of machine operations (or instructions) which realizes its statement part and by a representation of the environment (or context) in which this code must be actually executed. The environment is composed of

- an activation record made up from an argument frame through which the pro-cedure receives from its calling procedure (pointers to) its actual parameter values, and from a workspace frame which accommodates the local box vari-ables (and possibly temporaries) defined in the procedure block;

- the activation records of the enclosing procedures which hold the actual values for the global (or relatively free) box variables to which the procedure refers either directly or via reference parameters.

A procedure changes the values of the box variables which are defined in enclosing procedures and therefore belong to the calling environment. The activation record of the procedure which effects the changes may only contain pointers to activation records in which reference parameters are located.

In order to deal with (mutually) recursive procedures, a control flow engine must support run-time structures in which activation records are linked up in essentially the same way as is necessary for the argument frames of open λ-abstractions in our lazy graph reduction engine (see chapter 10). The structure becomes simpler insofar as all arguments of procedure (function) calls are passed on in evaluated form and thus need not carry environments with them. Exceptions arise only with procedures (functions) that are passed on to other procedures (functions) as actual parameters. They must be embedded in the environments in which their global variables are instantiated, i.e., they must be treated in the same way as unreduced arguments by our lazy graph reducer. However, since procedures (functions) can be freely substituted in other procedures but never be returned as results, they do not hold on to their environments beyond the lifetime of the procedure calls that created them. Thus, the entire run-time structure does behave like a stack: activation records are being created and released strictly in LIFO order.

13.2.1 The Run-Time Environment

The activation record of a procedure specified, say, as

$$\text{PROCEDURE } g(x\_1 : type; \ldots; \text{PROCEDURE } f\_name(\ldots);$$
$$\text{REF } x\_k : type; \ldots; \text{REF } x\_n : type);$$
$$\text{VAR } y\_1 : type; \ldots; y\_m : type;$$
$$\vdots$$
$$\text{BEGIN}$$
$$\vdots$$
$$y\_1 := expr\_1$$
$$\vdots$$
$$y\_m := expr\_m$$
$$\vdots$$
$$\text{END}$$

basically features the same layout as the composition of the argument frames generated by instances of a function

$$g(x\_1, \ldots, f\_name, \ldots, x\_n) = (\text{DEFINE}$$

$$\vdots$$

$$\text{IN } expr) \text{ WHERE } y\_1 = expr\_1$$

$$\vdots$$

$$y\_m = expr\_m$$

in our lazy graph reducer. We have an **argument frame** for instantiations of the formal parameters $x\_1, \ldots, f\_name, \ldots, x\_n$, followed by a **workspace frame** for the instantiations of the local variables $y\_1, \ldots, y\_m$. The workspace frame may include a number of temporaries for the storage of intermediate values and extend into processor-internal registers. Both frames are separated by a **control block** which contains the **link pointer** to the activation record of an earlier (enclosing) procedure call and some status information that belongs to the calling procedure.[48]

We remember that the interpreting lazy graph reducer generates these frames dynamically by pushing, in the course of performing β-reductions-in-the-large, argument pointers into a stack-like run-time structure. Since all argument pointers are of unit length, entries within a frame can be accessed using the second components of de Bruijn-index tuples $[\#k, \#i]$ as offsets relative to the frame bases. The frames themselves can be located following k levels of indirection along the pointer chain that links the frames belonging to a particular environment. The graph reducer, as all functional systems, never changes environment entries.

Control flow engines work with argument and workspace frames that are **prefabricated** by the **compiler**. They accommodate directly all box variables specified as value parameters in the procedure headings and in the local variable declarations parts. Reference parameters are represented in the argument frames as unit-length pointers (to the respective entries in the work space frames of the procedures (or functions) in which they are declared).[49] Instantiations of **procedure parameters** require two pointer entries in the argument frames: one points to the procedure code, the other points to its actual environment.

The compiler deduces from the type declarations of the formal procedure parameters and of the local variables their entry formats, places them in the order of descending addresses into the respective frames, and calculates their address posi-

---

[48] Alternatively, the link pointer is often set up as the first entry of an activation record, preceding the argument frame, in order to facilitate relative addressing within the record.

[49] We need no heap space to represent the data objects of the PASCAL kernel under consideration. There is also no notion of object descriptors since type and structural specifications become part of the compiled machine code. A heap would only become necessary if a full PASCAL with pointer types for the dynamic creation, modification and consumption of linked list structures would have to be supported.

tions relative to the frame bases. These relative addresses, in conjunction with the actual frame base addresses, are used by the machine code sequences to access the frame entries at run-time.

Fig. 13.2 depicts schematically the layout of the activation record for the procedure g specified above. In order to connect the pointer entries of this record to an existing environment, we assume here that

- the procedure g is local to a procedure f which in turn may be local to other procedures enclosing it;

- some of the reference parameters of g are local to f, others are local to procedures enclosing f;

- the procedure parameter of g is instantiated with a procedure, say s, which is assumed to carry the environment of the procedure f.

In a stack implementation of the run-time environment, the activation record for g is stacked up on top of the activation record for f which in turn sits on top of

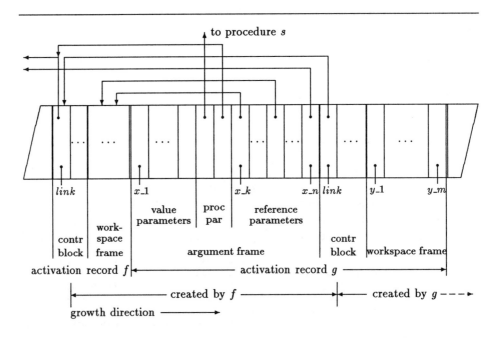

Figure 13.2: Activation record of a procedure invocation

the activation records of its enclosing procedures. These records are connected by a chain of link pointers held in the control blocks to form a contiguous environment for the evaluation of the statement part of the procedure g.

Since the linkage of the activation records by this pointer chain directly corresponds to the nesting of procedure (function) declarations in the high-level program text, it is also referred to as the **static chain**. All reference parameters in the argument frame of g are instantiated with direct pointers to the locations of the respective parameter values deeper down in the stack. The actual addresses of these locations are dynamically figured out at run-time. Likewise, the environment pointer(s) for the actual instantiation(s) of the procedure parameter(s) is (are) derived at run-time from the existing **link pointer** chain by means of the nesting level(s) of the called procedure(s) relative to the calling procedure(s). By convention, the run-time stack grows towards decreasing addresses and shrinks towards increasing addresses.

There are good reasons to place the **control block** of an activation record between its argument frame and its workspace frame. As indicated in fig. 13.2, the former is always created by the **calling procedure** which also establishes the link of the new activation record to the **calling environment**. From there, the **called procedure** takes over to save some vital status information of the calling procedure (which must be restored when returning from the called procedure) and to create its local workspace frame. Thus, the order of frames within an activation record and the order of entries within the control block complies with the order in which the calling and the called procedure may push the items they are responsible for into the run-time stack.

The **static link pointer** for a new activation record may be found by the following simple rules. Let a procedure p call a procedure q, and let

- p be declared at the same level as q, then copy the link pointer found in the activation record of p into the control block of q;

- q be a local procedure of p, then take over the address of the link pointer entry in the activation record of p as the new link pointer in the control block of q;

- p be defined some k nesting levels inside the procedure q, then follow the link pointer chain starting in the activation record of p through $(k - 1)$ levels of indirection and take the pointer found in this control block as the new link pointer.

These rules derive straightforwardly from those given in section 10.2.4 for locating the environment pointers for function calls in the actual environment structure created by β-reductions-in-the-large. The equivalence between these two environment concepts relates to the fact that in both cases we have to deal with **abstractions** (functions or procedures) defined in terms of relatively free (or global) variables that are instantiated somewhere else.

To illustrate these rules, we consider the following nested procedure declarations (formal parameters and local variables are not explicitly specified here since they are not of interest):

$$\begin{aligned}
&\text{PROCEDURE } f(\ldots); \\
&\quad \text{VAR} \ldots \\
&\quad \text{PROCEDURE } g(\ldots); \\
&\qquad \text{VAR} \ldots \\
&\qquad \text{PROCEDURE } h\_2(\ldots); \\
&\qquad\quad \text{VAR} \ldots \\
&\qquad\quad \text{BEGIN} \ldots g(\ldots) \ldots f(\ldots) \ldots \text{END} \\
&\qquad \text{PROCEDURE } h\_1(\ldots); \\
&\qquad\quad \text{VAR} \ldots \\
&\qquad\quad \text{BEGIN} \ldots h\_2(\ldots) \ldots \text{END} \\
&\qquad \text{BEGIN} \ldots h\_1(\ldots) \ldots \text{END} \\
&\quad \text{BEGIN} \ldots g(\ldots) \ldots \text{END}
\end{aligned}$$

When calling the procedure f with some set of actual parameters, we expect to get the following sequence of subsequent procedure calls:

f calls $g \parallel g$ calls $h\_1 \parallel h\_1$ calls $h\_2 \parallel h\_2$ calls recursively first g and then f.

This results in the environment structure depicted in fig. 13.3 whose activation records are linked up according to the above rules. Note that the two stacking sequences that develop on top of the first instance of h_2 are alternative.

Accesses to environment entries also follow the rules laid down in section 10.2.4 for the environment structures generated by the lazy graph reducer. However, rather than using de Bruijn index tuples to determine in a given environment the frames and the locations within frames, accesses are here performed by means of **relative** and **indirect addressing modes** based on address specifications that are figured out by the compiler.

The environment of a procedure instance is completely specified by

- a pointer each to the base of the argument framè and of the workspace frame,

- the static link pointer to the calling environment, which is held in the control block of the activation record associated with it.

The locations of all procedure parameters and local variables are specified as addresses relative to the respective frame bases, with reference parameters using one

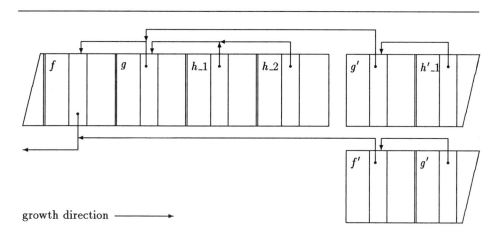

growth direction ──────→

Figure 13.3: Linking the activation records of nested procedure calls

level of indirection. The locations of global variables are specified indirectly via the static link pointer chain.

13.2.2 The Configuration of a Virtual Machine

The components that are necessary for the execution of a machine-level program include

- a static memory section which holds the constant program code itself;

- a dynamic memory section which accommodates the run-time stack at one end and, if necessary, a heap section for structured objects that are produced and consumed at run-time at the other end;

- a processing unit which realizes the control mechanism that traverses and thereby activates the operators of the program code on the one hand, and the operational mechanism that copies the operands into the operators and overwrites result locations on the other hand.

The layout of a memory region that accommodates both the static and the dynamic section has already been discussed in section 2.3 (see in particular fig. 2.3). The processing unit must include a set of registers of which some are used for dedicated purposes, whereas the remaining registers may be used as parts of the workspace frames of the active procedures. The dedicated registers comprise

- a **program counter** PC which holds the pointer to (or address of) the active operator within the machine code program;

- a register AFP to hold the **argument frame pointer** of the active procedure;

- a register WFP to hold the **workspace frame pointer** of the active procedure;

- a register ENV_PTR for the **pointer to the environment** of the active procedure;

- and a register TOS for the pointer to the actual **top of the run-time stack**.

Fig. 13.4 shows graphically where the contents of these registers point to in the memory region of a program. In fact, these pointers specify in large part the status of a control flow computation and thus a **process context**.

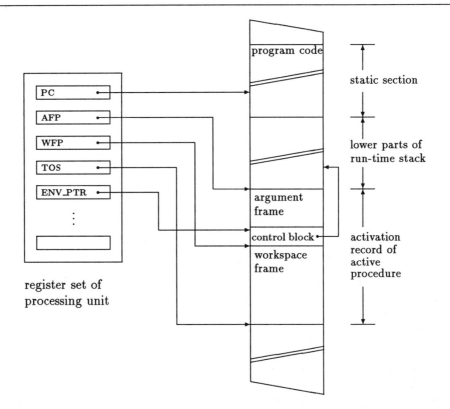

Figure 13.4: The context of a control flow computation

It is interesting to note that the set of dedicated registers necessary to govern control flow computations relates rather straightforwardly to a corresponding set of registers for the control of lazy graph reductions as described in chapter 10.

Differences with respect to the sequencing of operations are due to the fact that operators are fully ordered in control flow programs but only partially ordered in machine-level reduction programs. Thus, we need only one register, the program counter PC, to traverse the former, but three stack-top pointer registers to traverse the pre-order linearized tree representation of the latter.

Both engines also represent the environment structures in a slightly different form (compare here fig. 13.4 and fig. 10.10). The control flow engine distinguishes explicitly a pointer each to the argument frame and to the workspace frame of the active procedure, and a pointer to the full environment. The lazy graph reducer explicitly supports only a pointer to the latter. Thus, we have a correspondence between the registers AFP, WFP and ENV_PTR of the former and the register CURR_ENV_PTR of the latter engine.

The registers TOS of the control flow engine and TOP_OF_ENV of the lazy graph reduction engine correspond directly to each other: they both point to the topmost environment position where the next entry is to be made.

13.2.3 Machine Instructions

Control flow computations are at the machine language level specified as fully ordered sequences of state- (or value-) transforming operations which in incremental steps copy and update the environment. These sequences are interspersed with control operations which either conditionally or unconditionally transfer the focus of control to another but the next operation in sequence. Both kinds of operations are, in reference to their imperative character, also called machine instructions.

State- (or value-) transforming instructions have the syntactical form

$$val\_rator \ \{rand\}^n \ dest$$

where

val_rator   specifies the operation to be performed;

$\{rand\}^n$ specifies the sources of some n operands to which the operator must be applied;

dest   specifies the result destination.

Both *rand* and *dest* denote register or memory locations. The contents of operand locations are copied without destruction, whereas the contents of the destination

location is overwritten (updated) with the result value. It is common practice to
have either the first or the last operand location of an instruction coincide with the
result location, in which case *dest* is omitted.

Value-transforming instructions have in the overwhelming majority of control flow
architectures monomorphic function types based on formatted representations of
simple integer, real and boolean values and of character strings. Operands carry no
type identifications with them, e.g., in the form of tags or descriptors. The operand
types of a value-transforming instruction are inferred from the particular operator:
the bit strings found in the respective memory or register locations are interpreted
as operand representations of the required types and formats.

An important subclass of value-transforming instructions are transfer instructions
which simply copy values or pointers from memory or register locations to others.
These instructions play a key role in creating activation records for function and
procedure calls and in manipulating frame pointers.

Control instructions have the syntactical form

$$contr\_rator \ (predicate) \ \{label\}^n$$

where

contr_rator specifies a control operator;

(predicate) specifies a (tuple of) predicate value(s) to be inspected by the control
operator;[50]

$\{label\}^n$ specifies some n alternative labels within the instruction sequence, to
one of which control is transferred depending on the actual predicate
value(s).

Other than supporting a built-in sequencing mechanism for instructions, control flow engines provide very little structure else which would prescribe how to
organize computations. Control instructions are very elementary yet effective components for the construction of complex control structures from pieces of sequential
control flow threads. They are required to call and return from procedures and
functions, to enter, circulate within and exit from iteration loops, and to transfer
control to alternative branches of IF-THEN-ELSE clauses, CASE statements etc. Since

---

[50] The predicate value(s) is (are) commonly represented in implicit form as standardized condition
code which defines part of the machine status. This condition code indicates the outcome of
the most recent value-transforming operation in terms of characteristic numerical (arithmetic)
properties such as non-zero, non-negative or out-of-range results etc. Just which of these conditions
is relevant for a particular control instruction is specified as part of the operator. There is usually
no explicit predicate in a control instruction.

value-transforming instructions are only defined over simple types, loop controlling instructions in conjunction with indexed addressing modes also play a key role in generating and traversing array structures. Other control instructions in combination with indirect addressing modes are required to traverse complex data objects whose structures are defined by means of pointers.

Thus, a control flow engine is in fact little more than a rather amorphous substrate. It provides in the form of primitive value-transforming and control instructions just some elementary components for the organization of complex computational structures which define detailed work schedules. These structures are usually deduced by compilers from high-level program specifications and translated into appropriate machine instruction sequences (or machine programs). Since primitive instructions entail a considerable complexity in program design and increased insecurity about program correctness, machine level programming is largely confined to a few routines of an operating system kernel and to certain subroutines of real time applications which have to meet stringent run-time constraints.

13.3 A Control Flow Architecture

We will now define by means of a simple instruction set the architecture of a concrete control flow machine which realizes a dynamic execution model as outlined in the preceding section. Other than introducing some simplifications, this architecture is essentially identical with that of the VAX-11 systems.

We assume an underlying hardware configuration comprising

- a byte-addressable main memory which is physically laid out as an array of memory words of four consecutive bytes. The enumeration of bits, bytes and words is assumed to follow the scheme depicted in fig. 13.5. The addresses of byte locations have word format and thus define an address space of $[0 .. 2^k - 1]$ with $k = 32$. The memory is accessed in units of words;

- a processing unit which includes

  - a set of 16 word-sized general purpose registers $R0, \ldots, R15$;
  - a word-sized arithmetic/logic unit ALU for value-transforming operations and address manipulations;
  - a control unit which uses special registers to assemble, align and interpret instructions fetched from memory, and some of the general purpose registers to accommodate the program counter PC and the various pointers into the run-time stack.

The architecture supports the simple data types

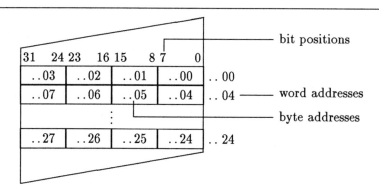

Figure 13.5: Enumeration scheme for bit positions, bytes, and words in a memory section

boolean   as byte format;

integer   as byte, half-word and word formats;

real   as word and double-word formats;

character as byte format and *character_string* as a sequence of up to 256 bytes.

Byte, half-word, word and double-word formats for data must begin at byte, half-word, word and double-word address locations, respectively, and stretch over the appropriate number of byte positions towards increasing address positions.

All **instructions** are either **monadic, dyadic** or **triadic,** i.e., they specify either one, two or three addresses of memory locations (registers) as operand and result locations or as control labels. Monadic instructions may implicitly refer to specific register or memory locations. Dyadic value-transforming or data transfer instructions use their second addresses as result destinations. Triadic instructions take the first two addresses as operand locations and the third address as result location. All control operations are monadic: they specify only one of two alternative control flow threads by an explicit label (address), whereas the other thread is assumed to be the continuation in sequence.

As for address specifications, we distinguish between

- a **register mode** to access the contents of general purpose registers within the processing unit, and

- a **memory mode** to access the contents of main memory locations by means of **offsets** (or **displacements**) relative to base addresses held in general purpose registers.

Machine instructions thus have the following simple syntax:

$$instruction := mon\_instr \mid dyad\_instr \mid triad\_instr$$
$$mon\_instr := mon\_rator\ addr$$
$$dyad\_instr := dyad\_rator\ addr,\ addr$$
$$triad\_instr := triad\_rator\ addr,\ addr,\ addr$$
$$addr := reg\_mode\ reg\ ([reg]) \mid mem\_mode\ reg\ (length)\ offset\ ([reg])\ ^{51}$$
$$offset := long\_offs \mid short\_offs$$
$$reg := R0 \mid \ldots \mid R15\ ^{52}$$
$$short\_offs := -2^7 \mid \ldots \mid +2^7 - 1$$
$$long\_offs := -2^{23} \mid \ldots \mid +2^{23} - 1$$

The operator codes are assumed to occupy one byte each. Likewise the combination of the mode specifications and of the registers to be used as data or base address locations can be packed into one byte each as well. Byte formats are also used for [reg] and length specifications, if required. Short offsets which cover the majority of cases take one byte, long offsets take three bytes. Both offsets are distinguished in order to utilize the memory space for the program code economically.

Thus, a monadic register mode instruction encoded in a half-word as

$$m_3 \ldots m_0\ r_3 \ldots r_0\ o_7 \ldots o_0$$

with

$o_7 \ldots o_0$ as binary coded operator,

$m_3 \ldots m_0$ as binary coded mode specification,

$r_3 \ldots r_0$ as binary coded register address,

is the shortest possible instruction format. A triadic instruction with indexed long offset memory modes for all three addresses which is encoded as

$$\{0000\ r_3 \ldots r_0\ d_{23} \ldots d_0\ m_3 \ldots m_0\ r_3 \ldots r_0\}^3\ o_7 \ldots o_0$$

where $0000\ r_3 \ldots r_0$ is a one-byte index register address,

$\quad\quad\quad\quad d_{23} \ldots d_0$ is a 3-byte offset,

---

[51] [reg] specifies an index register used only in index addressing modes, and length specifies the number of bytes in a character string, if applicable.

[52] For the program counter and for the registers that control the environment, we may also use the mnemonic identifiers PC, AFP, WFP, TOS, ... etc.

is the longest possible instruction format, requiring a total of 16 bytes. Other instructions may have any byte lengths in between. The layouts of the instruction formats follow the convention that instructions are by the program counter PC traversed in the order of increasing addresses, i.e., from right to left.

Instruction formats may be placed in all byte positions in memory so that they can be packed in sequence without any gaps. They may stretch over up to four word boundaries, requiring up to five memory access cycles to fetch, assemble and interpret them in the control unit of the processor. The control unit derives from the operator code the operation to be performed as well as the format (type) and the number of operands involved, if applicable. Thereupon it enters the micro-program which interprets the particular instruction. The addressing modes determine for each of the operands (labels) individually where they are located and how they must be accessed (i.e., from which components the addresses must be computed).

We will in this context forgo discussing the details of implementing instructions and addressing modes at the micro-programming level for conceptually this does not significantly differ from machine-level programming, which will be thoroughly treated in section 13.4.

13.3.1   Addressing Modes

Both the register mode and the memory mode split up into several addressing modes. They derive more or less directly from what is required to access entries in and to manipulate environment structures as outlined in section 13.2, or to traverse the instruction sequence. All addressing modes can be used direct (annotated as _dir) or indirect (annotated as _def (for deferred)).

In particular, we have

- the register addressing modes

    - *reg_dir* and *reg_def* which specify the contents of a register as a data value or as the memory address of a data value, respectively;

    - *incr_dir* and *incr_def* which are primarily used to increment by small pre-specified offsets pointers to stack-tops held in registers after the stack-top locations have been accessed, thus emulating pop operations;

    - *decr_dir* and *decr_def* which are used to decrement stack-top pointers by small offsets before accessing the stack-top locations, thus emulating push operations that complement *incr_dir* and *incr_def*, respectively;

- the memory addressing modes

- *x_offset_dir* and *x_offset_def* (where *x* stands for *short* or *long*) specify memory addresses obtained by adding the contents of registers to offsets as direct or indirect data locations (or labels), respectively;

- *x_offset_s* which specifies memory addresses computed as under *x_offset_dir* as locations of character strings of up to 256 bytes (the number of characters being determined by additional *length* fields).

The register addressing mode *reg_def* and the memory addressing modes *x_offset_dir* and *x_offset_def* are assumed to be extendable by index addressing which is annotated as *_ind*. Here the address defined by the regular mode is taken as the base of an array, and the contents of an additional index register identify an array entry relative to this base. In order to traverse the array entries, the index register may be incremented or decremented, under the control of an iteration loop, in small steps that correspond to the entry format.

The following table lists for all addressing modes the syntax used in machine-level programming and the address computation rules.

Mode	Syntax	Access to
reg_dir	Rn	Rn
reg_def	(Rn)	(Rn)
incr_dir	$(Rn)+$	(Rn) and then update $(Rn) := (Rn) + d$
incr_def	$@(Rn)+$	$((Rn))$ and then update $(Rn) := (Rn) + d$
decr_dir	$-(Rn)$	update $(Rn) := (Rn) - d$ and then (Rn)
decr_def	$@-(Rn)$	update $(Rn) := (Rn) - d$ and then $((Rn))$
x_offset_dir	$D(Rn)$	$(Rn) + D$
x_offset_def	$@D(Rn)$	$((Rn) + D)$
x_offset_s	$sD(Rn)$	$((Rn) + D)$

In this table, we use the symbols

Rn to denote a register with index $n \in [0..15]$;

$(\ldots)$ to denote an address specified by the contents of the memory or register location within the brackets;

$$d = \begin{cases} 1 & \text{for byte} \\ 2 & \text{for half-word} \\ 4 & \text{for word} \\ 8 & \text{for double-word} \end{cases} \text{formats}$$

to denote register increment and decrement steps which are specified as part of the operators;

@   to denote indirect (deferred) addressing;

D to denote an offset.

Index addressing extends the syntax of the addressing modes for which it is permitted by $[Rm]$ to specify the index register, and adds (Rm) to the address as specified in the table.

An important special case of the memory mode x_offset_dir is addressing relative to the register $R15$, i.e., to the program counter PC. This register holds the address of the instruction next in sequence to the one that is actually executed. When specifying the labels of all control operations and the locations of all constant data embedded in the instruction sequence as offsets (or distances) relative to this pointer position, the machine program becomes location-independent. It can thus be loaded anywhere into the memory for execution without updating addresses.[53] PC relative addresses may simply be specified as offsets D without naming a register. These offsets are then taken as distances relative to the instructions in which they are used.

PC relative addressing can only be applied within the program code. Since the program is assumed to be a constant object, this addressing mode may be confined to read (copy) accesses only in order to prevent the program from being changed either accidentally due to programming errors or willingly due to dirty tricks. We also rule out for the PC all addressing modes which cannot be applied to it in a meaningful way, e.g., all indirect and index modes.

In conjunction with a particular class of control instructions, we also have an addressing mode under which labels can be specified as absolute addresses. These addresses overwrite the actual program counter value directly.

13.3.2   An Instruction Set

The instructions to be introduced here are primarily those which are required to realize procedure calls, to control iteration loops, and to perform a few selected value-transforming operations.

---

[53] We will see later on that this is not entirely true if the program is made up from several modules (or segments) that must be linked together via external references.

As briefly mentioned before, all value-transforming instructions set a condition code of the form

$$(N, Z, V, C) \in \{0, 1\}^4$$

where

N indicates a negative result,

Z indicates a zero result,

V indicates an out-of-range result,

C indicates a carry-out condition,

with respect to a two-complement binary arithmetic. One of these conditions may be inspected by a subsequent control instruction to decide about the branching to an alternative control flow thread.

An instruction's operator specifies not only the operation to be performed but also type, format and number of operands (including a separate result location for triadic operators), or, in the case of a control operator, the status condition to be inspected. To do this in a systematic way, operators are denoted as

$$AB \, . \, . \, C\_X$$

where AB . . C is a mnemonic operator name and X defines

- either the format of the operands with $X := B \mid H \mid W \mid D \mid S$ for bytes, half-words, words, double-words and character strings, respectively;

- or a status condition, with

$$X := N \mid NN \mid Z \mid NZ \mid \ldots$$

for negative/non-negative/zero/non-zero/...results, respectively.

The most important instruction of our architecture is the transfer instruction

$$MOVE\_X \; addr\_1, addr\_2 \, .$$

It copies the contents of a format X from a register or memory location identified by $addr\_1$ to another register (memory) location identified by $addr\_2$. All addressing modes are permitted. What this instruction effects is illustrated in fig 13.6 by means of two examples, of which one realizes a memory-to-register transfer, the other realizes a memory-to-memory transfer where the destination location is assumed to be an indirectly addressed stack-top.

(a) MOVE_W $(R1), R2$

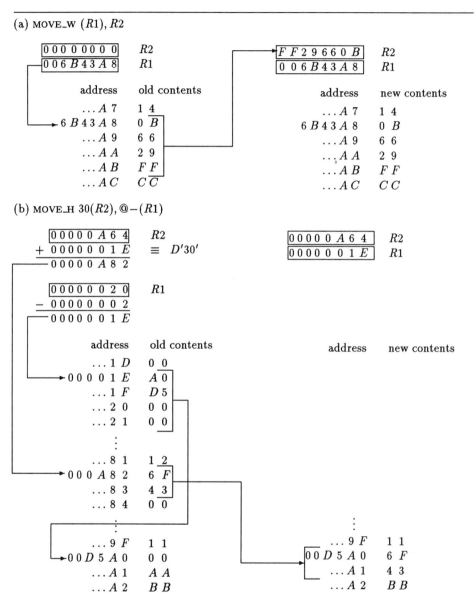

(b) MOVE_H $30(R2), @-(R1)$

Figure 13.6: Illustration of two MOVE instructions (all addresses and memory contents are given in hexa-decimal code)

An important special version of this instructions is MOVE_AD, which stores a memory address $addr\_1$ into the memory location $addr\_2$.

To push data items into or pop them out of the run-time stack, we have another two special versions of the MOVE_X instruction. They implicitly take the register $R14 \equiv$ TOS as the location of the stack-top pointer:

$$\text{PUSH\_X } addr \equiv \text{MOVE\_X } addr, -(\text{TOS})$$
$$\text{POP\_X } addr \equiv \text{MOVE\_X } (\text{TOS})+, addr \,.$$

Yet another version of push and pop instructions that involve the run-time stack efficiently support the saving and unsaving of register contents when calling and returning from procedures:

$$\text{PUSH\_REG } \# < Rn_1, \ldots, Rn_k >$$

(with $k \leq 16$) pushes the contents of the registers specified within the brackets in the order from left to right into the stack, and the complementary instruction

$$\text{POP\_REG } \# < Rn_1, \ldots, Rn_k >$$

loads the registers specified within the brackets in the order from right to left with word-formatted data popped off the stack.

Typical value-transforming instructions are

$$\text{ADD\_X } addr\_1, addr\_2 \quad \text{and} \quad \text{ADDT\_X } addr\_1, addr\_2, addr\_3$$

(with X := B | H | W) for integer addition, and

$$\text{ADFL\_X } addr\_1, addr\_2 \quad \text{and} \quad \text{ADFLT\_X } addr\_1, addr\_2, addr\_3$$

(with X := W | D) for floating point addition, where ...T denotes the respective triadic operators. Similar instructions exist for all other arithmetic and for various logical and relational operations, e.g.,

$$\text{COMP\_X } addr\_1, addr\_2$$

(with X := B | H | W | D | S) which compares two operands for equality and sets the status conditions N and Z accordingly for subsequent inspection by a control instruction.

MOVE_X and all value-transforming instructions can also be used with an immediate value, denoted as $\#number$, in the first operand position.

Control instructions partition into

- branch instructions which transfer control to labels relative to the actual program counter value;

- jump instructions which transfer control to labels specified as absolute addresses.

The former are used to branch conditionally or unconditionally to labels within the same program code, the latter are used to jump to labels outside the program, say to an operating system routine with a fixed entry address.

Branch and jump instructions have the general syntax

$$\text{BR\_CC } D \text{ and } \text{JP\_CC } \#D \,,$$

respectively, where CC denotes one of the status conditions and D denotes a displacement relative to the program counter in the former case, whereas $\#D$ denotes an absolute address in the latter case. The **program counter** is changed to

$$\text{PC} := \text{PC} + D \quad \text{by a branch instruction}$$
$$\text{PC} := \#D \quad \text{by a jump instruction}$$

if the specified status condition holds (is set to one), and left unchanged otherwise (i.e., the computation continues with the next instruction in sequence). Legitimate instantiations for CC are N | NN | Z | NZ | V | NV | C | NC (where NX denotes the negation of the condition X) and A (for branch/jump always), in which case the program counter is changed unconditionally.

To transfer control to the entry label of a procedure (or subroutine), we have the special instructions

$$\text{BSR } \quad D \qquad \text{(branch to subroutine)}$$
$$\text{JPSR } \#D \qquad \text{(jump to subroutine)} \,.$$

In addition to changing the program counter as specified before, these instructions also save on the run-time stack the current program counter as the point of return by performing implicitly the equivalent of the instruction PUSH_W PC. The complementary parameterless control instruction

$$\text{RTS} \equiv \text{POP\_W PC} \qquad \text{(return from subroutine)}$$

restores the contents of the current top-of-stack position as the new program counter value. This instruction is used as the last one in a procedure. It expects on top of the stack the program counter value pushed by the calling instruction BSR D (or JPSR $\#D$).

Finally, we have a special branch instruction of the syntactical form

$$\text{BR\_DEC } Rn, D$$

to control loop iterations. It is the last instruction of a loop. The register Rn is assumed to contain a loop index which is initialized with the number of iterations to be performed, and D is assumed to be the PC-relative address of the loop entry instruction. The instruction performs the sequence of micro-operations

$$Rn := Rn - 1;$$
$$\text{IF} \quad Rn \text{ GT } 0$$
$$\text{THEN PC} := \text{PC} + D;$$
$$\text{ELSE PC};$$

i.e., it decrements the loop index by one and thereon branches to the loop entry point as long as the index value is greater than zero, but continues with the next instruction following the loop otherwise.

13.4 Assembler Programming

Machine level programs, if not generated by a compiler, are written in a so-called assembly language. Programs of this language include

- sequences of machine instructions specified in terms of mnemonic operators and symbolic addresses which may be preceded by unique symbolic labels identifying their locations in order to improve the readability and to relieve the programmer of the tedious and error-prone task of manual address calculations;

- assembler directives (or pseudo instructions) which essentially are to control the conversion into machine code and to organize the composition of large programs from smaller modules (or segments).

Assembly language programs can be more or less directly transliterated to binary machine code since there is a one-to-one correspondence between the respective instructions. To do so, the assembler employs

- a pre-specified opcode table to convert mnemonic operators into binary codes;

- a location counter to dynamically generate symbol tables which assign to each symbolic address (or label) a numerical address value.

The location counter is a small subroutine of the assembler. In scanning an assembly language program from top to bottom, it counts the number of bytes necessary to represent in binary coded form all instructions and data encountered up to the current scanner position. This counter value is in fact equivalent to the address offset (or displacement) relative to the base of the program code. Having collected in the symbol tables the location counter values for all relevant labels, the assembler can subsequently compute concrete values for offsets that in the assembly program are symbolically specified relative to other locations, and insert them as binary codes in the machine level program. Binary coded addressing modes and register locations derive straightforwardly from the respective symbolic specifications.

Large assembly language programs usually consist of several **segments** which are programmed more or less independently of each other. These segments must be logically interconnected by **external (or global) references** in order to call procedures or to pass values across segment boundaries.

The assembler converts in a first pass all segments of a program separately into binary code, thereby generating **segment-internal addresses** relative to the segment bases. All external references are for the time being left unspecified.

A so-called **linkage editor program** subsequently arranges all segments contiguously in a program-specific **virtual address space**, updates all labels relative to its base, and establishes the **global references** (or links) among all segments.

Before execution, a **loader program** binds the virtual address space to the physical address space, say, of a memory region (compare section 2.3) in that it adds to all link addresses the base address of the region.

The assembler and to some extent the linkage editor are guided by **assembler directives** which specify

- segments and global references across segment boundaries;

- the conversion of symbolic into numerical addresses by means of the location counter;

- the allocation of memory space for buffer areas, constant values etc.

The assembler directives appear in the assembly program (or the **source code**) but disappear in the course of assembling the machine code program (or the **object code**).

13.4.1 Program Segmentation and Segment Linking

An assembly language program is generally composed of some $p \geq 1$ segments $S_1, S_2, \ldots, S_r, \ldots, S_p$. A **segment** is a fully ordered sequence of objects of the form

$$< label, instruction >$$
$$< label, data\_value > \ .$$

Let SN_r denote the set of object labels used in segment S_r, $<$ the ordering relation over the labels, n_r the total number of bytes necessary to represent all objects of S_r in binary coded form, $A_r = [a_r \ .. \ a_r + n_r - 1]$ with $a_r \in [0 \ .. \ 2^N - (n_r - 1)]$ the address interval in main memory into which S_r is loaded for execution, then we must have for each segment S_r a mapping

$$\alpha_r : SN_r \longrightarrow A_r$$

such that

$$(\forall x, y \in SN_r) \left((x < y) \Rightarrow (\alpha_r(x) < \alpha_r(y)) \right)$$

and

$$(\forall r, t \in [1 \ .. \ p]) \left((r \neq t) \Rightarrow (A_r \cap A_t = \emptyset) \right) \ .$$

With respect to global references from a segment S_r to another segment $S_{t \neq r}$, we may have the situations that

- a value-transforming instruction in S_r addresses a data object in S_t;

- a control instruction in S_r uses a branching label in S_t.

In both cases we must use in S_r a label x with $x \notin SN_r$ and $x \in SN_t$.

In order to help the linkage editor to establish the respective links, the assembler must explicitly distinguish in a segment S_r between

- objects which are exclusively referenced from within S_r and thus are called **local** to S_r;

- objects which are also referenced from somewhere else and thus are called **global** to S_r.

The assembler generates by means of the location counter for each segment individually a mapping

$$\alpha_r^S : SN_r \longrightarrow [0 \ .. \ n_r - 1]$$

into a segment-specific logical address space. The linkage editor binds all segments of the program to a continuous program-specific virtual address space $V = [0 .. (\sum_{r=1}^{p} n_r) - 1]$ such that for all segments S_r we have

$$\alpha_r^V : SN_r \longrightarrow V$$

with

$$(\forall r \in [1 .. p])(\forall x \in SN_r)\, (\alpha_r^V (x) = \alpha_r^S(x) + \sum_{i=1}^{r-1} n_i)$$

(where $\sum_{i=1}^{0} n_i = 0$). The loader program considers V a virtual memory region for which it subsequently realizes the mapping α_r with

$$(\forall r \in [1 .. p])\, ((\forall x \in SN_r)\, (\alpha_r(x) = \alpha_r^V (x) + abs))$$

and $abs \in [0 .. 2^N - (\sum_{r=1}^{p} n_r) - 1]$ which binds it to a region in main memory whose base address is abs (compare section 2.3).[54]

To establish the links between the segments of a program, the linkage editor requires information about the segmentation of a program and about the object labels defined in a segment and used externally, or referenced in a segment but defined somewhere else. This information is provided by the following assembler directives:

SEGMENT defines the beginning of a new segment, from where the location counter assigns new addresses, starting with the address zero, in order to realize the mapping α_r^S;

END follows the last object of a segment to terminate the assembler;

PUBLIC $b_0, \ldots, b_{q-1}$ with $b_0, \ldots, b_{q-1} \in SN_r$ explicitly declares the labels of all global objects of a segment S_r (which are referenced from other segments) as a segment-specific public domain;

---

[54] Alternatively, we may use the following solutions to realize the mapping α_r:

(i) The linkage editor, as before, binds the segments of a program to a contiguous virtual address space (or region) which is subsequently mapped into the main memory per paging. Virtual addresses are transformed into real addresses by means of a page table.

(ii) The logical segments of the program are directly and individually mapped into segments of the main memory. Logical addresses are translated into physical addresses by means of segment tables. To do so the linkage editor must create a so-called common area (or a public domain) via which all global references across segment boundaries are realized. The common area is just another segment.

(iii) (i) and (ii) may be combined (compare section 2.3).

EXTERN $c_0, \ldots, c_{q'-1}$ with $c_0, \ldots, c_{q'-1} \notin SN_r$ explicitly declares the labels of all objects referenced from within a segment S_r but defined in other segments.

The PUBLIC directive causes the assembler to create a so-called public symbol dictionary (PSD) via which the linkage editor establishes the links to the segments that refer to its entries. The EXTERN directive creates a corresponding external symbol dictionary (ESD). The assembler demands that all labels declared EXTERN be used with an indirect addressing mode.

When assembling a segment, location counter values relative to its base are assigned to all local and global (public) labels in their order of occurrences. The location counter values for all public labels are collected in the PSD. In addition, the assembler reserves word-sized locations at the end of the segment for all labels declared EXTERN which are enumerated by the location counter as well. These label/counter-value pairs are collected in the ESD.

The linkage editor maps all segments of the program consecutively into the virtual address space V, and updates the location counter entries in the PSDs and ESDs of all segments accordingly. If b denotes a public label in the segment S_r which is declared EXTERN in $S_{t \neq r}$, then the virtual address

$$\alpha_r^V(b) = \alpha_r^S(b) + \sum_{i=1}^{r-1} n_i$$

is retrieved from the PSD of S_r, and via the ESD of S_t it is written into the location reserved for b at the end of the segment S_t. Thus, the object labeled b is accessible from S_t in S_r through one level of indirection.

A program P with the segments $S_1, \ldots, S_r, \ldots, S_p$ is said to be completely linked iff all segments are completely linked. Let C_r be the set of external labels in the segment S_r and B_t be the set of public labels in another segment $S_{t \neq r}$, then S_r is said to be completely linked iff

$$(\forall c \in C_r) \left((\exists S_{t \neq r}) \, (c \in B_t) \right)$$

and for S_t the mapping $\alpha_t^V : SN_t \longrightarrow V$ is fully specified.

13.4.2 Allocating Address Space

To reserve within a segment address space for buffer areas, constant data etc. and to assign values to names (labels), the assembler provides the following directives:

LABEL: BLOCK_X. n

> with $n \in I\!N$ and X := B $|$ H $|$ W $|$ D allocates, starting at the symbolic address LABEL, a continuous address interval for the storage of n objects with format X;

NUMBERS: BYTE. $1, 2, a$

stores, starting at the symbolic address NUMBERS, the characters $1, 2, a$ in this order in three consecutive byte locations;

LIST: WORD. $1325, -76, 223, -11$

stores, starting at LIST, the binary coded values of the listed numbers in consecutive word formats;

CHAIN: STRING. $'ABC14abc'$

stores, starting at CHAIN, the specified character string in consecutive byte positions;

XYZ $= expr$

with $expr := name \mid value \mid expr \; arith\_op \; expr$ equates the symbolic name XYZ with the value of $expr$.

13.4.3 Converting Symbolic into Numerical Addresses, Linking and Loading

Converting an assembly language (or source code) segment into binary object code is usually done in two passes through the segment.

In a first pass, the location counter LCT assigns its actual value, denoted as (LCT), to all objects of the segment in the order in which they are listed, starting with (LCT) $= 0$ at the first object. The location counter in fact traverses the address space of the machine code to be assembled and always points to the position into which the next piece of object code must be placed. The LCT is moved forward by the lengths of the objects added, counted in bytes. This includes byte positions which must be left free in order to align data formats to permissible address boundaries.

While doing this, the assembler generates

- a local symbol dictionary LSD for all labels defined in the segment;

- the public symbol dictionary PSD for all global labels;

- the external symbol dictionary ESD for all labels declared under EXTERN, for which word-sized locations are allocated at the end of the object code segment.

The entries of these tables are all of the form $< label, (\text{LCT}) >$.

In a second pass, the source code can actually be converted into binary object code. The operator codes can be looked up in the opcode table, and the symbolic address labels can now be substituted by absolute addresses or offsets that are either directly taken or computed from the respective location counter values found in the above dictionaries.

To illustrate these ideas by means of an example, we consider a small subroutine which tests a block of 4096 bytes of memory, starting at some arbitrarily chosen base address, for the occurrence of faults. It does so by first writing the test pattern $H'AA' \equiv B'10101010'$ into each byte location of the block, and then comparing the actual contents of these locations against the original pattern. In case of a discrepancy, the subroutine branches out to an error-handling routine.

The assembly language version of this subroutine is as follows:

```
        SEGMENT
            (* subroutine for memory test *)
                    EXTERN BASE,ERROR
                    PUBLIC ENTRY
            (* definition of constants *)
INTERVAL:   WORD.       D'4096'
TESTPAT:    BYTE.       H'AA'
            (* save two working registers and load test pattern into block *)
ENTRY:      PUSH_REG    #< R0, R1 >     3
            MOVE_W      @BASE,R0        4
            MOVE_W      INTERVAL,R1     4
LOOP_1:     MOVE_B      TESTPAT,(R0)+   4
            BR_DEC      R1,LOOP_1       4
            (* read block and compare *)
            MOVE_W      @BASE,R0        4
            MOVE_W      INTERVAL,R1     4
LOOP_2:     COMP_B      TESTPAT,(R0)+   4
            BR_NZ       @ERROR          3
            BR_DEC      R1,LOOP_2       4
            POP_REG     #< R0, R1 >     3
            RTS                         1
        END
```

(The numbers to the right specify the lengths in bytes of the object code instructions.) This subroutine may be referenced from somewhere else by the label ENTRY. It receives the base address of the block to be tested through the externally defined label BASE.

After the first pass through this segment, the assembler has generated the following dictionaries:

LSD:	INTERVAL	0	(4 bytes)
	TESTPAT	4	(1 byte)
	ENTRY	5	$(3 + 4 + 4 = 11$ bytes)
	LOOP_1	16	$(4 + 4 + 4 + 4 = 16$ bytes)
	LOOP_2	32	$(4 + 3 + 4 + 3 + 1 = 15$ bytes)
PSD:	ENTRY	5	
ESD:	BASE	48	(4 bytes)
	ERROR	52	(4 bytes)

(The numbers in the parentheses to the right denote the distances from the current to the next label in sequence, as determined by the lengths of the intervening objects (instructions).)

From the contents of these dictionaries, the assembler generates in the second pass a machine program with the following address (offset) values (the address intervals into which the objects (instructions) are placed are shown in the brackets to the left):

$[0 . . 3]$	:	$H'00001000'$	
$[4]$	:	$H'AA'$	
$[5 . . 7]$	:	PUSH_REG	$B'00 \ldots 011'$ [55]
$[8 . . 11]$	:	MOVE_W	$@37(R15), R0$
$[12 . . 15]$	:	MOVE_W	$-15(R15), R1$
$[16 . . 19]$	:	MOVE_B	$-15(R15), (R0)+$
$[20 . . 23]$	:	BR_DEC	$R1, -8(R15)$
$[24 . . 27]$	:	MOVE_W	$@21(R15), R0$
$[28 . . 31]$	:	MOVE_W	$-31(R15), R1$
$[32 . . 35]$	:	COMP_B	$-31(R15), (R0)+$
$[36 . . 38]$	:	BR_NZ	$@13(R15)$
$[39 . . 42]$	:	BR_DEC	$R1, -11(R15)$
$[43 . . 45]$	:	POP_REG	$B'00 \ldots 011'$
$[46]$	:	RTS	
$[47]$	:	(* alignment *)	
$[48 . . 51]$	:	(* uninstantiated *)	
$[52 . . 55]$	:	(* uninstantiated *)	

Note that the address offsets are calculated relative to the byte positions at which the program counter PC will have arrived when computing the actual ad-

---

[55] The assembler transforms a register specification of the form $\# < Rn_1, \ldots, Rn_k >$ into a binary mask of 16 positions in which the positions $n_1, \ldots, n_k$ are set to one.

dresses. These are the byte positions immediately following the respective address specifications.

A segment thus converted into binary code may be linked up with all other segments of a program as follows:

- As described before, all segments are placed into the contiguous virtual address space of the program so that each segment $S_r \mid r \in \{1, \ldots, p\}$ receives a base address

$$a_r^V = \sum_{i=1}^{r-1} n_i \ .$$

This base address is subsequently added to the LCT value entries in the ESD and PSD of S_r so that for all $x \in B_r \cup C_r$ we get the new entries

$$\alpha_r^V(x) = a_r^V + \alpha_r^S(x) \ .$$

- For each entry $x \in C_r$ in the ESD of segment S_r, search the entries of all PSDs that belong to segments $S_{t \neq r}$ for a matching label $x \in B_t$. If successful, write the address value

$$\alpha_t^V(x) = a_t^V + \alpha_t^S(x)$$

found in this dictionary entry into the location with address $\alpha_r^V(x)$ in the segment S_r. This is the link location allocated for the external object $x \in C_r$ at the end of the object code of segment S_r which is left uninstantiated by the assembler. Since all references to external objects must be specified indirectly, the link is thus established.

Of course, for this to work correctly, it must be assumed that the labels of all global objects are unique throughout the entire program, i.e., they must occur only once in all PSDs. Otherwise, linking would become ambiguous.

In order to execute the linked program, the operating system must allocate a contiguous memory region of size $L \geq \sum_{r=1}^{p} n_r$. When loading the program into this region, its base address *abs* must be added to all virtual addresses specified in the ESDs of all program segments since all external references require absolute addresses. To start the program thus bound to physical address space, the operating system executes the instruction JP_A ABS to load the program counter register PC with *abs*, which is assumed to be available in the memory location ABS.

13.5 A Case Study: Quicksorting

We will now investigate how a non-trivial PASCAL program translates to machine code. We are particularly interested in the realization of procedure and function calls and in the interaction of the machine program with the run-time stack. A reasonably sophisticated example to discuss these aspects is the recursive *quicksort* procedure specified in section 13.1, which includes two local subfunctions.

We will here develop an assembly language version of this PASCAL program which directly translates into object code as it would be generated by a compiler in a very similar form. This version includes assembler directives to equate the symbols used in the PASCAL program for formal parameters and local variables with displacement values relative to the respective frame bases. To exhibit the interaction between two segments, we define artificially a segment each for the procedure *quicksort* and for both of its local functions *piv* and *part*, though a PASCAL compiler would place everything into one segment.

In this program, we use the following permanent register assignments:

$R15$	$\equiv$	PC	for the program counter,
$R14$	$\equiv$	TOS	for the stack-top pointer,
$R13$	$\equiv$	AFP	for the most recent argument frame pointer,
$R12$	$\equiv$	WFP	for the most recent workspace frame pointer,
$R11$	$\equiv$	ENV_PTR	for the environment link pointer,
$R0$	$\equiv$	RES	for passing a function value to the calling procedure (or function).

The register specifications or the symbolic names may be used alternatively.

The control block within the activation record of a procedure (function) call must generally include

- the link pointer to the calling environment which must be pushed into the run-time stack by the calling procedure (function);

- the actual program counter value PC and some status information such as interrupt mask and condition code etc. of the calling procedure (function) which are pushed into the stack as part of executing the branch-to-subroutine instruction BSR;

- the contents of the working registers to be used by the called procedure as well as the current contents of the registers ENV_PTR, WFP and AFP which must be restored when returning to the calling procedure;

which we will also order in this sequence.

Thus, the calling and the called procedure must generate on (and eventually remove in reverse order from) the run-time stack an activation record layout which includes a standardized control block as shown in fig. 13.7 (compare also fig. 13.2). All entries of the control block per definition have word size. Formats and positions of the argument and workspace frame entries, as said before, may be deduced by the

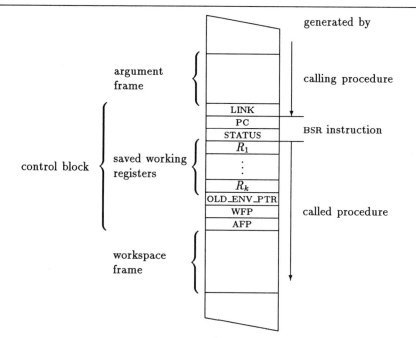

Figure 13.7: Activation record of a procedure call

compiler from the formal parameter and local variable declarations. When ordered in the same sequence in which they are listed in the high-level PASCAL program, the frames may develop holes of unused space since all data formats must be aligned to admissible address positions. For reasons of standardization, we also decide to make the sizes of all argument and workspace frames multiples word formats.

We also need to remember that the stack grows towards decreasing addresses and shrinks towards increasing addresses.

With this in mind, we are now ready to study the implementation in assembly language of the procedure *quicksort* in a segment separated from its subfunctions. To facilitate the discussion, we repeat here the PASCAL version of this procedure, disregarding subfunction declarations. At the beginning of the statement part, we have added an assignment $n := n + 1$ to a global variable defined in some enclosing procedure. When initialized with $n := 0$, this box variable simply counts the number of *quicksort* calls necessary to sort a given argument list. The purpose of this is to include a global reference which necessitates link pointers from the activation records of *quicksort* calls to the calling environments. If the procedure would have no global reference, as in the PASCAL program of fig. 13.1, an optimizing compiler would eliminate these links for they are then redundant.

PROCEDURE $quicksort(i, j : integer; \text{REF } list : array[1 .. maxsize] \text{ of } integer)$;
    VAR $pivot, pivot\_pos, k : integer$;

    $\vdots$

  BEGIN
     $n := n + 1$;
    IF i LT j
    THEN BEGIN
            $pivot\_pos := piv(i, j)$;
         IF $pivot\_pos$ NE 0
         THEN BEGIN
               $pivot := list[pivot\_pos]$; $k := part(i, j, pivot)$;
               $quicksort(i, k - 1, list)$; $quicksort(k, j, list)$;
         END
       END
  END

This procedure has two integer value parameters for which we allocate half-word formats and one reference parameter which requires a word format for the array pointer. Thus, the argument frame for *quicksort* takes two words. Relative to the frame base, we place the formats for i, j and *list* into the address positions $-2, -4$ and -8, respectively.

As for the local variables, we decide to make up a workspace frame for *pivot* only, and hold *pivot_pos* and k in working registers. All three items are assumed to require half-word formats, with *pivot* placed at the address position -4 relative to the base of a one-word workspace frame, whose first half-word remains empty.[56] At the head of the segment for *quicksort* shown in fig. 13.8, these offsets are defined by EQUATE directives. They also include an offset for the environment link pointer which must be placed right on top of the argument frame as the first item of the control block.

Following the declarations of public and external labels, the procedure starts at the label QUICK which is used as address specification for a BSR instruction either outside the segment, in which case it must be indirect, or within the procedure for recursive calls, in which case it must be direct. The first three instructions that follow QUICK are to save relevant register contents of the calling procedure,

---

[56]Putting the *pivot* variable into a workspace location in memory is a somewhat artificial measure which merely serves to create a workspace frame at all. Of course, *pivot* could be easily placed into a register as well

to instantiate $R11$ with the address of the environment link pointer position in the current control block, and to set the new workspace frame pointer to the position following the control block.

The points to be noted in this procedure are

- the direct passage of the environment pointer with the instruction PUSH_W $R11$ to the subfunction calls for *piv* and *part*, which must link up to the most recent instance of *quicksort*;

- the passage over one level of indirection of the environment pointer with the instruction PUSH_W $(R11)$ to recursive calls of *quicksort*, which must link up to the most recent instance of the procedure that calls *quicksort*;

- the indirect addressing via the external labels PIV and PART of the functions *piv* and *part* in another segment;

- the release of argument and workspace frames by simply resetting the top-of-stack pointer TOS by the respective frame sizes, using immediate operand modes.

The procedure terminates by popping the saved register contents of the calling procedure off the run-time stack, and by executing the RTS instruction which restores its status and its program counter.

Fig. 13.9 shows the basic structure of the segment in which the assembly language code for the functions *piv* and *part* is specified. In both cases, we decide to keep all local variables in working set registers; i.e., we need to specify by the EQUATE directives at the top of the segment only the layouts of the respective argument frames. The parameters defined in the headings

$$piv(i, j : integer) : integer;$$

and

$$part(i\_min, j\_max, pivot : integer) : integer;$$

require frames of word size for two half-word integers and of double-word size for three half-word integers, respectively. In addition, we define an offset LIST for the position of the list pointer in the argument frame of *quicksort* relative to the link pointer entry sitting on top of it.

We forgo being specific about the procedure bodies other than for the implementation of the sequence of statements that swaps in the function *part* the elements *list*[*i*] and *list*[*j*] by means of a temporary *h* (see the complete definition of *part* on page 379). The code shows how the global parameter *list* is accessed via the environment link of *part* that is held in register $R11$. It first copies the link pointer

SEGMENT QUICKSORT
(* displacements for argument and workspace frame *)
   I $= -2$
   J $= -4$
   LIST $= -8$
   LINK $= -12$
   PIVOT $= -4$
(* assumed displacement of the global variable n relative to the LINK entry of
the activation record in which it is instantiated *)
   N $= -20$
(* declaration of public and external labels *)
   PUBLIC   QUICK
   EXTERN   PIV,PART
(* entry into procedure *quicksort* *)
QUICK: PUSH_REG $\# < R1 .. R4, R11 .. R13 >$
   MOVE_AD LINK(AFP),$R11$
   MOVE_W   TOS,WFP
   SUB_W $\#4$,TOS
(* increment the global count variable n *)
   MOVE_W $(R11), R4$
   MOVE_H   N$(R4), R3$
   ADD_H $\#1, R3$ □
   MOVE_H $R3,$N$(R4)$
(* compute predicate $i < j$ and test branching condition *)
   MOVE_H   I(AFP), $R1$
   MOVE_H   J(AFP), $R2$
   MOVE_H $R1, R3$
   SUB_H $R2, R1$ □
   BR_NN   EXIT   □
(* set new AFP, prepare frame for *piv*, branch to *piv* and, upon returning,
remove the frame and re-store the AFP of *quicksort* *)
   MOVE_W   TOS,AFP
   PUSH_H $R3$
   PUSH_H $R2$
   PUSH_W $R11$
   BSR   @PIV
   ADD_W $\#8$,TOS
   MOVE_W 4(TOS), AFP
        (continued on the next page)

Figure 13.8: Assembler language program for the procedure *quicksort*

(* test function value *pivot_pos* in $R0$ for $\neq 0$ and branch to EXIT, or compute
pivot := *list*(*pivot_pos*) *)

SUB_H	#0, R0	□
BR_Z	EXIT	□
MOVE_H	R3, R1	
MOVE_H	R0, R3	
MOVE_W	LIST(AFP), R4	
MOVE_H	(R4)[R3], PIVOT(WFP)	

(* call and return from function *part* and move result to R3 *)

MOVE_W	TOS,AFP
SUB_W	#2, TOS
PUSH_H	R1
PUSH_H	R2
PUSH_H	PIVOT(WFP)
PUSH_W	R11
BSR	@PART
ADD_W	#12, TOS
MOVE_H	R0, R3

(* call *quicksort*($i, k-1, list$) with i in $R1$, k in $R0$ and $R3$, list pointer in $R4$,
and return *)

PUSH_H	R1
SUB_H	#1, R3
PUSH_H	R3
PUSH_W	R4
PUSH_W	(R11)
BSR	QUICK
ADD_W	#12, TOS

(* call *quicksort*($k, j, list$) with j in $R2$, k in $R0$, list pointer in $R4$, and return *)

PUSH_H	R0
PUSH_H	R2
PUSH_W	R4
PUSH_W	(R11)
BSR	QUICK
ADD_W	#12, TOS

(* remove workspace frame and return to the calling procedure *)

EXIT:	ADD_W	#4, TOS
	POP_REG	# < R1..R4, R11..R13 >
	RTS	

END SEGMENT QUICKSORT

Figure 13.8: continued

```
SEGMENT FUNCTIONS
      (* displacements for argument frames *)
            I = −2
            J = −4
            LINK1 = −8
            IMIN = −4
            JMAX = −6
            PIVOT = −8
            LINK2 = −12
            LIST = 4
      (* declaration of public labels *)
            PUBLIC      PIV,PART
      (* function piv *)
PIV:        PUSH_REG    # < R1 .. R4, R11 .. R13 >
            MOVE_AD     LINK1(AFP), R11

            ⋮

            POP_REG     # < R1 .. R4, R11 .. R13 >
            RTS
      (* function part *)
PART:       PUSH_REG    # < R1 .. R6, R11 .. R13 >
            MOVE_AD     LINK2(AFP), R11
            MOVE_H      IMIN(AFP), R1
            MOVE_H      JMAX(AFP), R2
            MOVE_H      PIVOT(AFP), R3
      (* local address of list to register R6 *)
REPEAT:     MOVE_W      (R11), R6
            MOVE_W      LIST(R6), R6
      (* swap contents of list[i] and list[j] *)
            MOVE_W      (R6)[R1], R4
            MOVE_W      (R6)[R2], (R5)[R1]
            MOVE_W      R4, (R6)[R2]

            ⋮

            POP_REG     # < R1 .. R6, R11 .. R13 >
            RTS
END SEGMENT FUNCTIONS
```

Figure 13.9: Segment for the assembly language programs of the functions *piv* and *part*

to the control block of the most recent *quicksort* call to *R*6, and then uses LIST = 4 as an offset relative to this pointer to access in this location the pointer to the list array and to copy it into *R*6. Now *list*[*i*] and *list*[*j*] can be accessed through the pointer in *R*6 in indexed addressing mode, using the contents of *R*1 and *R*2 as index values. The same addressing scheme for list entries is used in the function *piv* as well.[57]

A careful analysis of these assembly language programs reveals that to a large extent they serve no other purpose but to organize in a very elementary form a computational process on the primitive substrate provided by the machine architecture. Lacking more powerful machine operations and any structure other than the one induced by the sequential control mechanism, the programs consist almost exclusively of sequences of MOVE and PUSH instructions in combination with various addressing modes. They explicitly specify the details of creating and linking activation records, of copying data from memory to register locations and vice versa, and of de-referencing pointer chains. Explicit control and context saving/unsaving instructions are necessary to branch to and return from a subroutine in an orderly form. Even many of the arithmetic instructions do nothing but move the run-time stack pointer. Very few instructions, which in the program shown in fig. 13.8 are marked with □, perform operations that actually contribute to the solution of the problem.

The layout of the stack frames and accesses to them are statically fixed in terms of offsets relative to the frame bases. These offsets are determined by the number and formats of the frame entries. We may even have statically fixed references across the boundaries of activation records in the case of non-recursive procedures (functions).

The instructions primarily refer to formatted memory or register locations. Their contents are bit strings which have no meaningful interpretation of their own. The types of the objects represented by these bit strings are irrelevant in the case of all transfer instructions, and inferred from the operator types in the case of arithmetic, logic and relational instructions. For instance, what is addressed as operand of an ADD_W instruction is interpreted as a word-formatted 2-complement representation of an integer value, what is addressed as operand of an ADFL_D instruction is interpreted as binary representation of a floating point number in double-word format.

---

[57] Accesses to the global variable *list* can of course be had more directly in the particular case of the functions *part* and *piv*. Since both functions are non-recursive, they create only one activation record on top of the most recent record for *quicksort*. The list pointer location in the argument frame of *quicksort* is therefore always a fixed distance away, say, from the control block of *part* (*piv*) and can therefore be accessed directly, using this distance as offset relative to the link pointer held in *R*11. However, recursive functions or procedures require that global variables be accessed indirectly through the link pointer chain as specified in fig. 13.9, for then these distances change dynamically.

Control instructions refer to locations whose contents are assumed to be instructions. Their formats are determined by the operators which define the number of operand positions and by the addressing modes which for each operand individually define the length of the address (or immediate operand) representation. Binary coded instructions cannot be distinguished from binary representations of other objects. Just what is interpreted as an instruction sequence is solely determined by the fact that the program counter PC traverses the memory locations in which it is stored. Thus, the correct execution of a machine code program critically depends on the initialization of the program counter with the address of the first instruction. From there, the control unit infers step-by-step the entire structure and interpretation of the program, assuming that every piece of code is meant to be what it is taken for. No type checks to this effect are being performed at run-time.

Thus, machine-level programs, as variously stated before, realize static work schedules which expect every object to be in the right form (binary representation) in the right place at the right time. No deviations from this plan are possible. This precludes the application of procedures to actual parameters of changing types and formats, and also partial procedure (function) applications.

13.6   Some Pragmatic Aspects of Control Flow Architectures

Machine (or assembly) languages define the lowest level of programming that is commonly accessible to the users of control flow systems. We saw that at this level the programmer is primarily concerned with the details of organizing computations on a particular machine, given its rather primitive instruction set. Algorithmic aspects play an almost negligible role. Programming is extremely vulnerable to errors since even small programs cannot be understood without mentally executing them, which is nearly impossible for sequences of more than a few instructions. Hardly any programs other than small subroutines of the operating system kernel or of applications with tight run-time requirements are therefore written in machine (assembly) languages.

The role of assembly languages is generally reduced to that of a target for the compilation of high-level languages. Though compilation may simply be seen as a semantic-preserving transformation of programs from one language representation to another, its ultimate goal always is to obtain programs that can be directly executed on a concrete architecture. In the case of control flow machines, these **target** or **object code** programs are inherently procedural, specifying how the computation must be performed step-by-step. Every construct that occurs in a high-level program uniquely relates to a small piece of object code. For instance, in the assembly language program shown in fig. 13.8 we can readily identify the instruction sequences that realize the two nested conditional statements and the procedure (function) calls embedded in them.

Yet another procedural level is usually required to interpret on a concrete hardware processor the machine instruction set itself. These instructions, though generally rather primitive in terms of what they accomplish, are often quite difficult to implement even on a tailor-made register transfer structure, easily requiring more than ten elementary transfer operations (or machine cycles) to execute them. This is largely due to complicated address manipulations and alignment problems caused by varying instruction formats, addressing modes and effective data or instruction addresses that do not coincide with physical memory word or register boundaries.

The VAX architecture is a perfect example in kind [LeEc80, VAX81, KeBa84]. From a programmer's point of view, its instruction set leaves little to be desired. It is well adapted to the needs of a dynamic execution model, and highly flexible: all value-transforming or transfer operators can be combined with a variety of addressing modes and applied to several data formats. However, this flexibility comes at the expense of a rather formidable control unit which implements the instruction set on the arithmetic-logic and register part of the processing unit. It must execute fairly long micro-code sequences to identify step-by-step one of many different instances of a particular instruction, to interpret (decode) its components in dedicated instruction and data register positions, to compute effective operand addresses, and to perform the respective memory accesses. The most difficult and time-consuming part often is instruction fetching itself. Long instructions stretching over two or more memory words must be moved piecemeal into the processing unit where its logical components must be aligned and assembled in specific instruction register positions prepared for their interpretation by appropriate decoders. Depending on formats and actual byte positions of these components, this may require several processor-internal byte or half-word transfers from register to register. Thus, the micro-code sequences necessary to interpret machine instructions are primarily busy to move pieces of code (or data) and addresses (of addresses) back and forth between the memory and the processing unit, and to move things inside the processor from one place to another. The real action, e.g., adding two numbers, usually takes just one or two micro-instructions (or machine cycles) once the operands are finally in place.

We thus face at the micro-code level essentially the same problems as at the machine instruction level: unproductive transfer (micro-)instructions clearly dominate value-transforming (micro-)instructions. Lengthy and complicated micro-code sequences quite obviously arises from instructions whose formats and legitimate address positions are incompatible with the word-oriented physical structure (or bandwidth) of the memory and of the processing unit. While considerable efforts may be necessary to get things from the memory and to arrange them properly inside the processing unit, machine instructions generally accomplish very little in comparison to this overhead. Transfer instructions move just one data item of a simple type (format) at a time, and value-transforming instructions operate on at most two simple data values to produce another value of the same simple type and format. The overhead is particularly annoying in the case of highly repetitive computations such as iterations through a large array. Here the machine goes over and over again through the unproductive motions of fetching, aligning and decoding within a loop body the same instructions in the same way and of performing essentially the same address computations.

Architectures with these characteristics are therefore also referred to as complex instruction set computer architectures (or as CISC architectures for short).

To turn things around in favor of more useful computations, we obviously have the choice between two radically different approaches.

At one extreme, we have architectures based on very simple and uniform machine instruction sets which render interpretation by micro-code superfluous. These so-called reduced instruction set computer architectures (or RISC architectures for short) are mainly motivated by the problems we have just discussed of implementing traditional architectures, but also by observations on general program behavior, on the subsets of machine instructions commonly used as the targets for compilation, and on the frequency of executing certain instructions. Another important issue are the constraints imposed by VLSI-technology on the design of modern processing units [Hen84, Kat85].

The basic idea underlying RISC architectures is

- to include into the processing unit a fairly large set of working registers, say from at least 32 up to 256;

- to perform all value-transforming operations only from register to register, and to communicate data between the processor and the memory just by load/store register instructions;

- to use only direct offset modes for memory addressing (in load/store instructions);

- to hold, by means of a window technique, from two to eight of the most recent activation records of procedure (function) calls completely inside the register set;

- to restrict the set of instructions to those necessary as targets for high-level language compilation, which typically are about

    12 arithmetic/logic instructions;

8   load/store instructions;

6   branch (to subroutine) instructions;

6   miscellaneous instructions to handle interrupts, to load and change the
     program status, etc.;

- and, most importantly, to have all instructions trimmed to word formats, with
  just two or three different but fixed arrangements of subformats for operator
  and operand specifications.

The purpose of these measures, particularly of the last one, is to drastically
reduce the complexity of instruction execution and thus of the control unit – a very
important aspect when it comes to the on-chip VLSI-implementation of a complete
processor. All instructions can then be loaded in one piece, and without further
alignment, from the memory into the instruction register, wherein all components
can be decoded immediately. When complemented by instruction caching, pipelining
and pre-fetching, and by delayed branching techniques, the majority of instructions
(all register-to-register and branch operations) can in fact be completed at a rate
of about one per machine cycle; load/store instructions usually take two machine
cycles (not including any memory latencies). The gap between machine instructions
and micro-instructions is thus closed, and the micro-code level for all practical
purposes disappears. Without micro-code sequences, the control unit is basically
reduced to the program counter which governs the sequencing of instructions, and
to some combinatory logic circuitry which distributes within the register-transfer
structure the control signals that are more or less directly obtained by decoding
the actual contents of the instruction register.

Executing a high-level language program on a RISC machine thus takes only
one level of procedural code to which it must be compiled. RISC machine code is
usually made up from about 20% to 50% more instructions than, say, equivalent
VAX code, since the instructions are generally much simpler. For instance, arithmetic multiplication and division must be compiled to loops of add (subtract) and
shift instructions for there are no equivalent machine instructions (which would
have these loops realized as micro-code). However, since all unproductive transfer and alignment operations as well as complex address computations are largely
eliminated, RISC machine code nevertheless executes decidedly faster than equivalent VAX code. In fact, we may think of RISC machine programs also as direct
micro-program realizations of the respective high-level programs.

The RISC approach has proved to be very successful commercially. In modern
work stations, RISC processors have almost completely replaced the more traditional MC68000 and INTEL 8086 micro-processor lines. It is well established that
the former outperform the latter by a factor of about four to five, though part

of the performance gain must also be attributed to higher clock frequencies made possible by the simpler architectures. However, we have also wider gaps between high-level languages and the machine architectures. Large semantic gaps usually do not only increase the size of the machine programs but also the complexity of the compilers. In the particular case of RISC architectures, the compilers must generate code which more or less directly controls the register-transfer structure of the target machine. They require sophisticated code generators/optimizers which make efficient use of the processor-internal registers, of pipelining facilities, delayed branching etc.

At the other extreme, we have so-called high-level language (HLL) architectures [Car75]. They are attempts to completely close, at the expense of fairly complex machinery, the semantic gap between the machine languages and high-level languages, and to improve at the same time the performance relative to conventional control flow architectures. High-level programs are either directly processed as they are, or a pre-processor converts the constructs of the high-level language one-to-one into equivalent machine instructions which are directly interpreted by micro-code sequences on tailor-made hardware. Since compilation degenerates to transliteration, we have only a level of procedural interpretation.

Unfortunately, HLL architectures are not too well suited for systems which generally are expected to support a large variety of imperative high-level languages. There is simply too much syntactic and semantic disparity to define a machine language to which all of them can be easily transliterated. We can either have an HLL architecture adapted to the particularities of a few very similar languages (very likely only one), or we must settle for an intermediate machine language featuring fairly high-level instructions which requires simple compilation. The problem here is to identify a suitable set of instructions from which widely differing languages such as PASCAL, FORTRAN, C, PL1, ADA, COBOL or APL are likely to benefit, and thus justify their interpretation by micro-code on fairly sophisticated hardware. The criteria by which these instructions ought to be selected include the frequency with which they are being used and the extent to which they reduce the space and time complexity of the resulting machine code. Good candidates are composite instructions for subroutine calls and loop controls as, for instance, supported by the VAX architecture, and vector instructions which, in conjunction with pipelining techniques, are used in various high-performance number-crunching systems.

A more rigorous concept for a suitable intermediate machine language, which may also considerably improve high-level program design, are data type architectures [GiGu82]. In addition to simple types, they are to support as machine data types at least vectors, but preferably matrices and lists (of typed elements) as well, making available a large set of generic value- and structure-transforming instructions. The benefits of such an APL-like architecture are twofold:

- high-level programming becomes more concise when using APL notations rather than awkward iteration loops to specify operations on structured objects;

- at the expense of more sophisticated machinery necessary to perform run-time type checks, to pipeline data values, and to traverse structured objects by means of fast hard-wired address generating mechanisms, we obtain a higher run-time efficiency. This is mainly due to the elimination of time-consuming but unproductive instruction fetch-and-decode operations that would have to be repeatedly executed when iterating through a conventional loop.

Except for the Burroughs B5000, B6000 and B7000 series [Org83], which were designed with efficient support for ALGOL as the primary system and application programming language in mind, and for several *LISP* machines that entered the market in the early 1980's (see also the last chapter), the idea of HLL architectures has received little interest outside the research community. The case held against these architectures is largely based on the unattractive combination of complicated and hence costly hardware with lacking generality of instruction sets [Cra80]. The closer the semantic gap between a chosen machine language and a high-level language, the more are the syntax and semantics of the former dictated by the specific needs of the latter, which inevitably leads to diverging architectures. The demand for multilingual computers on the one hand and current trends in VLSI-technology on the other hand clearly point in the opposite direction. They strongly favor RISC architectures featuring simple low-level instruction sets. High-level languages may be compiled either directly to low-level machine code or to an intermediate language which, in turn, may be interpreted (or emulated) on a RISC machine by standardized machine-code macros. We may also settle for a mix of both approaches, implementing only a selected subset of composite operations by macros. The line between what is considered machine code and what is considered micro-code can be rather freely chosen.

However, it should be clearly recognized that current RISC architectures are primarily a target for the direct compilation of conventional imperative languages, not for the emulation (or interpretation) of possibly widely diverging architectures. Due to the preference given to operations on word formats and due to the lack of appropriate memory addressing modes, there is little support for efficient string manipulations and for computations involving stacks, queues or linked lists that may grow to considerable length. Thus, it is for instance difficult to emulate on RISC architectures with reasonable efficiency the interpreting reduction systems discussed earlier.

Interestingly enough, RISC architectures are not even too well suited to emulate more traditional control flow instruction sets. The poorer efficiency, say, of a VAX emulation as compared to a dedicated VAX processor can be offset only by the higher clock-frequencies with which RISC processors can be operated.

13.7 A Note on Concurrent Programming Control Flow Style

Executing imperative programs non-sequentially in control flow systems that comprise several cooperating processing sites has been and will continue to be the subject of intensive research and development efforts. They are to a large extent stimulated by advanced microprocessor technologies which are expected to render low-cost multi-processor or distributed system configurations that outperform sophisticated main frame mono-processors a reality. Adhering to imperative programming concepts in a non-sequential world, though not necessarily an immediate consequence of using control flow processors, obviously is widely considered an asset rather than a deficit when it comes to writing highly efficient programs. Unfortunately, the programming techniques that must be employed to achieve these ends [Brin77, AnSc83, ChMi88, Ben90, And91] are also the source of considerable insecurities about program correctness, particularly about the determinacy of results.

To illustrate the problem by means of a simple example, let us return to the *quicksort* program given in fig. 13.1. It derives its efficiency largely from the in-place sorting of elements in the array *list* that is handed over to the procedure *quicksort* as a reference parameter. This array is subsequently shared between and overwritten by two recursive *quicksort* calls specified inside the procedure body. If both procedure calls would be executed concurrently, using a divide-and-conquer scheme, the result would still be determinate for both calls (and recursively all concurrently executable calls of the emerging tree) update non-overlapping partitions of the array. However, the situation changes when switching to the modified *quicksort* procedure shown on page 416, where we introduced another global variable n which was to count the total number of procedure calls necessary to sort the entire array. When executing this program concurrently, we again get the array *list* correctly sorted, but the number of *quicksort* calls accumulated under n may be incorrect and even change when running the program several times with the same unsorted list as argument. The cause of the problem is that the box (or channel) represented by the global variable n is shared among all active instances of *quicksort*, some of which may try to increment it nearly at the same time on the basis of having read the same actual value. Thus, all but one of these updates are in fact lost.

Since in this particular case the sequencing of updates is irrelevant due to the associative property of addition, the problem can be easily rectified by turning the global variable n into a critical region, under which accesses are granted to several competing update operations in a mutually exclusive manner. In other cases, however, the order of inspecting and updating a shared variable may be relevant and thus must be strictly enforced.

It is generally impossible for a compiler to decide by a static semantic analysis of a high-level imperative program whether two procedure calls that share a global variable can be executed truly concurrently, whether this variable must be embedded in a critical region to do so, or whether both procedure calls must be executed strictly in a pre-specified order to ensure the determinacy of results. Abstract interpretation may help to arrive at fairly good approximations, but this method is inherently of an exponentially growing complexity and thus not very practical. Instead, the programmer is asked to make these decisions as an integral part of planning the organizational details of non-sequential program execution. To do so, imperative languages must be enriched by constructs which are to specify explicitly

- how a program may be statically or dynamically partitioned for concurrent processing;

- the flow of data and control in and out of concurrently executable program parts in order to protect them against unintended side effects;

- the orderly interaction among these parts, e.g., via global variables or by the direct passage of control signals or messages.

These additional organizational measures clearly are an inescapable consequence of using imperative programming concepts in the first place, not just a nice programming feature. They are absolutely necessary to properly control the effects of updating shared variables by concurrent operations. The programmer is thus forced to assume full responsibility not only for the correct algorithmic specification of an application problem but also for the correct implementation of a complete work schedule for concurrent processing. However, simply declaring two procedure calls concurrently executable or declaring a shared variable a critical region is by no means a guarantee that the program indeed behaves deterministically at run-time, and even less so that it is semantically correct. If it includes cyclic patterns of interaction, it may even deadlock.

When taking these aspects into consideration, the merits of concurrent processing based on imperative program specifications become rather arguable. While the speed of program execution may be substantially increased, the difficulties of establishing program correctness and liveness either by verification or, less ambitiously, by validation grow enormously. Nothing is, however, gained by executing programs with utmost speed but almost no confidence in the results they produce.

There are basically two concepts of introducing into imperative programs specifications that relate to concurrent processing.

In languages such as MODULA-2 and ADA [Wir76, Wir85, Geh84]. selected program segments (subroutines) may be explicitly declared concurrently executable modules or tasks which form the constituents of a more or less static process structure. These modules may communicate among each other by exchanging messages or by sharing in an orderly form global variables. Process synchronization is accomplished either by a so-called rendezvous-technique which controls the exchange of messages with a synchronic distance of one, or by transmitting special synchronization signals.

The most difficult semantic problem with modules arises from assignments to globally shared variables. They may cause a non-deterministic run-time behavior whose consequences are hardly comprehensible, particularly in the context of large programs where they may cause far-reaching effects.

Semantic models for these languages describe, in one way or another, the state transitions carried out by the underlying machinery. Correctness proofs must therefore consider every possible execution sequence among concurrent modules in order to determine whether or not shared variables are always correctly instantiated. Thus, proofs even for simple programs become extremely complex, and propositions about correctness and liveness are often only of a more or less speculative nature.

Processing module-based programs concurrently is a rather straightforward affair, which may explain the widespread acceptance of the respective languages. At runtime, a process is created for each module (or task) which can be allocated to any of possibly several processing units within the system. Process communication is realized by means of dedicated library functions of the respective languages.

Another established concept of concurrent programming in a procedural world is based on formal process calculi such as Milner's calculus of communicating systems (or CCS for short) [Miln80] and Hoare's calculus of communicating sequential processes (or CSP) [BrHoRo84, Hoa85]. Both use a variety of process operators and communication/synchronization primitives to define the communication structures of process systems. In contrast to process modules, the sharing of global variables among processes is outlawed. Processes are allowed to interact only by exchanging messages via special communication channels which establish synchronic distances of just one (i.e., a very tight coupling) between senders and receivers. Larger synchronic distances must be realized as special buffer processes. Non-deterministic operations, e.g., those on semaphore variables, may be specified by means of guarded commands. Programming languages that originate from these concepts are CSP, DP (distributed processes) and, most prominently, OCCAM – the language invented for transputers [May83, MaShKe86].

Semantic models for these languages are based on process algebras which use terms of the underlying calculi to define and formally reason about communicating processes. They include, besides more traditional operational and axiomatic approaches, trace models and synchronization graphs [Miln80, Old86] which abstract from the details of process-internal operations. Nevertheless, correctness proofs remain complex and difficult. Part of the problem with these models seems to be that they more or less reflect the position of an observer in that they do not distinguish between concurrency and choice. Different occurrences (or serializations) of concurrent operations are treated as alternative process traces, i.e. as non-determinism, and thus thrown into the same bin as traces emerging from the resolution of conflicts. However, in chapter 3 we learned that truly concurrent transactions always transform the state (constellation) under which they are enabled to take place into the same successor state, irrespective of the order in which they occur, i.e., they are completely deterministic and could therefore be folded into one trace.

A viable alternative therefore appear to be semantic models based on various forms of Petri-nets. They completely abstract from the position of an observer, clearly distinguish between concurrency and choice, are intuitively comprehensible due to their graphical representation, and also provide the algebraic apparatus that is necessary to formally reason about the stability and orderly behavior of system (e.g., the absence of deadlocks and chaos) in terms of well-defined invariance properties. However, little use has sofar been made of the analytical methods provided by the net theory. Decidedly more advanced are interactive graphical specification methods based on nets. They use composite operators written in a procedural or functional language as specifications of atomic processes, and define the communication channels among them by means of Petri-net graphs. An example of a rather sophisticated interactive design system which supports these features is DESIGN/CPN [Jen90, PiSh91]. It uses ML to specify process nodes and coloured Petri-nets to model the communication channels. However, the system is not yet supplemented by appropriate analytical tools, as one would wish.

14 Summary

At the end of chapter 4 we gave a rough classification of reduction, data flow, and control flow as basic models for the organization of deterministic computations. It was based on little more than the underlying operational and control disciplines.

Having had a close look at typical architectures and implementations, we are now ready to add to this classification a little more structure and another perspective. We do so by applying as a structuring principle some relevant semantic properties of the underlying language concepts. They relate to the basic issues of a functional versus an imperative paradigm, of high-level interpretation versus executing compiled code, of untyped versus typed languages, and of evaluation orders. Using as a primary ordering criterion what may be considered conceptual distance to a full-fledged λ-calculus, we thus obtain the diagram shown in fig. 14.1.

In this rhombus-shaped structure, the three interpreting reduction engines described in chapters 6 through 9 assume the topmost positions, forming a smaller triangle among themselves. All of them realize the reduction semantics of an applied untyped λ-calculus, at least with respect to their appearances at the user interface. They perform high-level program transformations governed by full β-reductions. Intermediate programs as well as normal forms can be made visible to the user in the same high-level representation in which the initial program was specified. Functions are truly treated as first class objects: they may be applied without restrictions to other functions or to themselves, and new functions may be returned as the results of (partial) function applications. Naming conflicts among free and bound variable occurrences are correctly resolved, and programs may also contain globally free variables, thus meeting some essential requirements for simple symbolic computations.

The string reduction engine, though inherently inefficient due to the $O(n^2)$ complexity problem, is placed slightly on top among equals. It performs at run-time full β-reductions based on textual substitutions, and it does so both in applicative and normal order. The kernel engine consists of a shunting yard made up from three stacks about which program strings are traversed in search for instances of reductions.

Both interpreting graph reducers emulate textual transformations largely by graph pointer manipulations. Since pointer substitutions are in fact naive, special measures must be taken to cope with potential naming conflicts.

The eager graph reducer resorts to supercombinator reductions at run-time so that nearly all substitutions of formal by actual parameters can be performed naively. It employs full-fledged β-reductions only on partial supercombinator applications left over after all other reductions are done. When converting these applications

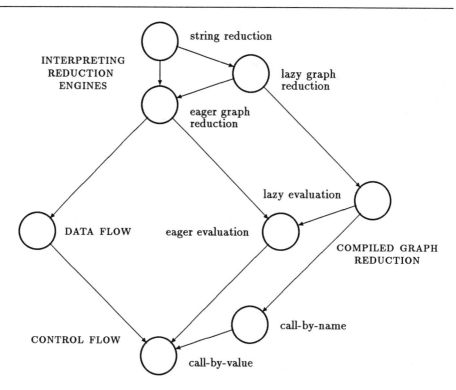

Figure 14.1: A classification of the computational models by programming concepts and their semantic properties

into new functions, naming conflicts may have to be resolved between free variable occurrences in argument terms and the remaining formal function parameters.

The kernel of the eager graph reducer, in addition to the shunting yard inherited from the string reduction engine, includes a run-time stack for the argument (pointer) frames of instantiated supercombinators.

The applicative order reduction regime demands that functions be applied to argument terms that are in normal form. The respective graphs can be conveniently shared among pointer occurrences replicated in the course of supercombinator reductions: they may only be copied or deleted but never be modified (overwritten). Thus, eager graph reduction is fairly easy to implement, lending itself particularly well to non-sequential processing since the subgraphs that may have to be shared among concurrent activities are constant. However, there is a subclass of programs which have normal forms but never reach them when reduced in applicative order.

The lazy graph reducer is bound to produce normal forms if they at all exist, and it generally does so with the least number of reductions, provided the programs do not contain redundantly specified subterms. Applications of λ-abstractions are reduced by full β-reductions-in-the-large. They are realized as delayed substitutions of pointers to argument graphs which generally are not in normal form. Actually substituting the graph pointers into abstraction bodies and subsequently reducing the graphs to canonical forms is postponed until it becomes absolutely necessary to do so. The reductions are shared among all pointer occurrences directed at the graphs. Lazy β-reductions-in-the-large require a fairly sophisticated run-time support which often degrades the performance below that of eager graph reduction.

There are also considerable coordination problems when performing lazy graph reductions concurrently. Unevaluated graphs that are shared among several processes should be protected against multiple attempts to reduce them, and the processes that are actually given the permission to do so must signal their completion to all other processes sharing these graphs.

The lazy evaluation regime supports an intriguing style of programming finite problems with infinite structures. For these semantic features it is rated in our diagram a little higher than the eager regime.

One level down, along the horizontal axis of our rhombus, we find the system architectures (or abstract machines) which execute, in one form or another, compiled versions of functional programs. This approach is based on the supposition that the acceptance of the functional programming paradigm primarily depends on a competitive speed of program execution, and that this can only be had when riding on the wave of steadily advancing conventional processor technology.

In following this line of reasoning, the idea of supporting the reduction semantics of a full-fledged λ-calculus must be generally abandoned for the following reasons: Compiling defined functions to executable code[58] means that they become static objects cleanly separated from the changeable program parts. Thus, while functions may still be applied to other functions (by passing the pointers to the respective code sequences), there is no notion of really computing new functions. Moreover, compilation to efficient code requires that all programs be well-typed. Though typing is emphatically praised as a means to introduce more formal rigor into program design and hence more confidence into program correctness, it must also be recognized that it forecloses self-applications, the use of certain higher-order functions in different contexts and, last not least, programs with globally free variables and thus truly symbolic computations. Evaluating partial applications is ruled out since

---

[58]Before compilation the functions are usually converted into (super-) combinators to facilitate the construction of and references to the environments (or contexts) in which they must be executed.

static function code must be supplied with full sets of (correctly typed) arguments in order to execute correctly. Whereas partial applications can be internally represented in the form of closures, there is no direct way of returning them in evaluated form to the user. Thus, higher-order functions cannot be fully supported. What can be produced as intelligible output are merely (sequences or structures of) elementary data values.

High-level program transformations as prescribed by a reduction semantics cannot be made visible to the user either. Intermediate states of code execution are usually distributed over several structures of the run-time environment, rendering it difficult to relate them to identifiable reduction steps, particularly if reductions are nested inside other reductions and the code has undergone optimizations. The same is true for data tokens distributed over the code representations of data flow graphs. Code must generally run to completion in order to produce meaningful results.

With most of the semantic properties of a full-fledged λ-calculus traded in for raw run-time performance, all there is left that distinguishes the functional from the imperative programming paradigm is the Church-Rosser property.

Data flow graphs exploit the Church-Rosser property at the level of primitive operations on atomic operands. All operators remain partially ordered as specified in the high-level program text. The activation of operators is solely controlled by the availability of operands, and all activated operators may occur in any order.

The tagged token model which we extensively studied in chapter 12 is the most general of the data flow execution models. It fully supports mutual recursions, including explicit iterations, and utilizes problem-inherent concurrency most extensively. Tokens belonging to different function (or loop) instances are distinguished by tags which uniquely identify the contexts in which the function (loop) bodies must be executed. A particular operator instance is activated by a set of operand tokens with identical tags.

In exploiting fine-grain concurrency, the tagged token model even permits computations to penetrate to some extent incompletely instantiated functions and iteration loops. Likewise, primitive value-transforming and structuring operations may be performed on (elements of) incompletely instantiated arrays. This is made possible by individualized link operators which pass actual for formal function (loop) parameters, and by the concept of I-arrays which separates the existence of an array as a structured object from its instantiation with valid elements (or entries).

Since data flow has no notion of sequencing operations in a particular order, it requires fairly sophisticated non-standard machinery to synchronize operands with operators, and to hide behind useful computations the rather substantial synchronization overhead inflicted by the fine-grain concurrency. In this respect data flow contrasts considerably with the compilation concepts supported by the abstract functional machines on the opposite side of the rhombus. The idea here is to compile functional programs to code for conventional control flow machines, i.e., the underlying execution models are essentially sequential.

Compiled code for high-level functional programs typically comprises a **top-level routine** which computes the outermost goal expression, and several **subroutines** which compute applications of the defined functions. All subroutines are individually code-optimized to make efficient use of the particular target machine.

Compilation to non-sequentially executable code is not substantially different. In order to take full advantage of subroutines as natural units of optimized code, program-inherent concurrency is utilized only at the level of defined function applications. In comparison to the fine-grain concurrency of data flow, this approach produces a decidedly lower synchronization overhead, and it also permits the implementation of organizational measures which prevent the explosion of computations in space (see chapters 7 and 10).

Compiled graph reduction as exemplified by the *G*-machine described in section 11.1 has become more or less a standard for the efficient execution of functional languages with a **lazy semantics**. The *G*-compiler accepts as input programs composed of flat sets of functions converted into supercombinators. It returns as output optimized supercombinator code which systematically constructs and transforms program graphs. These graph manipulations are effected by EVAL instructions which are included into the code wherever the canonical forms of subterms must be computed. The entire program code in fact specifies a composite program-specific reduction rule which **in one conceptual step** computes the program's canonical form, and in several subsequent reduction steps, under the control of PRINT instructions, its normal form.

The *SKI* reduction machine described in section 11.2 realizes another concept of compiled graph reduction. Functional programs are here compiled to *SKI* combinator terms whose graph representations are transformed in essentially the same way as in the *G*-machine. However, there is a significant difference insofar as this machine supports a full combinator reduction semantics. The combinators define atomic term transformations which in contrast to those effected by compiled supercombinators are not recursively nested in each other. Each combinator application returns a complete program graph with no status information left anywhere else in the run-time environment (e.g., on a dump). In this respect, the *SKI* reduction machine closely resembles the lazy interpreting graph reducer. Unfortunately, the combinator reduction semantics is too low-level to be of much use from a pragmatic point of view. Combinator terms of only moderate size are hardly intelligible, and with all bound variables irretrievably gone, a re-conversion of partially reduced combinator terms into high-level programs is not possible either. Further difficulties arise due to the fine grain of *SKI* combinator reductions: since it generally takes several of them to accomplish the equivalent of a single β-reduction, partially reduced combinator terms in most cases do not correspond one-to-one to intermediate high-level programs as they can be obtained when applying the reduction rules of an applied λ-calculus. Intelligible output can again only be produced in the form of data values or sequences thereof. Thus, the limitations from which the G-machine suffers for conceptual reasons are essentially the same as those from which the SKI reduction machine suffers for practical reasons.

Abstract machines for compiled versions of functional programs with an eager semantics, other than operating directly on elementary or structured data values rather than on unevaluated graphs, do not differ too much from their lazy counterparts. They both feature run-time environments which are more or less direct descendants of the $SECD$ machine. Their common basis, in addition to the program code, typically includes a stack for argument and local work space frames and a dump for machine states, usually reduced to a stack for subroutine return addresses.

Down to and including the horizontal axis of the rhombus, we thus have machinery which realizes a functional programming paradigm based on (if not directly realizing) the λ-calculus or a combinatory calculus. It is completely liberated from all elements pertaining to program execution, merely requiring the specification of abstract algorithms in the form of recursive function equations and function applications. Plans (or schedules) for their execution are either dynamically deduced at run-time by high-level interpretation or (at least to some extent) worked out by a compiler. The Church-Rosser property guarantees the determinacy of results irrespective of execution orders, rendering non-sequential program execution an almost trivial issue both conceptually and also from an organizational point of view. This is due to the principle of context-free and meaning-preserving substitutions, which entails an operational discipline governed by the orderly consumption and replication of (graph pointers to) operand objects by operator occurrences.

When moving to the bottom of the rhombus, we cross the line between the functional and the imperative (or procedural) world.

There we have the architectures (or abstract machines) which realize the conventional control flow model of computations. It is characterized by an operational discipline with an explicit notion of side effects, which necessitates a control discipline based on the orderly consumption and replication of control tokens to force the occurrence of operators in a particular order. The underlying idea is to share in sequence the same channels, implemented as memory locations, to pass several operand objects, represented as actual contents of these locations, among different subsets of operators. Different instantiations of these channels must therefore be distinguished by unique states of control in order to maintain the determinacy of results. The safest way of achieving these ends is to execute all operators strictly in sequence, i.e., along a single control flow thread. When sharing without restrictions channels among operators that belong to concurrently executable control flow threads, the Church-Rosser property cannot be guaranteed since these operators may then occur in any order.

The ensuing imperative programming paradigm is based on a state transition semantics whose formal properties are hard to understand. Having lost the Church-Rosser property, only rudimentary elements of a typed λ-calculus are left over, e.g., static scoping rules for identifiers of channels (memory locations).

Even high-level imperative programs, though abstracting to a considerable extent from the particularities of the underlying machinery, are sophisticated work schedules in which algorithmic and procedural aspects are closely intertwined. They prescribe sequences of incremental state transformations, realized as primitive copy-and-update operations on selected memory locations (the channels), which add up to global state changes. The results of computations are taken from the memory contents that represent the terminal states or specific intermediate states. It is solely the responsibility of the programmer to make sure that the right things are in the right places (memory locations) at the right time (states of control).

Control flow system architectures usually provide only a very basic substrate for the manipulation of formatted bit strings. It includes a set of primitive value-transforming and control instructions, a variety of addressing modes, and a hard-wired control mechanism for the traversal of instruction sequences which is realized by means of a program counter. The bit strings usually have no meaningful interpretations of their own. If they are referenced by the program counter, they are taken as instructions whose formats and interpretations are deduced from what is found in the respective operator code fields. Value-transforming instructions interpret the bit strings in their operand locations as type-compatible values, and control instructions take the contents of their operand locations as instruction addresses. Addressing modes are tailored to the needs of creating, linking and accessing the data structures (activation records) of a run-time environment and of transferring control within the instructing sequence.

Classifying abstract machines (or system architectures) in terms of their 'distances' to the direct realization of a full-fledged λ-calculus emphasizes their intimate relationships to basic language concepts. The particular order depicted in fig. 14.1 reflects the perspective of a programmer who is primarily interested in the machine support for an elegant and concise programming style based on a comprehensible semantics, rather than on raw run-time performance. Interestingly enough, the arrows in this diagram do not only point in the direction of decreasing expressive power and semantic simplicity, but also in the direction of increasing speed of program execution (though not necessarily proportional to the lengths of the arrows). High-level interpretation of untyped languages generally performs decidedly poorer than executing compiled code for typed languages, and functional languages, due to their abstraction from organizational details of program execution, are generally less efficient to implement than their imperative counterparts. Run-time performance crucially depends on the extent to which complete and near-optimal work schedules can be (or are being) statically inferred from high-level program specifications. This is primarily a matter of typing and of having at least critical parts of the schedules fixed by the programmer.

Our classification gives a somewhat idealized picture insofar as a clean separation of the functional from the imperative (or state transition) world is not what we find in reality, at least not outside the research community, and it may not even be desirable for a variety of pragmatic reasons. The conceptual flavors of purely functional languages and systems which derive from the simple semantics of the underlying formal calculi are widely considered a mixed blessing. Inferior run-time performance per sé may be one of the reasons for lacking acceptance, but it certainly does not in itself constitute the major obstacle. In fact, the performance deficits of compiled functional (or function-based) languages with an applicative order semantics (e.g., HOPE or SML) have become almost negligible for a many applications.

However, what really seems to matter, despite the supposedly higher expressive power of functional languages, is the absence of any notion of a state (or of a memory). Notwithstanding the ensuing semantic problems that are due to side effects, particularly the loss of the Church-Rosser property, the concept of updatable box variables undeniably is a considerable asset when it comes to writing in a reasonably concise and efficiently executable form complex application programs. Interacting with a state is often more straightforward and more efficient both in space and time consumption. This is particularly the case with operations on large data structures which make up the bulk of computational work in all serious applications. There is no doubt that it is much easier to just update a few elements whose values are no longer needed, rather than explicitly disassembling the entire structures to remove these elements, and subsequently to compose new structures from the remaining parts of the old structures and from the new elements, as a purely functional programming style would require.

Including into an otherwise functional (or at least function-based) language a notion of variables that are bound to a state definitely is one of the key factors in the continuing wide-spread success of *LISP*, a language that is primarily designed for the needs of non-numerical (or symbolic) computations. It is the major language used in artificial intelligence, but also in prototyping and experimenting with other languages, their compilers and run-time environments. Its appeal for the latter derives in large part from its list-manipulating capabilities and from the fact that *LISP* can be conveniently used to define its own operational semantics as well as that of other languages.

LISP is essentially based on an untyped applied λ-calculus with an applicative order semantics. Its kernel includes the constructs that can be typically found in all purely functional languages, e.g., in HLFL . However, variables may also be subject to assignments in a conventional sense. As with implementations of purely functional languages, *LISP* can be interpreted in a stepwise manner by program transformation similar to those prescribed by a reduction semantics, or compiled to code for one-shot execution.

Older versions such as *LISP 1.5* [McC62] realize a dynamic scoping rule. This is due to the implementation of function calls by means of a so-called **association list** of name/value pairs, from which always the latest entry for a particular variable is taken as its valid instantiation. Variable substitutions are thus carried out naively, i.e., binding levels may change when substituting free variables into the scopes of other binders. Strangely enough, this rather irritating feature has been (and still is) of considerable appeal to experienced *LISP* programmers. However, more recent *LISP* variants such as *CommonLISP* [Ste82, Ste84] and *SCHEME* [Dyb87] are **statically scoped**.

The imperative (or state transition) part of *LISP* enters the game through **global variables** and through so-called **program variables** or **special variables**, both of which represent values that can be changed by the program. Other operations with side effects change in-place the components of *S*-expressions, the basic constructs of *LISP* programs. Deterministic results can therefore only be guaranteed by a strictly sequential execution order. *LISP* must therefore be considered an **imperative language** based on a **control flow model** of computation, even though it incorporates a concept of functions and function applications similar to that of the λ-calculus. However, as an untyped language which primarily requires the manipulation of graph structures, it cannot be expected to run efficiently on conventional control flow machinery. With no hardware support to this effect available, the type checks that need to be carried out at run-time in order to determine the correct instantiations of the primitive built-in functions (many of which are overloaded) and the dynamic management of heap space for graph structures must be included into the interpreting or compiled code, which inevitably slows down program execution.

These deficiencies, together with the potential of *LISP* for symbolic computations, stimulated the design of special *LISP* machine architectures of which some even led to commercial products which at least for some time were quite successful in the market place. They include the *LMI Lambda LISP* machine [Smi84], the *Symbolics 3600* [Sym84, Moon85], and the *Compact LISP* machine of Texas Instruments [MaHeKr87], which are descendants of the *CONS* and *CADR* machines developed at MIT [Gre84]. They were designed as workstations with complete *LISP* implementations for operating systems, compilers, interpreters and other utilities, and, of course, with *LISP* as the dominating language used for application programming. What distinguishes them from conventional machines basically is extensive hardware and micro-program support for time-critical operations such as tag-based type-checking, dynamic memory space management (primarily heap space allocation and garbage collection), special buffer areas for the topmost frames of the run-time environment, and *LISP*-specific instruction sets tailored to the needs of efficient list manipulations.

However, with the availability of fairly efficient *LISP* implementations on UNIX-based RISC workstations which fully exploit advanced micro-processor and compiler technology, the demand for tailor-made *LISP* machines seems to have faded away. The machines mentioned above have fallen behind in the continuing technological and commercial race for more processor speed, the SPUR RISC processor (a type-tagged architecture designed with support for languages like *LISP*, SMALLTALK and PROLOG in mind) [Hill86, TaHi86] has become a highly successful product in SUN's SPARC workstations, and – what is even more important from a user's point of view – the amenities of a UNIX environment with its wide variety of other programming languages, utilities, system services and application programs seem to be more attractive than a *LISP*-centered environment. Moreover, a careful performance analysis based on a mix of *PSL* (portable standard *LISP*) programs on a MIPS_X RISC processor simulator showed that, contrary to what one would expect, the speed-ups due to hardware-supported type-checking versus doing as much of it as is possible by the compiler and by including the remaining type checks into the compiled code are just somewhere between 10% and 22%. Also, advanced garbage collection schemes based on life-time scavenging (see section 9.4) create only a marginal overhead when implemented as code. Thus, designing and continuously upgrading with the latest technology dedicated *LISP* machinery can hardly be justified [StHe87].

All of this seems to spell bad news for functional systems and for tailor-made hardware machinery supporting them. A purely functional programming paradigm seems to have no chances of survival on its own since a state transition environment apparently is indispensable, dedicated functional machinery is likely to suffer sooner or later the same fate as *LISP* machines, and on top of that there is a considerable acceptance problem from a very pragmatic and economical point of view. Huge investments have been made in the past to develop complex system software and voluminous program libraries for various application areas, using imperative programming languages (including *LISP*). There is no reason to assume that these often sophisticated and highly optimized programs can easily and as efficiently be re-implemented in a functional language (the functional programming style does not provide the best solution for all the problems), let alone that hardly anybody would be prepared to re-invest the manpower, time and other resources into such an endeavor.

The way out of this dilemma appears to be the fully symmetric coexistence and orderly interaction of purely functional and imperative subsystems within what may be called **hybrid computing systems**. Imperative subsystems (or program modules) must be capable of calling on functional subsystems (program modules), and vice versa.

The former case is the more common and also the simpler one. Calls for functional in imperative subsystems may occur at several levels, e.g., when invoking the execution of a functional program by the operating system, or when evaluating in imperative programs function applications. Calling functions in imperative subsystems does not change the semantic properties of the latter: the functional part remains purely functional, whereas the combined system realizes a state transition semantics. Both subsystems are therefore fully compatible in this particular caller-callee relationship.

However, things are quite different when calling an imperative in a functional subsystem. In order to preserve the functional semantics of the latter (which is essentially the Church-Rosser property) all side-effects must remain encapsulated in the former. The imperative subsystem must not change global variables nor must it pass on internal states from one function call to the next, or share it with other imperative subsystems.

Called subsystems of either kind must be treated as primitives of the respective calling subsystems, in which they are represented by names (identifiers). Their arguments are program terms of the calling subsystems (or languages) which must be converted to data that can be interpreted by the called subsystems. Conversely, the called subsystems return data which must be re-converted to terms of the calling subsystems.

A particularly interesting aspect of integrating in this orderly form imperative into functional subsystems is to exercise control over non-sequential computations which are largely specified in imperative form, say as *LISP* or FORTRAN program modules. Rather than trying to 'parallelize' these imperative programs with considerable effort but dubious results, it may often be more convenient and economical to have a simple functional program generate several concurrently executable instances of one or several modules written in an imperative language and to have it assemble the partial results returned by these instances. With this hybrid programming technique, we can fully utilize the conceptual advantages of the divide-and-conquer scheme for the concurrent execution of purely functional programs as outlined in chapters 6 and 9. The functional programs serve more or less just as control structures which guide the system in recursively partitioning, scheduling and balancing the workload, and they also guarantee the Church-Rosser property among concurrently executable parts. However, the bulk of the computational work can be specified in imperative form. This may not only avoid a great deal of re-programming but it can also be expected to yield a better run-time performance than corresponding functional programs.

Subsystems that realize abstract machines (or architectures) based on different models of computation, as we saw, are primarily distinguished by the implementation of the respective run-time environments. Tailor-made hardware machinery which efficiently supports specific architectural (or language) features as well as operations on the data structures that make up the environment may be highly desirable for performance reasons, but it is not really essential. All machine implementations, in spite of the seeming diversity of architectures, require some basic set of computationally complete value-transforming, structuring and control primitives, data structures such as stacks or heaps of argument (workspace) frames, queues, graphs and code sequences (either compiled or interpreting), and suitable addressing modes to traverse them or to access their elements randomly in memory. Control flow machinery which meets these basic needs reasonably well can be used to implement any of a variety of abstract machines (architectures) by emulation (micro-code), interpretation or compilation, though not in all cases with the best possible performance.

Supporting in a hybrid computing system several closely interacting subsystems based on different computational models is not primarily a problem of providing dedicated hardware machinery for each of them, but to map these subsystems onto the same machinery, and of switching quickly between the respective operation modes and run-time environments.

Supplementary Reading

Since this monograph primarily deals with functional programming and its impact on computer organization/architecture, we will here briefly review some supplementary textbooks and survey papers which relate to this subject and may or may not have been quoted throughout this monograph. They may be consulted on topics that are somewhat outside our scope of interest and therefore not treated in full detail.

There are basically two standard texts on the theory of the λ-calculus and on combinatory logic, Barendregt's *The Lambda Calculus, Its Syntax and Semantics* [Bar81], and Hindley/Seldin's *Introduction to Combinators and the λ-Calculus* [HiSe86]. A somewhat older text are the two volumes on *Combinatory Logic* by Curry, Feys, Hindley and Seldin [CuFe58, CuHiSe72]. As another theory, Backus introduces in his Turing Award Lecture FFP [Back78], a formal system for variable-free functional programming which is based on a fixed set of combining forms. For its engaged discussion of the conceptual shortcomings of the imperative programming style, this paper is also a highly recommendable reading to everyone interested in language concepts and their relationship to the underlying machinery.

Functional programming concepts are the subject of an early book by Burge on *Recursive Programming Techniques* [Bur75]. It introduces a sugared version of an applied λ-calculus as a programming language, and describes implementation techniques based on Landin's SECD machine. Another excellent introduction to the functional programming style is Henderson's textbook on *Functional Programming: Application and Implementation* [Hend80]. It centers around a purely functional variant of *LISP* called *LispKit* which serves as an intermediate target for the compilation of high-level languages. Implementing *LispKit* is based on compilation to code which executes in an SECD machine environment. Both texts advocate advanced programming with streams and delayed (lazy) evaluation techniques.

A fairly complete state-of-the-art survey as of about 1980 on functional (or function-based) programming languages, architectures and applications can be found in course material published in [DaHeTu82].

More recent books include those by Henson on *Elements of Functional Languages* [Hens87] and by Field and Harrison on *Functional Programming* [FiHa88]. The former is of a more theoretical nature, emphasizing program transformation and verification. It uses MIRANDA as a primary language, but also contains a chapter which outlines programming with Backus' FFP. The latter briefly addresses functional programming techniques supported by HOPE, but otherwise focuses mainly on implementation issues such as interpretation, (super-) combinator-based graph reduction, compilation and optimization techniques.

A textbook well suited for undergraduate courses on functional programming is

Introduction to Functional Programming by Bird and Wadler [BiWa88]. It emphasizes the derivation of programs from mathematical specifications and the elegance
of programming with recursive functions and with lazy lists. The program notations
closely resemble those of MIRANDA. Very little is said about implementations. Another textbook that may be used as course material on functional or function-based
programming is *Structure and Interpretation of Computer Programs* by Abelson and
Sussman [AbSus85]. The language used in this text is *SCHEME*, a cleaned-up variant of *LISP* with static scoping and functions as first-class objects, but still with
assignments and quotes.

Peyton-Jones' book on *The Implementation of Functional Programming Languages* has become more or less a standard text on compiled graph reduction
[Peyt87]. It addresses in depth compilation and optimization techniques, includes
two chapters on polymorphic type checking (contributed by Hancock), and also
contains a comprehensive description of the *G*-machine.

Another excellent textbook is *The Architecture of Symbolic Computers* by Kogge
[Kog91] which covers both function-based and logic-based models of computation
and systems. The functional part focuses primarily on abstract programming and
on the (self-) interpretation of λ-terms, using *LISP*-like program representations
and run-time environments. It also contains an up-to-date survey on function-based
computing systems, including a complete account of *LISP* implementations. As for
the logic part, the book deserves credit for a concise introduction into the theory
of logic computations and, even more important, for a comprehensible description
of Warren's abstract *PROLOG* machine.

There are also a number of survey papers and collections of selected papers in
workshop or conference proceedings, or in special issues of regular periodicals that
are worthwile readings.

A fairly recent survey by Hudak on the state of the art in functional programming
can be found in [Hud89], a somewhat older collection of papers on graph reduction
systems is contained in [FaKe87]. In [Thak87] is another selection of papers on
reduction and data flow systems. Still older is a 1984 survey by Vegdahl of papers
describing architectures for functional languages [Veg84].

As of now, there is no comprehensive textbook on data flow systems. A special
issue of IEEE Computer, edited by Agerwala and Arvind [AgAr82], was devoted to
data flow systems in 1982, a tutorial by Dennis on data flow execution models can
be found in [Denn84], Arvind and Culler have surveyed data flow architectures in
[ArCu85], and Gurd, Kirkbaum and Watson give a fairly thorough description of
the Manchester data flow machine in [GuKiWa85]. A chapter on data flow systems
is also contained in [FiHa88]. Contributions on the recent state of research and on
future trends in this area are collected in workshop proceedings edited by Gaudiot
and Bic [GaBi91].

References

[AbSus85] Abelson, H.; Sussmann, G.J.: *Structure and Interpretation of Computer Programs*, MIT Press, McGraw-Hill, New York, NY, 1985

[AcDe79] Ackerman, W.B.; Dennis, J.B.: *VAL – A Value-Oriented Algorithmic Language : Preliminary Reference Manual*, Technical Report TR-218, MIT, Cambridge, MA, June 1979

[Ack82] Ackermann, W.B.: *Data Flow Languages*, IEEE Computer, Vol. 15, No. 2, 1982, pp. 15–25

[AgAr82] Agerwala, T.; Arvind (Eds.): *Data Flow Systems*, IEEE Computer, Vol. 15, No. 2, 1982,

[AN66] *American National Standard FORTRAN*, American National Standard Institute, ANSI X3.9, 1966

[AmHa84] Amamiya, M.; Hasegawa, R.: *Dataflow Computing and Eager and Lazy Evaluation*, New Generation Computing 2, 1984, pp. 105–129

[AmHaOn84] Amamiya, M.; Hasegawa, R.; Ono S.: *Valid – A High-Level Functional Programming Language for Data Flow Machines*, Review of the Electrical Communication Laboratories, Vol. 32, No. 5, 1984

[Ama88] Amamiya, M.: *Data Flow Computing and Parallel Reduction Machine*, Future Generation Computer Systems 4, 1988, pp. 53–67

[AmBl64] Amdahl, G.M.; Blaauw, G.A. et al.: *Architecture of the IBM System /360*, IBM Journal of Research and Development, Vol. 8, No. 2, 1964, pp. 87–101

[AnSc83] Andrews, G.R.; Schneider, F.B.: *Concepts and Notations for Concurrent Programming*, ACM Computing Surveys, Vol. 15, No. 1, 1983, pp. 3–43

[And91] Andrews, G.R.: *Concurrent Programming : Principles and Practices*, The Benjamin/Cummings Publishing Company Inc., Redwood City, CA, 1991

[ArGoPl78] Arvind; Gostelow, K.P.; Plouffe, W.: *The ID-Report : An Asynchronous Programming Language and Computing Machine*, University of California at Irvine, Technical Report 114, December 8, 1978

[ArTh80] Arvind; Thomas, R.E.: *I-Structures : An Efficient Data Type for Functional Languages*, MIT Laboratory of Computer Science, Technical Report No. 178, 1980

[ArIa85] Arvind, Ianucci, R.A.: *Two Fundamental Issues in Multiprocessing : The Dataflow Solution*, Proceedings of the DFVLR Conference on Parallel Processing in Science and Engineering, Bonn-Bad Godesberg, Lecture Notes in Computer Science, No. 295, Springer, 1987, pp. 61–88

[ArCu85] Arvind; Culler, D.E.: *Dataflow Architectures*, Annual Review of Computer Science, Vol. 1, 1986, pp. 225–254

[ArNi87] Arvind; Nikhil, R.S.: *Executing a Program on the MIT Tagged-Token Dataflow Architecture*, Proceedings of the Conference on Parallel Architecture and Languages Europe (PARLE), Eindhoven, Vol. II, Lecture Notes in Computer Science, No. 259, Springer, 1987, pp. 1–29

[ArCuMa] Arvind; Culler, D.E.; Maa, G.K.: *Assessing the Benefits of Fine-Grain Parallelism in Dataflow Programs*, The International Journal of Supercomputer Applications, Vol. 2, No. 3, 1988, pp.

[Aug84] Augustsson, L.: *A Compiler for Lazy ML*, Proceedings of the ACM Conference on LISP and Functional Programming, Austin, Texas, August 1984, pp. 218–227

[AuJo89] Augustsson, L.; Johnsson, T.: *Parallel Graphreduction with the $\langle \nu, G \rangle$-Machine*, Proceedings of the Conference on Functional Programming and Computer Architecture, London, 1989, pp. 202–213

[Babb88] Babb, R.G.: *Programming Parallel Processors*, Addison-Wesley, Reading, MA, 1988

[Bach86] Bach, M.J.: *The Design of the Unix Operating System*, Prentice Hall International Editions, Englewood Cliffs, NJ, 1986

[Back72] Backus, J.: *Reduction Languages and Variable-Free Programming*, IBM Research Report RJ 1010, 1973

[Back73] Backus, J.: *Programming Language Semantics and Closed Applicative Languages*, Proceedings of the ACM Symposium on Principles of Programming Languages, Boston, MA, 1973, pp. 71–86

[Back78] Backus, J.: *Can Programming Be Liberated from the von Neumann Style? A Functional Style and Its Algebra of Programs*, Communications of the ACM, Vol. 21, No. 8, 1978, pp. 613–641

[Baer80] Baer, J.-L.: *Computer Systems Architecture*, Computer Science Press, Digital System Design Series, Rockville, ML, 1980

[Bak78] Baker, H.; *List Processing in Real Time on a Serial Computer*, Communications of the ACM, Vol. 21, No. 4, 1978, pp. 280–294

[Bar81] Barendregt, H.P.: *The Lambda Calculus, Its Syntax and Semantics*, North-Holland, Studies in Logic and the Foundations of Mathematics, Vol. 103, 1981

[Ben90] Ben-Ari, M.: *Principles of Concurrent and Distributed Programming*, Prentice Hall, Englewood Cliffs, NJ, 1990

[Berk75] Berkling, K.J.: *Reduction Languages for Reduction Machines*, Proceedings of the 2nd Annual Symposium on Computer Architecture, 1975, ACM/IEEE 75CH0916-7C, pp. 133–140

[Berk78] Berkling, K.J.: *Computer Architecture for Correct Programming*, Proceedings of the 5th Annual Symposium on Computer Architecture, 1978, ACM/IEEE, pp. 78–84

[BeFe82a] Berkling, K.J.; Fehr, E.: *A Modification of the Lambda-Calculus as a Base for Functional Programming Languages*, Proceedings of the 9th International Colloquium on Automata, Languages and Programming (ICALP 82), Aarhus, Denmark, Lecture Notes in Computer Science, No. 140, Springer, 1982, pp. 35–47

[BeFe82b] Berkling, K.J.; Fehr, E.: *A Consistent Extension of the Lambda-Calculus as a Base for Functional Programming Languages*, Information and Control, Academic Press, Vol. 55, Nos. 1–3, October/November/December 1982

[Berk86] Berkling, K.J.: *Headorder Reduction : A Graph Reduction Scheme for the Operational Lambda Calculus*, CASE Center, Syracuse University, Technical Report No. 8613, November 1986 and Lecture Notes in Computer Science, No. 279, Springer, 1986, pp. 26–48

[BiWa88] Bird, R.S; Wadler, P.L.: *Introduction to Functional Programming*, Prentice Hall, Englewood Cliffs, NJ, 1988

[BrReRo87] Brauer,W.; Reisig, W.; Rozenberg, G. (Eds.): *Petri Nets : Central Models and their Properties*, Lecture Notes in Computer Science, No. 254, Springer, 1987 and *Petri Nets : Applications and Relationships to Other Models of Concurrency*, Lecture Notes in Computer Science, No. 255, Springer, 1987

[Brin73] Brinch Hansen, P.: *Operating System Principles*, Prentice Hall Series in Automatic Computation, Englewood Cliffs, NJ, 1973

[Brin77] Brinch Hansen, P.: *The Architecture of Concurrent Programs*, Prentice Hall, Englewood Cliffs, NJ, 1977 and Communications of the ACM, Vol. 21, No. 11, 1978, pp. 934–941

[BrHoRo84] Brookes, S.D.; Hoare, C.A.R.; Roscoe, A.W.: *A Theory of Communicating Sequential Processes*, Journal of the ACM, Vol. 31, No. 7, 1984, pp. 560–599

[Bro85] Brownbridge, D.R.: *Cyclic Reference Counting for Combinator Machines*, Proceedings of the Conference on Functional Programming and Computer Architecture, Nancy, Lecture Notes in Computer Science, No. 201, Springer, 1985, pp. 237–288

[Bur75] Burge, W.H.: *Recursive Programming Techniques*, Addison-Wesley, Reading, MA, 1975

[BuGoNeu46] Burks, A.; Goldstone, H.H.; von Neumann, J.: *Preliminary Discussion of the Logical Design of an Electronic Computing Instrument*, Report on the Mathematical and Logical Aspects of an Eletronic Computing Instrument, Pt. I, Vol. I, The Institute for Advanced Study, ECP List of Reports, No. 1, 1946 – 1957

[BuMQSa80] Burstall, R.M.; MacQueen, D.; Sannella, D.T.: *HOPE : An Experimental Applicative Language*, CS Report CSR-62-80, University of Edinburgh, May 1980

[Card83] Cardelli, L.; MacQueen, D. (Eds.): *The Functional Abstract Machine*, Polymorphism, The ML/LCF/HOPE Newsletter, AT&T, Bell Laboratories, Murray Hill, NJ, 07974, USA, 1983

[Car75]   Carlson, C.R.: *A Survey of High-Level Language Computer Architectures*, in: Chu, Y.(Ed.): High-Level Language Computer Architecture, Academic Press, 1975

[ChMi88]   Chandy, K.M.; Misra, J.: *Parallel Program Design : A Foundation*, Addison-Wesley, Reading, MA, 1988

[Chur32]   Church, A.: *A Set of Postulates for the Foundation of Logic*, ANM, 33, 1932, pp. 346–366 and ANM, 34, 1933, pp. 839–864 (second paper)

[Chur36]   Church, A.: *A Note on the Entscheidungsproblem*, Journal of Symbolic Logic, Vol. 1, pp. 40–41, Correction, pp. 101–102

[ChRo36]   Church, A.; Rosser, J.B.: *Some Properties of Conversion*, Transactions of the American Mathematical Society, Vol. 39, 1936, pp. 472–482

[Chur41]   Church, A.: *The Calculi of Lambda Conversion*, Princeton University Press, 1941

[ClGl80]   Clarke, T.J.W.; Gladstone, P.J.S.; MacLean, C.D.; Norman, A.C.: *SKIM – the S,K,I Reduction Machine*, Proceedings of the LISP-80 Conference, Stanford, CA, August 1980

[CoDe83]   Coffman, E.G.; Denning, P.J.: *Operating Systems Theory*, Prentice Hall Series in Automatic Computation, Englewood Cliffs, NJ, 1983

[Col60]   Cohen, J.: *A Method of Overlapping and Erasure of Lists*, Communications of the ACM 3, No. 12, 1960, pp. 655–657

[Com84]   Comer, D.: *Operation System Design, the XINU Approach*, Prentice Hall Software Series, Englewood Cliffs, NJ, 1984

[CoCuMa87] Cousineau, G.; Curien, P.-L.; Mauny, M.: *The Categorical Abstract Machine*, Science of Computer Programming 8, 1987, pp. 173–202

[Cra80]   Cragon, H.G.: *A Case Against High-Level Language Computer Architecture*, Proceedings of the International Workshop on High-Level Language Computer Architecture, Fort Lauderdale, Fla, 1980, pp. 88–91

[Cur86]   Curien, P.-L.: *Categorical Combinators, Sequential Algorithms and Functional Programming*, John Wiley, New York, NY, 1986

[Curr29]   Curry, H.B.: *An Analysis of Logical Substitution*, American Journal of Mathematics, 51, 1929, pp. 363–384

[Curr34]   Curry, H.B.: *Functionality in Combinatory Logic*, Proceedings of the National Academy of Science of the United States of America, Vol. 20, 1934, pp. 584–590

[Curr36]   Curry, H.B.: *First Properties of Functionality in Combinatory Logic*, Tohoku Mathematical Journal 41, 1936, pp. 371–401

[CuFe58]   Curry, H.B.; Feys, R.: *Combinatory Logic, Vol. I*, North-Holland Studies in Logic and the Foundations of Mathematics, 1958

[CuHiSe72] Curry, H.B.; Hindley, J.R.; Seldin, J.P.: *Combinatory Logic, Vol. II*, North-Holland, 1972

[DaRe81] Darlington, J.; Reeve, M.: *ALICE a Multi-Processor Reduction Machine for the Parallel Evaluation of Applicative Languages*, Proceedings of the ACM Conference on LISP and Functional Programming, Wentworth-by-the-Sea, Portsmouth, New Hampshire, 1981, pp. 65–73

[DaHeTu82] Darlington, J.; Henderson, P.; Turner, D.A. (Eds.): *Functional Programming and Its Applications*, Cambridge University Press, Cambridge, 1982

[Dasgup89] Dasgupta, S.: *Computer Architecture : A Modern Synthesis, Vol. 2 Advanced Topics*, John Wiley, New York, NY, 1989

[Dav78] Davis, A.L.: *The Architecture and System Method of DDM1 : A Recursively Structured Data Driven Machine*, Proceedings of the 5th AnnualInternational Symposium on Computer Architecture, 1978, pp. 210–215

[Brui72] DeBruijn, N.G.: *Lambda-Calculus Notation with Nameless Dummies. A Tool for Automatic Formula Manipulation with Application to the Church-Rosser-Theorem*, Indagationes Mathematicae, Vol. 34, 1972, pp. 381–392

[Denn69] Dennis, J.B.: *Program Generality, Parallelism and Computer Architecture*, Information Processing , Vol. 68, 1969, pp. 484–492

[Denn74] Dennis, J.B.: *First Version of a Data Flow Procedure Language*, Symposium on Programming, Institue de Programmation, University of Paris, Paris 1974, pp. 241–271

[DeMi75] Dennis, J.B.; Misunas, D.P.: *A Preliminary Architecture for a Basic Data-Flow Processor*, Proceedings of the 2nd Annual International Symposium on Computer Architecture, IEEE, 1975, pp. 126–132

[Denn84] Dennis, J.B.: *Dataflow Computation*, in: Broy, M. (Ed.), Control Flow and Data Flow : Concepts of Distributed Programming, International Summer School, NATO ASI Series, Series F: Computer and System Sciences, Vol. 14, Springer, 1984, pp. 346–398

[Denn80] Dennis, J.B.: *Data Flow Supercomputers*, IEEE Computer, Vol. 13, No. 11, 1980, pp. 48–56

[Dyb87] Dybvig, R.K.: *The SCHEME Programming Language*, Prentice Hall, Englewood Cliffs, NJ, 1987

[FaWr88] Fairbairn, J.; Wray, S.C.: *TIM : A Simple, Lazy Abstract Machine to Execute Supercombinators*, Proceedings of the Conference on Functional Programming and Computer Architecture, Portland, Oregon, Lecture Notes in Computer Science, No. 274, Springer, 1987, pp. 34–45

[FiHa88] Field, A.J.; Harrison, P.G.: *Functional Programming*, Addison-Wesley, Reading, MA, 1988

[FaKe87] Fasel, J.H.; Keller, R.M. (Eds.): *Graph Reduction*, Lecture Notes in Computer Science, No. 279, Springer, 1986

[FrWi76] Friedman, D.P.; Wise, D.S.: *CONS Should Not Evaluate its Arguments*, in: Michaelson, S.; Milner, R.(Eds): Automata, Languages and Programming, Edinburgh University Press 1976, pp. 257–284

[GaBi91] Gaudiot, J.-L.; Bic, L. (Eds.): *Advanced Topics in Data-Flow Computing*, Prentice Hall, Englewood Cliffs, NJ, 1991

[Geh84] Gehani, N.H.: *Ada : Concurrent Programming*, Prentice Hall, Englewood Cliffs NJ, 1984

[GeLa78] Genrich, H.J.; Lautenbach, K.: *The Analysis of Distributed Systems by Means of Predicate/Transition-Nets*, in: Semantics of Concurrent Computation, Lecture Notes in Computer Science, No. 70, Springer, 1979, pp. 123–146

[GeSta80] Genrich, H.J.; Stankiewicz-Wiechno, E.: *A Dictionary of Some Basic Notions of Net Theory*, in: Net Theory and Applications, Lecture Notes in Computer Science, No. 84, Springer, 1980, pp. 519–535

[GeLaTh80] Genrich, H.J.; Lautenbach, K.; Thiagarajan, P.S.: *Elements of General Net Theory*, in: Net Theory and Applications, Lecture Notes in Computer Science, No. 84, Springer, 1980, pp. 21–163

[Gela81] Genrich, H.J.; Lautenbach, K.: *System Modelling with High-Level Petri-Nets*, Theoretical Computer Science 13, 1981, pp. 109–136

[Gen87] Genrich, H.J.: *Predicate Transition Nets*, in: Petri-Nets : Central Models and their Properties, Lecture Notes in Computer Science, No. 254, Springer, 1987, pp. 207–247

[GiGu82] Giloi, W.K.; Gueth, R.: *Concepts and Realization of a High-Performance Data Type Architecture*, International Journal of Computer and Information Science, Vol. 11, No. 1, 1982, pp. 25–54

[Gre84] Greenblatt, R.D.; Knight, T.F.; Holloway, J.; Moon, D.A.; Weinreb, D.L.: *The LISP Machine*, in: Interactive Programming Environments, McGraw-Hill, New York,1984, Chap. 16

[GrWo89] Greenberg, M.; Woods, V.: *The FLAGSHIP Parallel Reduction Machine*, Manchester University, FS/MU/MIG/005-89, 1989

[GuKiWa85] Gurd, J.R.; Kirkham, C.C.; Watson, I.: *The Manchester Prototype Dataflow Computer*, Communications of the ACM, Vol. 28, No. 1, 1985, pp. 34–52

[Harp85] Harper, R.: *Introduction to Standard ML*, Laboratory for Foundations of Computer Science, University of Edinburgh, January 1989

[HaMcQMi86] Harper, R.; MacQueen, D.; Milner, R.: *Standard ML*, Laboratory for Foundations of Computer Science, University of Edinburgh, March 1986

[HaMiTo88] Harper, R.; Milner, R.; Tofte, M.: *The Definition of Standard ML Version 3*, Laboratory for Foundations of Computer Science, University of Edinburgh, May 1989

[HaRe86] Harrison, P.G.; Reeve, M.: *The Parallel Graph Reduction Machine ALICE*, Proceedings of the Graph Reduction Workshop, Santa Fe, Lecture Notes in Computer Science, No. 279, Springer, 1986, pp. 181–202

[Hay78]   Hayes, J.P.: *Computer Architecture and Organization*, McGraw-Hill Computer Science Series, New York, NY, 1978

[Hell88] Heller, S.K.: *Efficient Lazy Data-Structures on a Dataflow Machine*, MIT Laboratory for Computer Science, Technical Report 438, 1988

[HeMo76] Henderson, P.; Morris, J.H.: *A Lazy Evaluator*, Proceedings of the Third ACM SIGACT-SIGPLAN Symposium on Principles of Programming Languages, Atlanta, Georgia, 1976, pp. 95–103

[Hend80] Henderson, P.: *Functional Programming : Application and Implementation*, Prentice Hall, Englewood Cliffs, NJ, 1980

[HeJoJo83] Henderson, P.; Jones, G.A.; Jones, S.B.: *The LISPkit Manual Vols. I and II*, Technical Monographs PRG-32/33, Oxford University Computing Labs, 1983

[Hen84]   Hennessy, J.L.: *VLSI Processor Architecture*, IEEE Transactions on Computers, Vol. C-33, No.12, 1984, pp. 1221–1245

[HePa90] Hennessy, J.L.; Patterson, D.A.: *Computer Architecture : A Quantitative Approach*, Kaufmann, 1990

[Hens87] Henson, M.C.: *Elements of Functional Languages*, Blackwell Scientific Publications, Oxford and London, 1987

[HiPe78] Hill, F.J.; Peterson, G.R.: *Digital Systems : Hardware Organization and Design*, John Wiley, New York, NY, 1978

[Hill86] Hill, M. et al.: *Design Decisions in SPUR*, IEEE Computer, Vol. 19, No. 11, 1986, pp. 8–22

[Hil87]   Hilton, M.L.: *An Architecture for Reducing the λ-Calculus*, CASE Center Technical Report No. 8715, Syracuse University, August 1987

[Hil90]   Hilton, M.L.: *Implementation of Declarative Languages*, CASE Center Technical Report No. 9008, Syracuse University, June 1990

[Hin69]   Hindley, J.R.: *The Principal Type-Scheme of an Object in Combinatory Logic*, Transactions of the American Mathematical Society, Vol. 146, 1969, pp. 29–60

[HiSe86] Hindley, J.R.; Seldin, J.P.: *Introduction to Combinators and λ-calculus*, Cambridge University Press, London Mathematical Society Student Texts 1, 1986

[HiSeShi89] Hiraki, K.; Sekiguchi, S.; Shimada, T.: *Status Report on SIGMA-1 : a Dataflow Supercomputer*, in: Gaudiot, J.-L.; Bic, L. (Eds.): Advanced Topics in Data-Flow Computing, Prentice Hall, Englewood Cliffs, NJ, 1991,

[Hoa85]   Hoare, C.A.R.: *Communicating Sequential Processes*, Prentice Hall, Englewood Cliffs, NJ, 1985

[Hom77] Hommes, F.: *The Internal Structure of the Reduction Machine*, GMD-ISF-77-3, D–5205 Sankt Augustin 1, March 1977

[Hom80] Hommes, F.: *An Expression Oriented Editor for Languages with a Constructor Syntax*, Proceedings of the International Workshop on High-Level Language Computer Architecture, Fort Lauderdale, Florida, May 1980, pp. 181–189

[Hom82] Hommes, F.: *The Heap/Substitution Concept – An Implementation of Functional Operations on Data Structures for a Reduction Machine*, Proceedings of the 9th Annual Symposium on Computer Architecture, Austin, Texas, IEEE, 1982, pp. 248–256

[HuWa88] Hudak, P.; Wadler, P. (Editors) et al.: *Report on the Functional Programming Language : Haskell*, Draft Proposed Standard, December 1988, Yale University

[HuAn88] Hudak, P.; Anderson, S.: *Haskell Solutions to the Language Session*, Problems at the 1988 Salishan High-Speed Computing Conference, Research Report YALEU/DCS/RR-627, 1988

[Hud89] Hudak, P.: *Conception, Evolution, and Application of Functional Programming*, ACM Computing Surveys, Vol. 21, No. 3, 1989, pp. 359–411

[Hugh82] Hughes, R.J.M.: *Super-Combinators – A New Implementation Technique for Applicative Languages*, Proceedings of the ACM Conference on LISP and Functional Programming, Pittsburgh, PA, August 1982, pp. 1–10

[Hugh82b] Hughes, R.J.M.: *Reference-Counting with Circular Structures in Virtual Memory Applicative Systems*, Programming Research Group, Oxford, 1982

[HwBr84] Hwang, K.; Briggs, F.A.: *Computer Architecture and Parallel Processing*, MacGraw-Hill Series in Computer Organization and Architecture, New York, NY, 1984

[IBM78] *IBM System/370 Principles of Operation*, IBM Corporation GA 22-77000, 1978

[Ill82] Iliffe, J.K.: *Advanced Computer Design*, Prentice Hall, Englewood Cliffs, NJ, 1982

[Jen90] Jensen, K.: *Coloured Petri Nets: A High-Level Language For System Design and Analysis*, in: Rozenberg, G. (Ed.): Advances in Petri Nets 1990, Lecture Notes in Computer Science, No. 483, Springer 1991, pp. 342–416

[JeWi75] Jensen, K.; Wirth, N.: *Pascal User Manual and Report*, Springer, 1975

[John83] Johnsson, T.: *The G-machine : An Abstract Machine for Graph Reduction*, SERC Chalmers University, Goeteborg, Programming Methodology Group, Internal Report, August 1983

[John84] Johnsson, T.: *Efficient Compilation of Lazy Evaluation*, Proceedings of the ACM SIGPLAN '84 Symposium on Compiler Construction, SIGPLAN Notices, Vol. 19, No. 6, 1984, pp. 58–69

[John85] Johnsson, T.: *Lambda Lifting : Transforming Programs to Recursive Equations*, Proceedings of the Conference on Functional Programming and Computer Architecture, Nancy, Lecture Notes in Computer Science, No. 201, Springer, 1985, pp. 190–203

[John87] Johnsson, T.: *Compiling Lazy Functional Languages*, PhD Thesis, Chalmers University of Technology, Goeteborg, 1987

[Kat85] Katevenis, M.: *Reduced Instruction Set Computer Architecture for VLSI*, MIT Press, 1985

[Katz71] Katzan Jr., H.: *Computer Organization and the System /370*, Van Nostrand Reinhold Company, 1971

[Katz76] Katzan Jr., H.: *Computer Systems Organization and Programming*, SRA Science Research Associations, 1976

[Kel85] Keller, R.M.: *Distributed Computation by Graph Reduction*, Systems Research, Vol. 2, No. 4, 1985, pp. 286–296

[KeBa84] Kenah; Bate: *VAX/VMS Internals and Data Structures*, Digital Press, 1984

[KeRi78] Kernighan, B.W.; Ritchie, D.M.: *The C Programming Language*, Prentice-Hall, Englewood Cliffs, 1978

[Kieb88] Kieburtz, R.: *Performance Measurements of a G-Machine Implementation*, Oregon Graduate Center, University of Oregon, 1988

[Klu79] Kluge, W.E.: *The Architecture of the Reduction Machine Hardware Model*, GMD-ISF-79-3, D–5205 Sankt Augustin 1, August 1979

[KlSc80] Kluge, W.E.; Schluetter, H.: *An Architecture for Direct Execution of Reduction Languages*, Prodings of the International Workshop on High-Level Language Computer Architecture, Fort Lauderdale, Florida, May 1980, pp. 174–180

[Klu83] Kluge, W.E.: *Cooperating Reduction Machines*, IEEE Transactions on Computers, Vol. C-32, No. 11, 1983, pp. 1002–1012

[KlSh85] Kluge, W.E.; Schmittgen, C.: *The π-System – A Concept for High-Performance Reduction Systems*, Proceedings of the 1st Autumn Workshop on Reduction Machines, Ustica, September 1985

[Klu86] Kluge, W.E.: *Reduction, Data Flow and Control Flow*, in: Petri Nets : Applications and Relationships to Other Models of Concurrency, Lecture Notes in Computer Science, Vol. 255, Springer, 1987, pp. 466–498

[Knuth73] Knuth, D.E.: *The Art of Computer Programming, Vol. 1 : Fundamental Algorithms*, Addison-Wesley, Reading, MA, 1973

[Kog81] Kogge, P.M.: *The Architecture of Pipelined Computers*, McGraw-Hill, New York, NY, 1981

[Kog91] Kogge, P.M.: *The Architecture of Symbolic Computers*, McGraw-Hill, New York, NY, 1991

[Krak88] Krakowiak, S.: *Principles of Operating Systems*, MIT Press, Cambridge, MA, 1988

[Lan64] Landin, P.J.: *The Mechanical Evaluation of Expressions*, The Computer Journal, Vol. 6, No. 4, 1964, pp. 308–320

[Lan65] Landin, P.J.: *A Correspondence Between* ALGOL 60 *and Church's Lambda Notation*, Communications of the ACM, Vol. 8, No. 2 , 1965, pp. 89–101, 158–165

[Lan66a] Landin, P.J.: *The Lambda-Calculus Approach*, in: Fox (Ed.): Programming and Non-Numerical Computation, Pergamon Press, 1966, pp. 97–141

[Lan66b] Landin, P.J.: *The Next 700 Programming Languages*, Communications of the ACM, Vol. 9, No. 3, 1966, pp. 157–166

[Lavi87] Laville, A.: *Lazy Pattern Matching in the ML Language*, INRIA Rapporte de Recherche, No. 664, 1987

[LeEc80] Levy, H.M.; Eckhouse, R.H.: *Computer Programming and Architecture of the VAX-11*, Digital Press, 1980

[LiSi86] Lippe, W.; Simon, F.; *Private Notes on λ-Calculus*, 1986

[LiHe83] Liebermann, H.; Hewitt, C.: *A Real Time Garbage Collector Based on the Lifetimes of Objects*, Communications of the ACM, Vol. 26, No. 6, 1983, pp. 419–429

[LoKu89] Loogen, R,; Kuchen, H.; Indermark, K.; Damm,W.: *Distributed Implementation of Programmed Graph Reduction*, Conference on Parallel Architectures and Languages Europe (PARLE), Lecture Notes in Computer Science, No. 365, Springer, 1989, pp. 136–157

[McC60] McCarthy, J.: *Recursive Functions of Symbolic Expressions and their Computation by Machine*, Communications of the ACM, No. 3, 1960, pp. 184–195

[McQMi87] MacQueen, D.; Milner, R.; Mitchell, K.; Sannella, D.: *Functional Programming in ML*, Laboratory for Foundations of Computer Science, University of Edinburgh, 1987

[Mag79] Mago, G.: *A Network of Microprocessors to Execute Reduction Languages, Parts I and II*, International Journal of Computer and Information Science, Vol. 8, No. 5, 1979, pp. 349–471

[MaHeKr87] Matthews, G.; Hewes, R.; Krueger, S.: *Single-Chip Processor Runs LISP-Environments*, Computer Design, May 1987, pp. 69–76

[May83] May, D.: *Occam*, ACM SIGPLAN Notices, Vol. 18, No. 4, 1983, pp. 69–79

[MaShKe86] May, D.; Shepherd, R.; Keane, C.: *Communicating Process Architecture, Transputer and Occam*, Proceedings of the ESPRIT Summer School on Future Parallel Computers, Pisa, Italy, Lecture Notes in Computer Science, No. 272, Springer, 1986, pp. 35–81

[McC62] McCarthy, J. et al.: LISP *1.5 Programming Manual*, MIT Press, Cambridge, MA, 1962

[Miln78] Milner, R.: *A Theory of Type Polymorphism in Programming*, Journal of Computer and System Sciences, Vol. 17, 1978, pp. 348–375

[Miln80] Milner, R.: *A Calculus of Communicating Systems*, Lecture Notes in Computer Science, No. 92, Springer, 1980

[Mil87] Milutinovic, V.M.: *Computer Architecture : Concepts and Systems*, North-Holland, 1987

[Miln84] Milner, R.: *A Proposal for Standard ML*, Proceedings of the ACM Conference on LISP and Functional Programming, Austin, Texas, August 1984, pp. 179–212

[Moon85] Moon, D.A.: *The Architecture of the Symbolics 3600*, Proceedings of the 12th International Symposium on Computer Architecture, Boston, 1985, pp. 76–83

[Mot88] *MC68000 : 8-/16-/32-Bit Microprocessors Programmer's Reference Manual*, Motorola, 1988

[Mot84] *MC68020, 32 Bit Microprocessor User's Manual*, 2nd edition, Motorola Inc., Prentice Hall, Englewood Cliffs, NJ, 1984

[Mye78] Myers, G.: *Advances in Computer Architecture*, John Wiley, New York, NY, 1978

[Nau60] Naur, P. (Ed.): *Report on the Algorithmic Language ALGOL 60*, Communications of the ACM, Vol. 3, 1960, pp. 299–314

[Nikh88] Nikhil, R.S.: *ID Version 88.1, Reference Manual*, MIT Laboratory for Computer Science, CSG Memo 284, 1988

[Org73] Organick, E.I.: *Computer System Organisation : The B5700/B6700*, Computer Science Series, Academic Press, 1973

[Org83] Organick, E.I.: *A Programmer's View of the Intel 432 System*, McGraw-Hill, New York, NY, 1983

[Org85] Organick, E.I. *The Multics System : An Examination of Its Structure*, MIT-Press, Cambridge, MA, 1985

[Old86] Olderog, E.R.: *Process Theory : Semantics, Specification and Verification*, in: deBakker, deRoever, Rozenberg (Eds.): Current Trends in Concurrency, Lecture Notes in Computer Science, No. 224, Springer, 1986, pp. 442–509

[PaCu90] Papadopoulos, G.M.; Culler, D.E.: *MONSOON : an Explicit Token-Store Architecture*, Proceedings of the 17th Annual Symposium on Computer Architecture, ACM, 1990, pp. 82–91

[PaTr91] Papadopoulos, G.M.; Traub, K.R.: *Multithreading : A Revisionist View of Data Flow Architectures*, Proceedings of the 18th Annual Symposium on Computer Architecture, ACM, 1991, pp. 342–351

[Peson81] Peterson, J.L.: *Petri Net Theory and the Modeling of Systems*, Prentice Hall, Englewood Cliffs, NJ, 1981

[Petri62] Petri, C.A.: *Kommunikation mit Automaten*, Technical Report No. 2, Institut fuer Instrumentelle Mathematik, University of Bonn, Germany, 1962; also in: Technical Report RADC-TR-65-377, Criffiss Air Force Base, 1966 (English Translation)

[Petri76] Petri, C.A.: *Interpretations of Net Theory*, Internal Report GMD-ISF-75-07 (second edition), D–5205 Sankt Augustin 1, Germany, 1976

[Petri73] Petri, C.A.: *Concepts of Net Theory*, Mathematical Foundations of Computer Science, Proceedings of Symposium and Summer School, Mathematics Institute of the Slovak Academy of Sciences, 1973, pp. 137–146

[Petri80] Petri, C.A.: *Introduction to General Net Theory*, in: Net Theory and Applications, Lecture Notes in Computer Science, Vol. 84, Springer, 1980, pp. 1–19

[Peyt87] Peyton Jones, S.L.: *The Implementation of Functional Programming Languages*, Prentice Hall, Englewood Cliffs, NJ, 1987

[PeClSaHa87] Peyton Jones, S.L.; Clack, C.; Salkild, J.; Hardie, M.: *GRIP – A High Performance Architecture for Parallel Graph Reduction*, Proceedings of the Conference on Functional Programming and Computer Architecture, Portland, Oregon, Lecture Notes in Computer Science, No. 274, Springer, 1987, pp. 98–112

[PiSh91] Pinci, V. O.; Shapiro, R.M.: *An Integrated Software Development Methodology Based on Hierarchical Colored Petri Nets*, in: Rozenberg, G. (Ed.): Advances in Petri Nets 1991, Lecture Notes in Computer Science No. 524, Springer 1991, pp. 227–252

[PiAr85] Pingali, K.K.; Arvind: *Efficient Demand-Driven Evaluation*, Part 1, ACM Transactions on Programming Languages and Systems, Vol. 7, No. 2, 1985, pp. 311–333, Part 2, ACM Transactions on Programming Languages and Systems, Vol. 8, No. 1, 1986, pp. 109–139

[Pi88] Pingali, K.K.: *Lazy Evaluation and the Logic Variable*, Proceedings of the International Conference on Supercomputing, St. Malo, France, ACM, 1988, pp. 560–572

[PlSc90] Pless, E.; Schluetter, H.: *The Reduction Language OREL/2*, Arbeitspapiere der GMD, 1990

[RaRu64] Randell, B.; Russell, L.J.: *ALGOL 60 Implementation*, Academic Press, London and New York, 1964

[ReAl80] Rector, R.; Alexy, G.: *The 8086 Book*, McGraw-Hill, New York, NY, 1980

[Rei85] Reisig, W.: *Petri Nets*, EATCS Monographs on Theoretical Computer Science, Vol. 4, Springer, 1985

[Ros84] Rosser, J.B.: *Highlights of the History of the Lambda Calculus*, Annals of the History of Computing, Vol. 6, No. 4, 1984, pp. 337–349

[Rudd76] Rudd, W.G.: *Assembly Language Programming and the IBM /360 and /370 Computers*, Prentice Hall, Englewood Cliffs, NJ, 1976

[SaYaHiKoYu89a] Sakai, S.;Yamaguchi, Y.; Hiraki, K.; Kodama, Y.; Yuba, T.: *An Archi-tecture of a Data Flow Single Chip Processor*, Procceedings of the 16th Annual International Symposium on Computer Architecture, Jerusalem, IEEE/ACM, 1989, pp. 46–53

[SaYaHiKoYu89b] Sakai, S.;Yamaguchi, Y.; Hiraki, K.; Kodama, Y.; Yuba, T.: *Pipeline Optimization of a General-Purpose Dataflow Multiprocessor*, in: Gaudiot, J.-L.; Bic, L. (Eds.): Advanced Topics in Data-Flow Computing, Prentice Hall, Englewood Cliffs, NJ, 1991,

[Schee86] Scheevel, M.: *NORMA : A Graph Reduction Processor*, Proceedings of the ACM Conference on LISP and Functional Programming, Cambridge, MA, 1986, pp. 109–139

[Schm86] Schmittgen, C.: *A Data Type Architecture for Reduction Machines*, Proceedings of the 19th Hawaii International Conference on System Sciences, Vol. I, 1986, pp. 78–87

[SmGeHa86] Schmittgen, C.; Gerdts, A.; Haumann, J.; Kluge, W.; Woitass, M.: *A System-Supported Workload Balancing Scheme for Cooperating Reduction Ma-chines*, Proceedings of the 19th Hawaii International Conference on System Sci-ences, Vol. I, 1986, pp. 67–77

[SmBlKl91a] Schmittgen, C.; Bloedorn, H.; Kluge, W.: *Structured Data Types in the Re-duction System* π-RED, in: Arrays, Functional Languages and Parallel Systems, Kluwer Academic Publishers, 1991, pp. 171–183

[SmBlKl91b] Schmittgen, C.; Bloedorn, H.; Kluge, W.: *π-RED* * *– A Graph Reducer for a Full-Fledged λ-Calculus*, New Generation Computing, OHMSHA Ltd. and Springer, Vol. 10, No. 2, 1992, pp. 173–195

[Scho24] Schoenfinkel, M.: *Ueber die Bausteine der mathematischen Logik*, Mathematis-che Annalen, Vol. 92, 1924, pp. 305–316; (English Translation in: van Heijenoort, 1967, pp. 355–366)

[SiBeNe82] Siewiorek, D.P.; Bell, C.G.; Newell, A.: *Computer Structures : Principles and Examples*, MacGraw-Hill Computer Science Series, New York, NY, 1982

[Smi84] Smith, S.: *The LMI Lambda Technical Summary*, LMI Inc., Los Angeles, CA, 1984

[Ste82] Steele, G.L.: *An Overview of Common LISP*, Proceedings of the ACM Conference on LISP and Functional Programming, Pittsburgh, PA, 1982, pp. 98–107

[Ste84] Steele, G.L.: *Common LISP : The Language*, Digital Press, Bedford, MA, 1984

[StHe87] Steenkiste, H.; Hennessy, J.: *Tags and Type Checking in LISP : Hardware and Software Approaches*, Proceedings of the 2nd International ACM Conference on Architectural Support for Programming Languages and Operating Systems (ASPLOS II), Palo Alto, 1987, pp. 50–59

[Stre78]   Strecker, W.D.: *A Virtual Address Extension to the DEC PDP-11 Family*, in:
           Bell, C.G.; Mudge, J.C.; McNamara, J.E.: Computer Engineering, Digital Press,
           Bedford, MA, 1978

[Stru75]   Struble, G.W.: *Assembler Language Programming : the IBM Systems /360 and
           /370*, Addison-Wesley, Reading, MA, 1975

[Sym84]   Symbolics Inc.: *Symbolics 3600 Technical Summary*, Symbolics Inc., Cambridge
           MA, 1984

[SyCoHi77] Syre, J.C.; Comte, D.; Hifdi, N.: *Pipelining, Parallelism and Asynchronism
           in the LAU-System*, Proceedings of the International Conference on Parallel Pro-
           cessing, August 1977, pp. 87–92

[TaHi86]   Taylor, G.; Hilfinger, P.; Larus, J.; Patterson, D.; Zorn, B.: *Evaluation of the
           SPUR LISP Architecture*, Proceedings of the 13th Annual International Sympo-
           sium on Computer Architecture, 1986, pp. 444–452

[Thak87]   Thakkar, S.S. (Editor): *Selected Reprints on Dataflow and Reduction Architec-
           tures*, IEEE Computer Society Cat. No. EH0260-0, 1987

[TrBrHo82] Treleaven, P.C.; Brownbridge, D.R.; Hopkins, R.P.: *Data-Driven and De-
           mand-Driven Computer Architecture*, ACM Computing Surveys, Vol. 14, No. 1,
           March 1982, pp. 93–143

[Tuc86]   Tucker, S.G.: *The IBM 3090 System : An Overview*, IBM Systems Journal
           Vol. 25, No. 1, 1986,

[Tur36]   Turing, A.M.: *On Computable Numbers, with an Application to the Entschei-
           dungsproblem*, London Mathematical Society, 2s. 42, 1936, pp. 230–265

[Turn76]   Turner, D.A.: *SASL Language Manual*, St. Andrews University, Technical Re-
           port, December 1976

[Turn79]   Turner, D.A.: *A New Implementation Technique for Applicative Languages*, Soft-
           ware Practice and Experience, Vol. 9, No. 1, 1979, pp. 31–49

[Turn81]   Turner, D.A.: *The Future of Applicative Programming, Trends in Information
           Processing Systems*, in Duijvestijn; Lockemann (Eds.): Proceedings of the 3rd
           Conference of the European Cooperation in Informatics, Munich, Lecture Notes
           in Computer Science, No. 123, Springer, 1981, pp. 334–348

[Turn85]   Turner, D.A.: *Miranda : A Non-Strict Functional Language with Polymorphic
           Types*, Proceedings of the Conference on Functional Programming and Computer
           Architecture, Nancy, Lecture Notes in Computer Science, No. 201, Springer,
           1985, pp. 1–16

[Turn86]   Turner, D.A.: *An Overview of Miranda*, SIGPLAN Notices, Vol. 21, No. 12,
           1986, pp. 158–166

[Ung86]   Ungar, D.M.: *The Design and Evaluation of a High Performance Smalltalk Sys-
           tem*, MIT Press, Cambridge, MA, 1986

[VAX81]   *VAX Architecture Handbook*, Digital Equipment Corporation, 1981

[Veg84] Vegdahl, S.R.: *A Survey of Proposed Architectures for the Execution of Functional Languages*, IEEE Transactions on Computers, Vol. C-33, No. 12, 1984, pp. 1050–1071

[Vui74] Vuillemin, J.: *Correct and Optimal Implementations of Recursion in a Simple Programming Language*, Journal of Computer and System Sciences, Vol. 9, No. 3, 1974, pp. 332–354

[vWi69] van Wijngaarden, A. (Ed.); Mailloux, B.J.; Peck, J.E.L.; Koster, C.H.A.: *Report on the Algorithmic Language ALGOL 68*, Numerische Mathematik 14, 1969, pp. 79–218

[vNeu45] von Neumann, J.: *First Draft of a Report on the EDVAC*, University of Pennsylvania, Report for the US Army Ordinance Department, 1945

[Wads71] Wadsworth, C.P.: *Semantics and Pragmatics of the Lambda-Calculus*, PhD Thesis, University of Oxford, 1971

[WaGu79] Watson, I.; Gurd, J.: *A Prototype Data Flow Computer with Token Labeling*, Proceedings of the AFIPS National Computer Conference, Vol. 48, 1979, pp. 623–628

[WaGu82] Watson, I.; Gurd, J.: *A Practical Data Flow Computer*, IEEE Computer, Vol. 15, No. 2, 1982, pp. 51–57

[Weg71] Wegner, P.: *Programming Languages, Information Structures, and Machine Organization*, McGraw-Hill, New York, NY, 1971

[Wil85] Williams, S.: *Programming the 68000*, Sybex, San Francisco, CA, 1985

[Wir76] Wirth, N.: *Modula : A Language for Modular Multiprogramming*, Report 18, ETH Zuerich, 1976

[Wir85] Wirth, N.: *Programming in Modula-2*, Springer, 1985

[YoNaNa84] Yoshida, M.; Naruse, T.; Nakamura, O.: *Hardware Implementation od a Dataflow Machine*, Review of the Electrical Communication Laboratories, Vol. 32, No. 5, 1984, pp. 803–812

[Yub84] Yuba, T.; Shimada, T.; Hiraki, K.; Kashiwasi, H.: *Sigma-1 : A Dataflow Computer for Scientific Computation*, Technical Report, Elektrotechnical Laboratories, Ibaraki, Japan, 1984

[Zim91] Zimmer, R.: *Zur Pragmatik eines Operationalisierten λ-Kalkuels als Basis fuer Interaktive Reduktionssysteme*, GMD-Bericht Nr. 192, Oldenbourg, 1991

Index

The MIT Press, with Peter Denning as general consulting editor, publishes computer science books in the following series:

ACL-MIT Press Series in Natural Language Processing
Aravind K. Joshi, Karen Sparck Jones, and Mark Y. Liberman, editors

ACM Doctoral Dissertation Award and Distinguished Dissertation Series

Artificial Intelligence
Patrick Winston, founding editor
J. Michael Brady, Daniel G. Bobrow, and Randall Davis, editors

Charles Babbage Institute Reprint Series for the History of Computing
Martin Campbell-Kelly, editor

Computer Systems
Herb Schwetman, editor

Explorations with Logo
E. Paul Goldenberg, editor

Foundations of Computing
Michael Garey and Albert Meyer, editors

History of Computing
I. Bernard Cohen and William Aspray, editors

Logic Programming
Ehud Shapiro, editor; Fernando Pereira, Koichi Furukawa, Jean-Louis Lassez, and David H. D. Warren, associate editors

The MIT Press Electrical Engineering and Computer Science Series

Research Monographs in Parallel and Distributed Processing
Christopher Jesshope and David Klappholz, editors

Scientific and Engineering Computation
Janusz Kowalik, editor

Technical Communication and Information Systems
Edward Barrett, editor

DATE DUE